SOCIETY AND POLITICS IN GERMANY
1500–1750

STUDIES IN SOCIAL HISTORY

Editor: **HAROLD PERKIN**

Professor of Social History, University of Lancaster

Assistant Editor: **ERIC J. EVANS**

Lecturer in History, University of Lancaster

For a list of books in the series see back endpaper

SOCIETY AND POLITICS IN GERMANY 1500–1750

G. Benecke

Department of History, University of Kent

LONDON: Routledge & Kegan Paul
TORONTO: University of Toronto Press

First published in 1974
in Great Britain
by Routledge & Kegan Paul Ltd
and in Canada and the United States of America by
University of Toronto Press
Toronto and Buffalo
Set in Monotype Bell
and printed in Great Britain by
Western Printing Services Ltd, Bristol
© *G. Benecke 1974*

RKP ISBN 0 7100 7842 0

UTP ISBN 0 8020 2174 3

Contents

CONTENTS

Maps

Maps

Preface

THIS book attempts a new interpretation of the Holy Roman Empire in Germany from the fifteenth to the eighteenth century. It makes use of regional printed materials and of unpublished state archives from north-west Germany, a large and important region of which no thorough study has yet been published in English. These materials tell us how the early modern Holy Roman Empire actually worked. The book shows how politics were conducted on a loose basis, wherein the federal Empire could only ever be as strong as its component territorial states wished. This strength was not dependent on any national myth or propaganda which would show the origins of a nineteenth-century *kleindeutsch*-Prussian or *grossdeutsch*-Austrian cause. Nor is the Empire an example of a chaotic system of society and politics, which it would be the destiny of nineteenth-century German national liberals to overcome by rationalization and centralization. Instead, the strength of the early modern German system of society and politics lay in the way in which the mass of small states co-operated in mundane day-to-day affairs, and the way in which matters were co-ordinated in bodies set up for that specific purpose at federal/*Reich*/imperial level.

The way in which the records survive dictates that, in order to arrive at a true assessment of the whole, the parts have first and foremost to be studied in their own right. This technical difficulty goes a long way towards explaining why historians have not yet made their long-overdue revision of the real nature of early modern German society and politics. This book is a first study in depth from those specific state archives that

ix

show how essential were federal bodies—such as the *Reichstag* and its committees, the *Reichskammergericht* and *Reichshofrat*, *Kreisdirektorien* and *Kreistage*, plus their system of *Römermonate*, *Türkensteuer* and *Kammerzieler*—to German society and politics at state and federal level. The question that this mass of new material above all poses is, how effective and mature was this early modern German system of government?

Part I provides a general introduction to early modern Germany and to its social groups, going on to outline the existing printed sources and monographs for the study of early modern German federalism, pointing to the difficulties of obtaining a coherent general picture of its society and politics. Part II shows in depth that in order to study the Empire as a whole, its component states have first and foremost to be studied in their own right. This has been done by taking thirteen north-west German states which are new material to the English-speaking world, and to the German-speaking world in so far as they have been studied here not as states of interest only to local history, but as states showing in detail the fullness and complexity of early modern German history. These states co-operated in federal affairs in their own internal interest, in order to gain support collectively from each other to build up each of their own administrations, judicatures and assemblies. This is shown in detail in Part III as regards one specific small state, the county of Lippe in eastern Westphalia, by exhaustive analysis of its archives. German society is here atomized. The relations between rulers and their officials, the Estates of nobles and burghers, and the needs of peasants-plebeians are worked out in terms of taxation and finance during the whole early modern era, and then tested specifically in the worst crisis of that era, in the Thirty Years' War period. Part IV relates state affairs to the federal institutions of the Empire from the archive materials that remain for the county of Lippe. The nature of a loose federal system is thus laid bare for the first time from the point of view of its effect on one state, providing, it is hoped, a foundation upon which future study and research into early modern German history can be based. Part V concludes by summarizing these findings and seeks to point the way to further studies in order to verify the picture obtained from one set of state archives, namely that the Holy Roman Empire provided an effective and mature system of government for early modern Germany that was attuned both to its own needs and to the wider needs of early modern Europe.

I wish to thank Staatsarchivdirektor a.D. Dr Kittel, Staatsarchivdirektor Dr Engelbert, their staff at Staatsarchiv Detmold, and Stadtarchivar Dr Hoppe in Lemgo for their interest and generous help, and especially to thank Staatsarchivrat Dr Sagebiel for introducing me to the palaeography, and for his willingness to discuss my work at all times. The views and any remaining errors in the work are my own responsibility.

I acknowledge research grants from St Andrews University and from the Carnegie Trust for the Universities of Scotland in the years 1966–9. The work presented here is a revised and extended 1970 Ph.D. thesis of St Andrews University, completed under the supervision of Mr. A. F. Upton, to whose guidance and friendship this study owes its existence. Original quotations in German are in the thesis, along with much more expansive footnotes to which attention is drawn.

The thesis also includes a volume in German of selected documents, most of them transcribed from archive originals for the first time. These documents have not been published, but they can be consulted in my thesis, 'Northwest Germany, Lippe, and the Empire in Early Modern Times', in St Andrews University Library, Scotland.

I also acknowledge with gratitude private assistance from Mrs W. L. H. Butchard, Detmold; Professor Åke Nilzén and Fru Britta Nilzén, Stockholm; Fräulein Rosa Steinbuch, Berlin; Herr K.-G. Brackemann, Detmold; the Misses Butchard, Cobham, Kent; and encouragement from my contemporaries, Dr Göran Nilzén, Stockholm; Dr Kurt Schuster, Wolfsburg; jur. kand. Anders Lindqvist, Uppsala. Dr David Turley generously saved me from many a pitfall with the text.

I am also indebted to my students at Kent, Jayne Elsmore, Laraine Rynham and Harry Robins, whose critical approach to a 'crisis' in early modern Germany has helped my work immeasurably.

My wife Karin checked, improved and cross-checked several drafts of this work. The final version is dedicated to her.

G.B.

Part One

Introduction

I

Early Modern Germany

THERE is no good textbook on early modern Germany. Perhaps the subject is unimportant and thus of little interest. The mass of work on Luther and the Reformation would seem to suggest otherwise. Is it because historians are lazy? To unravel the history of all the German states from the scattered and voluminous archives that survive in such a way that the parts do indeed effectively explain the whole is a superhuman task. Yet this is what a good textbook must finally be shown to have accomplished. No one is anywhere remotely near to being able to do this. The subject is wide open to the research worker. The groundwork has simply not been done.

At present what can be done is to provide a new framework to interpret sources in such a way that early modern Germany can be understood for what it was—not for what it had been in the medieval past, nor for what it was to become in the nineteenth and twentieth centuries. Whether or not even this turns out to be a philosophical and ideological impossibility, such a framework would enable us to look at specific states within their own regions, and also to say something significant about the interrelationship of each specific state and early modern Germany as a whole.

This study seeks to do that by showing the federal importance of the regional and local sources that have been examined. So this is not a textbook. The work was originally a doctoral dissertation. It assumed prior knowledge of background, structure and events in early modern Germany, which Part I of this book now briefly seeks to outline. What was early modern Germany?

What was the structure of its society? How did its politics function?

By 'early modern' we mean a period of time. This is not precise: yet it is not insignificant notation, if it is used to indicate new trends, movements, crises, real or abortive changes as well as any underlying or superficial continuities. It is insignificant only if we use it too literally as chronology. The dates for the beginning and end of 'early modern' must fluctuate according to theme and subject. For Germany 'early modern' could be thought to begin to apply from 1450 to 1550, although this could be pushed back earlier, and to end at about 1750 to 1850.

By the fifteenth century German territories were developing an identity of their own. They built up their own territorial assemblies, administrations, law courts, procedures and tax systems. State structures emerged, exercising internal power in new ways. New systems came into conflict with older beliefs about politics. This caused much of the tension that can be noted as the beginning of an 'early modern' period. Whilst German peasants and artisans increasingly rebelled in the name of the good old justice (*Das Gute Alte Recht*) of God and King, state officials were pioneering new forms of law (*Gesetz*) to bypass the old, unworkable ideal of justice (*Recht*). The official established his ruler's rights (*Gerechtsame*) and enforced legislation by prerogative (*Gesetz und Gebot*).

In theory feudal ties had been contractual, freely and voluntarily made. In practice they were subordinated increasingly to a new obedience and loyalty of subject (*Untertan*) to ruler (*Landesherr*). Although feudal law was retained in early modern Germany, it was employed to deal with fewer and fewer privileged families and their privileged properties, whilst state officials worked out greater and greater numbers of duties for the mass of the subject population (see Chapter VII).

Existing beliefs and systems were modified or allowed to linger on. Old was not replaced by new in any revolutionary or rational way. The early modern method of change was to claim to return to the true old way, as with Luther's appeal to the Bible and primitive church, or to exploit an existing institution in a new, harsher way, as demonstrated in the increase in serfdom and latifundia in regions such as those east of the lower Elbe.

In the fifteenth century the German territories already formed a loose federal unit. A fixed procedure for electing the German king was operating by the fourteenth century. The rulers of Mainz, Cologne, Trier, the Palatinate, Saxony and Brandenburg became the body of Electors and formed the first chamber of an imperial assembly which itself was fully operational as a federal body of arbitration and included most of the territorial rulers of Germany as members by the time of King Wenceslas in the later fourteenth century. The reign of his father, the Emperor Charles IV, marks the real beginning of this new federal system in Germany. By the fifteenth century all the territorial rulers, whether ecclesiastical and elected or lay and dynastic, who were below the rank of Elector, had become one body at the imperial assembly called the Council of Ruling Princes (*Fürstenrat*). The third and last group to form as a distinct body at the imperial assembly were those town councils from the chief centres of population, finance and taxation in fifteenth-century Germany called the imperial towns because they owed allegiance directly to the king or emperor.

These three groups of Electors, ruling princes and imperial towns discussed reform in royal administration, defence and taxation, internal security and law and order, ecclesiastical affairs and foreign war with the kings and emperors of Germany and the Holy Roman Empire. A better system of procedure and record was developing by the end of the fifteenth century and politics had become two-tiered. There were territorial assemblies within the German states, and imperial assemblies at national level where the heads of the German states themselves were the actual members, thus producing an overall federal discussion, direction and control of German politics.

This system was shaped by brilliant and far-reaching plans of reform in the 1490s, especially by arrangements over law and order and taxation made at the imperial assembly of Worms in 1495, influenced by the genius of the Arch-Chancellor of Germany, Count Berthold of Henneberg, Archbishop-Elector of Mainz. This is not to say that Berthold's federal system was fully successful. The federal system faced the crisis of early 'monopoly capitalism', the knights', peasants' and artisans' revolts defeated at the hands of the ruling princes in the 1520s and 1530s, and finally the reforms and civil wars of religion in the mid-sixteenth century and the first half of the seventeenth. But a federal system of some form or other always reasserted itself. 'Early modern' thus includes the concept of some kind of native German grass-roots federalism which developed in the fifteenth century and continued until the eighteenth century.

What of the term 'Germany' at that same period of time? According to a rather generous contemporary estimate for the first decade of the eighteenth century made by the Austrian Habsburg War Council, the German Empire, including Bohemia and the Spanish Netherlands, had a population of nearly 28 million, comprising:

65 ecclesiastical states with 14 per cent of the total land area and 12 per cent of the total population;

45 dynastic principalities with 80 per cent of the land and 80 per cent of the population;

60 dynastic counties and lordships with 3 per cent of the land and $3\frac{1}{2}$ per cent of the population;

60 imperial towns with 1 per cent of the land but $3\frac{1}{2}$ per cent of the population. The imperial knights (well over a thousand of them) finally managed to control 2 per cent of the land but only 1 per cent of the population of Germany.[1]

The kingdom of Germany was part of a religious and pseudo-classical myth, the Holy Roman Empire. The Holy Roman Empire was a piece of medieval ideology, a claim for universal rule and Christian concord. This myth was not abolished. It was cherished by early modern Germans. In the early sixteenth century, as the links with Rome became harder to uphold, the concept was elaborated as 'the Holy Roman Empire of the German Nation'. This was formally retained until the impact of Napoleon and his armies on Germany, and the title was finally surrendered by the Habsburgs in 1806. Yet this grand ideology never played any real part in the internal affairs of the kingdom of Germany. The Holy Roman Empire was an anomaly, useful as an appeal to encourage support for foreign war, wherever general defence was necessary, and for crusading whenever the European diplomatic situation allowed. The Holy Roman Empire was the residual medieval ingredient in the early modern concept of Germany and it contrasts with modern elements such

[1] See Chapter VII, note 2 and the Appendices.

as frontiers and sovereign nation states. Early modern Germany thus stands between the two concepts—medieval universalism and modern nationalism—containing elements of both but subject to neither.

Early modern Germany never had clearly defined frontiers. Too many feudal jurisdictions made such modern rationalization impossible. To that extent historical atlases oversimplify and mislead. Historical maps give useful impressions of where any German state was situated at any one point of time but cannot, except in a very detailed, piecemeal way, explain the whole overlapping complexity of feudal jurisdictions, overlordships, inheritances, partitions and alienations, which shifted the lines with such rapidity that no frontier could ever be fixed. Equally there was no clearly defined concept of state sovereignty for Germany as a whole. Loyalty was to a specific state within Germany. To the Hessian, 'fatherland' was Hesse, and 'abroad' was Bavaria. Similar views were held in all German states in early modern times. Thus early modern Germany was not a nation state. It was not a political unit like England. That does not mean to say it was not a political unit. It was just different: it fitted into no clear category of Aristotelian forms which states might assume, a fact which annoyed early modern German lawyers, publicists and political thinkers as much as nineteenth- and twentieth-century nationalist historians. Yet the reality remained: early modern Germany was not a nation state, and yet it was still a working political reality. Thus, to repeat, 'Germany' includes the concept of some kind of native grass-roots federalism synonymous with the German term, *Reich*, at this time, which developed in the fifteenth century and remained into the eighteenth century.

Where within the regions of Germany did power over the federal whole really reside, and how did this power shift? By the eighteenth and nineteenth centuries this power was the rivalry between Austrian Habsburg and Brandenburg-Prussian Hohenzollern administrations. But this was not the case in the fifteenth, sixteenth and seventeenth centuries. The Austrian Habsburgs were certainly at the centre of early modern German power politics; not so the Brandenburg-Prussian Hohenzollerns who were the holders of the poorest of the six German Electorates. The Habsburgs held power on the geographical fringes of

Germany, hence their continued need to keep the universalist ideology of the Holy Roman Empire alive.

How had this situation come about? Where were the German heartlands? The geographical boundaries of Germany have never for long been static. The early medieval stem-duchies produced internal regional expressions which were used in the sixteenth century independently of the German states that already existed as the Circles (*Reichskreise*) of a federal system of peace-keeping. Such were, above all, the regions between the Rhine and the Elbe, Lower Saxony, Westphalia, the Rhinelands, Swabia, Bavaria, Franconia, Hesse and Thuringia. With the eastward expansion of the twelfth century new marches were driven into Slav Europe. The Teuton took over in Mecklenburg, Pomerania, Brandenburg, Saxony and Austria.

The centre of German politics was originally the Rhineland and the south-west. It had an ecclesiastical-electoral basis. It was centred on the archbishoprics of Mainz, Cologne and Trier, and had the co-operation of the dynasties of the north-west and south-west, the Saxons and Swabians. The Saxons colonized eastwards and built up a state within a state. In the later twelfth century the greatest power contest between Saxon Henry the Lion and Swabian Frederick Barbarossa was resolved in favour of the latter's universalist ideals, which were in turn destroyed in the turmoil of Italian politics in the thirteenth century. With the help of the papacy the German ruling princes both ecclesiastical and lay had re-established in German internal affairs the equilibrium which had been threatened by Barbarossa's overmighty imperial dynasty of Hohenstaufen. When the Hohenstaufens disappeared in the 1260s the centre of German politics did not move back to the ecclesiastical principalities of the Rhineland. The Rhineland states indeed remained one of the most important factors in German politics, but they were joined increasingly by the new dynasties of the east—the Luxemburgers in Prague with their heirs the Habsburgs of Austria and to a much lesser extent the Hohenzollerns in Brandenburg, and finally the Wettiners in Saxony. These dynasts were rulers of the German colonial Slav east. It was from here that new economic power built upon extensive new farming and methods of colonial taxation could flourish unrestricted by the older allodial and feudal traditions of the west.

Added to this in the east was a development in the mining of precious and bulk metals for which fifteenth- and sixteenth-century Europe showed an insatiable appetite. The balance between old and new, between the ecclesiastical Rhineland of West Germany and dynastic Elbian-Danubian East Germany, was held by the dynasties of the centre—the Palatine and Bavarian Wittelsbachs, the Brunswick Guelphs, the Hessians, Württembergers and Franconian Hohenzollerns, each with their own regional sphere of influence. Quite independent of these and often in direct economic competition to them, came the imperial towns of the south-west as well as the Hansards, urban economic units of the north. In the fifteenth century, therefore, power was diffused regionally throughout the kingdom of Germany. It was balanced between the old elective ecclesiastical west, the new colonial east, the traditional dynastic centre and the important municipalities of south and north. This meant that there was no dominant centre of power from which strong policies could emanate in a European world which was getting more national, more aggressive, more bureaucratic, more centralized and more expensive to run. Against this fifteenth-century Germany offered an alternative, a loose federal co-operation of internally independent territorial courts and administrations. In that respect fifteenth-century federal Germany successfully went against above all the west European trend towards nation states. To survive with a weaker system of power politics meant, however, that a compromise had to be reached within federal Germany. The Habsburgs, a territorially strong dynasty, were repeatedly chosen as German kings and Holy Roman Emperors to take on the overall direction of German foreign policy, defence, and law and order—but they were never given full power. The German ruling princes, whether they inherited or were elected or were ecclesiastical or lay, or even urban town councillors, always retained their own freedom of action and yet remained within an overall framework of allegiance to Habsburg kings and emperors. This was because they as the ruling princes of the German states collectively determined what federal politics would be. They formed the early modern *Reich*, an untranslatable federal whole, that had little to do with the Hohenstaufen past, and certainly nothing whatsoever to do with the German *Reichs* of Bismarck and Hitler.

II

Early Modern German Society

BEFORE the birth of human rights in the eighteenth century, European society recognized as self-evident that there were basic inequalities at law between different groups of people and their dependants, according to wealth, birth and profession. Even so, early modern social structures were not rigid and caste-like, but movement within them was individual and erratic: one can talk of cumulative effects but not of rational changes. This applies above all to the sociology of the 1520s in Germany. The 1520s appeared as the great divide for large sections of the west German lower nobility with the abortive knights' revolt of Sickingen and Hutten. It was the end of the road for sections of the common people in market town and village with the abortive peasants' revolt, especially for the adherents of Thomas Müntzer. Only in the Austrian and Alpine lands did the tradition of peasant revolt for better conditions continue unabated until well into the nineteenth century. In the rest of the German lands 1525 was the end of a century and more of rural violence against the law and order of ruling princes and municipalities. For the clergy also it formed a great divide. Where it went Protestant, the clerical profession changed its social status: the way was opened for commoners with university degrees. The nobility moved out of the best clerical jobs because a Protestant church system made them the lackeys of ruler or town council, rather than granting them the status and freedom enjoyed by clerics in the old medieval and Catholic German system. Thus the Protestant clergy of the German states became a government department of trained commoners in the service of the prince or municipality. In the Catholic

10

German states the situation remained more complicated and more favourable to the nobility. The ecclesiastical states retained their aristocratic government, with cathedral chapters and bishops drawn from the German high and low nobility still in charge of their own politics. In the Catholic dynastic territories the papal hierarchy was still available to arbitrate for the clergy with the ruling prince. In practice, the clergy increasingly had the worst of the arrangement, as for example in counter-reformation Bavaria. But such dynastic control of the Catholic clergy was only one aspect of the early modern German Catholic system. The links with Rome remained: the freedoms of many of the German ecclesiastical states such as Cologne, Münster, Würzburg and Fulda remained to tempt Catholic nobles into the Catholic church because of the power and wealth they would enjoy. All this was closed to the Protestant noble: in the seventeenth century increasingly he had to turn to military, diplomatic and general administrative service with ruling princes. The Protestant church generally remained beneath his dignity.

For the burghers the 1520s also meant a split in their ranks. A few of the large, old, independent municipalities especially of the south-west like Augsburg, Frankfurt and Nuremberg made common cause with the ruling princes and helped to finance them in destroying rebellious market towns and villages. There was thus a wealth of difference between one burgher and another. The great monopoly capitalist Jacob Fugger of Augsburg started as a burgher but it would be meaningless to classify him with an Augsburg master cobbler because they had both taken the burgher oath of the city. The same distinctions apply to all the other ranks and orders of early modern German society. Status could be modified beyond all point of similarity by wealth and opportunity within each order of society. Thus where each individual stands within his order of society is extremely important, despite the fact that without the corporate law and protection of his overall social group, be it as noble, burgher or peasant–plebeian, he would have been very vulnerable indeed. This proviso modifies all attempts to class early modern Germans in social groups. But before turning to a detailed examination of the varieties within each social group, the general groups themselves must be differentiated.

Basically, early modern German society was made up of

clergy, nobles, burghers, and peasants–plebeians. The first three groups were more noted for the privileges they could exercise, and the last group more for the duties it had to perform. The last group always made up the vast majority of the population. But the first three groups also contained the decisive professions, the doctors of law, theology and medicine, the preachers and teachers, the financiers and administrators, both military and civil. Theirs was the monopoly of education, ideology, and propaganda; the Christians who ran affairs. They also owned most of the property and pre-industrial plant in such a way that they could organize and gain the profits from the work and life of the last group, the peasants–plebeians, the masses, the common people, the early modern mob. The complexities of job, training and conditions of tenure and family made the last group, the peasants–plebeians, undoubtedly the most complex and interesting group of early modern German men, women and children. This group of people survives as an endless pattern of inheritance, endeavour and merit, and frustration. It provided the motor that kept agrarian and mercantile early modern society going. Thus it should be the focal point of any analysis of early modern German society. Yet a real analysis of the records that remain of peasant–plebeian early modern Germany has hardly started. This last group can by no means be analysed lucidly as can the records of the first three groups, of the clergy, nobles and burghers. For the first three groups have always dictated their own terms. They controlled the records; they monopolized education, economy, law and politics. Thus the records that survive are the records of their own activities. The records that survive of peasants–plebeians have been made by clergy, nobles and burghers, hardly ever by the peasants–plebeians themselves.

Despite this basic weakness in the records of early modern German history some statistical generalizations have been compiled from the later part of the period. By the later seventeenth and eighteenth centuries social statistics became extremely important above all for the more efficient taxation of the common people, allowing the following speculations to be made about East Prussia, the Austrian provinces and the county of Lippe (Westphalia).[1]

[1] See Chapter IV, note 24.

From statistics produced in 1805 as part of the Stein reforms, rural East Prussia contained:

1,400 estate managers; with dependants, 7,000 people; 1½ per cent of the population.

109,500 domestics and serfs without land; with dependants, 115,000 people; 21 per cent of the population.

58,800 tenant-farmers and serfs with land; with dependants, 294,000 people; 53½ per cent of the population.

8,000 cottars; with dependants, 40,000 people; 7 per cent of the population.

8,000 village craftsmen; with dependants, 32,000 people; 6 per cent of the population.

60,200 others; 11 per cent of the population.

Total rural population 548,200, representing three-quarters of the whole population of East Prussia; the rest lived in townships.

The population of seventeenth-century Lower Austria (the two provinces Ob der Enns and Nieder der Enns) was about 600,000 of whom 100,000 may have lived in the towns, including 75,000 in Vienna and its New Town alone. Town dwellers were here some 17 per cent of the total estimated population.

In a simplified form the 1788 census in Lippe gave the Establishment (court, nobles, officials, clergy, army, estate managers, protected Jews and all their dependants) 5,200 people = 8 per cent of the total population; town dwellers (burghers and plebeians) 10,600 = 17 per cent, and country dwellers (peasants, serfs, servants and farm labourers) 46,000 = 75 per cent —total 61,800. The first census in Lippe in 1776 had given a total population of about 50,000 which represents a massive increase of 24 per cent over a period of twelve years. In the decade 1779–88 a staggeringly high death-rate was outpaced by an even higher birth-rate when Lippe recorded 5,860 weddings, 24,189 births, and 18,509 deaths.

Such general statistics tell us something about the way populations were divided between the social groups and how they grew. Those given here are only a brief indication of the work that has been done and of the work that still has to be done to clarify the picture of early modern German society from the records that remain. To give one result from the above survey:

the Lower Austrian group of town dwellers was already as large a percentage of the population as a whole by the seventeenth century as was the equivalent percentage in Lippe in the later eighteenth century. This shows how early modern German social history is still wide open to new research.

Early modern Germans believed in status, in *Standschaft*. What did they mean by it? What did it mean to be of the first Estate, clergy; the second Estate, nobility; third Estate, burgher; and the rest, peasant–plebeian?

The clergy were a professional group. No one was born a cleric, unlike the majority of nobles and burghers who were born as nobles and burghers. So here is a fundamental distinction between the three ruling groups. Nobility and burgher status were more fundamental than clergy status. Clergy status was an extra. The greater number of clergy that really counted for anything were born nobles or burghers before they became clergy. Even Luther's father gained burgher status and a stone-built town house, so young Martin was about as much of a peasant as Colbert was a bourgeois. Although clergy status was a less fundamental grouping than noble or burgher status, the clergy officially remained the leading social group, the first Estate, in the continued Catholic constitution of early modern Germany. The cathedral chapters of the ecclesiastical states of Münster and Paderborn were drawn from the Catholic nobility. They continued to elect their bishops also from the Catholic nobility as if the Protestant Reformation had hardly happened. The medieval tradition in West Germany, where the clergy had been a mainstay of local government and royal administration, was continued in the very considerable number of ecclesiastical states that survived the Reformation, right down to the time of Napoleon. These states were the truly conservative element in early modern German public life, which would be well brought out by a study of the bishops of Augsburg or Salzburg. No comprehensive study of the ecclesiastical states exists. It can only very partially be provided here, because much more preliminary work has yet to be done on the subject. However, six such ecclesiastical territories have been examined for the Westphalian region, and the complex pattern that comes to light for the north-west is an indication of the nature of ecclesiastical state-life for the other regions of Germany. All these six ecclesiastical territories were socially and economically backward, even perhaps stagnant territories. Each tried to cope in its own way with the problem of elective-aristocratic political survival with greatly varying degrees of success against the ever-present threats of Protestantism, mediatization and dynastic take-over.

The early modern German nobility were the most powerful group of all. Nobility was above all a distinction by birth, but it was also open to merit and wealth. Thus the riches of the Augsburg banking Fuggers allowed them to move out of burgher status into not only noble status but territorial ruler, high noble status as imperial counts and ruling princes with an actual state of their own during the course of the sixteenth and early seventeenth centuries. Such a development was highly unusual, but it did happen, showing that German nobility was not caste-like but open to incentive. Thousands of burgher families purchased titles of low nobility (*Briefadel*) all through the early modern period and beyond. Although most nobles were born with their title, there were very great differences between one title and the next, differences of law and custom as well as of wealth and property.

The basic distinction was between 'immediate' and 'mediate' status (*Reichsunmittelbarkeit und Reichsmittelbarkeit*). Immediate status meant high nobility, the top rung of the social ladder. It implied having no overlord except for the supreme overlord himself, the elected German king or Holy Roman Emperor. High nobles were those who had *Reichstandschaft*, federal status under the king or emperor. This group included all the electors, dukes, margraves, ruling princes, counts, lords, bishops, abbots, abbesses, priors, prioresses, who were the rulers of the German states, as well as all their legitimate families. It also included the burghers and town council families of the imperial towns, but no other burghers. Finally, it included the imperial knights, those that survived the rebellion of 1522 without being pressed down into the ranks of the low nobility. By the fifteenth century the imperial knights had formed local cantons within their own specific regions in the Rhinelands, Swabia and Franconia. Imperial knights operated under the protection of the kings and emperors, but their cantons were never joined to the federal institutions of the German Empire, and they had neither seat nor vote in the imperial assembly.

The low nobility were not of federal, *Reich* status. They were privileged only at territorial, state level. They were of mediate status and said to have *Landstandschaft*. Such nobles had no direct appeal to institutions or courts of the federal *Reich*, and took part in federal *Reich* activities only if they happened to be the representatives and servants of high nobles or territorial rulers—hence the great importance of formal protocol, a potent form of power politics in its own right. The greater number of all German noble families were of low noble status. They were the real descendants of feudal and allodial patterns of land-holding, and also of families advancing to ennoblement through investment in, and service to, territorial rulers' courts. Many could be traced back to the unfree *ministeriales* of the high noble dynasties and ecclesiastical rulers of the high Middle Ages. The low nobility were the most important social group within the German states themselves. They provided the membership of the leading Estate in territorial politics, and were the major link in a chain of command that stretched down from the federal high nobility (the territorial rulers over the German states) to the commoners (the mass of burghers and peasants–plebeians within those states).

Where did the burghers stand in this complex system? Although they were classed as commoners *vis-à-vis* the high and low nobility, the burghers were a complex group, distinct at law from the peasants–plebeians. Burgher status was achieved by a conscious act, an oath of loyalty to a specific town council. This gave the burgher protection under the town's specific code of law (*Bürgerrecht*) which was usually an inherited privilege and renewed *pro forma* in each generation of the family concerned, or it could be purchased by outsiders. Purchase was especially welcomed when town finances were low. Thus the sale of burgher status was a considerable item of town income in the fiscal records that survive of late sixteenth-century Lemgo in Lippe (Westphalia) and could similarly be traced in the records of all the German towns, for Lemgo was no unusual specimen of pre-industrial German urban development. But most burghers inherited their status from their burgher parents. They were born burghers, and burghers of one town only. Those who moved to other towns had to purchase, marry or otherwise recommend their way into the burgher status of their new town. Most towns had rules for this, usually residence for a number of years plus a fee for the oath.

The value of any burgher oath depended upon the political and economic standing of the town that issued it. Thus there was great variation between the federal *Reich* status of imperial town burghers, like that of Frankfurt-am-Main or Augsburg, at the one end, and small-state, market-town burghers like those of Brakel or Lügde (Westphalia) at the other end. The latter were even *Ackerbürger*, burghers with ploughed fields. They were small farmers with fields just outside the town and farmyards behind the town wall. They were little more than inhabitants of fortified villages, but with enough political and legal autonomy to be accepted as burghers in the German system. They had their own civic institutions, however crude these were when compared with those of great towns like Nuremberg. Thus there were great differences between one burgher and the next.

External differences were of two basic forms. Either the town had federal *Reich* status as an imperial town under the Emperor, or it had territorial *Land* status as a town under a ruling prince. The imperial towns were scattered over the west and south-west of Germany. Most towns had only territorial status. Some imperial towns were small and insignificant such as Isny, and some territorial towns were large and important, such as Leipzig. Thus legal and constitutional distinctions were not always necessarily in accord with economic reality. Whether a town was rich or not did not depend upon whether it was an imperial town by early modern times. Yet formally at law by federal *Reich* constitutions and customs, distinctions were kept by established tradition. Early modern Germany believed in tradition and custom.

Internal differences in the burgher group within any one town were very great. Burghers were of course only the smaller, privileged section of a town's permanent population. Numbers varied according to the rules of citizenship in each town. Generally the poorer the town, the cheaper its burgher oath, and the less privilege that it bought. Market towns had a majority of small farmers, tradesmen and craftsmen as burghers, as for example in the small Westphalian towns. But however modest burgher status may have been, it divided those of any standing from the plebs. To the common man achieving burgher status could be his greatest aim in life. Such achievement, for example, crowned Luther's father's successful mining career.

At the top of the burgher scale were the town council families (*Ratsverwandte*). They were an oligarchy of the most economically significant burgher families who asserted themselves politically whilst tolerating minor adjustments to their membership from generation to generation, against the majority of the burghers all through the early modern period and beyond. Thus, the burgher system seemed to ape that of the nobility. There were high and low burghers, like high and low nobles. There was a further distinction between town council relatives and the rest of the burghers in every imperial town and territorial town. Yet the standing of an individual town and of an individual burgher within it varied so greatly that the overall distinction of 'burgher' would seem to be little more than meaningless upon closer analysis. A double standard resolves this dilemma. The status of burgher meant a great amount to those who were looking in on it from below and outside. Burgher status was a uniform object of desire for the plebs. Once inside, of course, the individual differences took precedence over the uniformity with which the group faced the outside world.

Burghers were generally the lowest social group to have political power and privilege within the federal and state systems of early modern Germany. Burghers were the rearguard of the political nation. Those that were burghers of imperial towns provided representatives at imperial assemblies (*Reichstage*). Those that were burghers of territorial towns provided representatives to territorial state assemblies (*Landtage*). Burgher representatives to both types of assembly were chosen by, and came from, the group of town council relatives within each town. In this way, burghers were part of the élite that exercised political, legal, social and economic power, alongside the clergy and the nobles. Burghers were the butt-end of the ruling élite. What, then, about the peasants–plebeians, the ruled, the mass of the real people of early modern Germany?

In Lippe (Westphalia) the second census of 1788 showed that three-quarters of the population lived in the countryside. They were the peasants, serfs, servants and farm labourers of ruler, clergy, nobles and burghers. Only one-sixth of the population lived in the towns. What proportion of this one-sixth were the privileged burghers and what proportion made up the rest, the plebs, smaller artisans, craftsmen, street venders, day-labourers, servants and the poor is not yet clear. What is clear, is that rural and urban plebs made up the mass of the population in every German state, but that the countryside produced by far the greatest number of people.

The most common representative of this group was the peasant. Variations in legal and economic status of the peasantry are so extensive that they would fill hundreds of volumes. It can only be the task here to give a very brief sketch. Once again a double standard applies to the peasantry also. To those looking in from below and outside, a peasant was a manager, a man in business with responsibility over land and livestock. To labourers, living-in servants and farmhands, to become a peasant was a grand desire. Once inside the peasantry, the differences between tenure, rents and taxes plus all the natural uncertainties of farming took precedence for each individual. Peasant differences stemmed from a great variety of economic pressures, first, concerning size and quality of land. This was often a question of medieval tradition stemming from the breakdown of the high medieval *villicationes*, *Meierhöfe*. Generally speaking, the richest peasants with the best conditions of tenure were those serf families living in the *Esch* of the older villages. The *Esch* was the heart of the village and with a farmyard in the *Esch* there went the best pieces of land. The poorest peasants were generally those who had arrived the most recently as free families living in the forests, scrub, marshes or wasteland on the edge of the villages with small-holdings as cottars. Thus, at least for West Germany, the best lands and tenures went to unfree, serf families. The common countryman who was a freeman was not an enviable person. The rich serf-peasant in the village *Esch* was, however, enviable indeed.

Second, conditions of the tenancy (*Meierbrief*) varied greatly. Tenants' contracts generally ran for any period from three to twelve years and thus could be revised to protect the landlord against inflation. In return they gave the peasant certain rights of tenure: he could not be evicted or sold up unless he had failed to satisfy the conditions of his contract after a certain time, usually after one to three harvests, and then only under legal procedures presided over by a territorial ruler's judicial officials.

Where these officials were of course the same persons as the landlords, as in Paderborn for example, the peasant was in a very bad position.[2] But this was unusual for West Germany. In the colonized east, the position had been initially much better for the peasantry. From the twelfth to the fifteenth century peasant colonists had been enticed east of the Elbe by farming contractors, *sculteti*, who offered tax- and rent-free years of farming. But once these were over the peasant had no residual customary rights whatsoever. When large-scale farming increasingly became economically viable in the sixteenth century, the once privileged peasant became a rural wage-slave or *Robot*. However, there were exceptions in the German east. The rulers of Saxony above all protected their peasants against such economic degradation because they had no wish to see the bulk of their main rural taxpayers disappear. Equally, around the towns and market towns a local, peasant-run agriculture could still preserve itself, but the latifundia of the noble landlords who were also the ruler's local officials were the prevalent form of rural economic organization in early modern East Germany, once again quite unlike the West.

The peasants had no political representation in territorial state assemblies (*Landtage*), except in a very few quite untypical regions in the south and north-west, Tirol, Frisia and the Dithmarschen. Peasants provided the bulk tax revenues that were granted at territorial state assemblies which they did not attend. Their landlords, the clergy, nobles and burghers, attended (in fatherly fashion) on their tenants' behalf. Thus peasants had to pay traditional tithes as well as landlord rents as worked out in regularly revised *Meierbriefe*, and on top of this taxes granted at assemblies of clergy, nobles and burghers to their territorial rulers, which were assessed according to the quality and size of the peasant's land, called *Landschatz*. The records of this land tax form the bulk of what we can ever rediscover about the ordinary peasant in any region on his own farmstead in early modern Germany. The *Landschatz* was unwieldy and soon became out of date, but it gave rise to a bureaucratic interest in peasant life, peasant settlement and movement, patterns of production and consumption, regulation and exhortation to, rather than actual, improvement in the

[2] See below, Chapter V (ii).

science and literature of husbandry (*Hausvaterliteratur*), encouraged by improving landlords.

Peasants themselves were bosses. They employed their own nuclear families and wherever possible servants and labourers, usually poor, unmarried boys and girls who lived on the farm without any privileges of their own, called *Gesinde*. The same applied to the young urban poor in the houses of the burghers, craftsmen and shopkeepers of the towns. They received food, lodging and clothing plus annual or biannual pay, which was extremely low, perhaps paid in debased small-coin. In the sixteenth and seventeenth centuries it was felt that *Gesinde* were worth poll-taxing and thus bureaucracy began to fix their wages in *Polizeiordnungen* and to obtain their names and addresses for tax purposes. These policy-decrees also fixed the wage maximums of the traditional day-labourers, from the ploughman to the joiner.

The rest was charity. The Catholic concept of 'good works' maintained its force during the early modern period. A middle course was steered between Christian welfare and the 'Protestant ethic'. Early modern Catholic and Protestant attitudes to alms and begging were indeed different, but the difference was really only whether poverty should be open or hidden, a public spectacle or a private misery. The Protestants certainly tried to distinguish between the deserving poor and sturdy beggars. Healthy drop-outs were intolerable, and as the economic system was only a part of God-given law and order, those that were only common people, but healthy and different, be it by design or accident, had little or no place in the early modern order of things. At best, perhaps, they swelled the ranks and camp-followings of ever-increasing armies, first mercenary, then territorial. Of course many also *chose* a military career, war gave honour, glory, a fatherland, a leader and the chance of loot and betterment, plus a lot of excitement before death claimed the field; and that death would do, anyway. The early modern war industry was considered exciting and approved by society: of course those who were in it were warned to obey its rules, a warning popularized by Jacques Callot's eighteen prints of the miseries and bad times of war first published in Paris, 1633. Callot's message was not that war was horrible, but that marauding by soldiers who broke their military code was horrible and he shows that soldiers who became marauders suffered most horribly of all when the authorities caught up with them. Callot was not anti-war, he was against its lack of discipline, that is the popular Thirty Years' War form of it.

We have briefly moved through early modern German society from the top downwards. A minority of the population, the clergy, nobles and burghers, controlled affairs, but how? We have now to outline the political and constitutional system of early modern Germany.

III

The Problem of German Federalism

FEDERALISM is the main theme of German political history. An integral part of everyday politics and government has been the relationship of the territories to the Empire or Federation since later medieval times until the present day. Until very recently it seems to have been in the nature of federalism that at most times more decisions should have been taken at territorial, state level than at imperial, federal level.

German federal development itself has been twofold, as expressed in the terms *Kaiser* and *Reich*. What was *kaiserlich* pertained to the elected head of the Empire and his court, almost invariably a Habsburg ruler with his capital in Innsbruck, Prague or Vienna. What was prefixed *Reichs-* generally, but not invariably, pertained to the territorial rulers as peers of the Empire, as *Reichsunmittelbare Stände*, with west and south-west German towns, notably Frankfurt-am-Main, Nuremberg, Regensburg, Augsburg, Speyer and Wetzlar as its administrative centres. Here the Emperor was admittedly *primus inter pares* by virtue of his election and coronation, but his power was also thereby and by previous law and custom strictly limited. Thus at this federal level the peers of the Empire preserved their own liberties, privileges, rights and customs, which neither Charles V nor Ferdinand II was able to destroy or even permanently modify.

For the earlier period of federalism the *Reichstagsakten* (1956ff.), which cover at present parts of the late fourteenth, earlier fifteenth, and earlier sixteenth centuries, are of fundamental importance. Chronologically incomplete, they leave too

23

many gaps to present an overall picture of early federal development. They are unfortunately also difficult to use because of the complex editorial rules which they follow. This is perhaps an inevitable weakness of federalism, where the relevant documents are necessarily collected together from a considerable number of territorial archives, and not from a central archive in one capital city, although head of them all is undoubtedly now the Haus-, Hof-, und Staatsarchiv in Vienna.

It is thus necessary to use early modern legal compendia in order to understand this federal development, above all the *Neue und vollständigere Sammlung der Reichsabschiede* (1747), J. J. Moser, *Teutsches Staatsrecht* (50 vols plus additions and register, 1737–54), and the same author's *Neues Teutsches Staatsrecht* (20 vols plus additional parts and register, 1766–75).

Many constitutional histories of Germany have been written since the end of the eighteenth century. One of the earliest, J. S. Pütter, *Historische Entwicklung der heutigen Staatsverfassung des teutschen Reichs* (3 parts, 2nd ed., 1788), and one of the most recent, H. Conrad, *Deutsche Rechtsgeschichte*, 2, 1495–1806 (1966), are of particular importance. Conrad gives a fuller coverage of the federal institutions of the early modern empire than has been customary in works of this nature in the more recent past. A notable survey of the imperial constitution at the beginning of the eighteenth century is still H. v. Zwiedineck-Südenhorst, *Deutsche Geschichte im Zeitraum der Gründung des Preussischen Königtums*, 2 (1894, pp. 185–328). Although some of his interpretations are now revised, Zwiedineck-Südenhorst based his account on contemporary sources and literature. Notable also is the account in C. Bornhak, *Deutsche Verfassungsgeschichte* (1934, pp. 91–126). The basic handbook is still R. Schröder and E. v. Künssberg, *Lehrbuch der deutschen Rechtsgeschichte* (6th ed., 1919–22), which is the German equivalent of Taswell-Langmead for the medieval and early modern period.

A reflection on the crucial rôle that legal history plays in the overall study of German history is that federalism led to a complicated system of politics and government by continually creating constitutional courts and countless other boards of arbitration as the means of compromise in the keeping of law and order. This is well brought out in the articles of M. Heckel,

'Staat und Kirche', 'Autonomia und pacis compositio', and 'Parität', in *Zeitschrift der Savigny-Stiftung für Rechtsgeschichte* (1956–7, 1959 and 1963). Constitutional conflict was a speciality of German lawyers between the Peace of Augsburg and the Treaties of Westphalia, 1555–1648, as W. Schlesinger, *Die Herrschaft der Herren von Schönburg* (1954, p. 5), put it: 'as also in past centuries, the science of law was pressed into service to motivate political decisions'. But naturally pride of place in the direction of such a loose federal system of politics went to the peers of the Empire, who were the territorial rulers, the *sine qua non* of the federal Empire. 'The German State stems from the territorial principality. It is not by nature a monarchic state, as are the states of West Europe' (Schlesinger, 1954, preface).

Territories developed out of a complex of jurisdictions and lands controlled primarily by those members of the high nobility who achieved a position of autonomy under the Emperors with a responsibility for keeping peace, law and order, especially from the thirteenth century onwards. H. Angermeier, *Königtum und Landfriede im deutschen Spätmittelalter* (1966), examines the federal and imperial aspects of this development until 1555. V. L. v. Seckendorff, *Teutscher Fürsten-Staat* (1656, 5th ed., with additions, 1678), examined the state of the smaller territories. It became the standard handbook of politics at the courts of the post-1648 era. It was used as a textbook in the education of future territorial rulers. Its importance is well brought out by H. Kraemer, 'Der deutsche Kleinstaat des 17. Jahrhunderts im Spiegel von Seckendorffs "Teutschem Fürstenstaat"', in *Zeitschrift für thüringische Geschichte und Altertumskunde*, 25 (1922–4, pp. 1–16, 48–60, 84–97).

The standard collection of documents is P. Sander and H. Spangenberg, *Urkunden zur Geschichte der Territorialverfassung* (1922–6; reprinted 1965), although only four of the planned seven parts were published. K. Zeumer, *Quellensammlung zur Geschichte der deutschen Reichsverfassung in Mittelalter und Neuzeit* (2nd ed., 2 parts, 1913), is the standard collection of constitutional documents for university use. A new edition is badly needed. W. Ebel, *Geschichte der Gesetzgebung in Deutschland* (2nd ed., 1958, pp. 57–77), summarizes the growth of legislative power in the territories: see also F. Lütge, *Geschichte der deutschen Agrarverfassung* (2nd ed., 1967, pp. 116–18).

H. Thieme, 'Die Funktion der Regalien im Mittelalter', in *Zeitschrift der Savigny-Stiftung für Rechtsgeschichte* (1942, p. 84), called territories: 'states constructed from areas of land taken over by princely administrations and built up economically as well as politically'.

O. Brunner, *Land und Herrschaft* (1939) is still the standard secondary work on the development of the medieval territories but it is now best read with Angermeier, as Brunner was doing pioneer work at a time before historians generally began to appreciate that the weaker federalism of the Empire between 1250 and 1806 was a vital constitutional development of its own, providing the essential framework outside of which the politically more powerful territorial development towards statehood could not, and indeed did not take place. See the fourth edition of *Land und Herrschaft* (1959, pp. vii–viii, 440), and compare O. Brunner, 'Deutsches Reich und Deutsche Lande', in *Zeitschrift für deutsche Geisteswissenschaften*, 3 (1940, pp. 241, 248–9); also Angermeier, 1966, p. 3, and K. S. Bader, *Der deutsche Südwesten* (1950, p. 17). Bader's book is a regional study which never loses sight of the importance of the Empire to territorial development in Swabia.

In contrast, G. Tellenbach, 'Vom karolingischen Reichsadel zum deutschen Reichsfürstenstand', in T. Mayer (ed.), *Adel und Bauern* (1943, pp. 72–3), gives the traditional view that the early modern Empire was a Hohenstaufen failure in power politics and nothing much else. This is a view which in no way detracts from the importance of the main body of his essay, but it well expresses what Bader has called the *kleindeutsche* (Prussian or *Machtpolitische*) view of the early modern Empire and territories, exemplified in the essay of F. Hartung, *Volk und Staat in der deutschen Geschichte* (1940, pp. 4–27).

Any attempt to derive the origins of the modern sovereign state from only one of the two basic forms of constitutional life, namely the federal Empire or territorial state, must fail, for each is dependent on the other. Federal Empire and territorial state produced all those peculiarities which later sealed the fate of the German Federal Empire and its members, namely the territorial states. For the constitutional historian that myth of the Federal Empire which has been magnified until it has become hysteria, and for which there is then supposed to be only one form of unification for the Germans, leads to as distorted a picture as the view that tries to trace the development towards statehood solely from the territories or even from one or other specific leading territory.[1]

That confusion still exists as a result of the *kleindeutsche* view of German history coming into conflict with a *grossdeutsche* view that the early modern Empire was a vital federal unit which enabled a myriad of territorial political systems to operate in concord under Habsburg emperors, and to establish a tradition of *teutsche Libertät*, of co-operation between Emperor and peers, rulers and Estates, can be seen in a work like E. v. Puttkamer, *Föderative Elemente im deutschen Staatsrecht seit 1648* (1955). This collection of extracts from documents and texts devotes three pages (27-9) to the 1648 Peace of Osnabrück and *Jüngster Reichsabschied* of 1654, but ten pages (39-48) to extracts from Pufendorf and Leibnitz, neither of whom was a statesman, and whose political writings were of no practical importance in Germany outside Brandenburg and the Guelph lands, unlike those of Chancellor Seckendorff, who is not included in the selection. In the history of political thought some clarification has recently been given by O. Hauser, 'Deutsch-englische Missverständnisse', in *Geschichte in Wissenschaft und Unterricht*, 18 (1967, pp. 275-88).

The problem of empire has been acute again since 1949 when Germany has had two territories struggling against each other for reunification (*Wiedervereinigung*, not just *Einigung*), with which both in their own way keep a yearning for political and territorial continuity with Weimar and the second and third empires very much alive. This situation has some marked similarities with the divided Germany of the Reformation period, where Wittenberg and Ingolstadt were the centres of ideological conflict as in another way Bonn for the West and Pankow for the East are in our day.

Within its own territorial boundaries, however, West Germany has settled down to a federal system of parliamentary government. Hence there is great yearning to find federal, parliamentary roots in the German past:[2]

---

[1] K. S. Bader, 'Territorienbildung und Landeshoheit', *Blätter für deutsche Landesgeschichte*, 90, 1953, p. 110.

[2] O. Brunner, *Land und Herrschaft*, 4th ed., p. 443.

The States of the Federal Republic of Germany have been created according to the model of the individual states that united to form the North German Confederation in 1867. They go back to the territories, territorial states of the original pre-1806 Federal Empire, in which framework, one knows, the modern concepts of state organisation and state administration were developed. These territories at least became formally sovereign when this original Federal Empire disappeared in 1806.

In the Napoleonic era the traditional federal bond of empire which had given the territories a common ground for negotiation was broken. Since 1806 there has been a striving for federal continuity and solutions have come only in temporary fashion by *force majeure*. It is in this light that the post-war solution of German Democratic Republic–West Berlin–German Federal Republic, of division in reality and a clinging to reunification in theory, can perhaps be understood. This is enshrined in the preamble to the 1949 Constitution of the Federal Republic, which goes by the name of a *Grundgesetz*, or basic law, as if to stress the transitional quality of the state which it has called into being:

The German People in the States of Baden, Bavaria, Bremen, Hamburg, Hesse, Lower Saxony, North Rhine-Westphalia, Rhineland-Palatinate, Schleswig-Holstein, Württemberg-Baden and Württemberg-Hohenzollern, conscious of their responsibility before God and men, animated by the resolve to preserve their national and political unity and to serve the peace of the world as an equal partner in a united Europe, desiring to give a new order to political life for a transitional period, have enacted, by virtue of their constituent power, this Basic Law of the Federal Republic of Germany. They have also acted on behalf of those Germans to whom participation was denied. The entire German people are called upon to achieve in free self-determination the unity and freedom of Germany.

This preamble serves more as a link with the Prussian and Nazi past than as a contribution towards a solution of present German problems in the light of Germany's political heritage and tradition, for the Prussian and Nazi past is not the only tradition that modern Germany has.

A comment on the political tension that a clinging to the idea of reunification caused is the lecture of F. Lusset, 'Die Wiedervereinigung Deutschlands von den Nachbarländern aus gesehen', and the accompanying letter of K. D. Erdmann, in

Geschichte in Wissenschaft und Unterricht, 16 (1965, pp. 157–68). See also W. Hubatsch *et al., Die Deutsche Frage* (*1949–61*) (1961), which prints the 1949 constitutions of both the Federal and the Democratic Republics (pp. 185–249). Hubatsch's preface begins:

The 'German question' is as follows: how can the numerically strongest people of Europe reach a common political goal in becoming one nation, as has happened in France, England, Russia, Poland, Italy, the Iberian and Scandinavian states, without necessarily endangering the peace and freedom of the remaining European nations?

The myth of reunification, which has only in the last few years begun to be overshadowed by Chancellor Brandt's ambitious *Ostpolitik,* is thus in some ways similar to the myth of the Hohenstaufen failure and the myth of the stagnant empire, after Reformation, Counter-Reformation and warfare had ended their first, more violent, phase in 1648. However, the internal structure of West Germany today brings out federal traditions which in the past bound together territories both large and small, although the recent past still looms threateningly over this new development.

Following F. Dickmann, *Der Westfälische Friede* (1959), the peace treaties of 1648 have been subjected to intensive archive studies and found to have been very statesmanlike arrangements, creating a political stability which Germany had never before and seldom afterwards experienced. Equally F. L. Carsten, *Princes and Parliaments in Germany* (1959), has uncovered a territorial political tradition as more than just of piecemeal, antiquarian and local interest. The *kleindeutsche* and *machtpolitische* view of history which saw early modern German history as the struggle between Prussia and Austria for political supremacy is thus being put into a better perspective in the light of German federal history as a whole. See the lecture of C. Haase, *Das ständische Wesen im nördlichen Deutschland* (1964).

A reappraisal of the role of the early modern empire and of the smaller territories in the federal and territorial development of Germany is thus taking place.

For a reappraisal of the rôle of the permanent conference at the imperial assembly, 1663–1806, see W. Fürnrohr, *Der immerwährende Reichstag zu Regensburg* (1963, pp. 64, 74):

The historical value of the Permanent Conference at the Imperial Assembly lies in the fact that it contributed substantially to upholding the religious peace of the Federal Empire by hindering stronger forces of destruction working against the multi-lateral balance of religion. This assembly safeguarded and furthered the internal security of the Empire and it prevented to the end its break-up into innumerable individual parts. Wherever inner conflicts occurred, the Assembly localised them, and played them down. Against foreign enemies the Assembly on the whole was capable of upholding the existing political order, and if it did this in a merely peaceful way, then that is no thorn in our flesh, as it seems to have been for some historians of the German past ... Hartung, Meinecke and many others, including Haller.

If one recognises a German assembly of states in the Permanent Conference at the Imperial Assembly (from the 1660s), which one is fully entitled to do, even if thereby its nature is not fully perceived, then one can say that Germany has always had such an institution, even in those times when there was no German *Reich*. The constitution of the (Napoleonic) *Rheinbund* included a federal assembly, the *Deutsche Bund* and the Second Empire depended upon a Federal Council functioning opposite a *Reichstag* which was a House of Representatives, and the Weimar Republic, which depended on the *Reichstag*, had its own Federal Council as a body for its component States. Only Hitler negated federal as equally as democratic principles.[3]

The Holy Roman Empire was a federal unit whose politicians may have criticized its weakness, especially in foreign policy and defence, but overwhelmingly they did not say that they wanted to do away with it before the Napoleonic era: not even the Hohenzollern despots of the seventeenth and eighteenth centuries said that they wanted to do that. The territories were powerful and the Empire weak, whereby the dictum of Pufendorf that the Empire was a monstrosity and a degeneration of the classical forms which states could take, was used to save the bother of delving into a mass of especially legal records in order to discover what really was the basic form in which imperial and federal politics were conducted. Hence the fundamental importance was not often recognized of the *Reichskammergericht* and the *Reichshofrat* in German history as courts of arbitration

---

[3] W. Fürnrohr, reviewing in *Geschichte in Wissenschaft und Unterricht*, 15, 1964, p. 688n.

and negotiation in the early modern period, as well as of the circles, imperial assemblies and a myriad *ad hoc* committees and commissions and other expedients from the earliest *Reichsregiment* to the *Corpus Evangelicorum* and *Reichsdeputationstage*.[4]

The drastic changes of the 20th century have turned the aged problem of justice and power in history into an urgent question for today. Thus the jurisdiction of the pre-1806 Federal Empire becomes interesting once more. The significance of the highest Federal Imperial Courts and struggles to influence them, especially the *Reichskammergericht*, the way they varied in importance and were called into question according to the changing circumstances of Federal Imperial reform, religious differences, confessional and power-political conflict, needs to be more accentuated nowadays than formerly was the case when *Realpolitik* predominated.

With imperial and federal institutions and procedures, the security and further internal political development of the territories was assured. What the *weak* Empire really means is that the territories took over the powers of executive government, of *Gebot und Verbot*, whilst the Empire remained a general court of legal complaint, constitutional arbitration and political appeal, a forum where territorial rulers could negotiate with each other and where even territorial subjects could at times take their own worst grievances, if they dared to do so and provided they could afford it. Equally, new ways and means of legislation and taxation were very largely first worked out at imperial and federal level before they were developed in the territories. This applies to taxes raised for military expenditure from the fifteenth to the eighteenth centuries, the *Römermonate* and *Türkensteuern*, which actually made 3,300,000 fl. in 1594–8 and 1,600,000 fl. in 1713 (Conrad, p. 135), as well as to the *Kammerzieler* to pay for the staffing of the *Reichskammergericht*.

Bader outlined these developments more specifically for south-west Germany (pp. 14–15), and generally for the Empire (p. 196).

The German southwest is after all only a part of a larger whole. The development of state organisations in the whole region took place

---

[4] R. Smend in an introduction to a reprint (Aalen, 1965) of his still incomplete monograph, *Das Reichskammergericht, Geschichte und Verfassung* (1911).

within the framework of the Federal Empire in which the territories even in times of the most extensive separation were nothing more than parts of a greater whole. If the history of these territories is to have a deeper meaning, then this relationship of the whole to the part must remain recognisable even when we stress that the part was a law unto itself. Thus it becomes our task to describe the relationship between territories and Federal Empire without distorting the existence of territories as particular states.

Whereas in the time after the end of the Federal Empire in 1806 the constitutional importance of Federal Imperial bodies of state such as the *Reichskammergericht* and *Reichshofrat* was undermined due to the influence of a *kleindeutsch* writing of history, so nowadays research increasingly accentuates the continued importance of the loose federal system. This applies with the same force to the constitution of the Circles.

The same author has worked out an example from the 1770s of how the *Reichshofrat*, with the help of the imperial court in Vienna, played an important part in the politics of a territory (K. S. Bader, 'Die Rechtsprechung des Reichshofrats und die Anfänge des territorialen Beamtenrechts', in *Zeitschrift der Savigny-Stiftung für Rechtsgeschichte*, 65 (1947, pp. 363–79). The same applies to the *Reichskammergericht* which for example supported the Hohenzollern-Hechingen peasantry against their rulers in the seventeenth and eighteenth centuries. F. Hertz, 'Die Rechtsprechung der höchsten Reichsgerichte', in *Mitteilungen des Instituts für österreichische Geschichtsforschung*, 69 (1961, pp. 329–58), further gives cases from the territories of Sayn, Isenburg, Saxony, Hesse, Jülich, Anhalt, Corvey, Mecklenburg, Frisia, Reuss, Calenberg, Württemberg and Salm of both *Reichshofrat* and *Reichskammergericht* supporting territorial subjects and territorial Estates against specifically criminal territorial rulers and their peers. In three exceptionally serious cases two of the rulers were forced to abdicate and the third was actually imprisoned for six years. Admittedly the latter was a peer without a territory, a fact which he made up for by obtaining money under false pretences and then going bankrupt in the earlier eighteenth century (see Hertz, 1961, pp. 346, 350).

The circles have also recently received greater attention,

although an overall study is as yet not available. See R. Wines, 'The imperial circles, princely diplomacy and imperial reform, 1681–1714', in *Journal of Modern History*, 39 (1967, pp. 1–29). A. K. Mally in *Der österreichische Kreis in der Exekutionsordnung des Römisch—Deutschen Reiches* (1967, p. 7) describes the leading circles as 'Co-operatives of numerous neighbouring middle-sized, small and minute territorial states . . . at least concerning the role of ruling princes who acted as Directors of the Circles in the execution of verdicts given in the federal-imperial law courts.'

The wealth of material, however, imposes its own stricter limitations on any studies in early modern German history. It is the plan here to see what form territorial development took in the heart of north-west Germany, and to find out how territorial internal affairs related to the regional, federal and imperial institutions of the early modern Empire. This has been done by examining an area containing a number of diverse territories by way of introduction, and thereafter by concentrating on Lippe, Westphalia and the Empire, that is a territory, a circle and the federal whole.

The best monographs on early modern Westphalia are H. Rothert, *Westfälische Geschichte* (3 vols, 2nd ed., 1962), which is very well written, and A. K. Hömberg, *Westfälische Landes-geschichte* (published posthumously, 1967), which are brilliant lectures that go into social, legal and economic history, so vital to any real understanding of internal territorial politics. Rothert and Hömberg treated the political history of Westphalia in its full multi-territorial development. This included the history of many territorial governments and Estates, in and out of assemblies, all struggling to direct society and economics to their own greater advantage.

But what was Westphalia? It is perhaps best to see it as an example of how the question of sovereignty was never really solved by a federal system of politics which is so peculiar to the Empire before 1806. The ruling dynasties developed territories or *Flächenstaaten* within the region of Westphalia which were already strong political units by later medieval times, yet without closed frontiers. During the sixteenth century they were associated in a regional circle with the task of coercing every member to execute especially those common policies which the leading territories had worked out at federal and imperial level during times of particular crises.

As the territories and not the Empire developed into states, it was necessary to create regional bodies of arbitration, because at imperial level there were too many diverse territories for a real community of interest to produce everyday co-operation in politics. There was no execution of majority decisions except at regional level. Thus from 1500 to 1800 Westphalia became a political reality as a popular expression for the Lower-Rhenish-Westphalian circle. Westphalia was primarily a regional expression for an intermediate level of government between the territories and the Empire.

It was up to the territorial rulers to make what they would of the concept of Westphalia as an intermediate level of federal government. Although they retained the power of the state over their own territorial subjects, and although Westphalia was just one of a number of federal expedients, the territories were too small and scattered and above all too economically interdependent, for some federal co-operation in law, police, defence and economics not to be an absolute necessity for their own continued existence.

That the Germans developed an imperfect state-system which had to rely upon federal expedients like those of *Westfalen, Kaiser und Reich*, is naturally difficult to grasp in the light of a nineteenth- and twentieth-century state monopoly in politics, nationalism and sovereignty. It is, however, a fact that the vast majority of the territories in the early modern Empire were too weak to establish their own monoliths of state power and control. This was of course not because they did not vigorously try to do so, but because they did not have the necessary resources to assert their own sovereignty as states against the claims of all others. For they were generally too small, without natural frontiers, too economically vulnerable and without a complete legal system of their own. At some stage or other in any crisis they generally had to appeal for help to an imperial or federal instance of government outside their own territorial boundaries. This has been well brought out for mid-seventeenth-century Mecklenburg by E. Hofer, *Die Beziehungen Mecklenburgs zu Kaiser und Reich, 1620–83* (1956).

This structure of politics furthered sovereign power only to a limited extent. The Empire was a meeting ground for territories that were by virtue of a basic lack of resources incapable of going their own way and only ever tolerated as independent by their neighbours on the strength of their mutual co-operation at federal and imperial level. This is explained, for example, by the continued importance of ties under an imperial feudal system which was copied in the territories until the days of Joseph II and the Enlightenment. A 'balance of power' was thus a necessity both from within and from without in order to give stability to this complex federal system. The Holy Roman Empire supported so many small territories that only very few of them could develop into sovereign states. Thus, although the Empire guaranteed a system of law and government, it also prevented the growth of sovereignty in the great majority of its component territories. One of these components was the county of Lippe.

Lippe has been chosen in preference to larger territories because it was in the smaller, more numerous territories that federalism was necessarily more adhered to, as a form of protection without which they could not have remained independent. Lippe has lost none of its archive materials, nor have they ever been dispersed and moved to Münster or Berlin, Marburg or Hanover as happened in part to the archives of Lippe's neighbours, especially during the nineteenth century. The county can thus be studied comprehensively from its leading town of Detmold.

The internal politics of Lippe for the period 1650–1790 has been dealt with in several theses written in the last decade. They make use of archive materials in Detmold. The period before 1650 has so far not been dealt with in the same way, although much work has been done on mid-sixteenth-century Lippe in the 1958 Münster University thesis of R. Wolf, 'Der Einfluss des Landgrafen Philipp des Grossmütigen von Hessen auf die Einführung der Reformation in den westfälischen Grafschaften', *Jahrbuch des Vereins für Westfälische Kirchengeschichte*, 51–2 (1958–9, pp. 27–149).

The *Lippische Regesten*, 1–4 (1860–8), provide précis and commentary on the documents of medieval Lippe until 1536, although without archive reference. It is not really until after the reign of Simon V (1511–36) that it becomes possible to write the internal history of Lippe from archive sources. A suitable starting-point is the regency of Bernhard VIII (1536–1548) when more detailed records of the councillors and Estates of Lippe begin. From this period onwards documents survive that are more than disconnected fragments, as the county administration began to deposit written records, the letters and complaints, instructions and rough drafts, registers and minutes of its day-to-day business.

That the period 1536–1650 has not been studied in detail recently, apart from the work of Regula Wolf mentioned above, is no doubt partly due to the remarkable six-volume biography of Simon VI and his times (1563–1613) written by A. Falkmann in the later nineteenth century. As a whole it is hardly possible to improve upon this work. Falkmann is very readable and he used the archives in full, but unfortunately he gave no references to the sources which he used. So at least to some extent his work has to be done again. In the few cases where the findings of Falkmann have been checked, they have, however, been found to be accurate and extremely well formulated as narrative.

For reference to published works on all aspects of Lippe's history from the scholarly to the antiquarian, genealogical and journalistic level, see W. Hansen, *Lippische Bibliographie* (1957) and thereafter the annual bibliographies at the end of each volume of *Lippische Mitteilungen*.

However, there is no work which poses the question, how far were economics and politics shared out between ruler, officials and Estates in Lippe? And second, no overall study has been made of the question, what were the relations between Lippe and federal, imperial institutions in early modern times? In order to find out what were the internal politics of the early modern Empire and its territories it will eventually be necessary to ask questions of this type not only about one small territory but about each and every one of them. It is hoped that the work done here will be a preliminary answer to this wider question. For it is essential to try to bear the affairs of the early modern Empire as a whole in mind, to which an invaluable introduction are the later seventeenth- and earlier eighteenth-century federal annuals, A. Faber (C. L. Leucht), 'Europäische Staatskanzlei', and J. C. Lünig, *Teutsches Reichsarchiv* (24 vols, 1710–22).

An attempt has been made to find out what the study of

Landesgeschichte, territorial, local history entails, and to see how important it really is as a method for the study of German history. There has been a rebirth of *Landesgeschichtliche Forschung* in post-1945 Germany, possibly of an intensity unheard of since the eighteenth century. At that time much history was still written primarily by lawyers and civil servants for the use of governments which employed and supported them. It is thus important to evaluate what a post-war West German historian has said: 'And it seems to me to be one of the greatest advantages of research into territorial history, that it seeks to encompass all these things—the history of settlement, economy, society and constitution.'[5]

The use of language presents its own problems. These are thought to be at least in part incapable of satisfactory solution unless a great amount of unwelcome historical over-simplification is introduced into the English text. For an example of this problem see the *New Cambridge Modern History*, 3 (1968, p. 319n.), where Chapter X solves this problem by introducing simplification for the sake of greater readability. It is an invaluable exercise to try to understand German politics in the medium of another language. The technical language in which German politics was discussed and accepted is thus questioned at every turning as to its real meaning and influence on events, as every concept has to be translated and understood as matter-of-factly as possible in order to become at all meaningful in English.

An institution like the early modern *Reichstag* is thus not translated by 'Imperial Diet', however much this corresponds to contemporary Latin equivalents, because the term 'Diet' is something culinary or politically foreign in English usage. It helps little that its German-Latin meaning is that it was a day's meeting of peers of the Empire.

It is perhaps feasible to use the term *Reichstag* as a loan word or to translate it literally as imperial meeting, or assembly, and then it is essential to explain its meaning by its function, which varied considerably over the centuries. Thus at one point it was more a federal assembly of peers of the Empire and their representatives, to whom they gave strictly limited powers of negotiation; at another time a Catholic 'rump', and finally a more or

[5] A. K. Homberg, *Westfälische Landgeschichte*, Münster, 1967, p. 168.

less permanent mission of territorial rulers' diplomats and lawyers set up in the imperial town of Regensburg.

To translate *Reichstag* by 'Imperial Parliament' in early modern times might imply that it had the same social homogeneity and the same power of making and enforcing decisions in its own name as the English Parliament with its tradition of representation and *plena potestas*, so foreign to German federal politics. By this one should naturally not underestimate the legislation that came out of early modern *Reichstage*, when large numbers of territories could and did at times work harmoniously together with their emperors. Then indeed substantial grants of troops and money were made and legislation was produced in *Reichsordnungen*, *Reichsabschiede* and *Reichsexekutionen*. Grants and legislation were promulgated not in the name of Emperor and *Reichstag*, but in that of the Emperor and *Churfürsten*, *Fürsten und Stände des Reichs*.

A simplification has been made in the use of the term 'Estates', which is used to cover the German term *Stände*. Its compound, *Landstände*, is translated as 'territorial Estates'. German *Stände* may generally be thought of as persons of quality, sometimes equivalent to English 'gentry', although the German term has another more specialized use to denote something similar to the English 'Lords and Commons'. Another simplification is the term *Land*, translated often as 'territory'.

By failing to systematize the use of language, anomalies and perhaps even contradictions will appear, but it is hoped that some over-simplifications may thereby be avoided. German history needs clarification, but this is not achieved by over-simplification, if the latter can be reasonably avoided.

Part Two

Territorial States in North-west Germany

IV

The Region around Lippe

THE territory of Lippe was self-governing from the later twelfth century until the twentieth century. Its existence was due to the remarkable longevity of one dynasty. The first *Edelherren* or Barons and Lords of Lippe appear in the 1120s but the history of the dynasty and its holdings of lands and jurisdictions really begins with the activities of Bernhard II, who ruled from 1168 to 1196. Bernhard II was just one of some 150 other heads of local noble families, or *Edelfreie*, who saw a chance to carve out a territory for themselves during the general contest between Emperor and Papacy. Bernhard's territory was probably formed out of pickings which he got on the destruction of the duchy of Saxony, after the humiliation of his one-time master, Henry the Lion, in 1180.[1]

The Lippe dynasty was neither one of the first, nor was it one of the greatest of the *Edelfreie* but it was the longest lived of them all.[2] From 1196 to 1666 the descendants of Bernhard II passed their lands on from father to son for sixteen generations. Thereafter, until 1905, a collateral branch passed the territory on from father to son for eight generations. A distant relation then became the last ruler until the revolution in 1918 when Lippe became a republic within Weimar Germany.[3] In

[1] H. Kiewning, *Lippische Geschichte*, Detmold, 1942. E. Kittel, *Geschichte des Landes Lippe*, Cologne, 1957, *Lippische Mitteilungen*, 29, 1960, p. 248.

[2] H. Rössler (ed.), *Deutscher Adel 1430–1555*, Darmstadt, 1965, pp. 154, 179. W. Wittich, *Ländliche Verfassung Niedersachsens und Organisation des Amts im 18. Jahrhundert*, Strassburg, 1891, pp. 116–17.

[3] A. Falkmann, *Beiträge zur Geschichte des Fürstentums Lippe*, 1–6, Lemgo and Detmold, 1857–1902. Hopf, *Historischer-Genealogischer Atlas*, Gotha, 1858,

1936 Lippe was put under one *Statthalter* together with Schaumburg-Lippe. The British Military Government incorporated Lippe into the new state of North-Rhine-Westphalia in 1947, and Schaumburg-Lippe became part of the new state of Lower Saxony.[4] From 1949 to the present day North-Rhine-Westphalia has remained one of the richest and largest states of the Federal German Republic. The former boundaries of Lippe are kept in the two local government circles of Lemgo and Detmold. Detmold has also become the seat of the regional government of East-Westphalia-Lippe, an intermediate level between the state government of North-Rhine-Westphalia at Düsseldorf and the circles within its region.[5]

Lippe has always been a border territory, between Westphalia, Lower Saxony and Hesse. Situated in the western uplands around the middle Weser, it is cradled in the south and west by the high Osning forest range.[6] Its political geography remained basically unchanged from the later fourteenth century onwards. In the fifteenth century Lippe acquired the larger part of the neighbouring county of Sternberg, by virtue of which Simon V in 1528 took the title of Count. From 1440 the western enclave and town of Lippstadt was shared with the counts of Cleves-Mark, from whom the Hohenzollerns inherited in the seventeenth century. The Condominium of Lippstadt lasted until 1850. In Schwalenberg, the heavily forested southeastern corner of Lippe, the counts shared their jurisdiction with the bishops of Paderborn and the abbots of Corvey until the secularization of the ecclesiastical territories after 1803.

Otherwise Lippe was a compact unit of jurisdictions and lands held by the dynasty as feudal lords over the towns, nobles and peasants, and as protectors of the church. In 1517 Count Simon V did homage to the Bishop of Paderborn and to Philip of Hesse

[4] M. Knaut, *Geschichte der Verwaltungsorganisation*, Stuttgart, 1961, pp. 99–100. G. Engel, *Politische Geschichte Westfalens*, Cologne, 1968, p. 288.

[5] A. K. Hömberg, *Westfälische Landesgeschichte*, Münster, 1967, pp. 168–282. *Brockhaus*, 16th ed., Wiesbaden, 1955, vol. 7, p. 264.

[6] M. Kuhlmann, *Bevölkerungsgeographie des Landes Lippe*, Remagen, 1954, pp. 10–12.

pp. 138–9. E. Kittel, *Geschichte der Stadt Detmold*, Detmold, 1953, pp. 399–400. Staatsarchiv Detmold, D. 71. *Europäische Stammtafeln*, 1, Marburg, 1960, Tables 143–4. H. F. von Ehrenkrook, *Genealogisches Handbuch des Adels, Fürstliche Häuser*, 1, Glücksburg, 1951, pp. 64–75.

in order to escape an unfavourable inheritance pact, which the dukes of Brunswick had partly purchased from Maximilian I's chancellery and then forced on the Lippe dynasty in 1508 and 1515. Then, in 1547, Charles V with the use of military force made Lippe a fief of the Empire, detaching the county from its unwilling support of Hesse in the War of the Smalkaldic League. Ferdinand I allowed Philip of Hesse to resume lordship over the counts of Lippe in 1562. These feudal ties with Paderborn and Hesse remained in force during the seventeenth and eighteenth centuries. The imperial status, or *Reichsunmittelbarkeit*, of Lippe was in no way jeopardized by them.[7] They gave Lippe strong allies against any one power which tried to assert control over the county, as the dukes of Brunswick had tried to do, for both Hesse and Paderborn cancelled each other out in any bid which either made to gain control of Lippe, as they were too unlike each other in their aims to have ever produced a common policy against the county.[8]

The Lippe dynasty did not for long retain any important new inheritances, for although Simon VI married a co-heiress of Rietberg in 1577, she died childless in 1585. The dynasty did not embark on over-ambitious marriage alliances nor did it in any way seek to raise its status until very belatedly in 1789,

[7] The rulers of Lippe held their lands as of ancient right. The twelfth-century build-up of land by the dynasty may well have been achieved through their role as protectors (*advocati, Vögte*) of local ecclesiastics. There were no direct feudal ties with the Emperors. The status of Lippe rulers thus defies neat classification. That they had direct access to the Emperors and imperial assemblies like any tenants-in-chief of the Empire is clear from their appearances in fifteenth-century *Reichsmatrikeln* and from the notoriety Lippe rulers gained from the Eversteiner Fehde (cf. Kiewning, *op. cit.*). After the fifteenth and sixteenth centuries only a fraction of the land that Lippe rulers owned was held of Paderborn and Hesse, but enough to guarantee the independence of Lippe as a small buffer-state. The rest was allodial land. The complicated pattern of land-holding and of rights and jurisdictions that formed Lippe under its dynasty was by no means a tidy unit with the neat frontier that early modern Lippe finally managed to achieve. This medieval background (especially its legal and feudal aspects) falls outside the scope of this work, and it is covered by Kiewning, *op. cit.*

Reichsunmittelbarkeit is the quality of direct access to imperial affairs achieved by ancient prescription by the ruling families of Lippe, rather than by any grants from, or services rendered to Emperors or Empire.

[8] Kiewning, *op. cit.*, pp. 115–16, 118, 163–4, 168. W. Goez, *Der Leihezwang*, Tübingen, 1962, p. 90. Hömberg, *op. cit.*, pp. 244–5. R. Wolf, 'Der Einfluss des Landgrafen Philipp etc. . .', *Jahrbuch des Vereins für Westfälische Kirchengeschichte*, 51–2, 1958–9, pp. 79–81. V. Ernst, *Die Entstehung des Niederen Adels*, Stuttgart, 1916, pp. 81–7. T. Mayer, *Fürst und Staat*, Weimar, 1950, pp. 308–9.

when the ruling Count first paid to take up the title of ruling Prince, or *Fürst*, which was originally a Habsburg grant from 1720.[9] In fact Lippe quietly remained a buffer-state against the expansionist policies of Cologne, Münster, Paderborn, Hesse and the Brunswick houses of Guelph. During the seventeenth century its most powerful neighbour became Brandenburg-Prussia, which gained control of Minden and Ravensberg to the north and west of Lippe.

From the flat land of the north-west, through to Ravensberg, Lippe had its window on to the north German plain. It was here that Lippe had its closest economic ties with the outside world, from the Ravensberg-Lippe towns of Herford, Lemgo and Bielefeld. They were called 'the three towns' inside the Cologne quarter of the Hanseatic League.[10] Nevertheless Lippe, with the exception of Lemgo from 1300 to 1600, always remained an economic backwater. Its one outlet on the river Weser was a sliver of land below Varenholz, between the Rinteln and Minden stretches of the river. The barren Osning forest south and west of Detmold prevented extensive trade with the Westphalian plain around Paderborn, and the forested Weser mountains of Schwalenberg made difficult any really extensive trade with the Brunswick Weser lands around Hameln, or further afield with the Hessian valleys which lead into south Germany. With the longevity of its dynasty, with its secure geographical position and its economic backwardness, Lippe continued to exist as a minute, independent buffer-state in a world of much larger states. In this it was joined by minute Waldeck-Pyrmont and Schaumburg-Lippe in the north, south and east in the course of the seventeenth century.

In 1500 Lippe shared boundaries with the duchy of Brunswick-Calenberg, Wolfenbüttel, the bishopric of Paderborn, the abbey of Corvey, the counties of Ravensberg, Schaumburg and Pyrmont, and the bishopric of Minden.[11] During the next two centuries, although this patchwork quilt of medieval territories

[9] H. Kiewning, 'Der lippische Fürstenbrief von 1720', *Lippische Mitteilungen*, 1, 1903.

[10] *Der Raum Westfalen*, 2, part 1, Münster, 1955, map 20. P. Berghaus, *Währungsgrenzen des westfälischen Oberwesergebietes im Spätmittelalter*, Hamburg, 1951, pp. 6, 10.

[11] G. Wrede, *Die westfälischen Länder, 1801: Eine Übersichtskarte*, Münster, 1953.

remained, some of them were reduced to mere provinces of larger dynastic or ecclesiastical units, which meant that the independence of the area had been curtailed. In 1700 Lippe felt the presence of Brandenburg-Prussia from Minden-Ravensberg. The Brunswick frontier was more static, except for a small encroachment when Brunswick took a share of the Schaumburg inheritance in 1647.[12] However, Brunswick-Lüneburg had advanced across the lower Weser as far as Osnabrück and across the middle Weser up to Pyrmont and Lippe.[13] Paderborn and Corvey were at times part of the larger holdings of pluralist princes of the Catholic church, such as the Bavarian Wittelsbachs of ecclesiastical Cologne. The greater part of Schaumburg had fallen to Hesse-Kassel, and to a junior branch of the Lippe dynasty, who continued to rule the county of Schaumburg-Lippe quite independently of Lippe itself until 1918. At Rinteln, in 1653, Hesse set up a provincial government for Schaumburg, equipped with a strong military force to show Hessian presence on the middle Weser.[14] In the county of Pyrmont a junior line of the Lippe dynasty did not survive the sixteenth century.[15] Their share went to the counts of Waldeck, whilst Paderborn retained its share in the Catholic enclave of Lügde.

To the south-west of Lippe were the splinter-territories, lordships, or *Herrschaften* of Rheda, Wiedenbrück-Reckenberg and Rietberg, partly remnants of the one disastrous family partition of the Lippe dynasty, stemming from the mid-fourteenth century. Rietberg was an independent county run by a succession of insignificant noble families. It lay between Lippe and her part of Lippstadt, but, try as they would, the Lippe dynasty could not obtain Rietberg or Rheda by marriage or by conquest. Wiedenbrück-Reckenberg was part of Osnabrück, and Rheda was inherited by the counts of Tecklenburg near Münster, whose lands went to the Bentheim and Orange-Nassau dynasties, to be finally swallowed up by Brandenburg-Prussia in 1707.

The area thus retained that territorial complexity which it

[12] W. Maack, *Die Grafschaft Schaumburg*, 2nd ed., Rinteln, 1964, pp. 70, 74.
[13] G. Schnath, *Geschichte Hannovers*, 1, Hildesheim, 1938, pp. 38, 40. *Lippische Regesten*, 2530. E. von Lethe, *Grenzen und Ämter im Herzogtum Bremen*, Göttingen, 1926, p. 106. [14] Maack, *op. cit.*, p. 78.
[15] G. Schnath, *Die Herrschaften Everstein, Homburg und Spiegelberg*, Göttingen, 1922, p. 53. *Europäische Stammtafeln*, Table 144.

had developed in the later Middle Ages, and long after nearly all the founding dynasties had died out. In the religious upheavals of the sixteenth and seventeenth centuries further divisions into confessions and territorial churches developed in the area, so that by the later seventeenth century Lippe and Hessen-Schaumburg were the centre of the Reformed church (Calvinists), Brunswick, Minden, Ravensberg the centre of the Evangelical church (Lutherans), and Münster and Paderborn the centre of the Counter-Reformation church (Catholics). Power was thus diffused, and the area displayed in miniature practically all that variety which was to be found in the German Empire as a whole, especially in religion, but with the notable absence of imperial knights and imperial free towns. By 1700 the powers with whom the future lay could also be clearly discerned, although it took Napoleon, Bismarck and Hitler to break the barriers of territorial independence in the area.

Despite the aggressive foreign policy of Bishop Christof Bernhard von Galen in mid-seventeenth-century Münster, the ecclesiastical territories were as much on the defensive against the powerful dynasties of Guelph, Hesse, Hohenzollern, Wittelsbach and Habsburg as were the smaller lay territories. Ecclesiastical Münster, Paderborn, Corvey, Essen, Werden, the duchy of Westphalia and Vest Recklinghausen feared as much as did the rulers of Lippe, Schaumburg-Lippe and Waldeck-Pyrmont the especially powerful states of Brandenburg-Prussia, Brunswick-Lüneburg and Hesse-Kassel after the Peace of Westphalia in 1648.

Although politics varied from territory to territory, there was a general, overall pattern of development.[16] Each territory had at least one politically organized Estate, whom the ruler consulted for financial support. In the later Middle Ages the towns and clergy were among the leading political elements in the territories in and around Lippe as elsewhere in the Empire. During the sixteenth and seventeenth centuries the power of the rulers and of the nobility generally outdid the political impor-

[16] F. L. Carsten, 'The causes of the decline of the German Estates', *Studies presented to the International Commission for the history of representative and parliamentary institutions*, 24, 1961, p. 296, 'The Estates indeed belong to the main stream of German history, as they do in the majority of European countries.' Yet in Oldenburg the Estates were not politically organized until after 1848—very much an exception to prove the rule. Haase, *op. cit.*, pp. 10–11, 16–17.

tance of any other group. No bid by the lower nobility of the area to become imperial knights was successful, although their widespread freedom from all regular taxation, especially pronounced for the Lüneburg nobility,[17] made it necessary to provide specifically for each of them and their lands a seat and vote in the territorial assemblies, the *Landtage*, where the ruler would try to obtain their consent to extraordinary taxation. In all territories the same social and economic divisions by birth and thereafter by wealth and election held good in the eyes of the law of the land and of the Empire.[18]

The rulers, as *Reichsstände*, imperial tenants-in-chief, or peers of the Empire, were the leaders of German society and politics.[19] As territorial rulers they rigidly segregated themselves from their subjects and took on aspects of a caste-system. Below them, the landed nobility was organized separately within each territory, although its ranks were open to commoners of exceptional wealth, influence or talent, for the Emperor exercised the power of creating new nobles by diploma, the so-called *Briefadel.*[20]

The territorial nobility were in some ways the pillars of the social system. That they were a complicated group that tried to emulate their rulers as dynastic units of lands, rights, offices, privileges and personal law, has recently been examined in early-eighteenth-century Hanover, where three distinct subdivisions have been found, traditional landed gentry, court nobles and town patriciate. All three groups were to some extent in a state of flux because their members hunted for high

[17] A. H. Loebl, 'Eine ausserordentliche Reichshilfe', *Sitzungsberichte der phil.-hist. Klasse der kaiserl. Akademie der Wissenschaften*, 153, Vienna, 1906, p. 108n.

[18] Rössler (ed.), *op. cit.*, pp. 153–202.

[19] The term *Stand*, plural *Stände*, as in *Reichsstände, Landstände, Adelsstand, Bürgerstand, Bauernstand*, was used in the late medieval and early modern period to describe status, with the distinct legal and political rights that went with such designation. Thus it would be anachronistic to use the term 'class', as in the nineteenth-century compound *Arbeiterklasse*. O. Brunner, *Sozialgeschichtliche Forschungsaufgaben*, Vienna, 1948, pp. 336–7. T. Mundt, *Geschichte der deutschen Stände*, Berlin, 1854. *Allgemeine Deutsche Biographie*, 23, pp. 10–12 (on Mundt). H. Mitgau, 'Ständische Daseinsformen genealogisch gesehen', *Gemeinsames Leben, 1550–1770*, Göttingen, 1953.

[20] The nobility was an extremely complex group in German law and society. The importance of the *Briefadel* in early modern German society has still to be worked out. See G. Benecke, 'Ennoblement and privilege in early modern Germany', *History*, October 1971, pp. 360–70.

office, pensions and places under the rulers and councillors. They were also continually enriched, whether they liked it socially or not, by those who bought new titles in Vienna or from amenable and cheaper *Hofpfalzgrafen*, and thereafter invested heavily in lands, offices and marriages which were the traditional preserve of established noble families. Thus of eighty-two members of the ancient family of Münchhausen, forty-nine held office in Hanover in early modern times. Members of forty-seven noble dynasties took part in the Hanover central administration during 1714–60. In the seventeenth and eighteenth centuries well over a hundred new titles were recognized in Hanover alone.[21]

The next distinct social group were the burghers. The nearest imperial free towns were Dortmund and Cologne to the west, and Hanseatic Bremen on the lower Weser to the north, so that all towns in the Lippe region were subject to the dynasties and clerics who had founded them, or to their successors in office. These towns had a greater or lesser degree of self-government according to the number of privileges which they had been able to buy from their overlords during the time of their greatest prosperity especially in the fifteenth century. Yet the burgher Estate was much divided. Leading merchants, entrepreneurs and manufacturers usually set up oligarchic, self-appointed and self-perpetuating town councils, forming a narrow patriciate of birth and wealth, equal to the nobility, if not in status, then at least in wealth and opportunity.[22]

This opportunity was best expressed in the clerical, legal, medical and teaching professions, open almost exclusively to

[21] *Ibid.*, pp. 362–3.

[22] By 1700 the towns had so abused their privileges of self-government that it became fashionable for despotic rulers to abolish their charters. The Hohenzollerns were especially fond of this course of action in their Westphalian territories. F. von Klocke, *Das Patrizierproblem und die Werler Erbsälzer*, Münster, 1965, distinguished three groups of burghers—*Patriziat, Honoratorienschaft* and *Klein-bürgertum*. These are modern terms. Contemporaries used *Ratsverwandter* and *Bürger*, or, as the Imperial Police Order of 1530 put it, 'So vom Rath, Geschlechtern oder sonst fürnehmes Herkommens sind und von Ihrer Zins und Renthen leben: die Kauff- und Gewerbsleutt: die gemeine Bürger, Handwerker und gemeine Krämer', from E. Kittel, reviewing in *Lippische Mitteilungen*, 35, 1966, pp. 325–7. For a town council family oligarchy the modern term commonly used is *Patriziat*, and there is little doubt that such a family was part of the German territorial gentry. See F. Gerlach, 'Die Patrizierfamilie Cothmann in Lemgo', *Lippische Landeszeitung*, Supplements 1–9, 1951; 4, 1954. F. Flaskamp, 'Die Anfänge der Wiedenbrücker Patrizierfamilie Wippermann', *Die Glocke*, 30 June 1954.

members of the nobility and to the wealthier burgher families who could afford to pay for university studies and unremunerative vicariates. To these professions were added careers in expanding seventeenth-century administrations, judicial systems and armies within all the territories, so that by 1700 those medieval territories which had survived intact were becoming noticeably modern states no matter how insignificant their area and population.[23]

Those subjects without direct voice in politics were the peasants, divided between the free tenants, or *Pächter*, and serfs, or *Leibeigene*, below whom came the artisans, day-labourers, living-in servants and the poor of town and countryside.[24] It is important to emphasize that the much-used general term, *Bauern*, or peasants, denotes a tenant-farmer or serf, who rented a *Hof*, or farm, and invariably had a burgher, noble, or ecclesiastical lord, if not the ruler himself, directly over him. A peasant before the nineteenth century could be personally free or unfree but he hardly ever owned his own land, stock, buildings or tithes. He was a hired person, and the degree of his actual freedom and security was gauged by the terms of his contract, the *Meierbrief*.[25]

The Lippe area differed little if at all from any other part of early modern Europe, except for its extraordinarily high degree of independent government so very characteristic of the Holy Roman Empire. But how did independence work out in practice in the territories themselves? As the Estates made up only a part of the social and economic structure of the region, how far

[23] See G. Benecke, 'Absolutism and the middle class: the case of a Northwest German burgher family in the seventeenth century', *Histoire Sociale*, 9, Ottawa, 1972.

[24] There are no German equivalents to Gregory King's tables, so vital as an introduction to early modern English social history. But see E. Kayser, *Bevölkerungsgeschichte Deutschlands*, 2nd ed., Leipzig, 1941, pp. 365–83. G. Ipsen, 'Die preussische Bauernbefreiung als Landesausbau', *Zeitschrift für Agrargeschichte und Agrarsoziologie*, 2, 1954, pp. 51–2. W. G. L. von Donop, *Historisch-geographische Beschreibung der Fürstlich Lippeschen Landen in Westphalen*, Lemgo, 1790, pp. 143–52. At a point where tenant-farming and farm-labouring merged, a comparative study between north-west Germany and Scotland has been made by L. Hempel, 'Heuerlingswesen und Croftersystem', *Zeitschrift für Agrargeschichte und Agrarsoziologie*, 5, 1957, pp. 169–80.

[25] G. Franz, *Quellen zur Geschichte des deutschen Bauernstandes in der Neuzeit*, Munich, 1963, Documents 1, 11, 12. P. Wigand, *Provinzialrechte Minden, Ravensberg* etc. . ., 2, Leipzig, 1834, pp. 231, 489–92.

could they run the politics of their own territory in the sixteenth and seventeenth centuries? Here they were organized as the territorial Estates or *Landstände,* a term used in the politics of the age distinct from the territorial ruler or *Landesherr,* and from his government or *Regierung.* How did this affect the peasantry and labourers and how did ruler and Estates govern them?

The territories in the Lippe region provide their own materials to illustrate German particularism. They will show what degree of responsibility each territory had for its own society and economy: and point out to what extent aims and methods were similar in each of these territories, leading to a federal consensus of opinion. For why otherwise should there have been such a marked absence of agitation to abolish the Empire before Napoleonic times?[26]

[26] F. Merzbacher reviewing in *Zeitschrift der Savigny-Stiftung für Rechtsgeschichte, Germanistische Abteilung,* 1966, p. 389.

V

Rule by Election:
the Ecclesiastical Territories

(i) *Münster*

IN the bishopric of Münster an efficient, lucrative system of extraordinary taxation was established during the course of the sixteenth century. It was based on the co-operation of the rulers with the territorial Estates, notably with the Chapter and the nobility in the internal administration. This was achieved to some extent by means of annual, sometimes even biannual *Landtage*, meetings of Chapter, nobility and town council representatives. The Estates had their own *Pfennigkammer* or treasury, sufficient committees, and a number of nobles who as councillors of an occasional sort, as *Landräte* or *Verordnete*, acted as liaison officers from within Estates' assemblies and committees between ruling bishops and the territorial Estates. On the whole the Estates were administratively minded, rather than politically so. The vital part which they played in taxation, expenditure and audit continued until the end of Münster as an independent territory in 1802. The Chapter played a key rôle for it was the anchor of the constitution, and it chose the ruling bishop. It was thus in the ecclesiastical territories where fifteenth- and sixteenth-century forms of constitutional rule had possibly the best chance of survival in the seventeenth and eighteenth centuries.[1]

---

[1] A. Hartlieb von Wallthor, 'Die Verfassung in Altwestfalen als Quelle moderner Selbstverwaltung', *Westfälische Forschungen*, 9, 1956, pp. 31–2, 37, *Die landschaftliche Selbstverwaltung Westfalens*, 1, Münster, 1965, pp. 16–18, with review in

The Reformation in Münster took an unusually violent turn in the 1530s. The town of Münster was close enough to the Netherlands to be influenced by the Anabaptists, and yet also sufficiently distant from the sea and from the Rhineland to be counted as something of a backwater. In its somewhat isolated, and yet, to the determined traveller, very close position to the more important centres of economic and social activity in northern Europe, Münster town witnessed one of the most articulate rebellions of the common man in early modern Europe. As a movement especially of the craftsmen and artisans, Anabaptism was tolerated by neither rulers nor Estates. It was a threat to them both, presenting rulers and Estates, especially in Münster, with a common enemy from within.

During 1533–46 Bishop and Estates wiped out Anabaptism in Münster. Bishop Franz von Waldeck received notification from the *Ämter* and towns on the whereabouts of Anabaptists. Treating them rather like a revolutionary 'fifth column' to be stamped out, Franz discussed measures against them at assemblies of the Estates. In the name of the *Landschaft* he then sent written instructions for the capture and trial of Anabaptists in the localities. A judicial commission of members of the Estates was convened as *Verordnete der Landschaft* to deal summarily with riots and unauthorized meetings. Even so, only the *Gogerichte*, courts under the Bishop's control in the *Ämter*, were found suitable or pliable enough to deal with the Anabaptists harshly.[2]

It was at *Gogerichte* and in the houses of *Amt* officials that 150 men and 54 women were kept and tried as Anabaptists between 1533 and 1546. Nearly all were tortured under the new imperial laws against rioting which had been used to deal so effectively with the peasants of the Great Rebellion of the later 1520s, and

[2] F. Philippi, *Landrechte des Münsterlandes*, Münster, 1907, p. VI. Philippi was too lenient in his assessment of the role which the *Gogerichte* played in crushing the Anabaptists. See K. H. Kirchhoff, 'Exekutivorgane und Rechtspraxis der Täuferverfolgung im Münsterland, 1533–46', *Westfälische Forschungen*, 16, 1963, pp. 161–80.

For descriptions of early modern *Ämter*, E. Debes, *Das Amt Wartburg*, Jena, 1926. H. Kellinghan, *Das Amt Bergedorf bis 1620*, Göttingen, 1908.

Osnabrücker Mitteilungen, 73, 1966, pp. 116–17. K. H. Kirchhoff, 'Landräte im Stift Münster', *Westfälische Forschungen*, 18, 1965, pp. 181–90.

also under the canon law in heresy and possibly indirectly through the new criminal procedures established by the Corpus Criminalis Carolina in the later 1530s. At one point Philip of Hesse sent Lutheran ministers to Münster to try to obtain recantations, which showed how Lutherans could make common cause with the Catholics when they detected a threat to the social order.[3] Half the Anabaptists who went on trial were executed. This was an expensive method of 'justice', and the Bishop's officials would probably have been happier to pardon more Anabaptists had more of them been able to afford the fines of between 20 and 500 fl. with pledges up to 6,000 fl. to keep the peace which their richer co-religionists actually paid. Heirs of well-placed Anabaptists who had somehow been executed started lawsuits to get back their inheritance. The family of Kerckerinck even took their case to the *Reichskammergericht* where they obtained a favourable verdict.[4]

The Estates also granted Bishop Franz money with which to besiege the Anabaptists in Münster town. More important perhaps was the need to finance the Bishop's debts after his victory in 1535, made worse by the fact that in Münster town he had temporarily destroyed the only large trading centre in the whole territory. Then out of economic misery an excellent method of taxation was evolved, showing what could be done when Bishop and Estates found real grounds for co-operation. By 1538 a system of extraordinary levies on land had been worked out by the Estates, to be parcelled out in quotas to the *Ämter*, in which parishioners were responsible for making up a specified sum from among their own number. This parish tax or *Kirchspiel-schatzung* was the most notable of a variety of often inefficient plough-taxes, hearth, cattle, inheritance, capital, income, and

---

[3] R. Wolf, 'Der Einfluss des Landgrafen Philipp etc. . .', *Jahrbuch des Vereins für Westfälische Kirchengeschichte*, 51–2, 1958–9, pp. 27, 122–3.

[4] Kirchhoff, 'Exekutivorgane', *passim*. K. H. Kirchhoff, 'Die Wiedertäufer in Coesfeld', in *Westfälische Zeitschrift*, 106, 1956, pp. 113–74. H. Rothert, *Das tausendjährige Reich der Wiedertäufer zu Münster 1534–5*, Münster, 1947, p. 11. That Lutherans thought of themselves as law-abiding and by no means to be associated with sectarians as social revolutionaries is brought out twenty years later in a plea for toleration by the Austrian Estates to Ferdinand I, which he accepted by lifting the Interim of 1554 in return for 500,000 fl. Turk aid to be raised as capital tax from clergy, nobles, towns and their tenantry. J. Stulz, 'Ausschusstag der fünf niederösterreichischen Lande in Wien 1556', *Archiv für Kunde österreichische Geschichtsquellen*, 8, Vienna, 1852, pp. 162–4, 167, 171–2.

jewellery taxes, as well as highly dubious taxes on the rents of nobility and clergy.[5]

Thus in December 1538 the *Landtag* granted a tax for the payment of outstanding interest on the Bishop's debts. Each parish taxed itself under the supervision of its priest. The tax seems to have made about 35,000 fl., which was paid to the *Pfennigmeister*, as head of the Estates' own treasury. The hard core of Münster's finance was Estates' finance. This first levy was followed within a few months by another which did actually make just over 35,000 fl.[6] In February 1539 the *Pfennigmeister* had estimated the debts of the territory at 192,000 fl. It seems likely, however, that the Bishop was keeping quiet about many more debts, or alternatively that the Estates, notably the Chapter, were being very particular about which of the Bishop's debts to honour.

At the *Landtag* of December 1539 the Estates agreed to levy parish taxes annually for ten years until all the debts were paid, but by 1541 they were already planning to liquidate an outstanding sum of over 120,000 fl. at one levy. It is not known how successful this was.[7]

The parish tax was next adapted to imperial military purposes in the wars of Ferdinand and Charles against the Turks. In 1543 the Bishop was requested to pay for over 500 troops in the field against the Turks at a cost of nearly 3,000 fl. a month. The Bishop could not meet these commitments out of his own pocket and by September 1544 the Estates had taken over these expenses, as a 'great favour' to their Bishop. The military system was from now on to become the most important item of territorial finance, whether in money or men, whether for imperial, circle or purely territorial purposes. However ineffectual against Spain and France, the imperial military system with its territorial quotas of men and money kept the threat even if not the continuity of the *Reich* alive in the majority of the territories and produced the eventual victories over the Turks under Leopold I.[8]

[5] K. H. Kirchhoff, 'Die landständischen Schatzungen des Stifts Münster im 16. Jahrhundert', *Westfälische Forschungen*, 14, 1961, pp. 120–6.

[6] *Ibid.*, p. 126.

[7] *Ibid.*, pp. 127–8.

[8] See Loebl, 'Ausserordentliche Reichshilfe', *passim*, and his studies of the Turk Wars, 1593–6, *Prager Studien*, VI, X, Prague, 1906–10. Müller, *Steuer und*

Thus in 1544 the Estates of Münster again resorted to the parish tax, which at over 20,000 fl. seems even to have produced an immediate surplus.[9] Methods of assessment were simple and efficient because there seems to have been little conflict between the Estates, their tenantry and serfs, and the Bishop and his officials. Although this tax combined land and poll tax by now, it was not the only tax. Yet it was the most important, and the territory does not seem to have had an important excise or indirect tax system other than as local taxation levied by the town councils.[10] Whatever the tax was at territorial level, it was granted in the *Landtag* and thereafter administered through the Estates' treasury. This may explain why the development of the Bishop's administration was so slow when compared with other territories. It was simply not needed so early.[11]

From the time that Johann von Hoya became bishop in 1566 until the end of the century the parish tax was levied almost yearly, and it made about 30,000 tlrs each time. In the first three decades of the seventeenth century the tax was usually levied biannually. In 1633 it was levied eight times and in the following year eleven times. From 1695 it was fixed as a permanent, monthly levy, by which time it could hardly still be regarded as an extraordinary grant of the Estates, granted as tax on burghers, tenants and serfs.

The parish tax only indirectly covered the nobility and the higher clergy who were also of noble blood. For although the nobility were in fact exempted from the parish tax for themselves, their revenues, families, houses, gardens and those farms which they themselves ran, the tax was still assessed through

---

[9] Kirchhoff, 'Schatzungen', p. 128.

[10] J. Greve, *Das Braugewerbe der Stadt Münster*, Münster, 1907, pp. 41–2, 63. Excise on brewing made 3,300 marks in 1533, reaching an all-time peak at 34,000 marks in 1647, at the time of the peace negotiations.

[11] G. Jacob, 'Die Hofkammer des Fürstbistums Münster 1573–1803', *West-fälische Zeitschrift*, 115, 1965, pp. 8–9. H. J. von der Ohe, *Die Zentral- und Hofver-waltung des Fürstentums Lüneburg*, Celle, 1955, pp. 69–77. F. L. Carsten, *Princes and Parliaments*, London, 1959, p. 429. The Estates provided 'a practical alternative to the development of a bureaucratic machine by the state'.

Finanzwesen, *passim*. For later seventeenth-century imperial circle militarism, B. Sicken, *Das Wehrwesen des fränkischen Reichskreises 1681–1714*, Nuremberg, 1967. R. Wines, 'The imperial circles, princely diplomacy and imperial reform 1681–1714', *Journal of Modern History*, 39, 1967, pp. 1–29.

the *Ämter* and town councils on their tenantry, and it was presumably as landlords that they had the right in the first place to grant these taxes in the assemblies which their tenants and servants then generally also contributed to. Whenever the burden of taxation on the tenantry became too great, landlords could expect to find difficulty in collecting their rents and may indeed have felt the demoralizing effect of an agricultural economy that was dependent on a near-bankrupt tenantry.[12]

During the rule of Bishop Johann von Hoya two new departments of state were set up by negotiations with the Estates. They were the *Hofgericht* in 1572 and the *Rechenkammer* in 1573. At the *Landtag* of 1570 Johann asked the Estates to appoint a committee to deal directly with his creditors. This the Estates refused to do, but the Bishop had opened the discussion on his financial affairs in a way by no means unfavourable to the Estates, provided they were not forced into shouldering debts which the ruler would be free to contract in the future.[13] The Estates granted Johann further parish taxes, for they were as keen to obtain a supreme court of appeal, staffed by professional lawyers in permanent session, as Johann was to get out of his debts.

Over the creation of this court there was soon deadlock, for both Johann and the Estates expected the other to pay for its running. The Estates offered a beer excise to pay for it. It was opposed in the towns and *Ämter*, for fear of increasing Johann's powers of taxation. An *Ausschusstag*, a meeting of the Estates' standing committee which dealt with affairs between the end of one *Landtag* and the calling of the next, agreed to take on 15,000 tlrs of debts if Johann gave up the beer excise. This shows how Johann could exploit the blunder of the Estates in offering an excise in the first place. At last in 1573 the Estates agreed to fund the *Hofgericht* with a capital sum of 20,000 tlrs in order to pay lawyers' salaries out of the interest with the grant of another parish tax. In return Johann gave up the excise.[14]

At the same time a collegiate body was established by the

[12] Kirchhoff, 'Schatzungen', pp. 131–2.

[13] In a situation rather like this the Estates of Brunswick-Wolfenbüttel were also outmanœuvred in the 1590s.

[14] R. Lüdicke, 'Die landesherrlichen Zentralbehörden im Bistum Münster 1530–1650', *Westfälische Zeitschrift*, 59, I, 1901, pp. 67–9.

Rechenkammerordnung of 1573 for the administration of the Bishop's income. This showed the strength of the Estates, especially of the Chapter, for the new body restricted Johann's freedom of action in disposing of his own regular income.[15] The *Rechenkammer* included *Hofräte* and *Landräte*. It was led by the Chancellor and included members of the Chapter and leading *Amt* officials. These men were unlikely to have been hostile to the Bishop, although some of them also had duties to the Estates as nobles, and to themselves and their own families as influential landowners. Even so, Johann continued to have difficulty in borrowing money, and the Chapter had to stand security for the loan of 6,000 tlrs which he took in order to be able to set up the *Rechenkammer* in the first place.

However strong the hold of the *Rechenkammer* and Chapter over the Bishop's finances, it was only temporary. An expedient financial arrangement was hardly expected to remain in force should circumstances change. This was not a constitutional gain for the Estates. As soon as the Bishop was solvent once more, there would be no restrictions, and he would regain sole control over the *Rechenkammer*. Yet would future Bishops ever manage affairs without running into debt? This was hardly to be expected as long as the Estates insisted that the Bishop should live off his regular domain income and also pay for his administration from it. Yet despite the fact that this had never been a practical proposition, by not repudiating it the Estates may well have impeded any real freedom of political manœuvre which they may have had against their rulers' prerogative. It may have prevented them from keeping their political demands up to date, for endless demands for confirmations of privileges were not necessarily the be-all and end-all of politics that the Estates seem to have thought.[16]

The Catholics saw the danger of losing Münster to the Protestants from two sides, from an elected Bishop who might secularize the bishopric and found a dynasty, thus in some way upsetting the provisions of the Peace of Augsburg of 1555, or from the Protestants who at one time in the 1570s and 1580s had a clear majority in the Chapter, and who desired to elect a Protestant like the Archbishop of Bremen who was already a ruler elsewhere. By blocking this candidature, and then by

15 *Ibid.*, pp. 81, 70–1. Jacob, *op. cit.*, p. 9.   16 Lüdicke, *op. cit.*, pp. 80–1.

electing no resident Bishops between 1574 and 1650, and finally by getting over the problem of illegal election and pluralism in choosing only Administrators, the Catholics never lost the upper hand in the politics of the bishopric. They chose the Wittelsbach Archbishops of Cologne in default of any more suitable candidates who were staunch Catholics. Innovations in government under Johann were now given the long period of Estates' consolidation which they needed, in order to become permanent by custom, and Chapter influence in the *Rechenkammer* as well as control over the *Pfennigkammer*, the treasury into which the Estates directed all payments of the parish tax, possibly prevented Ernst of Bavaria as Administrator of Münster from 1588 to 1612 from totally ruining the finances of the territory.[17]

A new era opened in 1650 when the Chapter appointed its own treasurer as Bishop against the candidature of yet another Wittelsbach, and against the advice of its own Dean who, although he may have hoped for the title himself, certainly suspected a violent streak in Christoph Bernhard's nature. Christoph Bernhard von Galen was a member of the territorial nobility and a staunch Catholic priest with a university training in theology and canon law. He was extremely fortunate to rise so high in the social scale and to become a spiritual ruling prince or *geistlicher Reichsfürst*, second in rank only to the Emperor and the Electors.[18]

Christoph Bernhard had to swear to keep a particularly harsh *Wahlkapitulation*.[19] He agreed to choose a fixed number of his senior officials from the Estates and to seek the approval of the

[17] *Ibid.*, pp. 81–5, 141, 155. Loebl, 'Ausserordentliche Reichshilfe', pp. 71–3. H. Börsting, *Geschichte des Bistums Münster*, Bielefeld, 1951, pp. 89–118. K. Schafmeister, *Herzog Ferdinand von Bayern, Erzbischof von Köln als Fürstbischof von Münster 1612–50*, Münster, 1912. H. Feine, *Besetzung der Reichsbistümer*, Leipzig, 1923, p. 401. H. G. Schmitz-Eckert, 'Die Hochstift-Münstersche Regierung von 1574–1803', *Westfälische Zeitschrift*, 116, I, 1966, p. 58.

[18] T. Bading, *Die innere Politik Christof Bernhards von Galen*, Münster, 1912, p. 4. R. Steimel, *Kleine Geschichte des deutschen Adels*, Cologne, 1959, p. 28n. Feine, *op. cit.*, p. 402.

[19] *Wahlkapitulationen* were a combined 'Magna Carta' and coronation oath imposed on ruling German bishops since the thirteenth century and then adapted to bind the Emperors beginning with Charles V in 1519. They were the very essence of the electoral principle in German politics outside the dynastic territories until the end of the Empire. For lists of *Wahlkapitulationen* in the bishoprics and archbishoprics, see Feine, *op. cit.*, index; for the Emperors, F. Hartung, 'Die

Chapter for all senior appointments. Equally all officials were to be natives of the bishopric. The Bishop was first to obtain the consent of the Chapter to any loans that he wanted to raise to cover extra government expenses, especially in the military and diplomatic fields.[20] But just as the Chapter had severely curtailed the Bishop's power on paper, so now in practice Christoph Bernhard was ruthless in ignoring its stipulations.

He overcame the interference by Chapter and Estates in the choice of his officials by using an inner circle of trusted councillors, who took whatever business they wanted out of the hands of the Chancellery, dealing with it in secrecy on the sole instructions of the Bishop. What was perhaps new in this time-worn system was that although secret councillors might change, the inner circle was to remain as an institution which really ran the bishopric for the rest of its independent existence. This *Geheimer Rat* was completely at the mercy of the Bishop, but the privy councillors safeguarded themselves by isolating the Bishop from alternative sources of information and advice. In Münster with its strong Chapter and annual assemblies of the Estates, the privy council was not, however, able to squash the Estates and monopolize the internal and external administration in the same way as happened in the dynastic territories.[21]

Yet Christoph Bernhard retained the right to declare an emergency. This time-worn doctrine of *necessitas* in practice bound the Estates to help him after he had involved the territory in wars without having first got their consent to open hostilities or to make subsidy treaties. In this way Christoph Bernhard could escalate a war and get the Estates and the territory as a whole to pay for it once it was too late to withdraw. The *Wahlkapitulation* of 1650 was thus worthless as a check on the power of the Bishop.[22]

[20] Bading, *op. cit.*, pp. 5–6.
[21] Notably Hanover. See A. Köcher, *Geschichte von Hannover und Braunschweig*, 2, Leipzig, 1895, pp. 3–18. E. von Meier, *Hannoversche Verfassungs- und Verwaltungsgeschichte*, 1, Leipzig, 1898, *passim*.
[22] W. Kohl, *Christof Bernhard von Galen*, Münster, 1964, pp. 32, 36. C. Brinkmann, 'Charles II and the Bishop of Münster in the Anglo-Dutch War of 1665–6',

Wahlkapitulationen der deutschen Kaiser und Könige', *Historische Zeitschrift*, 107, 1911, pp. 306–44; also eighteenth-century publicists, Moser and Pütter. The Osnabrück Wahlkapitulation of 1424 and the Hildesheim one of 1216 are in P. Sander and H. Spangenberg, *Urkunden zur Geschichte der Territorialverfassung*, Aalen, 1965, Documents 141, 143.

Far from borrowing money only with the consent of the Chapter, Christoph Bernhard was one of the first to call professional financiers from outside the territory to his court. In 1651 they began to supply him with money at very short notice without asking any questions as to what he needed it for, as the Estates would have inquired, had he asked them for the money instead. Court financiers were interested only in whether or not the ruler's assets could be manipulated to cover the size of the loan. In order to ensure this, the ruler used his prerogative to protect the financier and to let him carry out any restrictive practices which he had been granted by the ruler to recoup himself on the loan. The system of monopolies was already there to assist them both. [23]

From the end of the seventeenth century territorial rulers in Westphalia were receiving large sums of money from their court financiers without losing political power to the Estates in the way that their predecessors had done, when subject to money grants from their Estates. The Estates and the tenantry could still be enticed into paying the larger amounts eventually, but the money needed to start aggression, live luxuriously and salve petty megalomania was immediately available in a way that no Estates' grants or methods of taxation had ever been. The tragedy was that the new system of finance did not merge with the old.

Court financiers had no rights in the territories. They lived on the ruler's prerogative as specialized second-class citizens, over-privileged one minute and under-privileged the next. The Estates did not open their ranks to them but remained their bitter enemies. As some court financiers were Jewish, a further virulence was introduced into territorial politics, which might have been avoided if the Estates had been prepared to accept rivalry and success as evidence of a mutual struggle for power

[23] H. Schnee, 'Stellung und Bedeutung der Hoffinanziers in Westfalen', *Westfalen*, 34, 1956, pp. 176–89.

English Historical Review, 21, 1906, pp. 686–98. O. Israel, 'Der Bielefelder Kreistag von 1671', *54. Jahresbericht des Historischen Vereins für die Grafschaft Ravensberg*, 1947, pp. 52–69. V. L. von Seckendorff, *Teutscher Fürsten-Staat*, 5th ed., Frankfurt-am-Main, 1678, p. 20. G. Brauer, *Die hannoversch-englischen Subsidienverträge*, Aalen, 1962, pp. 9–15, 187. Between 1742 and 1748 Hanover received £2½ million in subsidies from Britain.

and wealth under the territorial rulers of the day. This could have bound families of different social status and religious belief together. Instead it split them off into isolated hostile, rival groups.[24]

Between them, court financiers and privy councillors pushed the Estates into the background. They put a gulf between ruler and Estates, whose assemblies and committees became pliant and often subordinate departments of finance. They provided the ruler with a sham, alternative government. The ruler lost his traditional political contact with those who had a stake in the country. Only by fits and starts and by coercion could a ruler run his territory with the resistance of the Estates, without the leaders of property and wealth in his land. So *Serenissimus* became the prisoner of the secret councils which he kept. Why then did the Estates not rebel? They still provided the money. They still had whatever customary law that there was on their side. Yet their power had been undermined by politicians who were chosen for their servility as outside professionals, and not for their ability to reconcile a large stake in the territory with the needs of the ruler. The connection between politics and society became either so tenuous or so beset with rules and regulations that it encouraged furtiveness in private and stupidity in public. Rulers had sought for better financial arrangements at most times. In the seventeenth century old and new clashed but the problem of who had a greater stake in the territory and therefore a greater claim to political responsibility, ruler or Estates, was not faced.[25] Rulers and their servants won a pyrrhic victory over their Estates. Rebellion or passive resistance, both were an outcome of the same situation of non-compromise, mistrust and deadlock in politics. Yet territorial Estates seemed to produce evidence only of passivity.

[24] H. Schnee, *Die Hoffinanz und der moderne Staat*, 1–3, Berlin, 1953–5, *passim*. P. Baumgart, 'Zur Geschichte der Juden im absoluten Staat', *Vierteljahrschrift für Sozial- und Wirtschaftsgeschichte*, 51, 1964, pp. 101–7. H. H. Hasselmeier, *Die Stellung der Juden in Schaumburg-Lippe 1648–1848*, Bückeburg, 1968, pp. 18–19. W. Treue, 'Das Verhalten von Fürst, Staat und Unternehmer', *Vierteljahrschrift für Sozial- und Wirtschaftsgeschichte*, 44, 1957, pp. 31, 36. J. von Klaveren, 'Die internationalen Aspekte der Korruption', *ibid.*, 45, 1958, pp. 500–2. B. Kuske, 'Das mittelalterliche Deutsche Reich in seinen wirtschaftlichen und sozialen Auswirkungen', *Köln, der Rhein und das Reich*, Cologne, 1956, pp. 284–6. Kuske, 'Die Entstehung der Kreditwirtschaft', *ibid.*, pp. 67–73, 77.

[25] Early modern power politics is the subject of F. Meinecke, *Machiavellism,*

Why were the Estates passive and not rebellious? The answer may lie in political theories which the Estates never used, but the issue was never as simple as the question implies. In their opposition the Estates resorted to the traditional methods, to petitions, lists of grievances, memoranda—an endless stream of *gravamina*. Under the new conditions that prevailed, a petition had little chance of finding its way to the ruler without first going through the hands of a privy councillor, who was unlikely to let anything go unchallenged which would threaten his own position or power. Hence the need to bring petitions to assemblies, a valuable outlet for those territories that still had them in the later seventeenth and eighteenth centuries. The police state took care to keep resistance within bounds. Together ruler and councillor produced a brand of politics that demanded excessive regimentation and even brutality in the territories. Even in the ecclesiastical principality of Münster it was the army and the difficulty of financing it which became the central issue of home affairs after the accession of Christoph Bernhard.[26]

Assemblies played a crucial rôle in financing the army from the Peace of Westphalia until the end of the War of the Spanish Succession. In 1650 the *Pfennigkammer* presented accounts for over 90,000 tlrs which it had spent on the Bishop's army.[27] This compared with recognized debts of 700,000 tlrs and 370,000 tlrs of arrears in interest. Everyone had debts. The Estates had granted 336,000 tlrs more in taxes by 1648 than the country could afford to pay. With such a financial situation it was understandable that the Estates wanted to reduce the size of the Münster army, and they granted supply for two months only.[28]

[26] M. Braubach, *Die Bedeutung der Subsidien für die Politik im spanischen Erbfolgekrieg*, Bonn, 1923, pp. 5–25, especially p. 19. L. Beutin, 'Nordwestdeutschland und die Niederlande seit dem dreissigjährigen Krieg', *Gesammelte Schriften*, Cologne, 1963, pp. 236–7.

[27] T. Verspohl, *Das Heerwesen des Münsterschen Fürstbischofs Christof Bernhard von Galen 1650–78*, Hildesheim, 1909, p. 100.

[28] Bading, *op. cit.*, pp. 9–10. Beutin, *op. cit.*, *passim*. Braubach, *Bedeutung der Subsidien*, *passim*. M. Braubach, 'Holland und die Geistlichen Staaten', *Historisches Jahrbuch der Görresgesellschaft*, 55, 1935, pp. 358–70.

London, 1958. See H. Maier, *Ältere deutsche Staatslehre und westliche politische Tradition*, Tübingen, 1966, pp. 7, 9–10, using Reinking, *Biblische Policey*, 1635. C. Schmitt, *Die Diktatur*, 3rd ed., Berlin, 1965, pp. 24–5, 11–14.

Christoph Bernhard looked at politics in another way. Swedish and Dutch troops were still in parts of his territory. The Swedes in the fortress of Vechta received 18,000 tlrs tribute for the first six months of 1653, and pensions and bribes came to 22,000 tlrs. Compared with this, the Münster army obtained only 28,000 tlrs over the same period of time.[29] Either way the country was paying heavy extraordinary taxes for troops. Christoph Bernhard began to see to it that the Estates paid for his own mercenaries rather than for the troops of foreigners and Protestants.[30]

By 1655 the assembly had agreed that the Estates and countryside should take on the costs of 3,000 foot and 400 horse, although Christoph Bernhard had asked for more. Of the Estates' tax bill for the first six months of 1654, totalling 112,500 tlrs, the army alone took 75,000 tlrs. In 1660 the Bishop even mortgaged domains for 12,000 tlrs as payment for munitions. Another civil war between ruler and capital city led to another costly siege in 1661, at which army costs increased to nearly 270,000 tlrs for the operation. Then just when it seemed that real bankruptcy would bring an end to this vicious military system, it was perpetuated by foreign and inter-territorial subsidy treaties, which helped the Estates and the ruler to bear the cost of large armies, provided they danced to the tune of the paymaster, and there was no paymaster who did not have an enemy in the alliance system that prevailed. In such a situation ever-larger territorial armies were produced to entice foreign and other territorial paymasters, to threaten them and to play them off against each other.[31] This was the era of the *Armierte* and the *Nichtarmierte*.

Münster at least did not go in for an army recruited extensively from its own peasant and artisan families. Its recruiting sergeants did not scour the countryside as did the Hohenzollerns in neighbouring Mark, nor were the Münster nobility interested in becoming its officer corps. The mercenary system prevailed. The Bishop made the policy, the Estates and foreign paymasters provided the money, forage and munitions, which

[29] Verspohl, *op. cit.*, p. 100.
[30] The Peace of Westphalia did not, of course, take religion completely out of politics. J. Schmidlin, 'Christof Bernhard von Galen und die Diözese Münster nach seinen Romberichten', *Westfalen*, 2, 1910, pp. 1–17. [31] See note 28.

professional soldiers from all lands were employed to spend.[32]

Yet despite the despotic trend in government, in Münster assemblies of the Estates survived to grant money annually and biannually all through the period, and from 1650 to 1715 army supply was annually forthcoming. The Chapter survived to lay down further *Wahlkapitulationen* and to take over the government between the death of one bishop and its election of the next. The constitution was preserved because the handing on of political power was non-dynastic and institutionally elective. Thus despotism could not flower into absolutism.[33]

(ii) *Paderborn*

In the early years of the nineteenth century, Annette von Droste-Hülshoff described the former independent bishopric of Paderborn in two essays, 'Die Judenbuche' and 'Bilder aus Westfalen'. Annette was a member of the Münster nobility. She was brought up on the Münster-Paderborn frontier. In contrast to the economy of the Münster peasant she described that of the Paderborn peasant as pitiable. This was not that the Paderborn peasant was not himself to blame, for he generally married whilst too young and then for love, and he drank too much. The Prussians had since brought in a stricter form of government after the secularization of the Napoleonic era. Annette wanted to describe the old ways before they altogether disappeared. What the historian could not convey to the people, that the poet managed to do in his particular way. Just as the popular view of the *Reichskammergericht* is that of the disappointed ex-lawyer Goethe, so the view of early modern Paderborn is that of 'Die Judenbuche'.[34]

[32] A. J. Völker, *Die innere Politik des Fürstbischofs von Münster, Friedrich Christian von Plettenberg, 1688–1706*, Hildesheim, 1908, pp. 30–2, 72–3. W. Dahl, *Die innere Politik Franz Arnolds von Wolff-Metternich zur Gracht, Bischofs von Münster und Paderborn, 1707–18*, Münster, 1910, pp. 9–41.

[33] Seckendorff, *op. cit.*, pp. 21–2.

[34] Annette von Droste-Hülshoff, *Ausgewählte Werke* (F. Droop, ed.), Berlin, 1925, pp. 130, 192, 199, 202, 213. Anon., *Der westfälische Bauernstand*, Elberfeld, 1843, p. 20. J. W. Goethe, *Dichtung und Wahrheit*, 3, Deutscher Taschenbuch Verlag, p. 12.

The *Reichskammergericht* (*RKG*) was thought to have 61,233 pending cases in 1772. In 1556 it claimed 5,000 pending cases (*RKG* visitation, see Staatsarchiv Detmold, L 41a IV E 9 vol. 1). When the case of the peasants against their rulers in Hohenzollern-Hechingen was pending, due to the breakdown of the *RKG* in

In reality Paderborn produced a remarkable constitutional government for which the sources are still plentiful. From the fourteenth to the nineteenth century the territorial Estates of Chapter and nobility controlled the politics of the bishopric.[35] Bishop and Estates co-operated well and with a certain political maturity in avoiding civil conflict, which possibly only adherence to an unwritten constitution for many generations could produce. All the towns and many of the larger villages had access to the territorial assembly, so that a large number of *Ackerbürger* or peasants who were also citizens were represented by their mayors in the assembly.[36]

Those with real power were, however, only a handful of territorial noble families.[37] They controlled the prebends in the Chapter as also the seats in the curia of the noble Estates. In 1434 the Chapter was already informing the Council of Basel that no one had been accepted as a member of the Chapter in the previous hundred years who was not also of noble birth. In 1480 candidates to prebends were expected to show evidence of four noble ancestors, according to a statute which the Chapter itself issued. This was increased to eight by the middle of the next century. By 1580 the Chapter was asking for sixteen noble ancestors. This was four generations of noble blood on both sides of the family. The stipulation remained in force until the secularization of 1810. Thereafter prebends ceased to be political offices. In this way the older territorial nobility preserved a

[35] G. J. Rosenkranz, 'Die Verfassung des ehemaligen Hochstifts Paderborn', *Westfälische Zeitschrift*, 12, 1851, p. 55.

[36] W. Leesch and P. Schubert, *Heimatchronik des Kreises Höxter*, Cologne, 1966, pp. 122–4. F. Jacobs, 'Die Paderborner Landstände im 17. und 18. Jahrhundert', *Westfälische Zeitschrift*, 93, II, 1937, pp. 55–6, 106–12, made a case for the Estates as an effective co-government, without whose committees, curias and assemblies the Bishop, his privy councillors and officials could not have run the country between 1600 and 1800. [37] Leesch and Schubert, *op. cit.*, p. 124.

1704–11, the territorial ruler was forced by the *Reichshofrat* to give up the practices that the peasants were appealing against, until the *RKG* should be able to come to a decision, which it finally managed to do in 1731. F. Hertz, 'Die Rechtsprechung der höchsten Reichsgerichte', *Mitteilungen des Instituts für österreichische Geschichtsforschung*, 69, 1961, pp. 336, 356. Thus a pending case could be equitable in itself, although the plaintiff had to pay year after year to keep it pending, otherwise it would be shelved. Compare the Court of Chancery under attack in rebellious England in the 1640s. A. Harding, *A Social History of English Law*, Penguin Books, 1966, pp. 266, 278, '23,000 cases were believed to be pending before it . . . some of which had been there for thirty years and had involved 500 (contradictory) orders'.

privileged position in the face of three dangers—Protestantism, secularization and new ennoblements. Thus a wealthy man could buy a patent of nobility from the Habsburgs and their *Hofpfalzgrafen* and even a few mythical noble ancestors, as did the Dortmund military enterprisers, the Deggings, after the Thirty Years' War. Yet they could hardly expect any ecclesiastical establishment to accept sixteen mythical ancestors. [38]

There were twenty-four prebends in the Paderborn Chapter. New members were usually accepted from among suitable candidates between the ages of nineteen and twenty-five. Although unmarried, most members were only in lower orders. They wore the tonsure but were not sworn to celibacy or burdened with the performance of high office. Many resigned and married at later stages of their lives. Of the twenty-four in 1683 only four were fully ordained, in 1712 only three. Yet each had produced a list of sixteen authentic noble ancestors and two established territorial nobles had introduced each of them by standing also as surety. The system of co-option thus prevailed. [39]

In 1662 the Bishop, Ferdinand von Fürstenberg, who had come up through the ranks of the established territorial nobility and through the Chapter, issued a decree confirming the sixteen-ancestor rule for access to the noble curia in the assembly. His reason for this move was that so many foreign, non-noble officers had obtained noble lands during the previous war period that the remaining territorial nobility were threatened with loss of their privileged position to a mass of newcomers. The result was that only thirty-nine nobles were sworn in at the Chancellery in October 1662 as qualifying for a seat in the noble Estate of the assembly. The Bishop had thereby achieved a drastic cut in the number of politically important nobles whom he would always have to take into account in home affairs. In return the oldest noble families obtained a monopoly of power in Chapter and Noble Estate at the territorial assembly. The man of merit and wealth without birth was effectively excluded. A tendency to make a closed social group which monopolized power had

---

[38] W. Tack, 'Aufnahme, Ahnenprobe und Kappengang der Paderborner Domherren im 17. und 18. Jahrhundert', *Westfälische Zeitschrift*, 96, II, 1940, pp. 5–6. A. Meininghaus, 'Vom Adel der Dortmunder Deggings', *Westfalen*, 20, 1935; the von Deggings in their *Adelsbrief* also bought four mythical noble ancestors from Emperor Ferdinand III. [39] Tack, *op. cit.*, p. 8.

thus been accentuated among the older Paderborn nobility and it had become constitutionally established.[40] To be elected, a prospective bishop now had only to negotiate with twenty-four nobles in the Chapter.[41] Once he had been accepted, the Bishop and his councillors had to deal with another thirty-nine nobles and relatives of those in the Chapter who had elected him. The new Bishop would be expected to exercise enough patronage to satisfy this small number of political grandees. This left the Bishop with only the burghers to satisfy.

The towns owed their political influence to some extent to the aid which they gave to the Chapter in the fight against Dietrich von Moers, Archbishop of Cologne in the mid-fifteenth century, when he had attempted to incorporate Paderborn into his archdiocese. The oldest three towns of Paderborn, Warburg and Brakel were, however, already founded in the twelfth century. To them came Borgentreich in the fifteenth century, and thereafter nineteen other market towns that were really only villages, some of them not even being foundations of the Bishops.[42] The four larger towns had populations of between 2,000 and 4,500 before the year 1800. The rest of the towns had between 450 and 1,000 people.[43] Under the Emperors Maximilian I and Charles V, Brakel town, like Lemgo in Lippe, even got into the *Reichsmatrikel* or imperial tax register as if it were an imperial free town. When Brakel did not pay the imperial taxes for which it was assessed, it was cited before the *Reichskammergericht* by the imperial prosecutor. Brakel won its case and reaffirmed its status as a territorial and not imperial town (*Landstadt, nicht Reichsstadt*).[44]

[40] *Ibid.*, p. 24.

[41] Rosenkranz, *op. cit.*, pp. 69–70. Thus Hoffaktor Gomperz left a list of bribes which the Wittelsbach Bishop Clemens August had ordered him to pay to eighteen members of the Chapters of Paderborn and Münster in 1719, in order that he should be elected Bishop, which duly happened. Each of the *Domherren* received between 2,000 and 10,000 tlrs for his vote. Clemens August thus bought himself two imperial mitres for a mere 127,000 tlrs of which only 8,000 tlrs remained unpaid in Gomperz's accounts of 1746. Schnee, *op. cit.*, *Westfalen*, 34, pp. 179–81. Thereafter the position of Bishop-elect went for 60,000 tlrs to a candidate with support from the larger Protestant territories, Lücke, *op. cit.*, p. 16n.

[42] Thus the town of Büren, Rosenkranz, *op. cit.*, pp. 123–5.

[43] Leesch and Schubert, *op. cit.*, p. 138. E. Keyser, *Westfälisches Städtebuch*, Stuttgart, 1953, *passim*.

[44] Similarly the town of Lemgo in Lippe. The imperial tax arrears that such towns would have had to pay had they accepted imperial status would have

In the seventeenth century the Paderborn towns generally lost their charters of privileges, owing to Protestant infiltration which Counter-Reformation bishops were swift to stamp out. Paderborn became the centre of a Jesuit mission for north-west Germany. This was tolerated especially once the nobility had realized that the reformed Church of Rome would continue to support their monopoly of offices in church and state.[45] In 1604 Paderborn town was subdued by Bishop Dietrich von Fürstenberg. Although they were so numerous, in actual fact the political power of the Paderborn towns was very limited, and even so usually expressed only by mayors and councillors of Paderborn town itself, or at most by the ruling burgher families of all four larger towns. Even these were no match against either Bishop and his officials or Chapter and nobility.[46]

So the nobility were in the long run the real rulers of Paderborn. General tax exemption applied to all the nobility, to the new families as well as the old. The tax on their incomes from land rents was nominal only and ran at 700 tlrs *per simplum* in 1662.[47] In about seventy rural areas local noble landlords had control over the local courts, over the police and over petty crime, rather like gentry-J.P.s in rural England or the Junkers of East Prussia.[48] The nobility were represented on all committees and there were always two of them in the privy council. When acting in an official capacity all nobles were paid by the day through the Estates' treasury or *Landkasse*.[49]

In the seventeenth century the Bishop generally relied upon grants of direct taxation to tide him over the annual deficits which his administration produced. On the whole, Paderborn finances showed a similar development to those in Münster, only Paderborn was the poorer territory. The Chapter and nobility were exempted from paying land tax. Land tax was hopefully assessed in 1590–1 at about 6,800 tlrs *per simplum*, of which the lower clergy paid 724 tlrs, the burghers 2,705 tlrs

---

[45] H. Rothert, *Westfälische Geschichte*, 2, 2nd ed., Gütersloh, 1962, pp. 262, 264–7. [46] Leesch and Schubert, *op. cit.*, pp. 138–50.

[47] For *simplum*, see note 51.

[48] A. Voss, 'Patrimonialgerichte im Paderborner Land', *Westfalen*, 21, 1936, pp. 106–8. Rosenkranz, *op. cit.*, pp. 55–6. [49] *Ibid.*, pp. 122–3.

---

bankrupted them. Cf. Stadtarchiv Lemgo, later sixteenth-century accounts with imperial tax arrears demands in Staatsarchiv Detmold.

and the peasants 3,375 tlrs. At nearly every assembly petitions were presented for remission of tax arrears. In reality the full land tax was lucky to make 5,000 tlrs per month, which often meant that officials tried to levy a double land tax to meet the demands made upon them. However, the Bishop also issued tax remissions out of necessity to those burghers and peasants who were in real economic need.[50]

Why this heavy taxation? The Bishop did not control sufficient domains to cover the cost of the court and administration. The army was the largest single item of expenditure. Hence by about 1700 a gross annual expenditure of 100,000 tlrs could be reckoned with in Paderborn. To finance this up to 16 *simpla* of land tax were needed annually.[51]

During the War of the Spanish Succession the Paderborn army cost an average 36,000 tlrs annually, but costs fluctuated wildly. This fluctuation was particularly harmful to the delicate balance of an agricultural economy. To the unavoidable danger of a bad harvest was added the burden of a standing army. Thus the Paderborn troops serving with the other imperial contingents on the lower Rhine cost 18,750 fl. in the period of May–December 1709. With the coming of peace in 1715 the Estates pleaded for drastic army cuts, but the Bishop gave as reason the dangers of the Northern War for keeping up troop strength.[52]

[50] Dahl, *op. cit.*, pp. 21–4. G. Wrede, 'Familienforschung und Hofgeschichte', *Westfalen*, 18, 1933, p. 147.

[51] Taxation according to *simpla* was first introduced at imperial, federal level. That is how Turk taxes were assessed from the early sixteenth century onwards. A Register was made (*Matrikel*) where everyone was given a fixed assessment and then this assessment was doubled, trebled etc., according to need. The assessment thus became the fixed unit upon which all tax bargaining was based. This assessment was called the *simplum*. The *simplum* was a sophistication of the older system of *Römermonate*. Thus if the federal authorities demanded a *duplum zu 10 Römermonate*, the territories each paid $2 \times 10 \times$ their *Matrikel* assessment. Cf. Staatsarchiv Detmold, L 37 XVII, nos 1–7. The territories also began to make use of this system for their own internal taxation. The smaller the original sum, the greater its multiplication.

[52] Dahl, *op. cit.*, pp. 38–9. In the war year 1711 the Paderborn circle contingent was 162 horse and 332 foot. Basic rates of pay were 8 tlrs per month for a dragoon and 3 tlrs per month for a foot-soldier. Each man was expected to pay for his own food and keep (and for his horse) out of this salary. If the troops were stationed at home this money could to some extent be recouped by the subjects who had in the first place paid it out in taxation. In the *Reichsdefensionsordnung* of 1681 the Paderborn *simplum* was 18 horse and 34 foot. In 1702 Paderborn asked for permission to provide 819 foot at a cost of about 6,000 tlrs per month. Rosenkranz, *op. cit.*,

During the 1650s the Bishop obtained money from five basic sources of taxation, from the land tax on peasants and burghers, from excise, cattle tax, poll tax and occasional charitable grants from Chapter and nobility. The first excises were not introduced until 1655 and by 1659 the towns had already bought the Bishop off by commuting all excises on necessities to a tax on alcohol consumption, estimated at half a *simplum* of land tax.[53]

The cattle tax was not favoured by the Estates. Presumably it delved too deeply into the affairs of their own tenants and serfs. It did not become a regular source of income to the Bishop. Novel forms of taxation were thus resorted to. Such was a hearth tax which made nearly 10,000 tlrs each time it was levied in 1645, 1650, 1652 and 1669, but the real backbone of public finance remained the land tax.[54]

The land tax was granted in annual assemblies by the Estates and collected from the peasants and burghers in monthly quotas. Apparently the only time that the Estates refused to grant taxes at all to the Bishop occurred at the assembly of 17 March 1597, when an unspecified number of nobles and mayors said that they would grant a Turk tax only if in return they were given permission to worship freely according to the rites of the Augsburg Confession. In a rising Counter-Reformation state like Paderborn this demand failed miserably.[55]

The development of the Estates' sole right to grant taxes in assemblies was, however, slow. As late as 1548 the Bishop's *Rentmeister* or local treasury official in Dringenberg gave the mayor, council and commoners of Warburg town a receipt for half a local land tax which came to 100 fl., which they had granted and levied, presumably quite independently from the other Estates, in direct negotiations with the Bishop's local officials, for repairs to public buildings in Dringenberg. So the

[53] M. Gorges, 'Beiträge zur Geschichte des ehemaligen Hochstifts Paderborn 1650–61', *Westfälische Zeitschrift*, 50, II, 1892, pp. 48–51.

[54] A. Brand, *Die direkten Staatssteuern im Fürstbistum Paderborn*, Münster, 1912, pp. 94–9. Cf. H. Tümmler, 'Ein Bedeverzeichnis', *Zeitschrift des Vereins für Thüringische Geschichte*, 29, new series, 1931, pp. 190–1.

[55] Rosenkranz, *op. cit.*, p. 152. Brand, *op. cit.*, p. 35. Schaten, *Annales Paderbornienses*, Neuhaus, 1693, II, p. 588, for a brief anti-Protestant account.

---

p. 54. The advantage of this imperial, federal system was that it could turn troop-levies into money-levies or both at will, according to the wishes of each single territory.

land tax was adapted to purely local needs, as well as to territorial and imperial needs.

Yet when a tax demand was taken to the assembly, the Bishop did not try to obtain consent to it from one or other of the Estates only. Apparently only once was this rule broken. In 1606 he asked for consent from the Chapter only. This led to immediate protests from the nobles and towns. It seems that no Bishop ever tried to do this again.[56]

This was a truly unusual development for the seventeenth century as a whole. In the bishopric of Paderborn assemblies continued as a living institution until the secularization of the Napoleonic era.

From the fourteenth century onwards the majority of those clergy who were not members of the Chapter paid a charitable grant as well as a share of the *Willkommensteuer*, which was granted once only to each new Bishop. This subsidy seems generally to have been very small. Except in the case of the rare *Willkommensteuer* it did not reach four figures, although from 1664 onwards the smaller subsidy was levied annually. In 1661 Ferdinand von Fürstenberg was granted 24,000 tlrs *Willkommensteuer*, of which 19,000 tlrs were actually paid. Even the nobility contributed. However, it was the land tax which really financed the early modern state of Paderborn.[57]

In the early sixteenth century one or two *simpla* per annum were enough to keep the Bishop's administration from bankruptcy. Between 1650 and 1755 the records showed that between three and sixteen *simpla*, that is between 16,500 and 88,000 tlrs, were needed annually. The land tax went through the assembly without fail throughout the whole period.[58]

[56] Brand, *op. cit.*, pp. 34–6. Mayer, *op. cit.*, Sander and Spangenberg, *op. cit.*, 1, Documents 47, 49, 50.

[57] Brand used Codex 52 'Verzeichnis der erhobenen Steuern 1650–1755' in the Archives of the Paderborn Historical Society. From the earliest extant Paderborn land tax register of 1498–9, 4,309 fl. could be raised. The register (*Matrikel*) of 1760 totalled 5,500 tlrs *per simplum*; a remarkable tax stability over the centuries. Accounts were in two columns, what should be paid and what was paid. The towns and rural communities usually paid up to 60 per cent of their assessment. Only by modern standards could this be regarded as insufficient. Brand, *op. cit.*, pp. 36–44, 57, 100–9. Cf. Staatsarchiv Detmold, L 37 XVII no. 6, Lippe tax receipts for 1704–7 show that arrears were low.

[58] Brand, *op. cit.*, pp. 61–2. Rosenkranz, *op. cit.*, estimated that an average of 12 *simpla* of land tax were levied annually after the 1650s, bringing in 65,000 tlrs a year.

Normally each rural community had its own method of taxation. Taxes were raised internally and then sent on to the official Receiver, the *Stiftsschatzeinnehmer*. Self-assessment and collection could be lucrative for local officials and notables. Thus Nieheim town was assessed at 600 tlrs by the Receiver for the tax year 1560, representing four *simpla* of land taxes which the assembly had granted to the Bishop for that year. In actual fact Nieheim town council levied 22½ *simpla* of community taxes in that year. Each community tax ran at 44 tlrs per *simplum*, so that the town treasury took in nearly 1,000 tlrs, of which only 600 had to be sent to the Receiver.[59] This is an example of how taxes could be manipulated by local authorities. The town council families were doing well out of it at the expense of the lower orders in the town. It helps to show why rulers and Estates were always very eager to discuss the ways and means of taxation, rather than the constitutional principles upon which it may have been based, for the one was lucrative and the other laborious. It was thus important that members of the Estates should co-operate well with officials in every locality. At best the Estates were appointed as officials themselves, at least in an honorary capacity, so that Bishop and Estates could thereby convince themselves of the solidarity with which they ruled over the rest of the population.[60]

The local man who stepped forward as tax collector had to deposit a cautionary sum with the government. He had to find people with enough private means to act as surety for him. He was then allowed to keep 2 per cent of what he collected. This was not very much, but then it was by order of the central authorities and likely to have reflected the yearnings for a fiscal utopia of a cameralist councillor, rather than local reality.[61] Thus in 1753 the Bishop's Receiver paid a *Caution* to the Estates of over 10,000 tlrs. His salary was 150 tlrs per annum. This was three times the salary of the Receiver in 1614, but still represented a return of only 1½ per cent per annum on his *Caution*. This shows that the Receiver had to recoup himself out of his office by accepting favours, bribes and other suitable perquisites, for otherwise he was losing money on the 10,000

---

[59] *Ibid.*, p. 148. Brand, *op. cit.*, p. 63.
[60] This succeeded in Paderborn. It failed in Osnabrück under Ernst August.
[61] Brand, *op. cit.*, p. 65.

tlrs which he had deposited, and on which he could easily have got 5 per cent elsewhere.

Even so, the Receiver had to suit his methods to the demands of a joint Estates' committee of audit, which met prior to annual assemblies. That both Bishops and Estates were sometimes not satisfied with the accounts is shown by a complaint in 1599 that they were too scanty. They were sent back to the Receiver for clarification. The joint committee consisted of privy councillors and representatives of all three Estates, their secretaries and legal advisers or *syndici*.[62]

Between 1706 and 1717 Peckelsheim town should have paid out 15,600 tlrs in taxes to the Receiver. It actually paid 12,577 tlrs and was granted tax relief of a further 2,303 tlrs. Thus its tax arrears were well under 1,000 tlrs for the whole twelve-year period. The town fulfilled the tax demands made upon it by nearly 95 per cent. The Estates system of taxation seemed to have worked very well here.

A burgher of Peckelsheim had his house and garden sold up to pay for his tax arrears in 1771, but from the long lists of tax arrears which were issued each year by local and central authorities, this drastic method, let alone the really destructive system of military billet or *scharfe Exekution*, was used very rarely as a terrible example to the rest of the community to pay their taxes promptly and in full.[63] Did continuous tax arrears imply continuous over-taxation, or did they imply that subjects were generally unwilling to pay taxes in full because they were prepared to rely on a more efficient protection of private property at law against confiscation than the tax authorities would have wished?[64] The use of force was a matter for the

---

[62] *Ibid.*, pp. 66–7. Klaveren, 'Erscheinung der Korruption', pp. 292–3, 316. In bishopric Hildesheim in 1783 the *Caution* was 20,000 tlrs for the *Landrentmeister* and 5,000 tlrs for each *Schatzeinnehmer*, Lücke, *op. cit.*, p. 113. J. von Klaveren, 'Fiskalismus-Merkantilismus-Korruption', *Vierteljahrschrift für Sozial- und Wirtschaftsgeschichte*, 47, 1960, p. 338.

[63] Brand, *op. cit.*, pp. 68–71. Kuske, 'Entwicklung der Kreditwirtschaft', pp. 120–1.

[64] Property and its conservation were the basis of a legal system which territorial rulers could interfere with only by exploiting to the full their powers as judges, by arbitrary use of their regal powers, by use of armed force and coercion. H. Thieme, 'Die Funktion der Regalien', *Zeitschrift der Savigny-Stiftung für Rechtsgeschichte*, 1942, p. 86. K. Rauch, *Kapitalerhöhung aus Gesellschaftsmitteln und ihre Besteuerung*, Marburg, 1950, pp. 5–6. A. Eger, *Vermögenshaftung und Hypothek nach Fränkischem Recht*, Breslau, 1903, p. 14.

imperial courts, as breach of the peace was an imperial offence as *Landfriedensbruch*.[65] Territorial officials had to beware of litigation which wealthier and pluckier subjects could bring against them not only in the territorial courts of appeal but also at the *Reichskammergericht*. Thus tax arrears may have been a further sign of the sanctity of private property against the demands of the tax authorities.

The legal system still favoured property if only by virtue of complicated legal procedures for the recovery of debt. However, troops had to be billeted in wintertime. Tax arrears were good excuses for billeting. The local community was keen to avoid giving such an excuse to the central authorities, and would often borrow money to pay off its arrears. This debt had then to be recouped from the surplus of next year's levies. In the meantime interest had to be paid on it. So the local community could not afford to lose its right to assess and collect its own taxes to the ruler or any *ad hoc* officials whom he might appoint. When the local community could find no more credit, the army could be sent in. At all events people learned to live with their debts and tax arrears, and with the threat of violence which that left them open to from their own rulers' officials.[66]

What, then, was life like for the ordinary people, the peasants

[65] G. Aders and H. Richtering, *Das Staatsarchiv Münster und seine Bestände, 2, Gerichte des Alten Reiches, Reichskammergericht*, A–Z, 1966–8, p. VIII. Neither Paderborn nor Münster had a *privilegium de non appellando*. Their subjects were thus free to take appeals against decisions of their territorial courts to the imperial instance, Hertz, *op. cit.*, p. 334. W. Sellert, *Über die Zuständigkeitsabgrenzung von Reichshofrat und Reichskammergericht*, Aalen, 1965, pp. 37–40.

[66] Schmitt, *op. cit.*, pp. 58–64. A. Lück, 'Die scharfen Exekutionen gegen Kaan und Obersdorf im Jahre 1735', *Blätter des Siegerländer Heimatvereins*, 44, 1967, pp. 16–23. G. Grüll, *Bauer, Herr und Landesfürst, sozialrevolutionäre Bestrebungen der oberösterreichischen Bauern 1650–1848*, Graz, 1963, *passim*, especially Appendices 2, 4. The position of peasants and farm-workers was often so unsatisfactory that it inevitably led to tax evasion, thieving and poaching. Cf. G. Benecke, 'Labour relations and peasant society in Northwest Germany c. 1600', *History*, October 1973. For a successful imperial *Exekution* against a ruling Duke of Mecklenburg which ended in his forced abdication, 1716–28, and an *Exekution* of 1671–2 to collect tax arrears, see Hofer, *op. cit.*, pp. 69, 194–6. Kuske, 'Entstehung der Kreditwirtschaft', p. 99. In the *Lippische Hofgerichtsordnung 1593*, Section XLVII, printed in *Landesverordnungen*, Lemgo, I, 1779, pp. 276–7, paragraphs 3–5, the debtor on paper at least received some protection against distraint by use of excessive force. F. W. Schaer, 'Der Absolutismus in Lippe und Schaumburg-Lippe', *Lippische Mitteilungen*, 37, 1968, p. 190. Staatsarchiv Detmold, L 10 Titel 2 no. 14, Hofgericht, 26 May 1626, *Exekution* against the Varenholz Drost von dem Busch for unpaid medical fees of 20 fl.

of Paderborn? Bishops showed an ever-increasing fatherly interest in them. The first *Polizeiordnung* to cover the whole territory from 1655 showed a basic awareness of the inadequate arrangements that existed for the welfare of ordinary people. The officials who drew up this edict were, however, hardly aware that even the poor were individuals with a right to an identity of their own. The edict forbade all swearing, all drinking during the times of Holy Office and other religious festivals. The prices of bread, beer, meat, haberdashery and medicine were fixed. Wages of tailors, cobblers, smiths, goldsmiths, tinkers, saddlers, tanners, clothmakers, shepherds, wheelwrights, cartwrights, window makers, tilers, building labourers, messengers and innkeepers were fixed not at a minimum, but at a low rate which was at the same time an employers' maximum. All lawyers were to register with the authorities. They were to keep records of all their transactions, especially all usurious agreements and credit transactions on cereals and farm produce, on alienations and divisions of tenancies and lands, which were made without consent of the landlords. Mortgage books were to be kept. Guardians and trustees were to keep annual accounts. No marriages were to be contracted without the previous knowledge of parents. Twice a year all buildings were to be checked in the interests of fire precaution. All officials who did not keep this edict were to be fined, and fines had to be paid first, before a case could go before a court of appeal.[67]

Rulers, officials and landlords, Bishop, councillor, *Amtmann*, noble, cleric and burgher, all had an interest in the welfare of their tenants and serfs who ran the farms and did the work upon which the whole economy depended. These tenants were headed by the *Meier*.[68] As serfs and unfree men, *Meier* sacrificed their freedom of movement, freedom of marriage and inheritance. In

[67] Gorges, *op. cit.*, pp. 37–8. For social welfare, J. K. Heidenreich, *Das Armenwesen der Stadt Warburg*, Münster, 1909, pp. 32–6. Early modern begging was a full-time occupation and the town council issued edicts to supervise it, especially in the interests of its native professional beggars against ousiders by appointing red-robed wardens, *Bettelvögte*. Warburg also provided 15 marks per month to subsidize poor girls' dowries. The town was supposed to take care of the pregnant and sick. Medical fees were subsidized and artisans could collect free wood in the town's forest. They could also obtain a certain amount of cheap credit.

[68] Wittich, *op. cit.*, pp. 6–65, on the *Meier* of neighbouring Guelph lands in the eighteenth century.

return they received the best land and the largest farms. Estate management was directed from *Meierhöfe*, which were scattered all over the territory. *Meierrecht* was the key to a legal system which provided the peasant, the serf and the tenant-farmer with an increasing number of rights and privileges against the landlord. It also tied the peasant more firmly to the soil than ever before.[69]

The condition of the peasantry varied from territory to territory in north-west Germany and nowhere were the rights of the peasantry clearly established before the nineteenth century, nor indeed were the peasantry a cohesive group. Above all being a peasant meant having a lord, who was a protector at law. Protection as *Schutz und Schirm* was a necessity for free and unfree peasant alike. Those, however, who were protected by a lord or ecclesiastical foundation in a legal system where the ruler controlled all the law courts were better off than those who were protected by a lord who also owned the local law court. Thus although the majority of Paderborn peasants were farmers with a secure tenure, a considerable number of them had the same landlord and magistrate.[70] They had thus no chance to exploit landlord-ruler jealousies which naturally arose where the landlord had no power over the local law court. However, apart from Bishop and Chapter, there were only two territorial noble families, two monasteries and two other episcopal domains in the territory of Paderborn which possessed their own unfree persons or *Leibeigene*.[71]

The peasant, whether freeman or serf, was a tenant. He paid rent and did not own the land he farmed. The rent he paid was generally heavy, as were also the taxes he paid to the state.The few exceptions to this rule appear between 1500 and 1800 in the tax registers as *Eximierte*,[72] whose status was comparable to that of the territorial nobility, officials and burghers.

[69] P. Wigand, *Provinzialrechte der Fürstentümer Paderborn und Corvey*, 1–3, Leipzig, 1832. C. Grünberg, 'Leibeigenschaft', *Handwörterbuch der Staatswissenschaften*, 2nd ed., Jena, 1901. In return for good land the prospective tenant-farmer had to expect that he and his family would have to give up their personal freedom to the landlord and become his serfs. F. Lütge, *Geschichte der Deutschen Agrarverfassung*, 2nd ed., Stuttgart, 1967, pp. 94, 191.

[70] Wigand, *op. cit.*, 2, pp. 278n., 280. In 1595 the Bishop in a tax demand to a *Guts- und Gerichtsherr*, who was his vassal, talked of 'Eure Gerichtseingesessene, unsere Untertanen'. [71] Leesch and Schubert, *op. cit.*, pp. 150–2.

[72] Cf. T. Weddigen, 'Die freien Höfe und Häuser, die Exempten oder Exi-

Peasant tenancies were the basis of the rural economy, and the feudal tenures which were held by the privileged nobles, burghers and *Eximierte* were part of this selfsame economy.[73] Rents paid by vassals were light and they paid no taxes to the state. A fief did not hamper a vassal's freedom of movement. He was free to sell up, to move away, to give out his land as he thought fit, and to marry as he thought best.[74] As vassal and feudal tenant his privileges were great and his burdens were negligible. As landlord and estate manager, however, he made sure that the peasants as his tenants and serfs carried heavy burdens in return for negligible privileges. This applied even more strictly to labourers and menials to whom even the peasants were aristocrats of the land.

The peasant's tenancy tied him to the soil and to a landlord within a pseudo-feudal system of rents and services. When ruler and landlord joined forces in exploitation of the peasant, when rents and Estates' tax grants were collected by the same landlord-magistrates or pliable officials, then the peasantry could expect a harsh time, mitigated only by a crude paternalism.

Attempts were always made to improve tenant-landlord relations by legislation. Yet the problem was not tackled rationally, for no two rents were paid with the same kind of services, moneys or produce. *Meier* of the Altenau valley, south of Paderborn town, freed themselves of personal servitude, but this did not prevent them from having to render increased services with their horses and carts, although they were officially freemen. Services had just gone over from the person of the tenant to the tenancy itself. Either way the peasants were at a disadvantage against their local landlords and magistrates, the Chapter, the monastery of Abdinghof and the von Kalenbergs.[75]

The bishops of Paderborn had an interest in all peasants

[73] For the overlapping of *Meierhöfe* and *Rittergüter* in Swabia, see V. Ernst, *Die Entstehung des deutschen Grundeigentums*, Stuttgart, Appendix and pp. 96–7. In Lippe the *Amtsmeier* were in this privileged, in-between position.

[74] Cf. E. A. F. Culemann, *Mindische Geschichte*, Minden, 1747–8. Staatsarchiv Detmold, D 71 no. 19.

[75] A. Voss, 'Die Grundherrschaft im Altenautale, Ein Beitrag zur Geschichte des Bauernstandes im Paderborner Lande', *Westfälische Zeitschrift*, 92, II, 1935, p. 69.

mirten', *10. Jahresbericht des Historischen Vereins für die Grafschaft Ravensberg*, 1895, pp. 25–56. Donop, *op. cit.*, 146–52. Out of a population of 62,000 in neighbouring Lippe in the 1788 census 266 were *Eximierte*.

because they paid the largest share of the extraordinary taxes which were needed to keep the territory from bankruptcy. In this they had to see that the peasants were not so exploited or so badly mismanaged by any of their landlords that they would be in no position to pay the ruler. The surplus produced by an unmechanized agricultural economy was inflexible and minimal. Thus in 1528 Erich von Braunschweig, Bishop of Paderborn, tried to regulate landlord-peasant relations between Paderborn town and its *Meier*. In return for a 'suitable' and not excessive *Weinkauf*, or inheritance tax, the *Meier* were warned not to alienate land without their landlords' consent Landlords were also given the right to deprive a *Meier* of his tenancy, or *Meierbrief*, as soon as he was three years behind in his rent.[76] This showed well the power of the Bishop to regulate relationships between burghers and peasants as landlords and tenants as equitably as possible.

In 1570 a legal judgment was actually given by a *Gograf* in favour of the landlords against all *Meier* who had borrowed money on their tenancies without consent. The *Meier* were to be deprived of their holdings. This case established a precedent. Another decision in the patrimonial court of the Lords of Büren affirmed that no creditors who had lent money to *Meier* without the consent of the landlords were to be allowed to claim their money back. This ruling was also upheld by a *Gograf*, or Bishop's local judge.[77]

The ruler thus took an active part in the problems arising out of tenant-landlord relations. He was also, of course, the most prominent landlord himself. He empowered his local judges to make laws by precedent as each particular case presented itself. As each legal problem came up it was dealt with in question-and-answer form and then preserved in writing as local custom, a *Landesurteil* or *Weistum*.

A considerable amount of legal business concerned regulation of inheritance among the *Meier*. The ruling of a von Haxtern in his own patrimonial court of Bökendorf in 1579 was to refuse to recognize an inheritance claim of an unfree tenant who had previously been bought off by the rest of the family before coming to his inheritance. To this decision was added a warning against love-making among the youth quite out of context

[76] Wigand, *op. cit.*, 3, p. 12.   [77] *Ibid.*, Documents 4, 5.

seemingly from the business in hand. If the lovers were not prepared to marry each other they were each to forfeit two years' wages (5–10 tlrs). This shows that attempts were made to control the birth-rate among servants and labourers in a crude fashion, and to instil in them the principles of holy matrimony not by education but by threat of material deprivation.[78] Coercion in the name of society, the Law and the Church is noticeable in the *Polizeiordnung* of 1655, where elopements especially between those of unequal status were to be made an example of by fines and corporal punishment. The officiating priest was also to be fined.[79]

In 1724 Bishop Clemens August issued an edict for the *Meier* in the *Ämter* of Neuhaus and Delbrück regulating the endowment of brides and the size of the pension which a retiring peasant should be allowed to pay himself. The bride was to be allowed no cattle, no cereals and only one cart. The marriage price to be rendered was fixed at 150 tlrs for a *Vollerhof*, the largest farm that appeared with four horses when rendering services to the lords; 80 tlrs for a *Halberhof* and between 5 and 50 tlrs for the rest—plus one cow in every case. The honest poor were assessed according to circumstances. All marriage agreements had to be notified immediately to the Bishop's local officials and confirmed before the marriage was consummated. The marriage gift was regulated according to the number of children a *Meier* had. The more he had, the less it came to. No drinking was to be allowed when the marriage agreement was drawn up among the parents. Farmers were not to retire when still in their prime in order that their heirs should not be allowed to escape death duties or *Sterbfall*, which had to be paid to the landlord.[80]

Bishops' control over serfs possibly reached the highest point in 1725 when an edict was issued forbidding the felling of fruit-bearing trees on pain of a fine of 5 *Groschen* per tree. This included fruit-bearing oak-trees because pigs were fed on the acorns. Every farmer was ordered to plant ten new oaks a year.[81]

Did personal unfreedom prevent a man from playing a

---

[78] *Ibid.*, Document 6. [79] *Ibid.*, Document 9.
[80] *Ibid.*, Documents 13, 29. Lütge, *Mitteldeutsche Grundherrschaft*, pp. 19–20. W. Müller, *Die Abgaben von Todes Wegen in der Abtei St Gallen*, Cologne, 1961, pp. 43, 49, 102, 105. [81] Wigand, *op. cit.*, 3, Document 15.

responsible part in village society? Perhaps so during the seventeenth and eighteenth centuries, but hardly in the sixteenth century, which was a time of new settlement and agricultural expansion in Paderborn. Thus in the year 1589 the local judge of Brenken, who even exercised the death penalty, was an unfree man.[82] By the end of the sixteenth century few landlords still knew which of their tenants were free and which were unfree. Instead of quietly forgetting the difference, unfreedom was pressed with new vigour upon the tenantry. So serfdom was a process which ever renewed itself. It was not allowed to disappear quietly.[83]

The local community or *Gemeinde* was a unit of self-help run by free and unfree tenants alike. Under the auspices of its landlord it ran its own law court. Peasants were their own judges and procedure was oral. With the adoption of written procedure and trained lawyers the peasant ceased to play a part in regulating the legal affairs of the community and became increasingly dependent upon the landlord and his expert servants.[84] During the seventeenth century Bishop and Estates as landlords began to make agreements with each other concerning mutual exploitation of their tenantry. The peasant moved into a world of enforced tutelage quite distinct from the responsibilities that he had exercised previously.[85]

However, edicts forbidding tenants from running their farms into debt, from alienating their holdings and from dividing them up among their families were repeated with such monotonous regularity in the later seventeenth and earlier eighteenth centuries that it is doubtful whether they were really effective.[86] This is where paternalist policy in the last resort failed. The peasant was not a child who had to be kept in tutelage but a

[82] *Ibid.*, 2, p. 280n.

[83] *Ibid.*, p. 300, a document of 1589 relates that free tenant-farmers have fallen into debt and have been distrained. To escape expulsion and total ruin they become serfs of their landlord, who protects them against their creditors.

[84] *Ibid.*, p. 301. Wigand regretted the passing of common law, oral procedures and the jury system in the sixteenth century. W. Ebel, *Geschichte der Gesetzgebung in Deutschland*, 2nd ed., Göttingen, 1958, pp. 65–7, 72, 75. Lütge, *Agrarverfassung*, pp. 159–61. Schmitt, *op. cit.*, p. 58.   [85] Wigand, *op. cit.*, 2, pp. 269–71, 340–2.

[86] The *Meier* was allowed to run his farm into debt merely to the tune of 20 tlrs without consent of his landlord. R. Brinkmann, *Studien zur Verfassung der Meiergüter in Paderborn*, Münster, 1907, p. 37. G. K. Schmelzeisen, *Polizeiordnungen und Privatrecht*, Münster, 1955, *passim*, especially p. 17.

businessman who had to be given freedom of movement if he was to become a good estate manager. Such a policy was outlined by early-nineteenth-century reformers of whom Wigand was one.[87] This of course went hand in hand with the policy of giving peasants ownership of the lands they farmed. It forced those who farmed uneconomically off their land and created demands for social security on the land, still one of the acute problems of our own day.

(iii) Osnabrück

Territorial rulers are not absolute rulers but they are under the laws and customs of the Empire, under which they are guaranteed a privileged position. Territorial rulers exercise legislative power but they must see that the laws which they decree do not conflict with the laws which have been made at imperial level, and the *Reichskammergericht* is there to see that this is carried out.[88] This is what ruling families could read in a handbook of the imperial constitution which the Saxony-Gotha Councillor, von Seckendorff, published in 1656. But far be it for any subjects, however prominent, to presume to tell their rulers when they were transgressing the laws of the Empire. Under the

[87] F. W. Henning, *Herrschaft und Bauernuntertänigkeit*, Würzburg, 1964, pp. 101, 273, 281, 282–3, 326, 328. One-fifth (20,000) of the Paderborn population were still serfs in 1800. The French abolished serfdom there in 1808. Wittich, *op. cit.*, p. 39. R. L. Plöthner (ed.), 'Erbregister über das schriftsässige Ritterguth zu Clodra 1669', *Zeitschrift des Vereins für Thüringische Geschichte*, 29, new series, 1931, pp. 465–9, showed the plight of serfs on a Thuringian noble estate. Lütge, *Mitteldeutsche Grundherrschaft*, pp. 18–20, 298–9. Also the manumissions sold by the Lippe government to serfs especially numerous in the era of the Thirty Years' War as a source of extra revenue, Staatsarchiv Detmold. From C. O. Mylius, *Corpus Constitutionum Marcicarum*, Berlin, 1737–55, *passim*, it is possible to contrast the burdens of the peasantry with the privileges of the Estates in the detailed legislation of the period by use of the systematic register. If only because of the breadth of knowledge displayed, it is still valuable to read the nineteenth-century liberal views against serfdom in S. Sugenheim, *Geschichte der Aufhebung der Leibeigenschaft und Hörigkeit in Europa*, St Petersburg, 1864, pp. 1–18, 350–499, especially pp. 374–5. For a Stalinist approach to serfdom, see J. Nichtweiss, *Das Bauernlegen in Mecklenburg*, Berlin, 1954, pp. 7, 51–72. And for a survey of 'liberalized' agriculture, E. Hobsbawm, *The Age of Revolution*, New York, 1962, pp. 180–4, 188, 191–2. That the freeing of the peasantry failed to help them socially and economically does not mean to imply that the old emphyteutic system that was thereby replaced was anything but an evil itself. Both systems were bad.

[88] Seckendorff, *op. cit.*, pp. 21–2. H. Kraemer, 'Der deutsche Kleinstaat',

German system of peerage, subjects obeyed and only rulers sat in judgment upon each other. This meant that generally no scrutiny into territorial home affairs by anyone who was impartial to the ruler was possible.[89]

Despite the need to placate the Protestant Guelphs at the Peace of Westphalia, the Catholics were able to retain a considerable hold over the bishopric of Osnabrück. Their ruler, Franz Wilhelm von Wartenberg, an illegitimate son of a Wittelsbach ruler, regained control. The Swedes were bought off, and the Guelphs had to content themselves with an alternating régime between a Catholic and one of their younger sons. This was a remarkable arrangement, but far more remarkable was that it actually worked. In the imperial constitution after 1648 the position of Osnabrück was unique. When Franz Wilhelm died in 1661, Ernst August took over the government as the first Guelph Bishop. A new era had dawned.[90]

When Ernst August returned from Italy he had the immediate problem of negotiating with a predominant Catholic Chapter over his rights in the administration of the territory according to the *Instrumentum Pacis Osnabrugensis* and the *Capitulatio perpetua*. According to the latter the ruler was still expected to run the state from his own regular revenues with occasional extraordinary grants from the Estates.[91] As the chief landowners and landlords, the Chapter and territorial nobility especially saw to it that the ruler's demands for extra money never went unchallenged. Although the Estates were themselves exempt from extraordinary taxation, their tenants were not. In an agricultural economy there was a strict limit to how much farmers could afford in rent, and every increase in extraordinary taxation correspondingly threatened the land-

[89] P. Göttsching, 'Justus Möser und der Westfälische Frieden', *Der Friede von Osnabrück*, Oldenburg, 1948, p. 197.

[90] As regulated for the imperial constitution by the Peace of Osnabrück, text and translation, ed. E. Walder, Bern, 1952.

As regulated for the territorial constitution by the *Capitulatio perpetua* between Bishop and Chapter in 1650, J. Freckmann, *Die Capitulatio Perpetua 1648–50*, Münster, 1906. R. Renger, *Landesherr und Landstände im Hochstift Osnabrück*, Göttingen, 1968, pp. 143–6.

[91] M. Bär, *Abriss einer Verwaltungsgeschichte des Regierungsbezirks Osnabrück*, Hanover, 1901, pp. 55–6.

Zeitschrift des Vereins für Thüringische Geschichte, 25, new series, 1922–4. H. von Zwiedineck-Südenhorst, *Deutsche Geschichte*, 1, Stuttgart, 1894, pp. 200–1.

lord with a decrease in rent, and the creditor with a break in steady mortgage repayment.[92]

The *Landtage* which Ernst August and his Osnabrück officials called between 1662 and 1698 followed much the same pattern as before. The ruler demanded money because the territory was in danger of foreign attack or threatened by interterritorial hostility. A phrase used to express an emergency situation was *gefährliche Conjuncturen*, which implied also a perilous financial situation. The Estates generally replied with a policy of procrastination, followed by eventual grants. In cases of refusal, the ruler collected the money that he wanted by arbitrary and illegal methods. Despite the general lack of trust and co-operation between Ernst August and the Estates, a reorganization of the system of extraordinary taxation in Osnabrück was achieved in 1667. The cattle tax was changed into a monthly land tax, rather similar to the system in the neighbouring bishopric of Münster. Yet the need for a reassessment of actual land distribution among the peasantry was not fulfilled.

[92] G. Schöttke, 'Die Stände des Hochstifts Osnabrücks 1662–98', *Osnabrücker Mitteilungen*, 33, 1908, pp. 9–10. But Bär, *op. cit.*, did not think that the Estates paid enough taxes themselves. Statistics of taxation on the territorial nobility are hard to find. A rare example is G. Tessin, 'Wert und Grösse Mecklenburgischer Rittergüter zu Beginn des dreissigjährigen Krieges', *Zeitschrift für Agrargeschichte und Agrarsoziologie*, 3, 1955, pp. 145–57. In 1632 the Mecklenburg nobility were assessed for a one-half per cent capital tax. For this they produced their accounts and swore an oath as to the completeness of the declarations they had made to the treasury. These modern and 'drastic' methods may have had to do with the political situation, and 1632 was no ordinary year with Mecklenburg still caught in the cross-fire of Wallenstein and Gustavus Adolphus. Tessin examines the tax returns of 343 noble estates out of a total of 572. The average capital value of a noble estate is reckoned at 22,600 fl. and the largest was worth 135,000 fl. and gave an annual income of 8,000 fl. from rents. Capital values were assessed on an average 6 per cent yield per annum. At this rating the average landed noble had an income of 2,000 fl. yearly, and with a capital tax of one-half per cent, he thus had to pay one-twelfth of his annual income in taxes—a by no means paltry sum. Especially highly rated were the rents and services the nobility received from their tenants, labourers and serfs. These were taxed six times more heavily if they were rents from serfs, and three times more heavily if they came from free-tenants, than rents from other sources. These serf and tenant rents made up to 5–25 per cent of a nobleman's income (pp. 148, 153). The rent of a tenant-farmer was between 20 and 60 fl. yearly. A ploughman received 30 fl. per annum in wages and keep, a servant-girl 11 fl. The farmer usually paid land tax; labourers and servants paid poll tax out of their meagre wages. Compared with these wages landed noble income was of course huge, and thus when noblemen did pay taxes of a realistic nature, as seems to have been the case in Mecklenburg in 1632, then their contribution was a significant item in treasury finance. See also Zwiedineck-Südenhorst, *op. cit.*, p. 202.

However, the existing *Matrikel*, or tax register of farms drawn up according to tenant and locality, was rescheduled. Only farms that could be proved to have been tax-exempt in 1602 were declared tax-free after 1667. This penalized those noblemen who since 1602 had turned to farming themselves in order to evade the taxes levied when their lands had been farmed by tenants.[93]

The new tax made 90,000–120,000 tlrs per annum. The heaviest burden of taxation fell on the countryside. Despite Ernst August's ruthless collection by use of troops without the consent of the Estates, tax-arrears were widespread. Even so Ernst August had to depend almost totally on arbitrary taxation, for his income from domain in Osnabrück was small. For 1671–2 the chamber showed accounts for 15,000 tlrs. Compared with the ratio of domain income to extraordinary income in Brunswick-Lüneburg and Brunswick-Calenberg this was indeed a paltry sum. It goes some way to showing that in the remaining independent ecclesiastical territories the rulers had to rely far more on money from extraordinary levies on the Estates and tenantry than was the case among dynastic rulers who had kept their domains in better shape than the Bishops. Thus the Estates in ecclesiastical territories had possibly a better chance of survival than Estates in dynastic territories. This could be seen in the way in which constitutional changes were generally slower in taking place in ecclesiastical territories than in dynastic ones by early modern times.[94]

Between 1675 and 1685 no *Landtage* were called in Osnabrück and all taxes were levied by decree. The Estates produced a flood of complaints. Ernst August was a tyrant. He appointed his own local tax-collectors called *Vögte*, who infringed the rights of the *Rentmeister* in the localities. This was a case where a traditional office was arbitrarily and temporarily deprived of its power at the whim of the ruler. *Vögte* were even said to be infringing the rights of the *Landräte*, according to complaints

[93] Schöttke, *op. cit.*, pp. 8–9, 11–12.

[94] *Ibid.*, pp. 12–13. Bär, *op. cit.*, pp. 57–9, taxes were written out at the Chancellery and collected by *ad hoc* officials whom the ruler called *Vögte*. They received an official premium of 2–3 per cent on what they collected. See also the budget estimates in G. Droege, 'Die finanziellen Grundlagen des territorialstaates', *Vierteljahrschrift für Sozial- und Wirtschaftsgeschichte*, 53, 1966, p. 154n.

from the Estates.[95] At the *Landtag* of 1686 the Estates refused to grant taxes unless the ruler gave them the right to examine tax assessments monthly and annually in the *Ämter*. The ruler would concede the right of audit only to *Landräte*, whose loyalty to the ruler was, according to the Estates, possibly firmer than to the Estates themselves. Equally, *Landräte* were unlikely to examine all the local tax returns and it was this that the Estates particularly desired. This showed what lack of confidence the Estates had in Ernst August, his officials and their methods.[96]

The fight over tax assessments continued as well. Both sides made propositions and in the meantime the Estates refused all taxes so that the ruler continued to levy by decree. Each ensuing year made a rapprochement more difficult. In 1687 Ernst August offered the Estates monthly examination of tax registers in the parishes and annual audit in the *Ämter*. However, no member of the Estates could examine any registers if he owned serfs, which therefore made it meaningless for Chapter and nobility to accept the offer. Further demands by the nobility in 1692 and by all the Estates in 1695 led only to a promise to allow examination of chamber accounts, a promise which was not fulfilled. In 1673 Ernst August had already proposed an excise which was to be sufficiently large to replace all direct taxation. It failed, chiefly owing to the passive opposition of Osnabrück town, and to the general mistrust of the nobility. Thus Ernst August continued to levy by decree, using the antiquated tax registers for his assessments.[97]

Ernst August justified arbitrary taxation on the grounds of necessity and emergency. The imperial law of 1654 made by Emperor and imperial Estates covered only fortifications and garrisons as fields in which territorial Estates were compelled

[95] *Landräte* were 'the permanent representation of the Estates'. Six were chosen, two from each of the Estates (Chapter, nobles, towns), and then confirmed by the Bishop, Bär, *op. cit.*, pp. 54–5.

[96] Much had still to be done in this field of historical inquiry. C. L. Weber, 'Die Anfänge der Statistik in der Grafschaft Mark bis 1609', *Jahrbuch des Vereins für Orts- und Heimatkunde der Grafschaft Mark*, 23, 1908–9, pp. 1–104, who prints actual *Ämterrechnungen*. J. Germing, 'Geschichte der amtlichen Finanzstatistik der Grafschaft Mark', *ibid.*, 27, 1912–13, pp. 1–81, dealt with the early Hohenzollern period up to 1723. For an early land tax reform, W. Güthling, 'Die Vermessung im Siegerland 1717–26', *Westfalen*, 28, 1950, pp. 47–58.

[97] Schöttke, *op. cit.*, pp. 14–15.

to contribute whether they agreed or not. A further extension of rulers' rights to levy taxes without consent in their territories was vetoed by the Emperor in 1670. Hence Ernst August was breaking the laws of the Empire, and penalties existed for tyrants as Seckendorff had hinted and as the Mecklenburg Dukes had discovered to their cost.[98] Yet the Estates of Osnabrück do not seem to have made an issue of it. Perhaps they could not get access to any arbitrary assessments or accounts. They could not prove what the ruler actually spent arbitrary taxes on. Thus they could hardly make out a case against him at the imperial courts, even if they had had the inclination. They seemed never to have got the opportunity to oppose force with force in the first place.[99]

Ernst August forced his territory to pay for a wasteful militaristic foreign policy by despotic methods. The hallmark of his régime in Osnabrück was illegal taxation backed up by force. From 1679 he was an absentee ruler owing to inheritance of Brunswick-Lüneburg-Calenberg-Grubenhagen. He used his resources to obtain the ninth electoral dignity. As far as Osnabrück went, this policy of Guelph dynasticism was hardly as constructive a policy as the cheaper, non-militaristic form of government which the territorial Estates seem to have desired. Backed by the Westphalian Peace and the *Capitulatio perpetua*, the Estates settled down to await Ernst August's death before coming back to power. In 1698 he died and the Chapter ruled in the interregnum whilst it made arrangements to elect a Catholic bishop.

Ernst August's privy councillors were sacked and an insight into his long administration was finally gained unconditionally by the Chapter, but not, however, by nobles and burghers as well. Hence those secrets of government which were essential to despotic and absolutist rule could not be handed on intact to the succeeding ruler, as could more readily be done in a dynastic system. Even so, Ernst August had set the pace, and once the Chapter had chosen Catholic Charles of Lorraine as successor, it was only a matter of time before a new era of despotic rule started with the appointment of a new set of privy councillors.[100]

---

[98] See note 88. Also Kraemer, *op. cit.*, pp. 1–2, 6. Seckendorff's book came out in nine editions, 1656–1754. Hofer, *op. cit.*, *passim*. Bornhak, *op. cit.*, pp. 169–70.
[99] Schöttke, *op. cit.*, p. 18.   [100] *Ibid.*, pp. 24, 60–1.

A ruler like Ernst August was primarily able to play the despot because of the development of a technically involved apparatus of government since the sixteenth century, which could eventually exclude the Estates and their methods of conducting public affairs. The ruler's officials at the court and in the *Ämter* took on more and more executive responsibility until there was hardly anything left for the Estates. By the 1550s the *Landräte* were already being replaced by *Hofräte* when it came to exercising power during the Bishop's absence. Government methods now began to be regulated at law. The first *Kanzleiordnung* of 1588 established by decree of the Bishop a very definite legal routine in the handling of all government business. All decisions had to be made in writing. All business meant a laborious exchange of complaints, orders, minutes, concepts, final drafts and duplicates.[101]

A register of the salaries of all officials in the Bishop's service was compiled in the 1650s. The whole apparatus was expected to cost about 6,500 tlrs a year, of which 1,000 tlrs was still paid out in kind. This included a few ecclesiastical officials who dealt with the Bishop's religious duties.[102] The local government received its first code of conduct and competence in the *Amtsordnung* of Bishop Johann of Hoya in 1556. It stressed three important functions for the *Ämter*. They were units of defence. They were to administer the Bishop's local income, run the police and cope with crime. In the sixteenth century the *Amtshäuser* as centres of local administration were still fortified and the strongest of them at Fürstenau had a permanent garrison of thirty-five.[103]

The bishopric of Osnabrück was already divided into seven *Ämter* by the early fifteenth century. By the later sixteenth

---

[101] H. Rehker, 'Die landesherrlichen Verwaltungsbehörden im Bistum Osnabrück 1553–1661', *Osnabrücker Mitteilungen*, 30, 1905, pp. 4–5, 22, 52. Kraemer, *op. cit.*, p. 56. Cf. Staatsarchiv Detmold, Landtagsprotokolle and Regierungsprotokolle.

[102] Rehker, *op. cit.*, pp. 82–92, 57, the Chancellor received 540 tlrs a year plus corn and straw. In 1576 Chancellor Heusschen received 200 tlrs plus food from the ruler's table. A *Rentmeister* (local treasury official) had 38–54 tlrs plus a large variety of payments in kind. A *Vogt* (common bailiff) who received a salary in coin only, had a mere 18 tlrs a year in the 1650s. Some of these salaries were at least partly paid by the Estates, as for example the senior administration of the Osnabrück Lutheran church.

[103] J. Prinz, *Das Territorium des Bistums Osnabrück*, Göttingen, 1934, pp. 127–66, 172–7.

century the *Drosten*, who were leading local nobles with a seat on the rulers' councils and overall responsibility for the security of the *Ämter*, had become mainly grand honorary officials. Financial and general secretarial business was dealt with in each *Amt* by a non-noble *Rentmeister*, who had a basic legal training. The law courts were run by judges whose competence generally came under *Amt* surveillance during the course of the sixteenth century.[104] The police were under *Vögte*, and their subordinates in the parishes. Whilst the *Rentmeister* were only overworked, the *Vögte* were also badly underpaid, so it seems likely that they just had to recoup themselves out of their offices. The first *Vögteordnungen* in Osnabrück were issued in the early seventeenth century. By 1651 every official both high and low had his duties meticulously defined in writing (his *Dienstvorschriften*) as well as his salary fixed. Thus under Bishop Franz Wilhelm in the earlier seventeenth century the territory already supported a potentially well-organized administration fully under the Bishop's personal control.[105]

Even so, the Estates retained their own financial system. They had their own treasurer who ran their own treasury or *Landkasse*.[106] Internal government was thus still primarily a bargain between two sets of officials, those of the ruler and those of the Estates.[107] It was this system which broke down under Ernst August, who could thus rely only upon his own officials in his attempts to obtain extraordinary taxes from the Osnabrück peasantry. In this task he would probably have been more successful had he not also used methods which alienated the Estates, who were of course largely the landlords or creditors of the tax-paying peasants, and whose passive resistance was at least to some extent effective.

The Estate of the nobility was made up of seventy-seven families, who by the later seventeenth century had to produce a family tree with four generations of noble ancestors in the female as well as in the male lines, and possess a *Rittergut* or noble estate, before their right to attend assemblies was recog-

---

[104] *Ibid.*, p. 175. A. Rossberg, *Die Entwicklung der Territorialherrlichkeit in der Grafschaft Ravensberg*, Leipzig, 1909, pp. 91–2, 100. In neighbouring Ravensberg the Bishop of Osnabrück still exercised rights in the local legal administration until 1664. [105] Rehker, *op. cit.*, pp. 11–12, 26n., 28–9, 34. [106] *Ibid.*, pp. 33–4.

[107] F. Philippi, 'Zur Osnabrücker Verfassungsgeschichte', *Osnabrücker Mitteilungen*, 22, 1897, pp. 98–9.

nized by the Bishop and by their own fellow nobles. The twenty-six prebends of the Chapter were open especially to those noble families who had remained Catholics. The Chapter was in any case closed to all those who lacked an unbroken line of noble ancestry going back over four generations. This stipulation was introduced in 1651 in the assembly by the nobility themselves, but because of widespread opposition was not applied by the ruler until 1710.[108]

Society and economy developed slowly in the Osnabrück countryside. It has been estimated that in the parish of Lintorf (Osnabrück) the population increased by 80 per cent between 1500 and 1600, and by over 30 per cent up to 1670, which included the Thirty Years' War period.[109] Between 1670 and 1711 the increase was only 9 per cent and up to 1772 a mere 2 per cent more. An average of five to six persons per farm is estimated. Around the year 1700, of all the children born only half reached the age of fifteen. In the parish of Barkhausen (Osnabrück) there were 89 farms in 1500, 163 in 1604, and 177 in 1718, which perhaps shows that existing farms were being split up as well as the fact that new land was also being culti-vated. The average number of children born per marriage be-tween 1664 and 1741 was probably under four. Hence if there was any population increase, it had to come through peasant immigration, as the infant mortality rate was 50 per cent of those that survived birth. Yet in the early eighteenth century nearly half the total of recorded marriages were between boys and girls born and bred in the parish. Recorded illegitimate births were less than 3 per cent of all births.[110]

In Osnabrück social groups did not always correspond to economic groups. The distribution of land and property was

---

[108] L. Hoffmeyer, *Geschichte der Stadt und des Regierungsbezirks Osnabrück*, 2nd ed., Osnabrück, 1920, p. 137. H. Spangenberg, 'Beiträge zur älteren Ver-fassungs- und Verwaltungsgeschichte des Fürstentums Osnabrück', *Osnabrücker Mitteilungen*, 25, 1900, pp. 77–8.

[109] A prosperous peasant from parish Badbergen, Johann to Elting (1572–1653), left enough written records of his farming career to make possible a reconstruction of his fate during the war years; Johann prospered. H. Rothert, 'Ein Artländer Bauer zur Zeit des grossen Krieges', *Der Friede von Osnabrück*, Oldenburg, 1948, pp. 149–62. F. Flaskamp (ed.), *Die Chronik des Ratsherrn Andreas Kothe* (of Wiedenbrück town in the Osnabrück enclave of Reckenberg), Gütersloh, 1962.

[110] E. Keyser, *Bevölkerungsgeschichte Deutschlands*, 2nd ed., Leipzig, 1941, pp. 368–70.

often at variance with the distribution of rights and privileges at law among the inhabitants. From 1350 to 1450 the number of fiefs fell from around 450 to 230. In the Bishop's *Lehnbuch* of 1561, of 200 vassals, 43·3 per cent were nobles, 24·6 per cent burghers and town councils, 8·4 per cent clergy and ecclesiastical foundations, and 23·7 per cent peasants. So less than half the remaining fiefs were held by nobles and nearly a quarter of them by peasants. Between them, burghers and peasants held more fiefs than the nobility.[111]

The lordship of Rheda, which lay on the Osnabrück side of the enclave of Reckenberg, was held by the counts of Tecklenburg as a fief from the bishops of Münster after 1365. This gave rise to vicious conflicts over the demarcation of frontiers. By swapping fiefs with neighbouring rulers, and by giving special rights to those vassals who were natives of the territory in which they held their lands, such as sole access to the nobles' curia in the *Landtage*, or to the rulers' councils if they qualified as nobles by ancestry, the territorial rulers began to rationalize the frontiers and to get rid of enclaves and unwelcome pockets of low jurisdictions, farms and serfs which were in foreign hands.[112]

A substantial number of peasants in the Osnabrück countryside were freemen. They had, however, to find themselves a protector, otherwise they would have been outside the complex of private and local law. They thus sought protection with the ruler and the Estates, in order to fit into the legal system of the territory. For this they paid a small annual fee. Those under the Chapter paid half a thaler annually. They were called *Hodefreie* and their names were entered into special registers. These freemen were unevenly spread over the Osnabrück countryside. Their numbers seem to have grown steadily from the later sixteenth century to the end of the eighteenth century. In 1660 there were at least a thousand of them. They varied from the

[111] G. Theuerkauf, 'Das Lehenswesen in Westfalen', *Westfälische Forschungen*, 17, 1964, pp. 19–24. Fiefs were held by non-nobles in Westphalia in the fifteenth century. Vassalage was just a better form of tenant-farming from the point of view of the tenant than was serfdom. Wrede, *op. cit.*, pp. 151–2.

[112] J. Möser, 'Mitteilungen über die Grenzstreitigkeiten zwischen dem Bischofe zu Osnabrück und dem Grafen von Tecklenburg', *Osnabrücker Mitteilungen*, 2, 1850, pp. 1–19. Eickhoff, 'Osnabrückisch-rhedischer Grenzstreit, 1524–65', *ibid.*, 22, 1897, pp. 107–94. On the Osnabrück-Ravensberg land exchange of 1664, Rossberg, *op. cit.*, pp. 107–8.

wealthiest sort of farmer or *Vollerbe*, who farmed the richest and longest-cultivated soils in the peasant community, to the poorest sort of cottar, who farmed along the road or on the fringe of the common or forest, where he had little more than squatter's rights. Thus being a free peasant did not necessarily entail a better economic status than did being a serf.[113]

The abbey of Iburg owned serfs who were substantial *Vollerben*. The *Vollerben* inherited from generation to generation and played a vital part in village politics and administration. A serf could thus be in a better social and economic position than could many a freeman.[114] Serfs had, however, no freedom of movement. They were tied to the land, although their land could turn out to be the best in quality and quantity in their particular locality. They belonged to the landlord; they had to ask his permission before they could marry, although in fact their duties had been regulated so that their landlord had to get permission via ruler and assembly to increase them. Osnabrück serfs also had access to the Bishop's courts in the *Ämter*, where their landlords did not sit in judgment upon them.[115]

An example of this bondage was the register of Bishop's serfs compiled by the *Amtsrentmeister* of the enclave of Reckenberg in 1652–63. It contains information about 270 families of peasants and labourers who were owned as chattels by the Bishop. They were spread out over two *Vogteien*, or local police districts, and each *Vogtei* was divided into a number of *Bauerschaften*, basic units of peasant self-government. In Reckenberg about half the population in the earlier seventeenth century were serfs belonging to the ruler. Thus substantial numbers of archive materials deal with serf administration and with the problem of estate management and tenant farming. In Reckenberg

[113] A. Schulten, *Die Hodegerechtigkeit im Fürstentum Osnabrück*, Münster, 1909, pp. 7, 81–7. Lütge, *Mitteldeutsche Grundherrschaft*, pp. VII–VIII, 9, 20. This does not mean that serfdom was necessarily a desirable status to attain, for contemporaries certainly did not act as if they thought this. But legal distinctions between free and unfree peasants did not always correspond to economic reality. T. Mayer (ed.), *Adel und Bauern*, Leipzig, 1943, pp. 312–45. Staatsarchiv Detmold, D 71 no. 16, Wendisches Copialbuch, 3, Amt Varenholz, folio 312: L 9 vol. 1, folio 206. Wittich, *op. cit.*, *passim*, especially p. 27.

[114] E. Donnerberg, *Der Besitz des ehemaligen Klosters Iburg*, Münster, 1912, pp. 150–2.

[115] For a less rosy picture of serfdom, especially also of landless serfs, servants and *Gesinde*, G. Benecke, 'Labour relations and peasant society', *History*, October 1973.

there was a heavy migration of serfs into neighbouring towns and villages. The Bishop's serf-register was compiled to ensure that emigrants had lawfully bought themselves free, or that they had been lawfully exchanged with serfs of other landlords. From the register it can be seen that emigrants seldom rose in social status. One or two got into the lower clergy and one or two learned a trade in the towns. The majority were menial servants, the proletarians of the towns, the privates of the armies and the day-labourers of the farms.[116]

The older the farm, the greater the variety of taxes to which it contributed. Of 950 *Vollerben* in the bishopric of Osnabrück in 1800, 391 were still paying tithes. This oldest of taxes levied by the church was also partly in the hands of the territorial nobility by early modern times. The abbey of Iburg received tithes from 110 farms, and the territorial noble family of Ketteler zu Harkotten owned the tithes of 37 farms. By the fifteenth and sixteenth centuries tithes were usually fixed by short agreements renewed every three to twelve years, stipulating fixed annual payments in corn or money. Short agreements meant that owners could keep up with the movement of prices. According to mid-sixteenth-century custom, tithes were paid in Osnabrück only on land that was manured and under cultivation. Lawsuits arising out of tithes were generally by 1500 decided not in the ecclesiastical courts but in the *Gogerichte*, run by the ruler's *Amt* officials.[117] Tithe-selling was frequent, and in the late sixteenth century such a sale made 800 tlrs in one parish

---

[116] J. Bauermann, 'Die Eigenbehörigenkonskription des Amtes Reckenberg', *Westfalen*, 21, 1936, pp. 9–12. For the biography of the relevant Reckenberg *Amtsrentmeister*, see F. Flaskamp, *Ravensberger Blätter*, 1955, pp. 100–2, Flaskamp, 'Westfälische Bauernhöfe', *Westfälische Forschungen*, 13, 1960, pp. 59–71. G. Theuerkauf in Rössler (ed.), *op. cit.*, pp. 173–6. Wrede, *op. cit.*, pp. 143, 150–3. F. Flaskamp, *Untersuchungen zur Geschichte der Kreisstadt Wiedenbrück*, Wiedenbrück, 1934, pp. 19–23.

[117] 'Alles Land, auf das der Mistwagen kommt und das vom Hofe aus gedüngt wird, unterliegt dem Zehnten', *Weistum* of 1555, in A. Suerbaum, 'Der Zehnte im Landkreis Osnabrück', *Osnabrücker Mitteilungen*, 70, 1961, pp. 36–7, 45, 52–5. The *Weistum*, a mixture of oral and written procedure by question and answer, was an early form of legislation which was used in trying to solve the dilemma involved in the principle that law was only found by divine revelation and not manmade. Ebel, *op. cit.*, pp. 12, 15–16, 63, 71, 78. See also Angermeier, *op. cit.*, p. 3, who saw in the keeping of the peace in the later medieval Empire and territories a battle between two forms of law, between *Recht* and *Gesetz*. This is already very close to what in early modern territories became the victory of prerogative legislation over custom, of *Gebot* over *Herkommen*. A general survey is given in

alone. This is a large sum, considering that the debts of the abbey of Iburg after the Thirty Years' War ran to only 10,400 tlrs. Peasants themselves did not buy out the tithes on their farms until the nineteenth century, when the government helped them to do so.[118]

Osnabrück town was the only substantial stronghold of the burgher Estate in the bishopric. It is characteristic of the north-west German bishoprics that they each had one large town only. This applied to Osnabrück just as to Münster, Paderborn, Minden and Hildesheim. The population of Osnabrück town rose sharply to about 10,000 in the 1520s. Before the plague year of 1625 it was still over 9,000. When the town housed the Protestant powers at the Peace Congress of the 1640s the population was around 5,000 and in 1772 was still estimated at under 6,000. Five figures were then again reached in the early nineteenth century. This indicates that the later seventeenth and eighteenth centuries especially were not favourable to town life as much as were the later Middle Ages and as are modern times. From the accession of Ernst August onwards the town housed a permanent garrison. The rulers had levied regular excises since 1358 but direct taxes remained emergency levies.[119]

Despite continuous devaluation of the mark-schilling-pfennig currency, the town still used it to work out its economy. Not until the early seventeenth century did the town treasury go over to the thaler-groschen system.[120] The earliest surviving register of town income from rents set out against items of expenditure dates from 1414. In the fifteenth century the mark lost ground to the gold coins—*Goldfloren* or *Goldgulden*—but town rents remained in marks. Thus although income increased from about 1,230 marks in 1424 to 1,800 marks in 1460, the actual result was a decrease of revenue from 240 Gfl. to 210 Gfl. By 1503 income was over 3,000 marks, and it reached five figures in

---

[118] Donnersberg, *op. cit.*, p. 98. Suerbaum, *op. cit.*, p. 54.

[119] E. Kayser, *Niedersächsisches Städtebuch*, Stuttgart, 1952, pp. 279–82.

[120] C. Stüve, 'Das Finanzwesen der Stadt Osnabrück bis zum Westfälischen Frieden', *Osnabrücker Mitteilungen*, 11, 1876, pp. 1–118. Early seventeenth-century Osnabrück currency was 1 Taler of 21 Schillinge at 12 Pfennige, or 36 Mariengroschen at 7 Pfennige. The town law-court of Wiedenbrück reckoned the fines it imposed in Marks at 12 Schillinge, Flaskamp, *Chronik*, p. 12.

H. Planitz, *Quellenkunde der deutschen, österreichischen und schweizer Rechtsgeschichte einschliesslich des deutschen Privatrechts*, Graz, 1948.

1567. From then on it fluctuated between 9,000 and 16,000 marks. By 1601 it was back at 10,000 marks, which then became a steady 6,000 tlrs a year between 1602 and 1612. In 1618 it was over 7,000 tlrs and thereafter never much over 3,000 tlrs, except during the years of the Peace Congress.[121]

By 1670 the town had debts of 40,000 tlrs which rose to 76,000 tlrs and by 1740 stood at 54,000 tlrs. The heavy indebtedness of the town council of Osnabrück was a real feature of later-seventeenth-century and eighteenth-century civics. In this period the town had less people and less income but ever more debts which swallowed up about 50 per cent of the annual income in interest payments alone.[122]

The town had always financed itself by raising loans and by running into debt. In the fifteenth and early sixteenth centuries a favourite way of raising money was to sell rents for life only. Revenues were anticipated in order to raise large sums of money as the situation demanded. Thus in 1525 the burghers had to pay the Bishop a fine of 6,000 Gfl. for participation in

[121] In sixteenth-century Germany debasement of gold and silver coinage was not as significant as has perhaps been supposed. It cannot be said to have heavily affected prices and wages. In Munich and Augsburg coinage debasement averaged one-third per cent annually between 1500 and 1600; in Frankfurt-am-Main and Würzburg only one-eighth per cent. Of basic importance to prices and wages, wealth and income were fluctuations in population and productivity. Between 1500 and 1800 in five large towns of south-west and west-central Germany wages rose steadily but they were always well behind price increases. Food prices fluctuated wildly, increasing from two to eight times between 1500 and the first part of the seventeenth century, whilst wages increased by a mere 70 per cent over the same period of time. Thereafter prices fell, whilst the more modest upward trend of wages continued. However, only in good harvest years could wages be expected to outstrip prices at the norm of the year 1500, M. J. Elsas, *Umriss einer Geschichte der Preise und Löhne in Deutschland*, Leiden, 1936–49, II B, pp. 67–70, 88–92, I and II A, *passim*. A. Dieck, 'Lebensmittelpreise in Mitteleuropa und im Vorderen Orient vom 12. bis 17. Jahrhundert', *Zeitschrift für Agrargeschichte und Agrarsoziologie*, 3, 1955, pp. 159–60. W. Abel, *Geschichte der deutschen Landwirtschaft*, Stuttgart, 1962, pp. 168–75.

[122] Osnabrück town had 80,000 tlrs debt in 1650, of which 20,000 tlrs was owed to Osnabrück burghers, and the rest to the Osnabrück nobility, neighbouring Ravensberg nobles, Tecklenburg and Münster nobles, and burghers in Lingen, Cologne, Amsterdam, Hamburg and Bremen, Stüve, *op. cit.*, pp. 116–18. At the standard rates of 5 or 6 per cent, the interest payments, if paid promptly and fully, would have outrun total town-council income in any one year. In this impossible situation the town along with other public bodies in the Empire was allowed to remit debt and cancel war-time interest arrears by the *Reichsexekutionsordnung* following the peace treaties of 1648; a federal German equivalent of an 'exchequer stop'.

riots. This sum was greater than the whole town income for that year.

The rents which the town treasury paid out as interest on capital which had been borrowed were always a considerable total of all annual expenditure. Two hundred and seventy-six marks were paid out in rents in 1425. This represented 20–25 per cent of the town's total annual income. Many rents had been made out in *Goldgulden* and thus the town council was caught unfavourably by devaluation of the mark, in which it continued to assess its payments. By 1487 rents cost over 1,000 marks and interest rates reached 8 per cent. Thereafter they were down again to 4–6 per cent, usually 5 per cent. By 1531 the more favourable rents for life were almost all replaced by a more modern form of finance, by *Erbrenten*, rents that were inheritable. These were less advantageous to the town treasury, because debts were not liquidated on the death of the original donor.[123] Even so, in the later sixteenth century interest payments were down at one point in 1598 to a mere one-fourteenth of regular income. In 1620 they were still only one-twelfth.

Undoubtedly the bishopric of Osnabrück survived as an independent territory because it built up a state of its own and financed itself from its own internal resources. The favourable terms which it obtained at the peace of 1648 provided the outside guarantee for its continued independence in home affairs. A freak state in constitutional history, it was yet capable of its own distinct political development, and the driving force in Osnabrück politics came from inside the territory, even under Guelph-Hanoverian rule in early modern times.

(iv) *Minden*

Nearly every Westphalian territory has had the history of its Reformation and Counter-Reformation written, and this applies especially to the Protestant side.[124] Broadly speaking, the larger towns went Lutheran first of all and were already supported to a great extent by Philip of Hesse in the early 1530s.

[123] Stüve, *op. cit.*, p. 52; interest payments appear in sixteenth-century records as 'old and new grievance'.

[124] Rothert, *op. cit.*, 2, *passim*. E. A. F. Culemann, *Mindische Geschichte*, Minden, 1747–8. Wolf, *op. cit.*, pp. 141–6.

In the counties and lordships, where dynasties ruled, religious innovation was soon tolerated, especially by town councils. From here the territorial nobility took it up. There was a scramble for control over ecclesiastical rights, benefices and even land. Mostly, however, the stricter rules governing the present-ment of clergy to livings were broken, as patrons found an added interest and profit in appointing men freely as their 'consciences' told them, and not necessarily as their bishops or papal and imperial envoys directed.[125]

This freedom was again abolished by Lutheran *Kirchenord-nungen*, or church systems in the territories and leading towns, which rulers like Philip of Hesse were swift in making use of in order to prevent social upheaval and unrest. The era of the 1520s and 1530s was one of revolt when all people, according to a letter which Philip wrote to the Reformer, Bucer, were aspir-ing above the station in life to which they had been born.[126] Lutheranism to a ruler like Philip was a means of increasing his own power inside and outside his own territory whilst at the same time prohibiting sectarians and any other socio-religious programmes of reform that were not strictly authoritarian and uniformist or directed by God-given *Obrigkeiten*, territorial rulers and their councillors.[127]

In Münster and Paderborn there was no problem of how to transfer ecclesiastical power to territorial authorities because these territories were run by bishops and chapters. Above all the nobility already had control of the prebends, from which church and state were harmoniously directed. Thus there was no need for a take-over of the local church by ruler and Estates as occurred in secular territories. An ecclesiastical territory could thus conceivably be at a distinct advantage in an era when there was a conflict between spiritual and secular powers because its constitutional structure united these two essential ingredients of territorial politics. Whereas in the Lutheran territories the clergy became schoolmasters and servants of the secular authorities, in ecclesiastical territories like Münster and Pader-born the high clergy remained the ruling group and were recruited from the ranks of the Catholic nobility. Here an aristo-

---

[125] For neighbouring Lippe, see Wolf, 'Der Einfluss des Landgrafen Philipp etc. . .', *Jahrbuch des Vereins für Westfälische Kirchengeschichte*, 51–2, 1958–9, p. 76. [126] *Ibid.*, p. 56n., letter of 24 June 1539. [127] *Ibid.*, pp. 79–83.

cratic, perhaps almost 'Whig' system of government continued in church and state.[128] Those sections of ruling society that did go Lutheran or sectarian were eventually eliminated or brought to see reason by economic sanctions or by military means. This happened to the Protestants among the Paderborn nobility and to Münster town.[129] But this did not work out so well in the bishoprics of Osnabrück and Minden.

Osnabrück and Minden were Lutheran-Catholic mixtures until 1806, when the end of the Holy Roman Empire meant also the end of religion as a possible controlling factor in political and constitutional affairs. The town councils of both Osnabrück and Minden were Lutheran, the nobilities were mixed or even predominantly Lutheran. A hard core of Catholics retained power in the chapters. In Minden town the earliest Lutheran *Kirchenordnung* in Westphalia was promulgated in 1530.[130]

In both bishoprics the chapters remained the backbone of Catholic power and territorial independence. In neither bishopric did outspoken, Lutheran bishops predominate, instead a particular brand of 'waverers' was produced to balance between the religious groupings within the territories and outside, in the Empire at large. This lasted for several generations until the early seventeenth century.

Of the last eight bishops of Minden in the sixteenth and seventeenth centuries, none except Christian of Brunswick were irrevocably and boisterously Protestant. Two resigned to marry, in accordance with a Catholic interpretation of the 1555 religious peace. Equally, only the last Bishop was irrevocably Catholic, being also a Wittelsbach and an exile to boot.[131] Both Osnabrück and Minden came under Swedish military occupation

---

[128] C. Spangenberg, *Die Geistliche Haustafel | Wie sich ein jglich Gottselig Mensch in seinem Stande und beruff nach Gottes willen rechtschaffen halten solle*, Wittenberg, 1556. Here territorial society became self-contained, inward-looking and split into thirteen groups each following separate rules of behaviour. These groups are the (Lutheran) clergy, their congregations, the rulers, their subjects, married men, married women, parents, children, masters and mistresses, domestic servants, workers and day-labourers, the youth, widows, and the whole Christian community.

[129] See above, Chapter V (i), (ii).

[130] N. Kragen, 'Christlike Ordeninge der Erlyken Stadt Mynden, Lübeck, 1530', reprinted by M. Krieg, *Jahrbuch des Vereins für Westfälische Kirchengeschichte*, 43, 1950, pp. 66–108.

[131] T. Olpp, 'Die stellung der Mindener Bischöfe zur Reformation', *ibid.*, 48, 1956–7, pp. 34–43.

during the 1630s and 1640s but at the peace of 1648 the two bishoprics experienced very different fates.

In 1648 neither Osnabrück nor Minden went to Sweden, but whereas Osnabrück remained half Catholic and half Lutheran-Guelph by constitutional arrangement, Minden was swallowed up by Brandenburg as part-compensation for Hohenzollern claims elsewhere. Osnabrück's politically active Catholic minority had found enough support at imperial level to save the territory from total submission to the Guelph, Protestant dynasty. It remained at least a partially independent ecclesiastical territory. The Catholic minority in Minden was, however, abandoned to Elector Frederick William. Minden lost its independence although the Hohenzollerns continued to hold an independent seat and vote for the secularized principality of Minden at imperial assemblies and conferences.[132]

In 1649 Brandenburg troops moved into Minden. The old constitution was not, however, replaced by a new one, as Hohenzollern despotism made only piecemeal but telling alterations in the existing political system. Minden Chapter continued to function as a body of born noblemen with the largest stake in the immovable wealth of the territory but no longer able to elect a ruling bishop. According to the religious truce of 1648 the year of normalization (1624) was strictly adhered to in Minden Chapter, and this gave a constant figure of eleven Catholics to seven Lutheran canons. The number of noble ancestors that a prospective candidate needed was even increased to the preposterous level of thirty-two in 1713.[133]

To Elector Frederick William Minden was the key link in his chain of lands that stretched right across north Germany up to the Rhine in the west. Like the Belfort gap in Alsace, so the Porta Westfalica outside Minden town in Westfalia was of inestimable importance to the military strategist. It was up to the Elector to see that Minden paid for its own Brandenburg-Prussian garrisons and if at all possible also produced a surplus in order to finance the debts which the Hohenzollerns had to take on as the new rulers. It was estimated that as late as 1681

---

[132] Peace of Osnabrück, Art. II.

[133] K. Spannagel, *Minden-Ravensberg unter brandenburg-preussischer Herrschaft 1648–1719*, Hanover, 1894, pp. 73–5. H. Nottarp in *Westfalen*, 13, 1927, pp. 95–6. The four noble ancestor rule was first applied in 1611.

total Minden debts were 150,000 tlrs. Another estimate put the debts of Minden town alone with its population of about 5,000 at over 160,000 tlrs in 1659. One-third of this figure comprised arrears of interest. Another estimate put domain debt at 63,500 tlrs, of which the Estates took over a mortgage of 25,000 tlrs in 1667. With a total estimated population of under 40,000 at the beginning of the eighteenth century, this was a considerable but by no means hopeless burden. Without Prussian troops the territory could have been very well off indeed compared with some of its neighbours—that is under the existing system whereby Estates and local officials mutually granted and collected taxes and revenues.

Gross income from the domains and five *Ämter* of the territory was just under 22,000 tlrs annually in the early 1650s. It was thus imperative that Frederick William should negotiate with the Minden Estates if he was not to be bankrupted by his army establishment. It did mean, however, that had Frederick William been prepared to get rid of his army, his income from domain would, it seems, have been sufficient to fund the burden of debt on the territory and to pay for a modest number of officials to run the administration. It would, indeed, have left him with no surplus and it certainly allowed no standing army. Thus the Minden Estates were forced to acquiesce in a policy of regular taxation where they had either to be content with less rents and income from their tenantry, or to pay some taxes directly themselves.[134]

Yet the Minden Estates of Chapter, prelates, nobles and towns had been used to almost complete autonomy, except to some extent during the war years. They knew only that during the rule of the last ten bishops they had been able to assert their own tax-freedom with considerable success. Bishops had usually been outsiders, elected from neighbouring ruling families. They were expected not to interfere unduly in internal affairs. Whenever an emergency did arise, the Estates granted their bishops money in return for constitutional and financial concessions recorded in documents that were drawn up very much

134 Spannagel, *op. cit.*, pp. 86, 138–9, 160–7. H. Tümpel, *Minden-Ravensberg unter der Herrschaft der Hohenzollern*, Bielefeld, 1909, p. 193. E. A. F. Culemann, *Sammlung der vornehmsten Landesverträge des Fürstentums Minden*, Minden, 1748, Document 19, pp. 136–7.

as contracts between equals. In this way a vigorous trade in alienated *Ämter* was conducted, as the nobility settled down within the Chapter especially to control territorial finances. Although taxation of the tenantry thus remained fairly infrequent, this only meant that the landlord system was more fully exploited. Minden was one of the areas where serfdom was still very much a successful commercial proposition.[135]

In 1649 Frederick William had taken over Minden by virtue of imperial law and imperial treaty, and not by inheritance, as in neighbouring Ravensberg, nor by conquest or agreement with the Estates and Chapter of Minden themselves. He was thus technically not bound to recognize the rights, privileges and customs of the Estates. In fact he was only prepared to sell anew any privileges that the Estates had formerly enjoyed. In this he was helped by a traditional lack of co-operation between clergy, nobles and towns, who had indeed at times united to form a common front against the demands of previous rulers, but whose lack of social, economic and religious homogeneity was a notorious factor in preventing the growth of an aristocratic parliamentary tradition. The imperial sell-out to Brandenburg thus brought the Minden Estates together for the first time in a very real way.[136]

They started off well by granting Frederick William a traditional tax of 'welcome' as the new ruler. This was 25,000 tlrs in 1650 and it was given as if to imply that he was just another bishop who had been theoretically elected to take over the reins of government. Frederick William had, however, refused to confirm the Estates' privileges before receiving their homage which was the traditional *quid pro quo* for the 'welcome' tax. After homage had been rendered, he confirmed their privileges only with a let-out clause.[137]

As long as the Estates were the only financial source through which Frederick William could hope to stay solvent, he was prepared to let them run internal politics and finance as they had previously always done. In return he required them to pay as much as possible of the 3,000 tlrs a month which his Minden

---

[135] Culemann, *Mindische Geschichte*, 3, *passim*. Culemann, *Landesverträge*, Documents 5–29, 40. Spannagel, *op. cit.*, pp. 165–201. Wigand, *Provinzialrechte Minden-Ravensberg*, 2, *passim*.   [136] Spannagel, *op. cit.*, pp. 74–8.
[137] *Ibid.*, pp. 80, 36.

garrison already cost before 1655. He adopted another traditional method in 1649 and alienated two of the five Minden
Ämter for 25,000 tlrs to local financiers. He then made further
concessions in 1667 in order to get the Estates to take over this
debt and the interest at 6 per cent which had accrued on it. In
return the Minden nobility got a half-share in running the
treasury and the profits of tax-farming and tax-collecting from
the peasantry and tenantry that went with this.

Frederick William had embarked on a policy of divide and
rule. The nobility of Minden were taken into confidence and the
burghers were generally excluded. A process which had started
in the *Homagialrezess* of 1650 when noble *Landräte* were taken
into the government, had been concluded at the *Reinebergischer
Rezess* of 1667 when the nobility were turned into Hohenzollern servants by incorporating them into the financial
machinery of state.

The way was ready from the 1670s for pushing the Estates
out of politics and finance back into a sphere of private privilege
and public oblivion. In 1674 the towns' excise was introduced
with noble support. It was then collected illegally without consent, thus annulling Estates' privileges which had last been confirmed only seven years previously. Gone were the days when
rulers and Estates bargained for political and financial control in
the territory as equals. None of the Hohenzollern rulers in
Minden kept the privileges which they each in turn had confirmed. In this process only the Chapter made one last protest
before Minden itself was swallowed up by the new Prussia
which emerged under King Frederick William I.[138]

By the end of the seventeenth century the Hohenzollerns had
turned Minden Chapter revenues into rents for life which were
sold to the highest eligible bidder. In 1705 the Deanery was
offered at 10,000 tlrs, representing nine years of net income. A
vicar's post at 80 tlrs per annum was offered for 1,000 tlrs.
This reopened the whole question of how much the Chapter was
worth in real terms. In 1665 the Chapter had bought Elector
Frederick William off with nearly 23,000 tlrs paid in cash. By
1720 a Hohenzollern commission estimated that Chapter
property was worth 500,000 tlrs. The Chapter still owned 205
serfs who farmed lands bringing in 2,355 tlrs per annum. Land

[138] *Ibid.*, pp. 83–91. Culemann, *Landesverträge*, Documents 31, 35, 36, 38.

rents brought in 3,000 tlrs, tithes and labour services 3,400 tlrs, tithes from outside the territory 3,350 tlrs, external capital 50,000 tlrs, revenues from Minden town 1,700 tlrs, and its own domain farm 1,200 tlrs.

On the strength of this information Frederick William I asked for further payments, as in his estimation his grandfather had received too little in 1665. The Chapter refused and took out a case against the King at the *Reichshofrat* in Vienna. The Hohenzollern ruler used violent coercion and the Chapter in 1736 gave up its case at Vienna. The last vestige of ecclesiastical independence had disappeared from Prussian Minden. It was ready to play its rôle as an obedient province.[139]

(v) *Corvey*

The Abbot of Corvey ruled a territory one-quarter the size of Lippe with a population of 10,000 in the later eighteenth century.[140] Yet he also owned lands in the surrounding territories, which belonged to the abbey long before the neighbouring rulers developed their own states.[141] As did many another imperial monastery and nunnery (only very much later), Corvey from the eleventh century onwards accepted as monks members not only of the high nobility, but also unfree *ministeriales*, the later territorial nobility.[142] The Reformation threatened Corvey as much as any other ecclesiastical territory in north-west Germany, but it survived as a Catholic state with Protestant Estates until it was secularized in the Napoleonic era.

The Abbot and his monks ran the administration and by the mid-sixteenth century were co-operating with an assembly of Estates, consisting of three nobles, one town and one prelate. It

[139] Spannagel, *op. cit.*, pp. 91–7. Hohenzollern Frederick William I denied that the *Reichshofrat* had sufficient impartiality to decide the Chapter's case against him. It is noteworthy that he did not deny that a complaint of this sort should come before the imperial courts. A plea on the grounds of injustice as practised in a territorial court or by a territorial ruler nullified any *privilegium de non appellando*, even if it was held by an Elector. Frederick William's attitude bears this out. Sellert, *op. cit.*, pp. 31–40. Bornhak, *op. cit.*, pp. 137–8.

[140] Anon., 'Korvei', *Meyers Lexikon*, 6th ed., Leipzig, 1908.

[141] A. Schöning, *Der Grundbesitz des Klosters Corvey im ehemaligen Lande Lippe* (*Iggenhausen, Ahmsen, Meinberg*), 1–3, Detmold, 1958–60.

[142] Dersch in *Westfalen*, 3, 1911, p. 64.

is notable that no monks acted as a corporation within the Estates as a counterbalance to the rulers, as was the case with the chapters in the neighbouring bishoprics.

Corvey was really too small to have a very pronounced political independence of its own. Even its home affairs smacked of nothing more than gentry-like estate management. It was caught up in the religious conflicts of the sixteenth and seventeenth centuries as a pawn in the hands of the Wittelsbachs in Cologne and of the Bishops in Paderborn and Münster. Yet its vulnerable position near the frontiers of Protestant Brunswick and Hesse-Kassel enabled it to develop a constitutional peculiarity of its own. It had a Catholic ruler and administration who were generally the monks themselves. They had to co-operate with Protestant Estates in running the country.[143]

In a *Landbrief* which confirmed a tax-grant in 1558 the development of ruler-Estates relations can be seen. Most of the villages and farms in the territory belonged to the Abbot. In 1558 he asked for a grant to cover his debts. He did not turn to his vassals, and Höxter town acted only as honest broker between the Abbot and his tenant-farmers in fixing the size of the extraordinary grant which the tenantry would have to pay.[144]

We, Reinhard, by the grace of God Abbot of the Imperial, free, ecclesiastical foundation of Corvey, proclaim and recognize for Us and Our successors, herewith publicly that We, after Our arrival and taking on of government have found Our Abbey to be in considerable difficulties and heavy debt. As it has been quite impossible to pay these debts out of Our annual taxes, interests, rents, and income, We have appealed out of sheer necessity to the common country and especially to those that are bound to render Us services and duties and are thereby subject to Us. We have deigned to allow and graciously desire that they, Our tenants, should consider this, and over and above the established regular services, duties and taxes should pay Us annually for each tenant-farmer, and each cottar one-half Thaler harvest money, and the same from every *Morgen* of newly cultivated land one *Scheffel* of cereals from their lands which they have in this territory in order to help pay off Our debts, and this We ask them to grant Us. Secondly, Our tenants have granted Us a common land-tax namely that they and

---

143 Leesch and Schubert, *op. cit.*, pp. 170–84. The Estates comprised three noble families, one town and one Protestant priory.

144 Wigand, *Provinzialrechte Paderborn-Corvey*, 2, pp. 303–6. The actual *Landbrief* which follows in part translation is from pp. 182–5.

their heirs will pay 4,000 Joachimsthalers of good mint that are at present valid currency, in the next eight years from next Michaelmas onwards at 500 tlrs a year, and at every Michaelmas thereafter until the 4,000 is paid off, against a valid receipt for every instalment so paid. This grant to be used to pay off Our debts and also to be used on any other pressing needs for the good of Our territory.

The Abbot then affirmed, with the arbitration of Höxter town council, that his tenant-farmers had given him increased labour services on farms, in woods, in defence duties, building and cartage.

Höxter town had no qualms about giving the Abbot extended rights to services and land tax over his subjects to help bring the territory out of debt. The townsmen, as vassals and burghers and as a territorial Estate, had after all nothing to pay here and it was all for their own good if the ruler's serfs paid the extra that the ruler needed with which to develop the territory into a proper state and to honour his debts. This was an example of an Estate, in this case the burghers, siding with the ruler against the ruler's peasants in order to save its own pocket.

The Abbot acted with the full consent and connivance of his monks. To this was added a guarantee drawn up by Höxter town council that the villages would pay off the agreed sum in the correct number of years. When this was done the village representatives were to get this letter of guarantee as proof of payment.

What did the Abbot concede in return for all this? He swore that he would not demand any other services or make any more tax increases. This was hardly much of a concession in the face of the new increases which he had just made. However, the Abbot exempted once and for all certain of the lands belonging to the poorest farmers. The smallest cottars were now free from land tax but they had still to render a fixed labour service or *Handdienst* in person. Thus a certain amount of land became free for the cottar and only in his person was he still bound to his lord, the Abbot.[145]

(vi) *Herford*

That imperial and territorial constitutional development was not a matter of natural or harmonious growth is shown by the

[145] *Ibid.*, 2, pp. 363–71.

history of the nunnery and town of Herford, a potential territory that failed to develop, and that was between 1500 and 1800
neither territory nor province.

Herford and Corvey were ninth-century ecclesiastical foundations—Herford for women and Corvey for men. The nunnery
was intended for the daughters of the high nobility of north-
west Germany, as their school, refuge and place where they too
could take part in religion and politics in an otherwise patri-
archal society. As such it operated until 1803–8.[146] However,
Herford nunnery never developed an extensive high jurisdiction
or *Vogtei* over its lands or neighbouring countryside, unlike its
fellow foundations Corvey and Essen. The Abbess of Herford
never exercised her own *advocatia*; the high jurisdictions which
she should have had by virtue of her immediate status under
Emperor and Pope, she chose to leave in the hands of other
potentates, such as the medieval Counts of Schwalenberg and
the Archbishop-Electors of Cologne. In 1547 the Abbess invested the Dukes of Jülich, who were also Catholic rulers of the
county of Ravensberg, with the *advocatia*. This was a fatal move,
as Herford was practically enclosed by Ravensberg territory and
until then had survived by seeking protection from the Archbishops of Cologne against the Ravensberg rulers.[147]

The nuns were threatened by the Lutheranism of the burghers
of Herford, for their buildings were situated in the centre of the
town. They were also in debt by the early fifteenth century.[148]
This was despite rich lands and endowments which had made
possible the building of a church which is still today the most

[146] A. Cohausz, 'Ein Jahrtausend geistliches Damenstift Herford', *Herforder Jahrbuch*, 1, 1960, pp. 1–2. Similarly the nunneries of Gandersheim, Quedlinburg and Essen which had imperial status (*Reichsunmittelbarkeit*), like Herford, were open to the daughters of the high nobility only. H. Gaul, 'Aus der Geschichte von Stadt und Stift Essen', *Beiträge zur Geschichte von Stadt und Stift Essen*, 83, 1968, pp. 7–27.

For the territorial nobility and burghers each territory had its own religious foundation where their daughters could go into religion and estate management at more modest levels. Thus for the neighbouring county of Ravensberg there was Convent Schildesche; for Lippe the Convents Cappel and St Mary in Lemgo. On Schildesche, see H. Culemann in *50. Jahresbericht Historischer Verein Ravensberg*, 1936, pp. 35–108. E. Kittel, *Kloster und Stift St Marien in Lemgo 1265–1965*, Detmold, 1965. All three confessions, Catholics, Lutherans, Calvinists, ran such establishments.

[147] A. Cohausz, 'Herford als Reichsstadt und papstunmittelbares Stift', *42. Jahresbericht Historischer Verein Ravensberg*, 1928, pp. 9–12, 76–84.

[148] *Ibid.*, Appendix I.

impressive for miles around. But with the rise of an early modern state the nunnery was at a disadvantage in its estate management. Not having developed its own high jurisdiction into a state machinery, it was treated like any other landlord by the territorial governments in which its lands lay, with the added disadvantage of being a foreigner with no say in the neighbouring territorial Estates and assemblies or committees. Increasing financial difficulty thus played a part in the failure of nunnery and town to escape mediatization at the hands of Jülich. In 1547 the Abbess was hardly expected to know that the House of Jülich would die out within the next sixty years and that the Calvinist Hohenzollerns would claim the *advocatia* over Herford by right of inheritance combined with brute force. What she did know was that Jülich in 1547 would guarantee her protection against secularization.

Herford town developed at the foot of the hill upon which the nunnery was built. The Abbesses furthered and protected this civic development. The old town grew up in the twelfth century when the community obtained corporative rights and privileges. These were confirmed by the Archbishops of Cologne in the early thirteenth century and a town council began operating at about the same time. The town took up contact with Luther in the early 1520s. It fought the decision of the Abbess to invest the Dukes of Jülich with the *advocatia* but had to do homage to the Duke in 1557. From then on the town spent large sums of money in attempts to become an imperial free town, in order to have its submissions to Abbess and Duke annulled. This it achieved by judgment of the Emperor and *Reichskammergericht* in 1631 but only as a result of Hohenzollern-Habsburg rivalries at the time. This constitutional confusion was due to the opportunism of the Habsburgs from Charles V to Ferdinand II. As regards tiny Herford they at one time acquiesced in the activities of Jülich and Brandenburg and at other times supported the counter-demands of the Herford burghers, for their own wider reasons of state.[149]

The *Reichskammergericht* decision of 1631 enabled the burghers to avoid re-Catholicization which the Edict of Restitution had threatened them with after 1629, for as an imperial town they

[149] F. Korte, 'Die staatsrechtliche Stellung von Stift und Stadt Herford', *58. Jahresbericht Historischer Verein Ravensberg*, 1955, pp. 145–8.

now possessed the *ius reformandi* themselves, whereby they could choose between the Augsburg and the Catholic confessions.[150] The *Reichskammergericht* decision did not prevent Elector Frederick William from annexing the town. In 1647 Brandenburg troops occupied the town and forced the town council to recognize the Elector as overlord and protector of town and nunnery. The nunnery continued to exist under Calvinist Abbesses, the most famous of whom was a granddaughter of King James I.[151] The Hohenzollerns added Herford Nunnery to their patronage-list.[152] Although they continued to recognize the imperial status of the ruling Abbess, this was a formality. At imperial level she raised no protests against Brandenburg and conducted no anti-Hohenzollern policies. This protest was left to the Emperor himself and to the Herford burghers.

The Brandenburg occupation of 1647 was condemned by imperial *Mandat* which the Elector thought it wisest to obey in 1650. Having withdrawn his troops, he sealed the town off from the surrounding Ravensberg countryside. In a blockade from three sides Herford town lasted out for barely a year and had to capitulate in the face of economic necessity and was mediatized.[153]

The later seventeenth and eighteenth centuries were times of economic and political eclipse for the once powerful towns of the Lippe-Ravensberg area. Although contacts between the Herford, Bielefeld and Lemgo markets remained essential factors in inter-territorial trade between Lippe, Herford and Ravensberg, the three towns did not develop as quickly as the countryside

---

[150] Relations between Convent and Town were strained, see *Gründlicher und Wahrhafter Bericht: Was gestalt die unter Stift und Stadt Hervorde eingefallene Streitigkeiten und Gebrechen ihren Anfang genommen*, Rinteln, 1637. These are fifteen pamphlets and legal decisions plus an introduction. The same occurred between Convent and Town Essen 1561–1670, see Gaul, *op. cit.*, p. 17. Also Spannagel, *op. cit.*, pp. 53–71.

[151] G. E. Guhrauer, 'Elizabeth Pfalzgräfin bei Rhein, Äbtissin von Herford 1667–80', *Raumers Historisches Jahrbuch*, 3rd series, i, pp. 1–150, and 2, pp. 417–554, Leipzig, 1850. O. Wöhrmann, *Elizabeth von der Pfalz*, Herford, 1921.

[152] H. Schulz, 'Johanna Charlotte, Markgräfin von Brandenburg-Schwedt, Äbtissin des Reichsstifts Herford 1729–50', *Herforder Jahrbuch*, 1, 1960, pp. 35–58. Her absentee predecessor drew an annual pension of 12,000 tlrs from the nunnery in the 1720s (p. 41).

[153] R. Pape, 'Überblick über die Geschichte der Stadt Herford', *Herforder Jahrbuch*, 1, 1960, p. 21.

under the control of rulers and nobility. Although Herford town did not try to solve its internal problems by extensive witch-hunting to the same extent as did Lemgo,[154] it sank to the size of a large village where the wealthiest burghers were those who ran town houses that served as full-time farmyards.[155]

Herford had failed to convince Brandenburg of its imperial status and this in return did not offer Herford a responsible place in Ravensberg politics. From the point of view of its self-governing neighbours in Lippe, Herford town was indeed badly off. Out of its tutelage Herford was raised by Prussian local government reforms, the railways and the coming of industrialization to eastern Westphalia in the nineteenth century.

[154] Schacht, 'Der leibhaftige Teufel in Herford', *46. Jahresbericht Historischer Verein Ravensberg*, 1931, pp. 123–34. K. Meier, *Die letzte und blutigste Hexenverfolgung in Lemgo 1665–81*, Lemgo, 1949.

[155] E. Keyser, *Westfälisches Städtebuch*, Stuttgart, 1954, pp. 180, 51, 215. Herford had about 300 houses and a population of under 3,000 in 1719. The population of neighbouring Bielefeld may have been 2,500 at the beginning of the sixteenth century. In the eighteenth century it was still only 3,000. To this must be added an extra 1,500 Prussian soldiers as garrison based on the castle overlooking the town. Early seventeenth-century Lemgo had 1,000 houses, but a population of a mere 3,000 at the end of the eighteenth century. These figures for Herford and Bielefeld are more modest than those given by T. Weddigen in *12. Jahresbericht Historischer Verein Ravensberg*, 1898, pp. 102–4. Town statistics are notoriously unreliable before the late eighteenth century.

VI

Rule by Inheritance: the Lay Territories

(i) *Brunswick-Lüneburg*

In the lands of the Guelph Dukes of Brunswick-Lüneburg a vigorous political reorganization seems to have taken place at the beginning of the sixteenth century. From 1495 the Dukes called assemblies of Estates in order to obtain more financial aid for their ambitious military policies, especially those which arose out of the French candidature for the imperial title and out of the civil war called the *Hildesheimer Stiftsfehde* between members of the Guelph family in 1519–20. At frequent assemblies ducal officials successfully negotiated with prelates, nobles and town councils for extraordinary taxes. In the later fourteenth century and in the fifteenth these taxes had been negotiated in something like a greater ducal council, which was composed of selected members of the Estates, who were at the same time sworn councillors of the Dukes. By the sixteenth century the Estates seem to have lost influence or trust in this council, making it necessary for the Dukes to call assemblies of the Estates seemingly for the first time ever for the purpose of getting consent to taxes. These were then levied as excise on produce and on cattle for a fixed number of years.[1]

---

[1] W. Krosch, *Die landständische Verfassung des Fürstentums Lüneburg*, Kiel, 1914, pp. 12–22. H. J. v.d. Ohe, *Die Zentral- und Hofverwaltung des Fürstentums Lüneburg (Celle) und hire Beamten 1520–1648*, Celle, 1955, pp. 7–9. P. Sander and H. Spangenberg, *Urkunden zur Geschichte der Territorialverfassung*, Stuttgart, 1922–6, Document 163, 'Die Lüneburger Sate 1392', whereby landlords obtained tax exemption in return for concessions to their rulers in taxing tenantry and servants. The *Sate* was a committee of eight nobles and eight burghers which limited the prerogative powers of the Dukes in government. H. Angermeier, *Königtum und*

The territory was agriculturally poor and without overmuch commercial or industrial potential. It was bereft of large urban centres, except for Lüneburg town which played a rôle of independence against its Dukes, whilst at the same time remaining as aloof from the rest of the Estates as possible in the sixteenth century. In this it displayed a selfishness quite unlike neighbouring Brunswick town which was the centre of the Estates of Brunswick-Wolfenbüttel.[2] The rest of the Brunswick-Lüneburg Estates, three of nine prelates to survive the Reformation of 1527–48, the curia of nobles or knights, and the curia of five towns led by Ülzen and Celle, negotiated through assemblies to which their Dukes summoned them for the chief purpose of raising money.[3]

Resources were limited. In 1562 Lüneburg town bought itself free from all future ducal customs and excise by agreeing to pay an annual quitrent of 2,000 fl. In an agreement of 1576 the town paid a further 1,000 tlrs annually to the Duke for continued economic control over the neighbouring countryside. Yet this large Hanseatic town was forced to attend the assembly as a member of the curia of towns for the first time in 1639 because it could no longer afford to pay for its special tax exemptions.[4]

The whole ducal debt was 650,000 tlrs in 1616, which the assembled Estates agreed to liquidate.[5] Heavier excises were levied for limited periods of years and then renewed when they ran out. By 1637 the debt had been paid off but excises continued to be levied as a regular source of income for the Dukes. Assemblies became less frequent in the early seventeenth century and none was held after 1652. Sporadically since the mid-sixteenth century standing committees of the Estates had taken

[2] Similarly Hildesheim town in the neighbouring bishopric, which also took no part in territorial assemblies as an Estate, see J. Lücke, *Die Landständische Verfassung im Hochstift Hildesheim*, Hildesheim, 1968.

[3] Krosch, *op. cit.*, pp. 23–37. Ohe, *op. cit.*, pp. 9–11.

[4] Krosch, *op. cit.*, pp. 15n., 45–6.

[5] Including Counties Hoya, Diepholz (also ruled by the Dukes) total debt was 1,070,000 fl. in 1614. Money was owed to the territorial nobility, ducal officials, Lüneburg town, and even to the neighbouring Brandenburg nobility along the river Elbe. Ohe, *op. cit.*, pp. 6–7.

Landfriede, Munich, 1966, p. 308. G. Barraclough, *The origins of modern Germany*, Oxford, 1947, pp. 328–9.

on responsibility for satisfying ducal demands for money.[6] In 1624 the Estates themselves were asking the Duke to set up a committee as a more comfortable way of doing business than by assembly.[7]

It is thus important not to confuse the Estates with the assemblies that the Dukes had called them to attend in the sixteenth century. *Landstände* and *Landtage* were politically very different things. Assemblies ceased in the seventeenth century, but the Estates continued to enjoy their particular rights and privileges. Yet why did the ducal experiment of calling assemblies fail to establish these assemblies as an integral part of the constitution of Brunswick-Lüneburg? Perhaps rulers here were despots, but it is more likely that the Estates themselves were generally not keen on the assemblies.

Why did the Estates in the seventeenth century consider themselves fortunate that the Dukes still at least preferred to send their tax demands to Estates' committees and to the *Landräte* rather than to levy and collect taxes by force of decree? The clue seems to lie in the ducal use of the term *Landschaft* or country, which may well have prevented the legal recognition of both the Estates and the assemblies during the sixteenth century as the constitutional representatives of the duchy against their rulers. However, no neat development seems to have taken place.[8]

In the sixteenth century the Dukes obtained regular grants from their assembled Estates. These grants the Dukes accepted not in the name of the assemblies or collectively in the name of the Estates, neither in the name of the *Landtag* nor in the name of the *Landstände*. Instead, the Dukes accepted grants in the name of a legal fiction, the *Landschaft*[9] or country, or in a variety of shifting terms. It seems that by allowing no comprehensive nomenclature to become established by custom and

---

[6] Krosch, *op. cit.*, pp. 12–13. Ohe, *op. cit.*, p. 12.   [7] Krosch, *op. cit.*, p. 14.

[8] This is to suppose some special plan by the Dukes to preserve their prerogative powers in the face of continuous insolvency. The territorial Estates were by no means united. The leading nobles, usually ten *Landräte*, formed a vital link between Duke and Estates, for they were his officials as well as members of the Estates. Ohe, *op. cit.*, pp. 11–16. Thus the Estates may have wanted to wrest power and responsibility from the Dukes now and again, but they were not united and organized enough to do so with any lasting success. G. de Lagarde, 'La structure sociale de l'Europe au XIVe siècle', *L'Organisation Corporative du Moyen Age*, 2, 1939, pp. 104–5.   [9] Ohe, *op. cit.*, p. 9.

thereby to develop the backbone of an institution, the Dukes legally retained their prerogative powers fully intact.

In 1472 the *Bede*, a forerunner of Estates' indirect extraordinary taxation or excise of the sixteenth century, was granted by a greater ducal council of six abbots, thirteen knights and four Lüneburg town councillors. There was no assembly or *Landtag*.[10] The 1495 tax grant was again made by a council.[11] In acknowledging the 1509 tax grant the Duke named the Estates more specifically. The council had disappeared now for this tax-granting purpose, but there was no acceptance of the grant by use of any collective terms such as Estates or assembly.[12] However, in acknowledging the 1518 tax grant, the Duke for the first time used the term *Landschaft* or country.[13] To make matters more ambiguous still, the term *Landschaft* was used to denote the towns or towns and *Ämter*. The Duke accepted a 1594 assessment in this way.[14] Other addresses used by the Dukes in the 1590s were similarly confusing.[15] It is at least as likely that so much confusion was intended by the Dukes and their officials, as that it occurred out of a merely haphazard and confused system of government and politics within sixteenth-century Brunswick-Lüneburg.[16] Yet it also shows that it is not possible to give a simplified picture of territorial constitutional development.[17]

[10] Krosch, *op. cit.*, p. 21.

[11] The Duke accepted a grant 'from our faithful councillors, ecclesiastical and lay, and the honourable town council of Lüneburg, Krosch, *op. cit.*, p. 21.

[12] *Ibid.*, p. 22n.   [13] *Ibid.*, p. 21n.   [14] *Ibid.*, p. 23.

[15] In sixteenth-century Hesse only the towns were called *gemeine Landschaft*. H. Siebeck, *Die landständische Verfassung Hessens im 16. Jahrhundert*, Kiel, 1914, pp. 4n., 20. Krosch, *op. cit.*, p. 28n.

[16] *Ibid.*, p. 28, 'Prälaten, Räthe und Landschaft'; 'wegen Räthe und Landschaft'.

[17] Cf. H. Krause, *System der Landständischen Verfassung Mecklenburgs*, Rostock, 1927, pp. 1–7. E. Hofer, *Die Beziehungen Mecklenburgs zu Kaiser und Reich*, Marburg, 1956, pp. 64–74. *Quellen zur Neueren Geschichte*, 17, Bern, 1951, Document IV, 'Der Vergleich des Markgrafen von Brandenburg mit den Landständen', 24 August 1472. F. L. Carsten, *Origins of Prussia*, London, 1954, p. 141. Sander and Spangenberg, *op. cit.*, Documents 174–81, showing the variety and complexity in the political development of territorial Estates. H. J. Cohn, *The Government of the Rhine Palatinate in the fifteenth century*, Oxford, 1965, p. 195. It is not really possible to generalize about the political position of territorial Estates because of the ambiguous terminology in constitutional documents of each individual territory. Thus Otto Brunner's dictum in *Land und Herrschaft*, 'die Stände sind das Land' (The Estates are the Country), repeated by C. Haase, *Das ständische Wesen im nördlichen Deutschland*, Göttingen, 1964, is an over-simplification.

By the seventeenth century the Dukes were ready to refuse to call assemblies of the Estates for extraordinary taxation, for reasons of emergency, necessity and the threats of war and invasion of the territory, by exercise of the ducal prerogative.[18] Although in practice the Estates had a right to be asked by the Dukes to grant all taxes in assemblies as of custom established over some hundred years, they had no case at law against the ducal prerogative by which to back up this privilege and present concrete proof of it in writing. Grants had been accepted in the name of the *Landschaft* by the Dukes, but who could claim at law to be the *Landschaft?* Not the Estates alone. A mere counting of subjects' heads or of taxpayers' heads could quickly show that they were just the privileged few. The Estates in assemblies may have granted the money but the Dukes accepted it from the *Landschaft*.

This legal fiction may well have played a part in preventing the Estates from insisting on their assemblies and may have also prevented them from opposing the ducal prerogative when taxation was demanded directly from committees of the Estates.[19] There were no legal grounds for constitutional opposition in Brunswick-Lüneburg, and there was no constitutional conflict between rulers and Estates over the discontinuance of assemblies. The Estates managed to retain executive responsibility over extraordinary taxation through their committees, and the wasteful system of taxation by decree seems to have been mutually avoided. Thus the Chancellor could afford to reply to a request of the Estates' committee for an assembly, in 1658, that the times were not suitable for the holding of assemblies of the Estates.[20]

(ii) *Brunswick-Calenberg*

Is it realistic to assess absolutism according to the ability of territorial rulers to suppress the assemblies of the Estates? For

[18] H. Kraemer, 'Der deutsche Kleinstaat', *Zeitschrift des Vereins für Thüringische Geschichte*, 25, new series, 1922–4, p. 60.

[19] The Dukes were actually helped by the territorial Estates, *Landtagsabschied*, 30 August 1610, 'dass oft die Sachen also beschaffen, dass sie keinen langen Verzug leiden konnten oder wollten, und Seine Fürstliche Gnaden die Ehrbare Landschaft in der Eile nicht gefuglich convociren konnte, so hat die Landschaft bey itzigen Conventu sich eines gewissen Ausschusses verglichen und nachbenannte Personen verordnet . . .'. The committee of ten was cut down to six nobles and one burgher from Celle in 1638, Ohe, *op. cit.*, pp. 10–11.   [20] Krosch, *op. cit.*, p. 12.

the political power of influential propertied subjects was not necessarily bound up in any one institution like the *Landtag*. Even when *Landtage* were assembled, the Estates did not act in the name of the *Landtag* but in their own names, as corporations of nobles and towns and sometimes still as clergy, or in the name of a legal fiction, the *Land* or *Landschaft*. Because rulers forbade *Landtage* from time to time, this does not automatically imply that they destroyed the power of the Estates. In the principality of Calenberg the Guelph ruler, Duke Johann Friedrich, could forbid the customary assembly of Estates in 1673, but grants and levies of extraordinary taxes remained the responsibility of Estates' committees, whose decisions the *Landtage* were still from time to time called upon to endorse.[21]

In the 1670s, when relations between ruler and Estates were not good in Calenberg, the Estates still produced a regular monthly quota of 20,000 tlrs to help pay for the army.[22] When this is compared with the 200–350,000 tlrs per annum which the ruler obtained from his Calenberg-Grubenhagen domains alone, it seems a modest sum indeed. The system of taxation was inefficient and the clergy and nobility especially wished to ensure that their tenants paid as little as possible in *Kontribution* to the state.[23] But equally the high tone which ruler and chancellery used with the Estates may possibly not have helped to bring about the trust and confidence in each other that would have been needed to get the Estates to grant as much money as was economically bearable.

With an army of up to 15,000 men costing over 800,000 tlrs per annum, Johann Friedrich had an annual deficit of at least one-third of that sum. As he chose not to flatter the Estates, other ways of covering his debts were to obtain foreign subsidies and to increase his own revenues from domain. Hence a refusal to share political responsibility with the Estates went hand in hand with a chronic lack of financial support from his wealthy subjects. In this way despotism proved to be a capri-

[21] Haase, *op. cit.*, p. 14.

[22] According to poll tax lists to provide aid against the Turks in the 1660s and 1680s, the taxable population of Calenberg-Grubenhagen was 130,000 of whom just over 12,000 lived in small townships and about 18,500 in the towns of Göttingen, Hameln, Hanover and Northeim. E. Keyser, *Bevölkerungsgeschichte Deutschlands*, 2nd ed., Leipzig, 1941, p. 377.

[23] G. Schnath, *Geschichte Hannovers*, 1, Hildesheim, 1938, pp. 37–9, 44–7.

cious, weak and economically dangerous form of government.[24] The rulers kept a close eye on Estates' finance committees. Whilst the committee system was resorted to whenever rulers and Estates were deadlocked, few of these committees were free from the ruler's supervision. If a committee proved intractable the ruler could starve it of business by taking his demands elsewhere. It was this that Duke Friedrich Ulrich promised not to do in a *Landtagsabschied* of 1628.[25] An *Abschied* of 1636 established a large committee with seventeen members of clergy, nobles and towns. Yet even here the ruler could divide and rule, for the largest towns of Hanover, Göttingen, Hameln and Northeim refused to join the committee. By 1638 Duke George was already able to call *ad hoc* committees of friendly members of the Estates to decide matters of taxation in his favour. Thereupon until 1641 the Estates were, however, able to make some opposition, although their success was short-lived.

A serious crisis developed in 1650–1, when the Estates fought the costs of the army, for they expected that the peace made in 1648 would be followed by general disarmament. Instead the ruler increased his army. Estates' committees refused to grant supply and a *Landtag*, called also a *plenum der Landschaft*, granted only sufficient money to pay for the army for a few months at its full strength. The privy council then entered the fray and demanded that the Estates show obedience to the ruler. This was a baldly authoritarian argument under the circumstances, and it was given in reply not to the full *Landtag* but to a group of the Estates, whom the ruler had chosen especially for their willingness to please him.[26]

The weakness of privy council and chancellery is here shown, for if they had been able to produce a good policy argument against the plea of the Estates for disarmament, it is unlikely that they would have needed to tell the Estates what mere subordinates the Estates were. The ruler, it seems, wanted his army and he was prepared to destroy his relations with the Estates to get it. How much was this his own personal wish? Was it not rather the policy of the privy council and chancellery to

[24] Cf. F. L. Carsten, *Princes and Parliaments in Germany*, London, 1959, pp. 428–9. J. Petersohn, *Fürstenmacht und Ständetum in Preussen während der Regierung Herzog Georg Friedrichs 1578–1603*, Würzburg, 1963, p. 184.
[25] A. Köcher, *Geschichte von Hannover und Braunschweig*, 2, Leipzig, 1895, p. 5.
[26] *Ibid.*, p. 7.

encourage the exclusion of the Estates from politics in order to increase their own power? Hence in the Estates' eyes councillors may have easily become evil councillors, but it is unlikely that any of the Estates ever went further than demanding that government officials be natives of the territory. To demand the dismissal of an official was, after all, to oppose the prerogative of the ruler who had appointed that official. The Estates seem to have attempted no political trials, and infringement of the ruler's prerogative was a matter of treason, which the ruler dealt with by *lettre de cachet*.

The Estates were not prepared to leave it at that, however. They assembled on their own initiative and produced a memorandum which was handed to the ruler, reaffirming their rights in taxation. They stressed especially their right to collect their own taxes. They talked about their *ius collectandi* rather than about their more dubious rights to grant taxes.[27] They affirmed that just as the Emperor could not levy arbitrary taxes on the imperial Estates, so the imperial Estates of which their ruler was a member could not levy arbitrary taxes on them, the territorial Estates.[28]

The ruler was impressed and he received the deputies in person. The chancellor, however, repudiated the alleged similarity between the ruler's position at imperial or federal level and the territorial Estates' position at territorial, state level, as implied in the memorandum. The chancellor knew that the Duke in fact exercised correspondingly greater power in his territory than did the Emperor in the Empire. Yet the outcome of this conflict over supply was that the ruler did not call another *Landtag* until 1656. Between 1651 and 1656 he continued to authorize his officials to deal with finance through *ad hoc* committees of the Estates.

The plea of the Estates to have a *Landtag* in 1657 was countered by officials who pleaded absence of the ruler from the territory together with the necessity of dealing swiftly with a dangerous foreign situation as the excuse for asking for taxes from another *ad hoc* committee. To both these excuses the

[27] *Ibid.*, p. 8.
[28] Kraemer, *op. cit.*, pp. 11, 87. G. Löhneiss, *Aulico-Politica*, Brunswick, 1624. G. K. Schmelzeisen, *Polizeiordnungen und Privatrecht*, Münster, 1956, *passim*. C. Bornhak, *Deutsche Verfassungsgeschichte*, Stuttgart, 1934, pp. 138–9.

Estates could hardly object without violating the ruler's prerogative.

In 1658 the officials established a standing committee of the Estates rather as the *Landtagsabschied* of 1638 had decreed. The ruler had the right to confirm the election of all committee members whom the Estates elected, and the officials used this to assert themselves over the Estates by refusing to accept the Estates' own first choice of candidates. Standing committees had in the past failed to be browbeaten into giving the rulers' officials the money which they wanted. In 1658 the committee also refused to make a grant without reference to a full *Landtag*. On this point the officials had to accept a defeat but they still demanded full powers for the committee in case of serious emergency.

Once the Estates agreed to this their power would be over, for only the ruler and his officials decided matters of policy and emergency. It was an easy matter to declare a state of emergency whenever money was needed from the territory. In the ensuing conflict in 1658 it is interesting to note that the Estates did not counter officials' demands for emergency powers by an attack on 'evil' councillors or on 'upstarts and foreigners' estranging the ruler from his Estates.

In practice, the 1658 standing committee took over the real business of the *Landtag*, which retained all its powers in theory alone.[29] The standing committee contained the smaller finance committee of the Estates, the *Schatzcollegium*, reinforced by thirteen other clergy, nobles and burghers. The ruler chose them from among the members of the Estates and he made alterations as he pleased. From now on the officials called *Landtage* only in order to formally endorse the arrangements made with this committee. *Landtage* thus became grand and formal occasions whilst the Estates were made to conduct their politics in committees carefully supervised by the ruler and his officials.

Even on the question of emergency powers the Estates gave way. It seems that they gave their standing committee sufficient powers to grant money without immediate reference to the assembly whenever the Duke and his privy councillors decreed an emergency. The ruler and his officials retained the sole prerogative right of saying when there was an emergency.

[29] Köcher, *op. cit.*, p. 11.

The Estates had also themselves made their position worse by often not attending a *Landtag* when it had been called, thereby saving the expenses they would have incurred. Officials were also swift to condemn *Landtage* as too costly. The committee system saved money and this seemed to be an important consideration to both ruler and Estates, although actual assembly costs can only have been a tiny amount of the money that was involved in a normal tax grant. The Estates even agreed to assemble in the chancellery in Hanover. The ruler no longer attended their meetings and he no longer signed their agreements. From 1651 the Estates were no longer presented with *Abschiede*; instead the chancellery left the results of negotiations in their raw state as scattered minutes. Should the Estates prove intractable, they were pushed into the corridors of the chancellery building, where crowds of common folk, waiting to petition officials, often forced them into the public square outside.

Even in the confirmation of their privileges the Estates had to witness the chicanery of the ruler.[30] The next step the ruler took was to prevent all informal meetings of members of the Estates, in order not to be further plagued with their petitions and complaints. The Estates replied by assembling on their own in Hanover in 1673, thus openly defying the ruler's order. Freedom of assembly was affirmed by the *Abschied* of 1639 according to the Estates. Again the privy council resorted to authoritarian methods. The leaders of the Estates, an abbot, a *Schatzrat*, a mayor, a town *Syndicus* and the *Landsyndicus*, were summoned to appear before the privy council. 'In order not to spoil the good relations between ruler and Estates', as they put it, the privy councillors resolved that the Duke should allow this meeting of the Estates, but that all future meetings would be expressly illegal unless previously consented to.[31] Thereafter the Estates did not dare to assemble again without permission. They appealed to the Emperor but reaffirmed their wish to obey the Duke. The finance committee thus asked and obtained permission to meet in May 1675.

Rulers had exchanged dependence upon the Estates for dependence on their own officials, who in turn still depended on the

---

[30] *Ibid.*, pp. 14–15, Appendix. J. Lampe, *Aristokratie, Hofadel und Staatspatriziat in Kurhannover*, 1, Göttingen, 1963, p. 215.

[31] Köcher, *op. cit.*, p. 17.

money which they could obtain from Estates' committees in order to pursue any viable policies at all.

Rulers called in experts trained in Roman Law to form their councils of state. Although ruler and territorial nobility still met socially and still co-operated in appointments to many of the offices of state, there was no self-made, separate and distinct place for the Estates in this new bureaucratic state, let alone for an independent nobility in politics. The Estates did not become watch-dogs of the constitution, nor did they develop political institutions which the ruler was forced to appeal to. Instead a bureaucratic development took place as the rulers' expert councillors pushed the Estates into the background and formed executive institutions, which were also the places where politics were decided without reference to the Estates or to their assemblies.

Admittedly the Estates were left their personal privileges in legal protection and tax reduction or exemption for themselves, but if they wanted to discharge any comparable duties, they could no longer do this through their own traditional assemblies to which former rulers had called them. Instead they had to go to court and get into the council of experts, or be satisfied with a sinecure or carefully supervised local post which they had inherited, gained by marriage or otherwise purchased with favours, service or money from the ruler and his clique. A parliament could not exist here.[32]

(iii) *Brunswick-Wolfenbüttel*

The Estates of Brunswick-Wolfenbüttel, who came under the same Duke but retained a distinct organization from the Estates of Calenberg in 1584, reached their period of greatest political influence in the sixteenth century, when they made a bid to extend their sole right to grant taxes to include also allocation, collection and audit. The latter had always been carried out by the Dukes' officials.

In 1505 the Duke allowed his Estates to appoint a committee of six to audit those ducal accounts which recorded the spending

---

[32] Lampe, *op. cit.*, pp. 216–35. W. Ohnsorge, 'Zum Problem: Fürst und Verwaltung um die Wende des 16. Jahrhunderts', *Blätter für deutsche Landesgeschichte*, 88, 1951, pp. 150–74.

of a grant which the Estates had made for liquidating ducal debts. Sixteenth-century Dukes needed the support of their Estates primarily to take over bad debts and to act as security for new loans, rather than to grant money for intended policies. By the 1560s both Duke and Estates began to place much reliance on committees of finance, composed of members of the Estates. These are to be distinguished from the more traditional committees which generally stayed behind after a full assembly of the Estates to deal with judicial business arising out of petitions and complaints brought to the assembly and often directed against specific ducal officials and their local practices.[33] The large committee of the Estates took on ducal debts of 300,000 fl. in 1572, which it spread out over twelve years and raised in special taxation.

Finance committees could not, however, obtain full or even regular scrutiny of ducal accounts. Having little idea of the actual items which made up ducal expenditure, they could hardly expect to control it. Yet control is what they seemed to desire perhaps even more than the right to make grants in assembly, for extraordinary taxation was becoming more and more frequent. The Dukes saw to it that not only the unprivileged but also the Estates should contribute, in the proportions of one-half from the towns and approximately one-quarter each from the prelates and nobility.

Thus the Estates began to desire above all a permanent committee of finance which could tell them more precisely where all their money went to. Special committees of audit were convened in the sixteenth century, but by skilful management in the early and late 1580s and again in the early 1590s the Dukes were sufficiently well off not to require grants from their Estates, and they refused to show accounts to the Estates even for grants which had been made many years previously. Yet in 1586 Duke Julius had conceded that a committee of audit should meet, but even as late as 1597 the Estates were still asking to be allowed to audit the accounts of a grant of 300,000 tlrs which they had made in assembly in 1586.[34]

[33] H. Koken, *Die Braunschweiger Landstände um die Wende des 16. Jahrhunderts unter den Herzögen Julius und Heinrich Julius, 1568–1613, im Herzogtum Braunschweig-Wolfenbüttel*, Kiel, 1914, pp. 28, 43, 46. Calenberg was under the Wolfenbüttel Guelphs from 1584 to 1634. [34] *Ibid.*, pp. 13, 27–9, 47.

The treasury into which the Estates paid their grants was in the ducal town of residence, Wolfenbüttel, a town which never gained even the right to send a councillor to the assemblies. By 1597 the time was ripe for a new arrangement to settle the claims of the Estates to allocation, collection and above all audit of taxes which they granted in assembly. As no assembly ever seemed to totally starve its Duke of money, and as no Duke ever seemed to refuse to take a grant,[35] however inadequate it may have been, the fight for rights over extraordinary taxes between Duke and Estates centred not so much on political and constitutional issues involving the granting and further demanding of money, as on those aspects of assessment, collection and accounting of tax grants which were purely executive matters.

As grants were usually made to pay off debts, there was also no need for conflict over allocation policies between Duke and Estates, other than at the lucrative, executive level.[36] It was for this reason that Duke and Estates agreed to set up a treasury council or *Schatzrat* when they assembled in Schöningen in 1598, for in the previous year the Estates had pressed home their demands with a gift of 200,000 fl.[37]

The treasury council consisted of seven members of the Estates and two ducal officials, elected to serve for life. The council controlled all aspects of extraordinary taxation after the Estates had granted it. The treasury moved from the ducal stronghold of Wolfenbüttel into the Estates' stronghold of Brunswick town, where it was kept in the College of St Blaise, whose Dean was the leading spokesman of the Estates at the assembly. The treasury council received its own seal from the Duke, a sign of administrative responsibility which the Estates themselves never possessed. Yet all decisions taken by the treasury council had to have the approval of the Duke.

So the Duke retained control over taxation without taking on the executive duties which had been the responsibility of his predecessors, for the Estates had been manœuvred first through *ad hoc* finance committees and then through the treasury council into taking on this executive responsibility. The Estates had

---

[35] *Ibid.*, pp. 12, 44–6.
[36] *Ibid.*, *passim*. G. Droege, 'Die finanziellen Grundlagen des Territorialstaates', *Vierteljahrschrift für Sozial- und Wirtschaftsgeschichte*, 53, 1966, pp. 147–55. For another point of view, Kraemer, *op. cit.*, p. 56.   [37] Koken, *op. cit.*, pp. 29, 43.

thereby lost their political freedom to judge ducal financial policy as interested outsiders. In 1598 the Estates had accepted a place in the executive under the Duke. In return for the profits to be made out of a place in the executive, in return for staffing the leading finance department in the Duchy, the Estates left the Duke with all the political power and in absolute control over financial policy. His was now to decree, and theirs was to do and to obey. This arrangement lasted until 1807.[38]

In this victory over the Estates the Dukes were aided by a complete lack of defined political aims and institutions, and by a lack of precise political language on the part of the three Estates of prelates, knights and towns in Brunswick-Wolfenbüttel. Their *Landtage* met neither regularly, nor without ducal permission, nor in a fixed place.[39] It was not more than an important gathering without formal powers as an institution. Conclusions were not drawn up in the name of the assembly, but remained in the name of the Estates or of the Duke and Estates. Outside the assembly all other business not pertaining solely to the Duke and his officials was conducted in the name of the country or *Landschaft*, and not in the name solely of the Estates or *Landstände* as might have been expected, unless it had specifically to do with one of their privileges or duties.

The treasury council of 1598 was to act in the name of 'the whole common country', according to the ducal order which established it, and each and every member of the Estates was to grant this power to the treasury council.[40] The Duke was thereby avoiding any reference to the Estates and assemblies, which could in any way have been interpreted as implying that they were the 'country' or that they did represent the whole land. There was no dualism of political power between Duke and Estates which the Duke could not emphatically deny, and if he ever needed to do this, if the Estates demanded constitutional power from him, then it seems likely that the ambiguous term

[38] *Ibid.*, pp. 29–32, 44–5, 47–8.

[39] It often met in the village of Salzdahlum an hour's ride from the Duke's palace in Wolfenbüttel town, where the assembly used the church if the weather was bad, and where the rule of sanctuary helped to keep hot tempers from attempting any violence during meetings, *ibid.*, pp. 15–16.

[40] *Ibid.*, pp. 32–4. Koken was perhaps too ready to identify the country with the Estates. If this had been so, it would have been hardly acceptable for the Duke to continue to use the terms *Landschaft* and *Landstände* in distinct separation from each other.

Landschaft which he used would give him the loophole through which he could slip.

Thus the Duke seems to have been prepared to let the Estates speak for the whole country when it suited him, such as for the purposes of raising money, but he was careful to keep a distinction between the country with its common needs for welfare on the one hand, and the Estates and their privileges on the other.[41] Yet the Estates did make themselves indispensable to their Dukes, which meant that although no assemblies were called between 1682 and 1768, the Estates were assured of survival if only in the guise of life-members of the treasury council in government and politics. 'They had become subservient to the prince, and he saw no reason why he should abolish them altogether, as they performed useful services as collectors of taxes, in billeting and recruiting and in the sphere of local government.'[42]

(iv) *Schaumburg*

A small territory like the county of Schaumburg could maintain its independence only if it continued to fulfil two basic needs, even before the fortunes of politics and warfare were entered into. The dynasty which ruled should continue to produce male heirs, and the territory should remain financially solvent. In both these fields Schaumburg produced striking if not altogether satisfactory results in the sixteenth and seventeenth centuries.[43]

In the dynastic field the main line of Holstein-Schaumburg made important marriage alliances with daughters of Guelph dukes, Hessian landgraves and Lippian counts. When the line died out, the two junior lines that succeeded each other contracted marriages with a Guelph duchess and a Lippian countess. In 1640 the dynasty died out in all its male lines. The inheritance was then claimed through three Schaumburg widows, Hedwig of Hesse-Kassel, Katharina Sophia of Brunswick-Lüneburg-Harburg, and Elizabeth of Lippe.[44] Hesse also

---

[41] *Ibid.*, p. 31.
[42] F. L. Carsten, 'The causes of the decline of the German Estates', *Studies presented to the International Commission . . .*, 24 (Louvain), 1961, p. 291.
[43] See K. S. Bader, *Der deutsche Südwesten*, Stuttgart, 1950, p. 16.
[44] A. Halliday, *A general history of the House of Guelph*, London, 1821, table III a, b. H. bei der Wieden, *Schaumburgische Genealogie*, Bückeburg, 1966, pp. 132–43. H. bei der Wieden, *Fürst Ernst*, Bückeburg, 1961, p. 186.

claimed escheat of the whole county by virtue of the Landgraves' lordship over the deceased Counts of Schaumburg. To this were added claims by the bishopric of Minden to ecclesiastical lands in Schaumburg. In 1647 all the claimants except Minden got a share of Schaumburg in a partition treaty which was ratified in the Peace of Westphalia a year later.[45]

The Guelphs took Schaumburg lands near their own territory and incorporated them into their new state ruled from Hanover. Hesse shared out the rest with a new dynasty of Schaumburg-Lippe, for which the Counts of Schaumburg-Lippe did homage to the Landgraves in Kassel. At Rinteln town Hesse set up a chancellery for its part of Schaumburg, which saved Hesse-Schaumburg from full incorporation into Hesse-Kassel until the nineteenth century. The arrangement here was perhaps legally comparable to Stuart rule over Scotland and England before the Union. Until 1668 Schaumburg-Lippe and Hesse-Schaumburg still jointly administered many revenues and jurisdictions. The Estates of Schaumburg still existed as a united body. Duties such as the upkeep of the University at Rinteln were still shared until 1668. In that year both sides seem to have split on the recommendation of the Count of Schaumburg-Lippe and the Hesse-Schaumburg Estates. The ancient county of Schaumburg had then ceased to exist. Its position of territorial independence was now taken by one-third of its original size, the new county of Schaumburg-Lippe with its tiny capital at Bückeburg.[46]

Schaumburg-Lippe then began to fear domination by Hesse-Kassel. Co-operation between the two territories gave way to obstruction and distrust. During the imperial wars against Louis XIV, Hesse demanded the right as feudal overlord to protect Schaumburg-Lippe and to provide her imperial and circle military quota, but Count Friedrich Christian (b. 1655, d. 1728) was skilful enough to buy military support from Hanover from 1683 onwards in short-term agreements that cost him about 300 tlrs a month. These remarkably cheap arrangements

[45] G. Schmidt, *Die alte Grafschaft Schaumburg*, Göttingen, 1920, pp. 61–74.

[46] Wieden, *Fürst Ernst*, pp. 65–6. W. Maack, *Die Grafschaft Schaumburg*, Rinteln, 1964, pp. 71–81. F. W. Schaer, *Graf Friedrich Christian zu Schaumburg-Lippe*, Bückeburg, 1966, pp. 4–6, and *Lippische Mitteilungen*, 37, 1968, pp. 181, 184–6. Schmidt, *op. cit.*, pp. 86–7.

freed Schaumburg from imperial and circle military taxes and also from the necessity of a standing army and police force at home. After personal disagreements between Friedrich Christian and Elector Georg Ludwig of Hanover in 1710 these military treaties lapsed. Friedrich Christian replaced them with military treaties with the Catholic Bishops of Münster-Paderborn for varying sums of 3,000–4,500 tlrs a year between 1712 and 1726. Hesse was successfully given the cold shoulder when Lippe and Prussian-Minden allowed safeconducts to troops moving between Paderborn and Schaumburg-Lippe. When Friedrich Christian died in 1728 Hesse immediately occupied Schaumburg-Lippe but the new Count soon broke free to pursue an independent policy which, if not free from the influence of neighbouring powers, at least was free from Hesse.[47]

The independence of the former county of Schaumburg was thus to some extent preserved, but it goes to show that if a small territory was to survive fully into the eighteenth century, then it really needed a ruling dynasty of its own which would not cease to produce normal male heirs. Yet it equally needed the reasonable co-operation of these heirs not to dissipate the revenues of the territory in extensive family partitions, lawsuits and wars of inheritance.

Count Otto IV (b. 1517, d. 1576) had embarked upon an ambitious military career in the 1560s and 1570s on the side of Philip II of Spain against the rebellious Dutch. As a soldier of fortune Otto had, however, spent more money than he received in subsidies from Spain. He had to mortgage his own lands and revenues. At his death in 1576 the burden of debt on Schaumburg was 150,000 tlrs. Despite the efforts of Otto there was no primogeniture by law in the dynasty and conflict broke out among Otto's children over the inheritance. Yet they seem to have realized that if they quarrelled over their inheritance at that time, so much land would soon have been lost in lieu of unpaid mortgages, that there would have been nothing left to inherit. Instead the Estates of Schaumburg were allowed to set up an administration to save as much of the county from alienation as possible. Nine territorial nobles, including a Mengersen, a family to feature often in Schaumburg credit operations,

[47] Schaer, *Friedrich Christian*, pp. 119–40, especially pp. 130–1, 173. W. Dahl, *Die innere Politik Franz Arnolds*, Münster, 1910, p. 17.

then formed a regency council which did indeed save the territory from oblivion.[48]

In 1582 Adolf XIV (b. 1547, d. 1601), an elder son of Otto IV, took over the administration from the Estates. The ruling family now felt more certain of being able to pursue inheritance claims with a real chance of success. Adolf's younger half-brother Ernst (b. 1569, d. 1622) made a partition treaty with Adolf in 1595, although Adolf's son (b. 1585, d. 1601) was alive at that time to ensure the succession.

Ernst had exceptional talent as a financier. He began to reduce the Schaumburg debt and by 1600 only 38,000 tlrs remained of Otto's outstanding 150,000. In this the Estates helped by taking on 40,000 tlrs of the debt in 1596. This meant, however, that three-quarters of the debt was still managed by Adolf and Ernst from their own revenues, without help from the Estates. The Estates seem to have played only a minor rôle in Ernst's world of high finance. From 1601 to 1622 Ernst was sole ruler of Schaumburg and he knew how to make that extra amount of money if he wanted to live above the means provided by his regular revenues.[49]

There was a limit, which Ernst soon reached, to the duties on trade and monopolies on necessary commodities like salt and cereals imposed upon his subjects. The traditional extraordinary taxes obtainable by grant of the Estates were small. The single *Landschatz*, which the Estates were assembled to grant, brought in 10,000 tlrs each time in the sixteenth century and about 14,000 tlrs a time in the seventeenth century. Of this sum the Estates of about twenty territorial nobles, six prelates and eleven towns and markets contributed only one-quarter. Three-quarters came from subjects directly under the jurisdiction of local comital officials. These subjects were the *Amtsuntertanen*, so called because the local comital administration was divided into small territorial units or *Ämter*, which usually comprised several villages or a parish or two. This was a very common form of internal territorial organization in the early modern Empire.

In Schaumburg the most lucrative part of the *Landschatz* was

---

[48] Wieden, *Fürst Ernst*, pp. 19–22. T. Dissmann, *Die Landstände der alten Grafschaft Schaumburg*, Kiel, 1938, pp. 50–60.
[49] Wieden, *Fürst Ernst*, pp. 23, 33–4, 173–82.

the cattle tax, which included a tax even on poultry. A complementary source of income for the Counts was a tax on the commercial production and sale of beer and spirits. By themselves none of these particular sources of revenue ran into five figures. They were puny amounts compared with the sums that Ernst handled.[50]

By 1600 Ernst was building up a sum of capital with which to go into money-lending. He borrowed favourably from the Mengersens. He sold unprofitable lands, unprofitable fixed rents and unenforceable rights and jurisdictions on a large scale to the highest bidder. To Hamburg he sold ancient rights for 32,000 tlrs. To Lippe he sold farms and rents for 20,000 tlrs. Ernst made money available at 5 and 6 per cent per annum. He lent his brother-in-law, Count Simon VI of Lippe, a total of 60,000 tlrs, of which Lippe still owed 50,000 when Ernst died in 1622. To another brother-in-law, Landgrave Maurice of Hesse-Kessel, he lent 10,000 tlrs at 6 per cent. To the nephew of his half-brother Adolf's widow, ruling Duke Friedrich Ulrich of Brunswick-Wolfenbüttel, he lent 100,000 tlrs at 6 per cent in 1614. When Friedrich Ulrich had repaid this in 1617, Ernst made available a further 200,000 tlrs within the space of a year. On this Ernst seems to have had a regular 6 per cent for the rest of his life. At 12,000 tlrs, this alone brought him in as much as a whole *Landschatz* every year.[51]

Ernst was not one to have hidden his light under a bushel. He is estimated to have spent a total of 300,000 tlrs on building programmes and 60,000 tlrs on his court in a single year.[52] With his rare talent for literally getting his money back, and also with the possibility that he may have believed in the faster circulation of precious metals than was customary at that time, we may better understand the huge discrepancy between the sums of money that Ernst disposed of and the sums that his Estates made available to him.

The crowning achievement of Ernst's life was to obtain the title of *Reichsfürst* or ruling prince of the Empire from Emperor Ferdinand II. This left Ernst open to the accusation at that time

---

[50] A large Estates' grant of 20,000 tlrs was given to Ernst in 1602 as a gift when he succeeded to the government of the whole county. Wieden, *Fürst Ernst*, pp. 169–72. Dissmann, *op. cit.*, pp. 61–7. [51] Wieden, *Fürst Ernst*, pp. 175–80. [52] *Ibid.*, pp. 36, 39.

of being the first Protestant to openly betray militant Calvinist policies against the Habsburgs. Ernst's *Hofrat* Goldast had not openly suggested the possibility of a loan to Ferdinand's officials at the Frankfurt Imperial Election of August 1619, yet the title of ruling prince had been conferred by Ferdinand II in September, followed by a request to Ernst for a loan of 100,000 fl. In fact Ernst paid 7,300 fl. chancellery dues via Leipzig town council to Ferdinand for registration of his new title in October 1620. This included a present of 1,000 fl. for the good services of *Reichsvize-Kanzler* von Ulm. In January 1621 Ernst paid a further 6,000 fl. for the good services of *Reichshofrats-Präsident* von Hohen-zollern through a Walloon banker. Finally Ernst paid 17,700 fl. to Ferdinand via an English merchant adventurer in Hamburg. Ernst had more than kept his word when in March 1620 he had offered to pay 15,000 tlrs for the title, of which Ferdinand eventually received well over half. Officially Goldast admitted that Ernst had paid only imperial chancellery dues of 6,000 fl. Rumours that Ernst had paid 100,000 fl. were not thereby stilled, although we now know that Ernst paid much less for the title.[53]

A measure of the anger which this affair roused in Protestant circles is shown by the objection which King Christian IV of Denmark as ruler of Holstein took to Ernst's new title of *Fürst und Graf zu Holstein-Schaumburg*. Ernst bought himself out of this by rephrasing the title and paying Christian an immediate compensation of 50,000 tlrs in the summer of 1621. Ernst's strength seems thus to have been in finance, not in diplomacy and politics, and his vanity was perhaps stronger than his devotion to the Protestant cause. Yet he got what he wanted. He had

[53] H. bei der Wieden, 'Die Erhebung des Grafen Ernst von Holstein-Schaumburg in den Fürstenstand 1619', *Schaumburg-Lippische Mitteilungen*, 18, 1967, pp. 47–55. On coinage, L. W. Hoffmann, *Alter und Neuer Münz-Schlüssel*, Nuremberg, 1692. C. L. Lucius, *Verbot der Guldiner; Neuer Münz-Tractat*, Nuremberg, 1692. Talers were silver and Gulden were gold, or if they were money of account, they corresponded to their respective precious metal market prices. J. Müller, 'Das Steuer- und Finanzwesen des Reiches im XVI. Jahrhundert', *Neue Jahrbücher für das klassische Altertum*, 5, Leipzig, 1902, pp. 665–78, on Reichspfennigmeister Geizkoffler's currency dealings. H. Grote and L. Hölzermann, *Lippische Geld- und Münzgeschichte*, Leipzig, 1867, *passim*. A. Luschin von Ebengreuth, *Allgemeine Münzkunde und Geldgeschichte*, 2nd ed., Munich, 1926, is the standard work of reference. Carsten, *Princes and Parliaments*, preface, 'In the later seventeenth century the thaler was reckoned as equivalent to 1½ guilders, or 3 French livres, or about 4 English shillings.'

also in April 1619 bought an imperial charter for his new Calvinist university at Rinteln, for as little as 400 tlrs, from the hereditary Imperial Vicar, Frederick V of the Palatinate, who by custom ruled a section of the Empire in the interregnum which followed the death of Emperor Matthias and before the election of Catholic Ferdinand.[54]

All this wealth was lost in the ensuing war years, and in the inheritance uncertainties of the following decades. The last two successors of Ernst's dynasty both saw the inside of imperial army prisons.[55] Yet there is no clear view on the effect of the war on the people of Schaumburg.[56] The middle Weser was a front between Westphalian-based Imperialists, and the Swedes and their Hessian and Hanoverian allies based on Lower Saxony.[57] This meant that there was considerable fighting and billeting in Schaumburg.

The burghers and town council of Oldendorf in Schaumburg were in a particularly vulnerable position between the armies of the two sides, and one of the great battles of the war was fought outside their walls in 1633. Yet even in this year the town chamber presented very favourable accounts. They show an income of 2,000 tlrs and an expenditure of 1,900 tlrs. The excise on alcohol provided 900 tlrs and war costs to the town were a mere 700 tlrs. By 1639 the town chamber was paying interest on a debt of 3,350 tlrs. The town council seemed to welcome loans from army officers to pay for war contributions, for it gave these

---

[54] Wieden, 'Die Erhebung . . .', pp. 51, 54–60. [55] *Ibid.*, p. 64.

[56] A traditional 'horrors' monograph is H. Stünkel, *Rinteln im dreissigjährigen Kriege, eine Chronik*, Rinteln, 1952, especially graph of births, p. 110. Town records are used without bearing in mind that it was in the town's interest to produce high losses in order to obtain tax remissions from its Hessian rulers especially in the 1640s. G. Benecke, 'The problem of death and destruction in Germany during the Thirty Years' War', *European Studies Review*, July 1972. G. Franz, *Der dreissigjährige Krieg und das deutsche Volk*, 3rd ed., Stuttgart, 1961, pp. 2, 9. H. Kamen, 'The economic and social consequences of the Thirty Years' War', *Past and Present*, 39, 1968, pp. 49–50. A bid to get off lightly is a document from 1649 which was printed and uncritically used to prove huge war devastation, *Schaumburger Heimatblätter*, 1952, p. 24. It is not that there was no devastation and disruption during this period, otherwise it would not have been warfare. Yet the extent of this devastation is not brought to light by indiscriminate use of the sources. See the warning implicit in W. Maack, 'Kriegsnöte vor 300 Jahren', *Schaumburger Heimatblätter*, 1960–1, p. 47. H. Jäger, 'Der dreissigjährige Krieg und die deutsche Kulturlandschaft', *Wege und Forschungen der Agrargeschichte*, Frankfurt-am-Main, 1967, pp. 142–3. G. Benecke, 'Labour relations and peasant society in Northwest Germany c. 1600', *History*, October, 1973. [57] Stünkel, *op. cit.*, maps pp. 114–15.

officers an interest in the protection of town property. It was hoped that they would thus be unwilling to let their soldiers plunder or otherwise damage property when they were billeted in town. The places that were plundered were more likely to be those localities that could not or would not pursue such sensible policies. The soldiers' economy and safety depended on the walled town at some time during the long and sporadic period of hostility. If burghers knew how to deal with the soldiers' needs, then they could survive occupation with considerable success.

In 1633 the amount of beer produced and sold by Oldendorf burghers had a value of 16,500 tlrs. Wages and prices did not rise, nor did petty crime, and weights and measures were carefully kept at full value. The recorded increase of births over deaths in the town was 328 during 1600–23, with a decrease of 290 during 1623–41, and an increase again of 69 during 1641–8. Real losses of population seem to have been caused by plague in 1626 and 1636, and by emigration of about one-quarter of the burghers of the town. Emigrants were often penalized for not remaining by impositions on the immovables that they had deserted. This shows that war devastation has to be examined with much caution.[58]

When Schaumburg was split in 1668, Hesse-Schaumburg was given a small and seemingly politically insignificant Estates' representation along with a ruling chancellery in Rinteln. There was one representative of the Calvinist clergy and two representatives each of nobility and towns. Whatever the real political future which remained for the former Estates of Schaumburg, it now lay with the five noble families and four towns and markets of Schaumburg-Lippe.[59]

The Schaumburg-Lippe Estates made a stand against the misrule of Count Friedrich Christian by appeals to the *Reichshofrat* in Vienna between 1702 and 1710. They obtained the sympathy of the Countess and of Elector Georg Ludwig of Hanover, and helped to prevent the sale of the county to Hesse,

---

[58] F. Kölling, 'Hessisch-Oldendorf im dreissigjährigen Kriege', *Schaumburger Heimatblätter*, 1951, pp. 24–8. For an outline of plague and population loss, Franz, *op. cit.*, pp. 5–7. M. J. Elas, *Umriss einer Geschichte der Preise und Löhne in Deutschland*, Leiden, 1936–49, 1, pp. 52–7. Kamen, *op. cit.*, pp. 48–53.

[59] Maack, 'Kriegsnöte vor 300 Jahren', p. 78. Schaer, *Friedrich Christian*, p. 65.

which Friedrich Christian seems to have been planning in 1702. The Estates obtained a decision from the *Reichshofrat* ordering Friedrich Christian back home to Bückeburg from Venice in order to take over the government of the county in person, and advising him to confirm the privileges of the nobility. Friedrich Christian knew better than the Estates how far to go with the lawyer-politicians in Vienna. A brief return to Bückeburg in 1708 produced a short-lived reconciliation between ruler and Estates, and the privileges of the nobility were at last confirmed. But by 1710 the Estates were asking the *Reichshofrat* for protection against Friedrich Christian and his rapacious officials by suggesting that Hanover be given control over the internal affairs of Schaumburg-Lippe. This was no solution for the Emperor, who was as loth to give the Hanoverians control as he had been to let the Hessians run the county. The right of Friedrich Christian to appoint his own commission for dealing with his subjects' grievances was upheld.

Friedrich Christian had won. The leader of the Estates fled to Hanover and the records of the Estates seem to have come to an end in 1715. No records seem to have survived of the actual terms of the *Reichskammergericht* agreement which was reached in 1718 on the long-standing conflict between nobles and towns over contribution to defence costs. This case had been temporarily suspended whilst they joined forces to fight Friedrich Christian at the *Reichshofrat*.[60]

The states of Schaumburg-Lippe had made a dramatic appeal at imperial level against the tyranny of their ruler and his officials which had failed through lack of support from Vienna, thus causing the political eclipse of the Estates. Yet how far could Friedrich Christian afford to play the profligate in Vienna, Paris and Venice on resources that were less than half of Ernst's meagre revenues from his subjects, and without Ernst's banking skill?

Friedrich Christian cut the cost of government by understaffing the administration to the point of real negligence, whilst at the same time over-exploiting his revenues.[61] In the last few years of his life he was forced to live on credit raised at times on personal and household effects like jewellery and furniture, as there was no more money to be found in the county.[62] The

[60] *Ibid.*, pp. 69–79, 84–93, 145. [61] *Ibid.*, pp. 144–5. [62] *Ibid.*, pp. 142–9.

financial situation had, however, been a sound one under Friedrich Christian's father.

Count Philip, the youngest son of Simon VI of Lippe and first ruler of Schaumburg-Lippe from 1646 to 1681, had just been able to support an administration and a very modest and obscure court without running into financial difficulties.[63] In 1646 the Chamber took in 10,000 tlrs. Three years later this had doubled, and by 1673 takings were 26,000 tlrs. Philip was also promised 2,000 tlrs a year as inheritance compensation from Lippe, and by 1651 Lippe had debts of 21,000 tlrs with him. When Friedrich Christian took over he was assured by the Chamber that he could well afford to live according to his status as a small territorial ruler but without luxury. This was hardly likely to appeal to the young Count, when he had already spent a decade visiting Paris, Versailles, Vienna and Italy. It soon became clear that he was not content to remain at Bückeburg as his father had done. He was not interested in ruling the county. He would much rather spend as much time and money as possible at the courts of his better-endowed social equals in the south.[64]

Friedrich Christian knew how to make the most of his position. To secure his inheritance in the family an order for primogeniture in Schaumburg-Lippe was bought from Emperor Leopold, and his *Reichshofrat* in 1687 confirmed this. A mentally unstable younger brother was left to run the village-sized enclave of Alverdissen in Lippe under Friedrich Christian's wardship.[65] Chamber revenue fell to 24,000 tlrs in 1684–5, increased to 34,000 tlrs in 1700–1, and made an artificial 84,000 tlrs in 1716–17. This latter figure included loans of 30,000 tlrs. In the financial year 1716–17 Friedrich Christian spent almost 30,000 tlrs on travelling and on his court, excluding any expenses of his wife and children who had fled to Minden, Hanover, and on to England. It also excluded the costs of running the administration. A further 20,000 tlrs was paid as interest on outstanding debts. Compared with all this the total wage-bill of his officials was a mere 5,500 tlrs. This was

[63] In 1647 Hesse and Schaumburg-Lippe agreed upon an equal division of the revenues of seven Schaumburg *Ämter*. Philip of Schaumburg-Lippe obtained the administration of four *Ämter* not on the river Weser, where for reasons of military strategy Hesse would brook no rival. Both powers hoped to make 20,000 tlrs a year from their share of the property. Schmidt, *op. cit.*, pp. 78–9.
[64] Schaer, *Friedrich Christian*, pp. 7–9.　　[65] *Ibid.*, p. 10.

even cut down to 3,600 tlrs in 1722–3. The Count's pocket money by itself came to 3,200 tlrs in 1716–17. Taxes remitted to the Estates in previous years in lieu of regular interest were demanded in full in 1695, but of the 47,150 tlrs the Count got barely 13,000.[66] The Estates continued to pay interest on the remaining capital. In this way the Estates very modestly did prevent Friedrich Christian from dissipating all his assets.

Friedrich Christian dealt with money-lenders in Bückeburg, Hanover, Augsburg and Vienna who served him well enough as long as he had real assets.[67] It is a reflection on the development of the territories into states that the indebtedness of Schaumburg-Lippe in the early eighteenth century did not threaten its further existence as an independent unit in the same way that the debts of Otto IV had threatened to dismember Schaumburg in the sixteenth century. Schaumburg-Lippe was treated as a state, despite the lack of responsibility shown to it by its ruler, Friedrich Christian. His insolvency stopped well short of the disintegration of his county, although it did not prevent the political failure of the Estates when they tried to put an end to his mismanagement.

(v) *Rietberg*

There seems to have been a lower limit below which the constitutional development of a territory was an illusion or even a nightmare. The fourteenth-century county of the Empire, Rietberg, is perhaps an example of this. Ruled by twelve generations of the dynasty of Arnsberg, it then passed in the 1560s through female inheritance to the Counts of East Frisia. After five generations it again passed through female inheritance to the Austrian Counts of Kaunitz. Its history illustrates the value of *Reichsunmittelbarkeit*, of nobility with regal status. Its size is only that of any other gentry property with its tenants, farms and rents so common all over early modern Europe. Yet its owners had self-government, and like all ruling princes of the

---

[66] *Ibid.*, pp. 145–7, also *Lippische Mitteilungen*, 37, pp. 158, 164–5, 167n., 172. Schaer called Friedrich Christian a psychopath.

[67] Heine, Behrens, von Raumer, von Münch. Schaer, *Friedrich Christian*, pp. 150–156. H. H. Hasselmeier, *Die Stellung der Juden in Schaumburg-Lippe 1648–1848*, Bückeburg, 1968, pp. 99–123.

Empire their own private family law. Rietberg's history is thus primarily one of family history.[68]

There was no primogeniture. Property was managed between brothers and sisters, between the in-laws, by a tribal pattern of kinship and marriage based on the profits of landlordism.[69] Large sums of money were lent on expectancy of inheritance, like the projected 300,000 tlrs lent to the house of East Frisia, which the houses of Liechtenstein and Kaunitz regulated from Vienna in 1726.[70]

Westphalia had few splinter territories compared, for example, with the Rhineland, Franconia and Swabia. Rietberg was a poverty-stricken backwater, a burden to any family that had nothing else to live on, should such a family also have the ambitions that generally went with regal status. The Kaunitz family clung to their Rietberg inheritance and remained in Vienna, living off their far more extensive Austrian lands and playing their rôle at the imperial court. Rietberg gave them the highest status that they could wish for, their Austrian lands gave them their wealth.

Built up by a vigorous family in the thirteenth century, Rietberg retained its territorial boundaries and independence until the end of the Empire. In 1377 the ruler turned it into a free county of the Empire. A descendant in 1456 became a vassal of Hesse in return for 600 fl.[71] Except for the period after the defeat of the Smalkaldic League, Rietberg remained a Hessian fief for the next 350 years. Yet this in no way changed its rights as an independent county under the imperial constitution. Only interterritorial politics were somewhat hampered by the periodic need to seek homage from the court in Kassel. On the death of Johann II without male heirs in 1562, Philip of Hesse with the approval of Ferdinand I occupied the county. Three years later the daughters were allowed to inherit on payment of 12,000 fl. to Kassel. Another enfeoffment in 1645 cost 16,000 tlrs. It was thus probably more lucrative for Hesse to have an independent ruler for a vassal than one who was just a territorial noble, who

[68] W. Leesch, 'Die Grafen von Rietberg aus den Häusern Arnsberg und Ostfriesland', *Westfälische Zeitschrift*, 113, 1963, tables pp. 352–3. P. Wigand, *Provinzialrechte Minden-Ravensberg*, Leipzig, 1834, 2, pp. 489–92.
[69] Leesch, *op. cit.*, pp. 354–76.   [70] *Ibid.*, pp. 368–70.
[71] *Ibid.*, pp. 287–8. K. E. Demandt, *Geschichte des Landes Hessen*, Kassel, 1959, p. 160.

would have exploited his position within the Estates to gain general tax exemption.

There were very good reasons for the expenses which the ruling families in Rietberg were prepared to shoulder. They were interested in obtaining, extending or just preserving regal status, whilst in fact only practising very modest estate management.[72] To the Kaunitz family it meant the acquisition of a cheap regal status, including membership of the Westphalian circle and of the Westphalian College of Counts with a voice in the imperial assembly in Regensburg. It also indirectly gave the Habsburgs a window on to a part of north-west Germany that was dominated by Brandenburg-Prussia, Hanover and Hesse.

With a compact estate of thirty-two fiefs, one town and a strong fortress, as well as their own serfs, extending even into the neighbouring Osnabrück enclave of Reckenberg, the rulers of Rietberg were undisputed masters in this small part of the Empire. Thus no family would part with such a convenient passport into the best circles, and Rietberg on the failure of its dynasties did not cease to find new families to pay the expense of continued independence. Needless to say the Rietberg administration was at one notorious point at least a real scandal.[73]

The rulers of the Moravian house of Kaunitz from 1699 to 1815 governed Rietberg from Vienna on the strength of weekly reports sent to them by three officials stationed in the county. No subject had direct access to the ruler. All complaints had to come by post via the officials. These officials had no viceregal powers; everything which was not immediately suppressed was referred back to Vienna. It was thus possibly best for the subjects if the officials fell out with each other and sent complaining letters about each other's incompetence to Kaunitz. Only in this way could abuses come to light.

The militia was run by a garrison officer. He had presumably bought his office, and he used his seventy men (the Rietberg

[72] The local districts of Bokel and Druffel, *Siedlungskundliche Entwicklung*, Gütersloh, 1968, pp. 7, 42–6, 211–19.

[73] O. Merx, 'Aus einem westfälischen Kleinstaate', *Westfalen*, 1, 1909, pp. 9–24. Leesch, *op. cit.*, pp. 288–93. F. Flaskamp, 'Westfälische Bauernhöfe', *Westfälische Forschungen*, 13, 1960, p. 63. Of 444 farms in the neighbouring *Amt* of Reckenberg the Bishop of Osnabrück ran 169 with his serfs, and the Count of Rietberg 43, mostly the larger farms. Of 943 farms in Rietberg itself the Count owned 921.

imperial circle contingent after the increased quotas of the 1680s and 1690s) as his own menials to fetch and carry for his family and to run his farms. He had no love for the officials running the general administration. It was the bad fortune of these officials to have captured four bandits, two highwaymen and their women in 1738. The men were offered to various rulers with large armies and fleets. Kaunitz presumably did not want the expense of a trial and execution, for his administration was hardly equipped with the necessary legal apparatus for that. One man was accepted into the Prussian army. The other was put under sentence of death. The garrison officer was to guard him.

Both men seemed to have liked each other and the prisoner led a very satisfying and free existence. He escaped from confinement, but being a native he went to his village and not over the frontiers which were everywhere within such easy walking distance. Finally he was sent to a mock execution, like the hero in Kleist's *Prinz Friedrich von Homburg*. The Rietberg prisoner's attitude was blasphemous and possibly obscene, hardly the response that *Serenissimus* Kaunitz had hoped for. Finally the prisoner was accepted into a Prussian labour camp. The ruler continued to pay 220 tlrs a month for the Rietberg army. The garrison officer retained his post.[74]

(vi) *Ravensberg*

What happened to territories that lost their indigenous ruling dynasties, and were ruled thereafter by strangers or absentees? Scotland lost its rulers to London in the seventeenth century. Scotland did not thereby become an English province. Yet it was in part the fear that the Protestant Stuart-Hanoverian succession should fail which helped to bring about the Union of 1707. A 'country' was called into being to help bind together the two kingdoms of Scotland and England. The patriotic myth of North and South Britain was created.

The county of Ravensberg was already ruled by a foreign dynasty in the fifteenth century. It did not thereby cease to exist as a separate territory. It survived four successive dynas-

[74] Merx, *op. cit.*, thus confirms the dismal picture set out in Justus Gruner, *Meine Wallfahrt zur Ruhe und Hoffnung*, Frankfurt-am-Main, 1802.

ties, those of Jülich, Cleves, Pfalz-Neuburg and Brandenburg. It was not until the first years of the eighteenth century that Ravensberg was also subjected to a union. The county became a part of the new kingdom of Prussia, the vehicle of Hohenzollern dynasticism. This kingdom had nothing to do with the organization of the former duchy of East Prussia, which had been a fief of the Polish crown from the fifteenth century to the mid-seventeenth, and which the Hohenzollerns had first inherited and then destroyed in the 1650s and 1660s.

In 1723 Ravensberg was put under a provincial government responsible for war and finance at Minden, along with the former bishopric of Minden and the counties of Tecklenburg and Lingen, by decree of Frederick William I. The Ravensberg nobility were bribed into accepting this in return for a privileged position in the army and civil service of the new Prussia along with the noble Estates of the other Hohenzollern territories. Ravensberg had been a classic example of local noble domination which was almost totally unchecked in practice because of the lack of a competent central government within the county itself. It eventually became just another part of the Prussian province of Westphalia.[75]

Territories, kingdoms and states still came under the archaic rules of dynastic inheritance in early-eighteenth-century Europe, as is shown by the wars for the succession to Spanish Habsburg Carlos II. Although the concepts of 'Britain' and 'Prussia' were both created within a decade of each other in order to incorporate ancient, independent units of government into a larger whole, the similarity stops there. For there was a great difference as to who was in control at Westminster, and who was in control of power in Berlin. In Britain the nobility and burghers were the ruler's equals in politics. In Prussia they were the ruler's underlings.

Ravensberg was an outlying part of Jülich-Berg-Cleves-Mark

[75] K. Nitzsch, 'Die ravensbergische Territorialverfassung bis 1535', 17. *Jahresbericht Historischer Verein Ravensberg*, 1903. K. Spannagel, *Minden und Ravensberg unter brandenburg-preussischer Herrschaft 1648–1719*, Hanover, 1894. H. Tümpel, *Minden-Ravensberg unter der Herrschaft der Hohenzollern*, Bielefeld, 1909. von der Horst, *Die Rittersitze der Grafschaft Ravensberg und des Fürstentums Minden*, Berlin, 1884. F. E. Hunsche, *250 Jahre Landkreis Tecklenburg*, Lengerich, 1957, pp. 21–2. H. Rothert, *Westfälische Geschichte*, 2nd ed., Gütersloh, 1962, 3, p. 306.

in the sixteenth century. The ducal central government at Düsseldorf appointed local officials who ruled with the help of the territorial nobility and town council of Bielefeld. Ravensberg was an enclave, stretching to the banks of the middle Weser, a long way from the Rhine. It was thus never an integral part of the Jülich-Berg-Cleves-Mark complex on the lower Rhine, but it had the same rulers, the same political and economic problems in government and a similar fate after 1609, when the Cleves dynasty died out. [76]

When the Hohenzollerns obtained the bishopric of Minden as a secularized principality in part compensation for the Pomeranian inheritance which had gone largely to Sweden at the peace of 1648, it was natural that they should attempt to unite Ravensberg with Minden to form a solid block of land on the middle Weser and to lay the foundations of a land-bridge between Berlin and the new possessions on the Rhine. Minden and Ravensberg were put under one *Statthalter*, or Viceroy, rather as Cleves and Mark were also grouped together. Yet there was no tradition of co-operation or real exchange of ideas, not even in tariff or trade policy between secular Ravensberg and ecclesiastical Minden. It took three generations of Hohenzollern rule for an amalgamation to succeed finally in 1718-23. Even then Ravensberg subjects retained the right to appeal directly to the privy council in Berlin over the heads of the councillors running the *Kriegs- und Domänenkammer* in Minden. [77]

[76] Nitzsch, *op. cit.*, pp. 108-9.

[77] Rothert, *op. cit.*, 2, pp. 262; 3, p. 304. Spannagel, *op. cit.*, pp. 98-103, 133-4, 141-2. Carsten, *Origins of Prussia*, pp. 254-5; *Princes and Parliaments*, pp. 258-340, left Ravensberg out of his description of the Jülich-Berg-Cleves-Mark rulers and Estates. Yet Ravensberg was part of this complex, although there was no tie between the nobility of Ravensberg and those of any of the other four territories, as there was for example between the nobles of Cleves and Mark.

C. O. Mylius, *Corpus Constitutionum Marcicarum*, Berlin, 1737-55, pp. 54-5, published the agreement between Elector Frederick William and the Estates of Ravensberg (only in fact the nobility), concerning abolition of the Chancellery in Bielefeld and establishment of a Court of Appeal in Berlin, 29 April 1653. This Court of Appeal was a dead letter from the start. The Ravensberg nobility controlled local courts of first instance from which the Bielefeld Chancellery had taken away much business after it was founded in 1647. These local courts now obtained jurisidiction over civil cases as well. In return the Ravensberg nobility gave up all rights of appeal to the *Reichskammergericht*. The Ravensberg burghers and peasants were not consulted, and it made no difference that the whole deal was against the constitutional customs of the county of Ravensberg and against the laws of the Empire. It was a good example of how the Hohenzollerns did business. E. A. F.

Ravensberg developed its own distinct system of government, despite the interminable rule of absentees. On accession, the absentees ordered *Lehentage* to assemble in order to receive homage from leading territorial vassals, the landowning nobles and burghers. Such a gathering was held in 1511 on the accession of Duke Johann of Cleves. Assemblies of all the nobles and of the towns of Bielefeld and Herford were called only in emergency situations involving threats of war, invasion or insolvency. Such a gathering was the *Landtag* of Jöllenbeck in 1535, which was convoked to discuss administrative reforms, to bring venal *Amt* officials to trial and to combat the Anabaptists. On most other occasions the ruler's officials, the *Drosten* and *Amtmänner*, negotiated with a committee of the Estates, either in Bielefeld or in an imposing castle on the Sparenberg, overlooking the town.[78]

In 1470 the Estates formed a tribunal for keeping the peace and for minimizing the threat to life and property entailed in the system of *Fehde*, or the execution of justice which the allegedly injured party set about obtaining for himself by a summary declaration or *Fehdebrief* backed up by force of arms. The tribunal called to prevent this primitive judgment by battle and feud contained six Ravensberg nobles, the mayor of Bielefeld as spokesman for the burghers, and the *Landdrost* as the ruler's lord lieutenant of the county. As late as 1535 the decisions of this tribunal were being sought by noble plaintiffs as an alternative to *Fehde* and self-help by force of arms.

Equally, a deputation of six nobles and the councils of Bielefeld old and new towns in 1496 added their seals to the Jülich-Cleves dynastic union. Documents appointing *Amt* officials survive from 1493. The first written instructions to *Amt* officials date from 1535.[79] This shows that an independent growth of politics and administration in Ravensberg was not only possible but was also in some ways facilitated rather than hindered by the absence of a native court and ruling family.

A system of taxation and territorial finance was also worked out by close co-operation between rulers, officials and the

[78] Nitzsch, *op. cit.*, pp. 86–93.   [79] *Ibid.*, pp. 38, 95–7.

Culemann, *Ravensbergische Merckwürdigkeiten*, 2, Minden, 1749, pp. 42–6. W. Sellert, *Über die Zuständigkeitsabgrenzung von Reichshofrat und Reichskammergericht*, Aalen, 1965, pp. 37–40.

Estates. A standard tax, the *Bede*, was levied on the ruler's own tenants and serfs directly by *Amt* officials. The Estates had originally no say in this. Yet by the middle of the fourteenth century these revenues were no longer sufficient to cover the gap between income and expenditure. A policy of *Verpfändung*, or short-, medium- and long-term alienation of lands, offices, rights, jurisdictions and domain revenues, was resorted to by the rulers in order to remain solvent. These alienations were mainly to territorial nobles and burghers. The first whole Ravensberg *Amt* was already alienated in 1319. Only once was a whole *Amt* alienated to a foreigner, to the Count of Tecklenburg in 1375. Apart from this, the Ravensberg Estates seem to have had a monopoly on taking up alienations. This gave them such a tight hold over the *Ämter*, ruler's revenues and officials' appointments that they had generally no need to insist upon an *Indiginatsrecht*, or the appointment of only natives to offices, as was common in most other territories.[80]

Alienation was lucrative for the creditor. In return for lending the ruler a lump sum of money at either 5 or 6 per cent interest per annum, the creditor obtained land or jurisdictions which he could exploit for his own profit until the ruler had repaid him in full. The interest rate was fixed so as to avoid breaking the canon law of usury which Lutherans applied as much as did Catholics. Five per cent was regarded as fair compensation, 6 per cent was tolerated. To make lending to the ruler at all attractive, alienations had to be added. This shows how bad the credit of late-medieval territorial rulers generally was. But under the system of alienation the ruler got his money and the creditor a high return on his capital outlay, and the law of usury was circumvented. Repayment of capital was thus not an essential matter, and a bloated creditor, who was perhaps also a member of the Estates, could well afford to take on these rulers' debts after a number of years of very high returns and thus keep the whole system going.

The administration of law and order suffered badly under this system of large-scale alienation, for the creditors were naturally interested primarily in profit and not in guaranteeing justice and equity for their temporary subjects and neighbours in the *Ämter*. The rulers themselves had alienated any right to inter-

[80] *Ibid.*, pp. 38n., 98–9, 103.

fere as long as the capital sum was not repaid. To this also came unpaid interest which also prevented the redeeming of *Ämter*. Thus rulers lost control especially over their own local officials and generally over internal territorial affairs.[81] It is natural that the Estates of Ravensberg, as the rulers' wealthiest subjects, should have been extremely willing to become the rulers' creditors under these conditions.

The system of alienation could not, however, guarantee that rulers obtained increased revenue for more than a very short time. The ruler remained financially weak, operating from one expediency to the next, and generally dreading to meet the treasury bills that fell due for payment at every Easter and Michaelmas. A system of emergency taxation was developed to prevent total bankruptcy at least, and this the Estates were called upon to help to organize. The Estates in turn agreed that taxes be levied on their own tenants, who were traditionally free from *Bede*, which only rulers' tenants had paid.[82]

The Ravensberg Estates made these emergency grants very infrequently at first, but from the sixteenth century onwards they increased in frequency until they became annual or bi-annual levies. Grants were voluntary and always accompanied by a guarantee from the rulers never to levy them again. In fact these grants were needed increasingly to keep the rulers from bankruptcy. As the Estates were among the rulers' chief creditors, it would have been disastrous for them to let the rulers go

---

[81] Kuske, 'Die Entstehung der Kreditwirtschaft', *Köln, der Rhein und das Reich*, Cologne, 1956, pp. 102–4. In the fifteenth century there was no non-violent way of recouping a debt when repayment was not forthcoming. This was the chief cause of *Fehde*, which itself was only a last resort of self-help by direct force. To prevent a breakdown of the availability of credit and of the public confidence that it entailed, the system of fiefs was incorporated into capital finance as part of a system of pawn and mortgage, whereby fiefs and offices went among other things to the highest bidder. L. Lettenbauer, *Gläubiger- und Schuldnerbegünstigung*, Breslau, 1931, p. 1. This was gradually backed by a system of bank credit control as described by P. J. Marperger, *Beschreibung der Banquen*, Leipzig, 1723, pp. 126–7, *passim*. But whatever harmony there may have been between rulers and Estates in the German territorial-federal system of the fifteenth and sixteenth centuries as regards keeping the peace (*Policey des Landfriedens*), there can in fact have been little permanent success until such a vital matter as debt liability, libel and bankruptcy had been effectively brought under due and swift process of law.

[82] Herford and Bielefeld towns later paid one-thirteenth of the taxes granted. The nobility were exempted. The tenantry and labouring population paid the rest. R. Reinert, *Die Besonderheit der preussischen Städtischen Verwaltung*, Münster, 1968, pp. 55–6.

bankrupt. It is in this light that the recurrent phenomenon of territorial Estates taking on rulers' debts can perhaps be understood. This also enabled the Estates to get their own tenants to help to pay for the rulers' expenditure, over and above the standard rents and services which these tenants continued to render. This applied also to imperial taxation which rulers could not afford to pay without reimbursement from their territorial subjects.

The Estates granted taxes in 1359 and 1497 to redeem alienations. These grants came presumably from the Estates' own tenants and went into the pockets of those members of the Estates among others who were the most pressing creditors as holders of the alienations in question. In 1489 and 1522 grants were made in order to pay off debts incurred in ducal military and diplomatic embassies at the Habsburg court. The 1526 tax paid for marriages in the ducal family. The 1533 grant was to pay the county's quota of the imperial war effort against the Turks. The 1535 tax was used to pay for the suppression of the Münster Anabaptists; it had been granted at imperial assembly and was a circle tax contribution.[83]

Tax grants now became so frequent that the Estates began to seek power over tax collection and audit, in order that money should be spent only on that for which it had been granted. The Estates thereby came into conflict with the prerogative powers of the rulers. The rôle of the Estates as creditors changed to one of political engagement, the more frequent demands for further grants became. Engagement of this sort brought its own responsibilities; above all, it increased a desire among the members of the Estates to secure an economical administration which would, however, also be strong enough to secure the capital which they had invested with the rulers. A public sector of finance was thus emerging as a bone of contention between rulers with their councillors and secretaries on the one hand and the Estates on the other. The question arose in the sixteenth and seventeenth centuries of how best to incorporate this into an older structure of politics. This question was an essential ingredient in the contemporary yearning for *Die gute Policey*. The government was reorganized and enlarged. Ravensberg began to develop into a state.

[83] Nitzsch, *op. cit.*, pp. 106–8.

Poll tax registers survive from 1533 as lists of those eligible for holy communion, indicating the executive part played by village priests in local government. Lists of tenant-farmers assessed for land tax date from 1537, and the records of cattle taxes go back to 1535. In 1574 the Estates granted 17,000 fl. to pay off rulers' debts in return for a say in its allocation, although this concession was not to be taken as a precedent. The ruler made it once only. This shows that the ruler was as cautious with his concessions as the Estates were with their grants. Both sides feared a loss of power through the establishment of new laws and customs by precedent.[84]

In 1535 the ruler opened a lawsuit against his own Ravensberg officials. It involved the *Amtmänner* Lüning and Schack. Lüning was accused of using public services for private purposes, settling his own serfs on the ruler's land, omitting to collect dues for forage in the ruler's woods, exchanging serfs without consent, and molesting the poor. Schack was said to have sold wood from the ruler's forest for his own profit, manufactured lime in the ruler's kilns that was not accounted for, expropriated death and inheritance duties, demanded illegal services, been excessively hard on debtors, and protected refugees and even taken outlaws into service against the decrees of the rulers. Both officials were dismissed, and Lüning's wealth was impounded. Neither seems, however, to have been further punished. They were apparently not subjected to imprisonment or physical violence.[85] Seemingly a Sheriff of Nottingham atmosphere prevailed.

This case opened a twenty-year period of reform, during which new registers were drawn up of the distribution of wealth among the tenantry upon which future taxes could be more equitably assessed. New government posts were created. *Amt* finances were put under newly installed *Rentmeister* and overall control was given to a new *Landschreiber*. There opened a new era of government by *Ordnung*, by decree of the ruler, haphazardly with or without prior consultation with the Estates in full assembly or select committee. A new *Urbar*, a survey of the property held in the *Ämter* as a whole by taxpaying peasants and labourers, was undertaken in 1550–6, largely under the

[84] *Ibid.*, pp. 106–7.
[85] F. Herberhold, 'Das Ravensberger Urbar von 1550', *Westfalen*, 21, 1936, p. 3.

auspices of new officials with the co-operation of members of the Estates and the clergy.[86]

In contrast with the rest of the population, rulers and Estates had one great common interest in that they were landlords. This bound them together and separated them from the rest. It also made the struggle of the wealthier burghers to enter the ranks of the nobility look like an irrelevancy, a luxury with which they and their families could amuse themselves.[87] Rulers and Estates co-operated increasingly in regulating the affairs of their tenants, serfs and servants to their own mutual advantage by compromising over the conflicting needs of private landlords and the tax demands of the rulers. Decrees were issued with monotonous regularity from the mid-sixteenth century until the Napoleonic era, which theoretically at least forbade tenants from leading a private, enterprising life of their own. The duties of tenants and serfs were precisely defined. Their lives came under strict supervision in the spiritual sphere by the Protestant clergy and for the rest by the landlords' and rulers' officials. This view of the world is well expressed in a preamble to the *Landpolizeiordnung* for Ravensberg, decreed by Elector Frederick William in 1687.[88]

After we have heard that our subjects in the countryside of our County of Ravensberg have been spending considerable and excessive amounts on food and drink at funerals, weddings and baptisms, and overmore also on heavy drinking and harmful gatherings such as for the filling of wedding-carts with gifts, entertainments and eating out at inns and suchlike, whereby our subjects have become not only impecunious and short of everything but that also considerable excesses in behaviour have been caused, but that such insolence and wastefulness is totally against our previous decrees and completely unsuitable to the present serious times, through which the Lord God is likely only to be provoked to greater anger and punishments against the Country, so we

[86] Nitzsch, *op. cit.*, pp. 109–10. Herberhold, *op. cit.*, pp. 1–8. G. Griese, 'Die Meierhöfe und ihre Entstehung', 47. *Jahresbericht Historischer Verein Ravensberg*, 1932, pp. 112–13. F. Herberhold (ed.), *Das Urbar der Grafschaft Ravensberg von 1556*, Bielefeld, 1960. Wigand, *op. cit.*, Documents 1–3, 5–6, pp. 285–91.

[87] A. Hoffmann, 'Die Grundherrschaft als Unternehmen', *Zeitschrift für Agrargeschichte und Agrarsoziologie*, 6, 1958, pp. 130–1.

[88] Document, K. Spannagel (ed.), *13. Jahresbericht Historischer Verein Ravensberg*, 1899, p. 136. O. Brunner, *Neue Wege der Sozialgeschichte*, pp. 34–6, Lütge, *Die mitteldeutsche Grundherrschaft und ihre Auflösung*, 2nd ed., Stuttgart, 1957, pp. 19–20, 298–9.

have decreed this new Police Order in addition to previous decrees *in order that our subjects shall not be allowed to render themselves incapable of paying the common taxes of the land* . . .

This order aimed at making tenants, serfs and servants lead a frugal and thrifty existence. They were the chief taxpayers in the Hohenzollern territories. On their rents ruler, official and noble alike had to a large extent to depend. Their labour and produce guaranteed the system. The less the peasants and labourers consumed, the more they could render in rents and services.[89] That peasants retorted to this by irresponsible management is only to have been expected. A *Meyer* of Stukenbrock on the Paderborn-Ravensberg frontier ran his holdings into considerable debt in the later eighteenth century in order to give money, and a chance to buy a way to a better existence with it, to his brothers, sisters and children. He paid 400 tlrs to his son to study at university for a period of eleven years.[90] This farmer was naturally more interested in providing for his family than in the future of his tenancy, which he could never hope to own or regard as his property, although it is true, his children could probably inherit it under the same conditions of

[89] See the final chapter of A. K. Hömberg, *Westfälische Landesgeschichte*, Münster, 1967; the Hohenzollern Ravensberg domain administration produced a surplus, and the Estates were manœuvred into taking a substantial proportion of the county debt, of just under 100,000 tlrs in 1693. They were half paid by 1719. In 1651-2 Hohenzollern income from the county was 21,400 tlrs. Expenditure was a mere 6,000 tlrs. By 1714-15 these figures had both doubled. Ravensberg was thus worth 15-30,000 tlrs net profit annually to Berlin, and could thus play a notable part, considering its size, in paying for the bloated Hohenzollern military machine. Spannagel, *op. cit.*, pp. 166, 186. With a total population of under 50,000 in the 1680s this was quite an achievement, Tümpel, *op. cit.*, p. 193. P. F. Weddigen, *Historisch-geographisch-statistische Beschreibung der Grafschaft Ravensberg*, 1-2, Leipzig, 1790, *passim*. E. A. F. Culemann, 'Geographische Beschreibung der Grafschaft Ravensberg (1745)', G. Engel (ed.), *54. Jahresbericht Historischer Verein Ravensberg*, 1948, pp. 85-187.

[90] F. W. Henning, 'Die Verschuldung Westfälischer Bauernhöfe', *Festschrift für W. Abel*, Hanover, 1964, pp. 11-25. On the tenant farms of later eighteenth-century Paderborn, the total debt usually outran the total market value of the land. On seventy-five farms the average number of creditors was six to seven. Most individual debts were under 100 tlrs in capital. At 5 per cent these were often life assurances and old-age pensions for the small investor, who generally lived close by. Debts probably took priority over rents and taxes, although this naturally depended on the legal skill of the creditor. W. Grothaus, *Die Lage der Eigenbehörigen in Minden-Ravensberg im 18. Jahrhundert*, Münster, 1934, pp. 12-29, attempts to justify serf and tenant farming in the earlier eighteenth century. For a balanced general survey, see W. Abel, *Massenarmut und Hungerkrisen im vorindustriellen Deutschland*, Göttingen, 1972.

tenancy. It was the inevitable result of serf and tenant farming that it did not foster enough interest in the economic well-being of the farm itself. Thus, in a way, repeated decrees forbidding the lending of money to peasants were necessary, but this was only the thin end of the wedge. An early example is the order of Duke William of 1560, following a decree of ruler and Estates of Ravensberg which was worked out at an assembly of the previous year and read out in all the parish churches of the county.[91]

William Duke of Jülich, Cleves and Berg, Count of the Mark and Ravensberg, Lord of Ravenstein, etc.

Dear Councillor and loyal followers, as we have previously agreed with the nobility of our County of Ravensberg and those who have inheritable lands and serfs on them, that a serf shall not have the power, without our or the landlord's prior knowledge and permission, to contract any debts on the lands (which he rents and farms), nor to burden these lands, but if anyone should try to raise money, then he should not pledge the tenancy which he has inherited and which belongs to the landlord, but only the movable property which he owns himself, so We have noticed that many people take up money against the above rules and burden their holdings to a disastrous extent. The result is also that the creditors can not be paid, that the debtors can not render to us and their other landlords the just rents and services which they owe, and that a considerable number of them resist with force the measures which by noble and ancient custom their landlords take against them. In order that such ruin of the land be in future avoided, and that the necessary measures against resistance by force can be taken, we command that the existing rules and regulations be strictly kept, as has also been decreed to be read in public in all churches ... with the addition that, if anyone do anything to the contrary, he be deprived of the money he has raised.

The collection of laws and decrees that Mylius published between 1737 and 1755 gives an impression of how peasants and labourers were dragooned by their landlords and masters in a

[91] Translated from Wigand, *op. cit.*, pp. 286–7. Wigand traced the history of family and property law among the tenantry in the rural districts of eastern Westphalia from the sixteenth to the early nineteenth century. His commentary is based on decrees and laws that territorial governments published from time to time, but it also includes relevant decisions of common courts, legislative and advisory bodies such as rulers' councils and Estates' committees. Wigand performed the task of social historian as well as lawyer and reformer. He published many documents that are available nowhere else.

truly mercantilist way. How far these regulations were effective is, of course, a moot point, but it seems likely that the peasant had to develop a natural cunning not to fall foul of a large number of 'do's and don'ts'. Mylius's documents thus illustrate social mores rather than actual facts. [92]

In his second Repertorium, Mylius, under the heading of 'peasant', started with a long list of what was forbidden to the peasant by decree. In contrast, under the heading of 'Estates' a long list of privileges was given. Each reference denoted a legal right or legal duty, which was then printed in the main parts of the *corpus*. [93]

The peasant was forbidden to have more than three godparents; he was not allowed to carry arms, go hunting, fell young trees, import bad corn, carry on trade or commerce, exercise the rights of a burgher, export or buy cereals, trade in wool or cattle, take on living-in servants without the consent of the lord's officials, drive his carts recklessly in town, sell spirits, take lodgers, brew beer, or buy it from other territories; and if he had an only son, this boy could not become a craftsman, should he or his father so desire, without the consent of their lord.

It was the duty of peasants to do all their buying and selling in market towns, to pay their rents, to plough fixed quotas of land per day, and to report all begging Jews to the local authorities. Where there was an over-abundance of children, each farm was to accommodate two families. The farmer who ran into hopeless debt should, however, be allowed a minimum to keep body and soul together. Peasants were to renew their tenancies at appropriate local offices or chancelleries. Yet it was forbidden to swindle peasants on market days. When peasants ran away, special rules were to be followed for dealing with the culprits. Any peasant or cottar who was one year or more in arrears with his rents and services had legally forfeited his tenancy. No new tenants were to be taken on without credentials. The problem was discussed whether a peasant could issue a valid bill of exchange. Peasants were forbidden to reside in towns without the consent of their landlords. Rules by which

[92] Grothaus, *op. cit.*, p. 5.
[93] Mylius, *op. cit.*, Repertorium II, pp. 115–18, 595–6, registers the duties of peasants and the privileges of the Estates.

tenants were protected were followed by regulations under which they could be sold up. Those who started lawsuits against their landlords without good reason for doing so were to be imprisoned, and no litigant was to obtain legal protection until the defence plea of his landlord had first been heard. Peasants were, however, free from military service. Those who did bodily damage to themselves were not punishable. Each peasant should give local officials twelve sparrow-heads annually. A peasant who was sentenced to prison had to serve his time and was not allowed to buy himself free. Soldiers were, however, forbidden to harass peasants. Landlords had first option on the labour services of their peasants' children.

In return, peasants were permitted under certain conditions to move to other villages and towns. They could keep a certain number of sheep and goats, and export limited amounts of their own cereals. They were directed to sell their wool at certain places, and to brew their own beer only on certain feast-days. They could do their own building, decorating and weaving but only to cover their own personal and family needs.[94]

These decrees applied to individual Hohenzollern territories, and Mylius grouped them all together. Thus they did not necessarily all apply in Ravensberg. It would need quite a stretch of the imagination to think that they were all in fact enforceable. Although these decrees were to some extent the distant fore-runners of modern bye-laws, they made as yet no distinction between the private lives of peasants and their civic duties. Only the members of the Estates, the nobility, wealthier burghers and their equals, the clergy, academics and higher officials were privileged to lead unmolested, private lives.[95]

[94] *Ibid.*, pp. 84–5, 178. Ravensberg *Landesordnung*, 1655; *Landpolizeiordnung*, 1687, Spannagel (ed.), *13. Jahresbericht Historischer Verein Ravensberg*, 1899, pp. 124–39, regulating the hours of work and leisure, and wages to be paid, to the best advantage of the employers. Cf. G. Benecke, 'Labour relations and peasant society', *History*, October 1973, *passim*. Schmelzeisen, *op. cit.*, *passim*. *Lippische Landesverodnungen*, 1. Staatsarchiv Detmold, L 10 Titel 2 no. 14 Appendix A.

[95] Mylius, *op. cit.*, *5*, part 1, p. 59, police order for Berlin and Cölln of 1580. The townsfolk were divided into: (a) patricians, rentiers, judges, councillors, treasurers, and those with university degrees, (b) wealthy tradesmen, master-craftsmen and guildsmen, (c) ordinary burghers and craftsmen, (d) servants and artisans. Cf. Culemann, *Ravensbergische Merckwürdigkeiten*, *3*, pp. 107–28, Frederick William's police order for Bielefeld, 1662, including sumptuary laws on clothing, denoting status—as in the satirical novel, G. Keller, *Kleider machen Leute* (Reclam), in mid-nineteenth century.

The Estates were protected at law and exempt from local, *Amt* jurisdiction. They had access to special privileges when they fought lawsuits against the ruler's officials. Their pleas were to be heard, and their rights, privileges, liberties, competences and properties were to be confirmed. They retained hunting rights, and the right to present to livings and ecclesiastical fiefs. They were to be provided with food and fodder at territorial assemblies. They were to be cited to assemblies where they were provided with *Reverse* which acknowledged in writing the conditions under which they had made grants to their rulers, and *Abschiede* which were written, formal accounts of what the rulers and officials had proposed and what was finally agreed between them and the Estates at the end of an assembly. In return, pledges by the Estates to take over rulers' debts were to be carefully preserved until the debts had been duly liquidated, and then the pledges could be returned to the Estates. If the Estates had to make payment out of their own incomes, then they could recoup themselves by increasing their tenants' rents. Some Estates had the right to export cereals and import salt without paying customs duty.

Territorial Estates formed committees and handed in petitions, complaints and memoranda at the ruler's chancellery. They had to pay an emergency subsidy out of their own private incomes when really necessary. They were to be left in peace to exercise their own jurisdiction over their serfs, but in cases of injustice their decisions could be annulled. The ruler promised not to make important decisions without seeking their prior advice. Estates were to be consulted over taxation. They owed tax on each horse with which they were duty bound to do military service. They should pay a roof tax and a beer tax in order to obtain tax exemption from everything else. They negotiated for fiefs and economic concessions with the ruler. In return they acted as *Bürgen*, or underwriters of his debts, and made their own credit available to him and his officials.[96]

It is in the light of a social background such as this that disagreements between rulers and Estates can perhaps best be understood. For these were largely internal conflicts within a privileged sector of society over divisions of political power and responsibility, which rulers and their officials refused, to a

[96] Mylius, *op. cit.*, Repertorium II, p. 139.

greater or lesser extent, to share with the nobility and burghers by insisting on a prerogative right to rule and take decisions all by themselves, or literally 'by the grace of God alone'. The relations of Elector Frederick William with the Ravensberg noble Estate are an example of this inside contest for political power. Essentially each side needed the support of the other to keep the system going. The ruler needed the financial expertise of the Estates to remain solvent. The Estates needed the executive power of the ruler to guarantee their own social and economic ascendancy at parochial level. This did not deter Elector Frederick William from blowing hot and cold in his policy towards the Ravensberg Estates.[97]

By the later sixteenth century Ravensberg was already run largely by its local nobility, an oligarchy of about twenty-five families with whom absentee rulers were prepared to negotiate in assembly and committee over the running of internal affairs. This was a very small part of the total number of noble families involved in one way and another with Ravensberg. The *Recess* of Düsseldorf in 1609 confirmed the privileges of the nobility, which included recognition of their Lutheran religion, their right to grant taxes, personal tax freedom and freedom from imprisonment. Yet an indication of Hohenzollern power to come was a conflict over the appointment of a *Rentmeister*, or local treasury official, in 1615, when the Brandenburg Viceroy on the Rhine declared that the privileges of the Ravensberg nobility should be accepted and understood *cum grano salis*.[98] However, it was not until the later 1640s, when Elector Frederick William had become more certain that the Ravens-

---

[97] *Ibid.*, 2, part 4, pp. 54–5, Recess of 1653. Spannagel (ed.), *13. Jahresbericht* . . ., pp. 133–5. In 1652 the Ravensberg nobility threatened to unite with Mark-Cleves nobles in opposition to the Elector if he did not abolish the Ravensberg Chancellery set up in 1647. They finally granted him 10,000 tlrs to help him make up his mind to close the Chancellery.

[98] Spannagel, *ibid.*, pp. 100–2, 170. von der Horst, *op. cit.*, gives a list of nobles eligible for seat and vote in the Ravensberg territorial assembly of 1647. The sixteen noble ancestor rule applied from 1692. Hohenzollern favourites who did not qualify could still be accepted with ruler's support, however, as happened to the Danckelmanns and Meinders. The latter started as Ravensberg county treasurers in the 1650s, achieving ennoblement in the third generation for services to the Hohenzollerns. Spannagel (ed.), *13. Jahresbericht* . . ., p. 136. W. Zuhorn, 'Stammtafel Meinders', *Ravensberger Blätter*, 1907. Also list of 175 noble families in Culemann, *Ravensbergische Merckwürdigkeiten*, pp. 138–43. Carsten, *Origins of Prussia*, pp. 258–9.

berg inheritance was to be his alone, that he could dismiss all fears of losing the support of the Ravensberg nobility to his main rivals, the Catholic Pfalz-Neuburgers who were now coming to Düsseldorf.

With the consent of the nobility, Elector Frederich William opened a chancellery for Ravensberg at Bielefeld in 1647, staffed by two non-noble lawyers and two native nobles as councillors. Its cost was to be 3,250 tlrs yearly, and the Estates were to pay this sum annually. Wages were good and even the chancellery scribe was promised 100 tlrs. This itself was as much as each of the six members of the standing committee of the nobility received. The chancellery soon began to interfere with the power of the nobility in local affairs. The non-noble experts especially gave offence. The nobility offered the Elector and certain of his privy councillors bribes of 16,000 tlrs if they would silence the chancellery, but to no immediate avail. One of the chancellery experts, Dr Schlipstein, had previously been the legal adviser of the Ravensberg nobility and one of the noble councillors was from the leading noble family of Ledebur. This is an indication that the Elector was supporting an ambitious faction within local Ravensberg politics when he set up the chancellery, a case of the policy of divide and rule so often favoured by despots.

For 1651–2 the nobility granted 24,000 tlrs in return for re-dress of certain grievances, and for getting the Elector to pay the cost of the chancellery out of domain revenue for one year. This sum was probably a bribe to get rid of the chancellery, for it was large enough to cover its cost not only for one year, but for seven. The Elector badly needed local money to finance his garrisons at Bielefeld, Minden and Lippstadt, and to pay for the recent violent subjection of Herford town to Hohenzollern rule. Yet what finally seemed to make the Elector move in the chancellery affair was the threat of the Ravensberg nobility to unite with the Estates of Mark and Cleves in February 1652. The chancellery was abolished in the next year and the Ravensberg nobility dropped their union plans. The nobility regained control over local affairs until their final eclipse as an independent factor in home affairs in 1719–23.[99]

In 1714 King Frederick William I started to amalgamate

[99] Spannagel (ed.), *13. Jahresbericht . . .*, pp. 129–31, 133, 139.

Minden, Ravensberg, Tecklenburg and Lingen. Ravensberg was now finally considered to be too small an economic unit to be run separately. The Ravensberg nobles and towns made a final remonstrance at an assembly in April 1719 which they apparently did not dare to send on to the King. Herford and Bielefeld especially were jealous of the economic advantage Minden town would now have over them in becoming the seat of a new multi-territorial administration. The Ravensberg treasury or *Amtskammer* was dissolved and its councillors sent to Minden. A new provincial government began work there in 1723. It had taken the Prussian king nine years to get what he wanted, a more centralized administration at least in his domains, in taxation and support of the military machine, and to some extent a simplification of the legal system and tariff systems. Alongside the Cleves-Mark complex the nucleus of Prussian Westphalia had been created. Although the liberties of the Ravensberg Estates remained untouched, the county ceased to be an autonomous state and its nobility ceased to run its affairs through institutions, committees and other local arrangements of their own creation. The nobility had ceased to play an independent role in territorial politics.[100]

True, some politics at communal or *Bauerschaft* level continued free from bureaucratic interference in Ravensberg, but this may have been due only to the fact that the Hohenzollerns were not in control of a sufficiently specialized, complicated and expensive civil service to have achieved such thorough supervision. However, self-determined government had ceased at territorial level in Ravensberg.[101] If the territorial nobility took part in Ravensberg politics, it was from now on as Hohenzollern officials or representatives. It was, as a non-noble Prussian assistant councillor who had been active in neighbouring Tecklenburg boldly put it, one year before the outbreak of the French Revolution:[102]

I have told this story not intentionally as if the Estates still now had as much say as in the days of the ruling Counts, for herein the German

[100] *Ibid.*, pp. 140–2.
[101] R. Meyer, 'Die geschichtlichen Grundlagen der westfälischen Landgemeindeordnung 1841', 47. *Jahresbericht Historischer Verein Ravensberg*, 1933, pp. 10–58.
[102] A. K. Holsche, *Historisch-topographische-statistische Beschreibung der Grafschaft Tecklenburg*, Berlin, 1783 preface.

territories are generally rather alike, if one excepts the Bishoprics. For today such an aristocratic constitution just could not manage to exist, and if it did, it would do the Estates no service, for they now live much more quietly [*ruhig*] than in the days of the Counts, when there was always a shortage of money. For the Estates have preserved their privileges, prerogatives and exemptions, at least the significant [*sic*] parts of them. Only [*sic*] in the legislative and executive power do they no longer share. Other bodies of state have developed and are running the state in a different way. Thus I find it absurd when subjects uphold privileges and rights which they had a hundred or a thousand years ago, and which they mostly usurped, for the conditions of those days no longer prevail today.

The irony of the situation is clear. In Ravensberg just as in Tecklenburg the Estates of the nobility especially continued as a privileged body in the later seventeenth and eighteenth centuries, but politics were conducted somewhere else. Although nothing was abolished, there was also no self-determined political development.[103]

(vii) *Tecklenburg*

In the backwoods of Westphalia, astride the hill-forests that run across the road from Münster to Osnabrück, one may perhaps be surprised to find a tradition of co-operation between ruler and Estates in a very small county of its own.

The medieval dynasty of Tecklenburg had steadily built up a territory for itself but had not been able to keep control of more than some scattered pieces after the private wars of the fifteenth and early sixteenth centuries, in which the Tecklenburgers had notoriously taken part. When this dynasty died out in the male line in the sixteenth century, there was a scramble for the remaining scattered pieces, for Tecklenburg, Lingen and Rheda. The inheritance went to Bentheim and Nassau-Orange, which brought involvement with Spanish troops who accordingly occupied Lingen in the 1560s as part of an effort to encircle and crush the Nassau-Orange-led revolt of the Netherlands. Tecklenburg subjects were faced with several foreign rulers, endlessly fighting for their inheritance in and out of the imperial

---

[103] R. Brandis, *Die historische Entwicklung und die heutige Stellung des westfälischen Amtmanns*, Göttingen, 1928, pp. 13–18.

courts, before finally being sold to the new Prussia of Frederick William I and suffering the same fate as the county of Ravensberg.

In the middle of the sixteenth century Tecklenburg left minutes of discussions held between rulers and Estates. It is a reflection on the area's backwardness that no towns were politically active as Estates. Tecklenburg and Lengerich towns were not called to territorial assemblies and they seem to have had no autonomous town councils. Tecklenburg town is a collection of houses cascading down an imposing hill upon which the ruler's castle stood. It had a town judge who was the ruler's official and who also gave account at one stage to the Estates on the spending of a grant. But who, then, were the Estates?

They were the heads of nine families of *Burgmänner*, or castellans, who owed their positions to hereditary military service to the rulers. This seems to have been a feasible arrangement in the fourteenth century but must be regarded as archaic in the mid-sixteenth century. More surprising is the fact that these castellans were capable of making remarkable political deals with their rulers whilst still keeping the old feudal ties alive. These deals were partly religious and judicial in content but overwhelmingly they dealt with finance and the profits to be made out of an agricultural economy.[104]

In 1562 the Regent, Countess Anna, confirmed the privileges of the castellans and for the first time seems to have provided them with a constitutional document. Anna promised to support the castellans in any private wars which they might get involved in with outsiders and to give them refuge in her castles. This, it must be remembered, occurred seven years after the crucial

---

[104] Holsche, *op. cit.*, is the only monograph on Tecklenburg. It was written from the sources when the author was a Prussian official there. His section on the rulers and Estates, 1554–1622, is a précis of the *Landtagsprotokolle*, pp. 146–73, 265–9. Cf. Staatsarchiv Detmold, L 9, L 10, L 37 XVII no. 2.

Such records provide a direct insight into ruler-Estates politics, and they are a starting-point for assessing the relations between territorial and federal politics, see G. Benecke, 'Relations between the Holy Roman Emperors and the Counts of Lippe as an example of early modern German federalism', in *Westfälische Forschungen*, 1972.

The case of Tecklenburg shows that an obscure territory with absentee rulers could also produce its own internal political development with Estates keeping it from bankruptcy and disintegration. Cf. the study of castellans in neighbouring county Bentheim, H. Voort, 'Burgmannen zu Bentheim', *Osnabrücker Mitteilungen*, 76, 1969, pp. 1–38.

Reichsexekutionsordnung, and two generations after the first crucial *Landfrieden* were published at imperial level expressly forbidding private war.

Tenants and servants of the castellans were not to be taxed in any way by the rulers without the consent of the castellans. Nobles were to be allowed to let their pigs fatten on any common land that they pleased. If differences arose between a castellan and the ruler or among the castellans themselves, then the ruler was to meet all the castellans together to decide the issue. The ruler promised not to appoint outsiders as *Drosten* or *Amtleute*, but instead was always to appoint Tecklenburg nobles *where available*. (The castellans were of course themselves the nobles referred to.) The phrase 'where available' is perhaps a typical ruler's let-out clause, for it cannot have been very feasible or practical to try to build up a territory into a state on the services of nine families only. Yet this concession showed that at least the nine families concerned wished for this to be tried.

Tecklenburg was not to be alienated, mortgaged or sold without the consent of the castellans. Only they were to make emergency tax grants, as a group, and they were to have an equal share with the rulers in collecting any such grants from the county's tenants, serfs and labourers.

A contract of Count Arnold of Bentheim-Tecklenburg with the castellans in 1580 restricted the number of cartage and labour services which Arnold could annually still demand from the castellans' tenants as general overlord.

Count Eberwien of Bentheim-Tecklenburg seems not to have been able to intimidate the castellans. He could not get them to grant him money unless they could have full control over its expenditure. An assembly at Lengerich in 1559 never got beyond discussion of the castellans' grievances, expressed as a remarkable financial proposal to Eberwien.

The castellans demanded that the treasure which Count Conrad of Tecklenburg had hoarded in Tecklenburg castle be restored; that 4,000 fl. lent to the Count of Mansfeld be used to pay dowry arrears demanded by the Count of Solms, which ran at 5,000 fl. and were to lead to a *Reichskammergericht* lawsuit for which regular payments to keep it pending were made for a century; that the 1557 tax grant levies be reimbursed because they were spent on that for which they had not been granted. The castellans then proposed that Eberwien alienate the whole county to them for five years against a fixed annual rent of 2,000 fl. For this they would grant five years of taxes to be paid by the peasants, servants and labourers. The castellans, however, wanted more control over tax-collection and also demanded that the county treasurer swear an oath of loyalty to them as well as to the ruler. If Eberwien demanded higher tax payments than were actually allowed in the granted quotas, then the castellans demanded power to cut these back. Finally in any financial agreements with their Bentheim rulers the castellans insisted that the Counts of Oldenburg and Waldeck act as guarantors.

Four months later Eberwien gave his reply to the castellans' package deal. Count Conrad had made over in writing 'many' thousands of *Gulden* to his son-in-law Eberwien, who had spent 3,000 fl. alone on just one military campaign. The right to demand repayment of the Mansfeld debt was not his and so Solms could not be satisfied from this source in the foreseeable future. The judge of Tecklenburg town had given an account of what the latest tax grant had been spent on and Jürgen Harde, along with the Ledeburs, leaders of the castellan opposition, were fully aware of this. The castellans had greatly overestimated the value of Tecklenburg revenues to the rulers, and Eberwien had thus to decline their bid to take over because there would not be enough left to pay the debts if they paid him; and they also presumably wished to recoup themselves. He was, however, delighted to accept their five-year tax grant, but would not bargain away the county in order to get it. He also refused the unprecedented demand that the ruler get other rulers to guarantee loans which he got from his own Estates. Such a diabolical twist was allowed to the Estates of Tecklenburg, to the nine castellans. What then could the Estates of Germany's bigger territories have proposed during this century of their greatest extension of power?

Finally, the castellans made another bid in 1559 and offered to take on 8,000 fl. of Eberwien's debts if the Counts of Oldenburg and Waldeck would act as guarantors and if one-half of the Lordship of Rheda was alienated to them. Eberwien refused. Negotiations between ruler and Estates had broken down. For two more years Eberwien asked in vain for financial support. Then he died in 1561 and his widow took over. Countess Anna immediately called the castellans together and asked for a circle tax. It was refused. Two months later it was granted. What caused the volte-face?

Already in the autumn of 1561 Anna had set up her own armed band by borrowing 3,000 fl. It was ostensibly her Westphalian circle contingent. It seems much more likely, though, that she used it to intimidate her Tecklenburg castellans. Anna's regency lasted from 1561 to 1579. Of the fifteen assemblies reported in this period, eleven granted substantial taxes. There were six territorial grants, to pay off debts, to pay for the suitable upkeep of the ruling family and to fight inheritance disputes in the imperial courts. There were five grants of a federal, imperial nature to pay for the upkeep of the *Reichskammergericht* and to pay taxes originally granted at imperial and circle assemblies by the rulers themselves.

Those who seem to have paid up were the tenant-farmers, servants and agricultural labourers, tenants and employees of both rulers and castellans. Taxes were on types of farms, classified according to the amount of labour-service owed from them, and also on wage-earners as poll taxes, and on the head of cattle each peasant owned. Even the castellans overestimated the wealth of this tax-source and by 1620 there were nearly 17,000 tlrs of tax arrears. Even so, the position during this period in Tecklenburg is clear. The ruler's leading social position as feudal overlord was one thing, but his economic situation showed quite another picture in all its naked truth. Basically, everything depended on the Estates. The ruler was only *primus inter pares*, and even this seemingly only on the strength of the fact that at one time at least he had had more serfs and tenant farms than anyone else in the county.[105]

Conclusion

It has been shown that the small territories dealt with in Part II have all at some point in the early modern period possessed an

[105] Holsche, *op. cit.*, *passim*. R. de Vries, 'Die Landtage des Stifts Essen', Münster, 1934, Chapter 6 and Appendix. M. Ritter, 'Zur Geschichte deutscher Finanzverwaltung im 16. Jahrhundert', *Zeitschrift des Bergischen Geschichtsvereins*, 20, 1884, pp. 11, 28–31, showing the crucial part played by imperial federal tax

identity of their own. We have seen how internal affairs were being worked out in thirteen territories in the Lippe region. The differences between constitutional practices, between ecclesiastical and secular powers, episcopal and monastic, princely and comital forms of government do not outweigh the similarities of territorial politics. Each territorial society was essentially composed of the same social groups and was facing the same problem of how to finance its own court, administration and defence to the continued advantage of the legally privileged orders, the territorial nobles and burghers. In some territories the Estates retained more control than in others, but essentially rulers and Estates had to co-operate within each territory to retain local independence.

These small units were capable of an autonomy of their own which was basically uneventful and orthodox if not always socially stultifying. But within what kind of a framework did this separate territorial existence take place? What prevented early modern Germany from falling in like a house of cards? Does the answer still lie with the great power of a few large dynasties and territories, or can one see more that is of value in ties between more of the small territories and the federal Empire? For why otherwise did the large territories not swallow up their small neighbours without further ado? In terms of military organization, taxation, and justice, what was the relationship between small territory and imperial whole? Was it at all distinctive, or did the large territory predominate over the small territory as well as over the Empire as a whole, as has usually been assumed without much further inquiry?

We have outlined the vigour and diversity as well as some of the absurdities of internal territorial affairs in the Lippe region. Even if they were unprogressive, local people were overwhelmingly in control of their own affairs. We now turn to a detailed study of Lippe itself and of Lippe's own rôle within its region, its circle and the Empire. For by studying this in depth we come to the vexed questions of how 'weak' really was the early modern German Empire and, most important, what contribution did the German small states in their own right make to the German tradition of federalism?

---

demands in the development of territorial Estates' tax methods in Jülich between 1521 and 1548. Carsten, *Princes and Parliaments*, pp. 269–72.

Part Three

◇◇

Society and Politics in One State: the County of Lippe

◇◇

VII

Lippe Society

WILL it ever be possible to understand the early modern Empire piece by piece, territory by territory? A recent survey in English gives 7 Electors, 80 ruling princes, 150 ruling counts and lords, about 2,000 imperial knights and 66 imperial free towns.[1] This makes a total of 2,303 territories and jurisdictions. To write the history of Germany as a whole becomes an impossible task. To make things worse, the particular federal structure of politics prevents a useful division into central and regional affairs. German history is thus at one and the same time rather similar to what would be a history of Westminster combined with a Victoria history of all the counties of England, plus, where appropriate, the rest of the British Isles right down to the Isle of Man, the Channel Islands and Lundy. Equivalently, it is as if England had continued under the Heptarchy and never experienced the unifying Danes and Normans.

If early modern Germany had had a stronger central government, then the history of the county of Lippe would in a way perhaps be similar to the history of a small English county. As it is, no simplifications can be made, and German history has to be recognized for what it is, a vigorous entanglement of component parts. This needs unravelling. Before that has been done, no history of Germany can do justice to the course of

---

[1] D. Hay, *Europe in the fourteenth and fifteenth century*, London, 1966, pp. 187–203. R. B. Wernham (ed.), *New Cambridge Modern History*, III, pp. 327–8. There were still 278 territories in the imperial assembly list drawn up by Joseph II's tutor in mid-eighteenth century, H. Conrad (ed.), *Recht und Verfassung des Reiches in der Zeit Maria Theresias*, Cologne, 1964, pp. 530–40. Cf. Appendices 2 and 3 below.

events. Condemnations of the early modern Empire do not clarify, just as the concept of the 'sick man of Europe' does not illuminate the Eastern Question or Turkish history. German history is thus at the outset a mass of uncertain statistics and an endless search into historical atlases.

According to a rather generous contemporary estimate for the first decade of the eighteenth century, the Empire, including Bohemia and the Spanish Netherlands, had a population of something under twenty-eight million. Sixty-five ecclesiastical territories covered 14 per cent of the land and had 12 per cent of the population. About forty-five dynastic principalities covered 80 per cent of the total area with 80 per cent of the total population. Approximately sixty dynastic counties and lordships shared 3 per cent of the land and $3\frac{1}{2}$ per cent of the whole population. This left about sixty imperial towns with 1 per cent of the land but $3\frac{1}{2}$ per cent of the population. The imperial knights finally managed to control 2 per cent of the land but only 1 per cent of the population of the Empire.

Thus ecclesiastical territories had $3\frac{1}{4}$ million subjects, ruling princes $22\frac{1}{4}$ million, counts and imperial towns one million each, and the knights half a million.[2]

The territories of north-west Germany which have here been dealt with in the last two chapters covered 7 per cent of the land and had 6 per cent of the population of the whole Empire. This worked out at under two million people in 1700. Of this Lippe made up 2–3 per cent of the regional whole in both land area and population. This was only one-fivehundredth of the imperial whole. Even this figure is high, for it reckons the population of Lippe at 50,000 at the beginning of the eighteenth century.

Lippe covered a compact area of 1,200 square kilometres, not including four enclaves in the near south and west. A thirty-mile journey or a day's steady riding would on the whole suffice to traverse the county of Lippe. The total population, according to another estimate, was about 35,000 in 1590, rising to over 40,000 before 1620. It may have been down to 30,000 in the 1640s and back at 35,000 by 1700. One-third of the popu-

[2] H. v. Zwiedineck-Südenhorst, *Deutsche Geschichte in Zeitraum der Gründung des Preussischen Königtums*, Stuttgart, 1894, 2, pp. 179–84, following statistics produced by the Austrian War Archive to assess the campaigns of Prince Eugène.

lation lived in the villages of the flat north-west. Moderate numbers lived in the central hill country, which was more easily fortifiable and thus included the main towns. The Osning forest and the sandy wastes of the Senne, running into the county of Ravensberg, were barely habitable. Its fame lay in the rearing of a very fine strain of horses.[3]

Between one-sixth and one-fifth of the population lived in the towns. They were said to have suffered especially during the later 1620s, 1630s and 1640s as a result of being just within the imperialists' zone of occupation, where they faced the Swedish front across the middle Weser at Minden and Hameln.[4] Five walled towns, Lippstadt, Lemgo, Horn, Blomberg and Detmold, were founded by the Lords of Lippe in the late twelfth and early thirteenth centuries. To them was added Uffeln, grown rich on its salt industry, in the fifteenth century. The oldest was Lippstadt, an enclave since the fourteenth century. It was partitioned as a result of inter-territorial warfare in the fifteenth century between Lippe and Mark.[5] Only Lemgo gained full local autonomy. Yet an integral part of Lippe politics was a civic tradition and Lemgo was even strong enough at the beginning of the seventeenth century to rebel against the introduction of Calvinism within its walls by Count Simon VI.[6]

Lippe had slowly but surely gone over to Lutheranism after the death in 1536 of Simon V, the last ruler to cling to the old faith. The religious change had occurred under the general direction of Philip of Hesse, as Lippe's overlord and protector. Like Hesse, Lippe survived the Catholic despotism of Charles V. The Lutheran victory in Lippe was sealed by a *Kirchenordnung*,

[3] M. Kuhlmann, *Bevölkerungsgeographie des Landes Lippe*, Remagen, 1954, pp. 10, 27, 40, 108. G. Wegemann, 'Grösse und Volkszahl Lippes im Wandel der Zeit', Staatsarchiv Detmold, manuscript C 308.

[4] H. Stünkel, *Rinteln im dreissigjährigen Kriege*, Rinteln, 1952, maps pp. 113–15. A 'war horrors' account is E. Stegemann, 'Die Grafschaft Lippe im dreissigjährigen Krieg', *Lippische Mitteilungen*, 3, 1905, pp. 1–155. Cf. Staatsarchiv Detmold, Knoch, Repositur Dreissigjähriger Krieg, L 56–60.

[5] H. Klockow, *Stadt Lippe—Lippstadt*, Lippstadt, 1964. E. Kittel, 'Die Samtherrschaft Lippstadt', *Westfälische Forschungen*, 9, 1956, pp. 96–116. Lippstadt retained its lords until 1366–76. Between 1445 and 1609 it was shared with Jülich-Cleves, thereafter until 1851 with Brandenburg-Prussia, *Lippische Mitteilungen*, 33, 1964, p. 313.

[6] A. Falkmann, *Beiträge zur Geschichte des Fürstentums Lippe*, Lemgo and Detmold, 1857–1902, 6, pp. 316–75. The Lemgo rebellion of 1607–17 led to litigation at *Reichskammergericht* and *Reichshofrat*.

or decreed church-system, produced with the help of the Estates during the regency of Simon VI in 1571. This date has also been generally regarded as marking the beginning of government by proclamation and decree in the county.[7]

Between 1603 and 1639 Lippe went Calvinist, not because Simon VI, a councillor and servant of Rudolf II, was an ardent admirer of the Heidelberg court and its political extremism, but because Simon seems to have been genuinely convinced of the rightness of Calvinist doctrine. However, he was not strong enough to convert Lemgo, which successfully resisted by force of arms until Simon's successor admitted the failure of his father's policies by making an uneasy peace in 1617. At a period when Calvinist and Jesuit extremists were taking over federal politics, Lippe could still stage a Calvinist-Lutheran civil war of its own, in which the traditionalist burghers won and their innovating rulers went empty-handed.

This burgher victory was, however, won at a price. Lemgo remained Lutheran with its own church and school government, but it lost the seat of the comital administration of justice to Detmold. Lemgo in the sixteenth century was the capital of Lippe, especially whilst Simon VI made Brake castle, just outside its walls, his main residence.[8] In the seventeenth century the Counts moved into their castle within Detmold town, which from now on expanded at the expense of Lemgo. In this Lemgo paid heavily for asserting its religious freedom against the Counts. Yet having forfeited the economic advantage of being the seat of court and administration to Detmold, Lemgo was free to play an independent rôle in Estates' politics, and it remained the centre of the county's overall trade and finance.[9]

There were only two Estates in politics, those of the local nobility and of the six towns. There was no Estate of the clergy.

[7] *Lippische Landesverordnungen*, 1, preface and pp. 1–172. The Calvinist system was finally promulgated in the long-overdue *Kirchenordnung* of 1684. For earlier decrees, H. Stöwer (ed.), 'Die lippische Amtsordnung vom 11. März 1536', *Lippische Mitteilungen*, 31, 1962, pp. 145–7. *Ibid.*, 26, 1957, pp. 48–78. Staatsarchiv Detmold, D 71; L 9 vol. 1–3. R. Wolf, 'Der Einfluss des Landgrafen Philipp etc. ...', *Jahrbuch des Vereins für Westfälische Kirchengeschichte*, 51–2, 1958–9, pp. 94–6.

[8] W. Süvern, *Brake, Geschichte des Schlosses und der Gemeinde*, Lemgo, 1960. O. Gaul, *Schloss Brake und der Baumeister Hermann Wulff*, Lemgo, 1967.

[9] E. Kittel, *Geschichte der Stadt Detmold*, Detmold, 1963, pp. 48–181. K. Meier, *Geschichte der Stadt Lemgo*, Lemgo, pp. 23, 73–81, 123–31, 147–83.

Until the Reformation Lippe was not an ecclesiastical unit of its own. Before the 1530s the old faith ran an archdeaconry in Lemgo which came under the Bishops of Paderborn. This covered only part of the county, where the ecclesiastical rulers of Minden, Osnabrück, Münster, Corvey and Herford also had rights, lands, tithes and jurisdictions.

There were native abbeys and nunneries, which came partly or wholly under the rulers of Lippe, at Falkenhagen, Cappel, Blomberg, Möllenbeck and Marienfeld, among others, as well as in Lemgo and Detmold.[10] Most of these survived the Reformation, continuing to exist as endowments especially for unmarried daughters of the ruling dynasty, territorial nobility and wealthier burgher families. Such an establishment was the convent of St Mary in Lemgo, which was founded in the thirteenth century for Lippe's 'higher daughters' and survived the doctrinal changes and secularizations of both Lutherans and Calvinists.[11] A similar establishment was Convent Cappel, situated in an enclave near Lippstadt. At Falkenhagen the Jesuits established themselves during the Catholic ascendancy in the Empire in 1626, a fact that led to litigation between Lippe and Paderborn in the imperial courts and at the Protestant section of the imperial assembly until the expulsion of the Jesuits in the 1770s.

The religious foundation in Blomberg town did not survive the Reformation in Lippe. Its religious trade was based on pilgrimage and healing rather than on the provision for the genteel, which is what the other foundations specialized in. Some of its land went to the territorial nobility and other ecclesiastical fiefs and lands were exchanged or purchased by the rulers as part of the perpetual trading in feudal and allodial property which was a general feature of medieval and early modern times.[12]

[10] Staatsarchiv Detmold, D 71 no. 66, folios 37–8. Religious houses paid nobility tax.

[11] E. Kittel, *Kloster und Stift St Marien in Lemgo 1265–1965*, Detmold, 1965; 'Das Kreuzherrenkloster Flakenhagen', *Festschrift G. Schreiber*, Münster, 1963, pp. 137–66.

[12] Staatsarchiv Detmold, D 71 no. 66, folios 30–2. The lands of the noble family of Wend were bought by the regency councillors of Count Simon VI on advice of the Estates of Lippe in 1563. The cost was 100,000 tlrs of which nobles and towns, according to Archivarius Knoch, contributed 15,000 tlrs and 30,000 tlrs respectively. The peasants paid the rest. Staatsarchiv Detmold, L 1 E XVIII 3.

In 1542 the nobles' and burghers' deputies, together with the regency councillors of Bernhard VIII, met representatives of the clergy to discuss ways and means of protecting religious houses which clung to the old faith.[13] There were other exceptions during these troubled times when clergy joined the councillors and Estates in assembly to discuss the state of religion, but they seem to have soon disappeared from the Estates' assemblies and committees. When the special case of religion came up, the clergy were naturally on call as experts, but wider political powers they did not have.

One of the earliest lists of those present at a territorial assembly in 1538 includes the Lutheran pastors of Horn and Detmold, although the latter's name was erased from the minutes.[14] This assembly discussed specifically religious affairs, but the Lutheran towns of Lippstadt, Lemgo and Saltzuffeln stayed away from it. The pastors of Horn and Detmold were cited to give an account of themselves and their new faith. A particularly large number of nineteen nobles appeared, along with the town councils of Horn, Blomberg and Detmold. As late as 1538 Lutheranism had still not got a full hold on the county, as Lippe balanced between Reformation Hesse and traditionalist Jülich, Paderborn and Cologne. Yet the future lay with the new faith as it obtained increasing support from Philip of Hesse, at whose court in Kassel young Count Bernhard VIII was getting an otherwise traditional, chivalrous upbringing in the 1540s.[15]

Through this Lippe came under the interdict of Charles V and had to pay 'compensation' for supporting Hesse after the Habsburg victory over the Smalkaldic League in 1547.[16] It was of little avail that ruler and Estates pleaded their loyalty to the Emperor. They had rendered military service to their Hessian overlord as early as 1542 and even after the declaration of treason in 1546, although with barely a score of knights,

[13] Staatsarchiv Detmold, L 9 vol. 1, folio 114.

[14] Magister Mentz was active as an adviser on religion and on Reformation doctrine for the inner circle of the Estates' regency government in the 1540s.

[15] Staatsarchiv Detmold, L 9 vol. 1, folio 41 verso. W. Butterweck, *Die Geschichte der lippischen Landeskirche*, Schötmar, 1926. F. Gerlach, *Der Archidiakonat Lemgo*, Münster, 1932. Wolf, *op. cit.*, pp. 50–96.

[16] H. Kiewning, *Lippische Geschichte*, Detmold, 1942. pp. 158–69. The original fine was 30,000 fl. Lippe actually paid 10,000 tlrs. Staatsarchiv Detmold, L 37 XVII. H. Berentelg, *Der Schmalkaldische Krieg in Nordwestdeutschland*, Münster, 1908, pp. 39–42.

instead of the fifty that Philip had demanded.[17] Yet Lippe had also sent a contingent to the Turkish wars in 1543 and had raised the appropriate imperial taxes to pay for wages and equipment.[18] It helped little, however, that the regency councillors and deputies of the Estates had supported both sides: they could not preserve neutrality. They were forced to contribute first to the Hessians and then to the Habsburgs, according to the fortunes of war and federal politics.

An example of how financial policy drew Lippe into the web of politics spun by the big territories appears in 1542, when the Duke of Jülich-Cleves was attacked by the Habsburgs in a war over possession of Gelderland. The Duke, as a creditor and holder of alienated Lippe lands, sent one of his Ravensberg nobles with powers to demand financial aid from the regency councillors in Detmold. The Estates' deputies were consulted. They wanted the Counts of Hoya and Mansfeld, the former as regent, the latter as a kinsman, to agree to help, by paying their own debts to Lippe. The county would then be able to redeem its alienations, notably Enger and Lippstadt, from Jülich-Cleves, whilst the latter so badly needed money, and whilst the terms were thus very favourable. There was, however, a real fear of acting too openly in case this should further displease the Emperor.

In the outcome, Hoya and Mansfeld delayed and failed to pay up. Yet leading territorial nobles in Lippe invested 3,000 fl. of their own with Jülich-Cleves, and the mayors of Lemgo and Blomberg also pledged sums of money, which they were wise enough to leave unspecified in the minutes which the regency councillors took. The chance of a favourable investment was thus too good to miss, even at the risk of offending the Habsburgs.[19]

Jülich-Cleves asked Lippstadt to pay an emergency tax along with the other towns in the county of Mark. This led to complaints before the regency councillors and Estates in Detmold, yet the town had to pay up. It hoped to raise 700 tlrs or 650 fl.

[17] Staatsarchiv Detmold, L 9 vol. 1, folio 128 verso.
[18] Staatsarchiv Detmold, L 9 vol. 1, folios 31–2, 130.
[19] Staatsarchiv Detmold, L 9 vol. 1, folios 134–6. Wegemann, *Die Bevölkerung Lippes* (*Handschrift*), folio 3. P. F. Weddigen, *Historisch-geographisch-statistische Beschreibung der Grafschaft Ravensberg*, Leipzig, 1790, 1, p. 20.

by selling winter cereals at a price that was exactly twice that of an official corn-rent paid into the county of Ravensberg by Lippe one month later.[20]

What numbers and what sort of people ran Lippe's affairs? An unofficial source may serve here as a useful introduction. Calvinist clergyman Jacob Sartorius was active up to 1608 in Lippe and he published a list of 'praiseworthy nobles, officials and towns' which he had noted whilst in office in Lippe. His list contains twenty noblemen, of whom seven were *Drosten* and two were leading courtiers, one as *Hofrichter* and the other as *Landdrost*. The rest lived on their lands. Thus nearly half the nobles that Sartorius mentioned were also ruler's officials.

There then followed nineteen *Amtmänner*, of whom several were members of well-established Lippe burgher families. One was *Oberamtmann*, and another concurrently held the posts of judge and scribe in Blomberg town. The official heads of *Vogteien*, units of local government below that of the *Ämter*, were also being given the title of *Amtmänner*.

There were no privy councillors or university-trained lawyers in the list and Sartorius did not remember any beyond one confidential treasury scribe. He also scorned his own ecclesiastical colleagues, for there were no ministers or pastors in his list. Sartorius had lost his job because of conflict with his colleagues. Among the towns, Horn was omitted but five market towns were added. These were the *Flecken* who paid taxes along with the nobility, as distinct from the proper towns with their burghers and the villages with their peasants.[21]

The twin pillars of Lippe society were its two Estates. But there still existed a feudal structure containing both nobles and burghers which was in the hands of the ruling dynasty. The resilience of this way of life provided the sheet-anchor in early modern as in medieval times.

In the sixteenth and seventeenth centuries, there were any-

[20] Staatsarchiv Detmold, L 9 vol. 1, folios 138–9. What the Lippe dynasty owed to the Lünings was again owed to Lippe by the Regent, Count Jobst of Hoya. Hoya went 'bankrupt', and the Lünings were bought off by Lippe with cheap cereals. Staatsarchiv Detmold, L 43, Hoya. Measurements for Lippe, 1 Fuder = 4 Molt = 48 Scheffel = 2,400 Litres. F. Verdenhalven, *Alte Maasse Münzen und Gewichte*, Neustadt, 1968, p. 23.

[21] F. Flaskamp, 'Eine abseitige Statistik der Grafschaft Lippe', *Lippische Mitteilungen*, 32, 1963, pp. 197–8; *Lippische Mitteilungen*, 33, 1964, p. 281; *Lippische Blätter für Heimatkunde*, 2, 1964, p. 7.

thing up to sixty noble or equally tax-privileged establishments in Lippe. About thirty of these were run by families that resided permanently in the county. A good attendance of nobles at an assembly was twenty. A comital administration could find suitable office for about ten of these.[22]

Up to the sixteenth century most noble families preferred to live in the towns. Between 1200 and 1500 some ninety feudatories lived in town houses, as against only twenty-one in castles and towers that were scattered over the county. This speaks against a military background for the majority of Lippe's feudatories and later nobles. During the sixteenth century many noble families moved on to their lands where they built themselves fortifiable mansions. They took to farming, got rid of their larger tenants and made good their claims to tax exemption and evasion in the face of new comital and federal demands for money.[23] The wealthiest kept on their town houses, but there was a steady shrinkage as town councils became less generous to exempted nobles within their walls. Only Lemgo kept its grandest families, enriched by a successful patriciate of its own.

There were twenty-four noble fiefs in Lippe, of which twelve were held solely of the ruling dynasty. There were thus far fewer fiefs than tax-exempted establishments. The latter included ecclesiastical and strictly non-noble holdings as well as lands held by outsiders only indirectly under the jurisdiction of the Lippe rulers. Between the sixteenth and eighteenth centuries only five fiefs escheated through the failure of heirs, and a further eight were sold to the rulers. This meant that there was usually one marketable fief per generation. The top rung of Lippe landed society was static and stable.

Despite the coming and going of families, a hard core of Kerssenbrock, Donop, Friesenhausen, Exterde, Grote remained as farmers and rentiers, and they moved in and out of office under the early modern rulers. New families like Hammerstein, Piderit, Hofmann, Hofmeister, Heyderstedt, Schmeriemen. and Kötzenberg arrived or obtained ennoblement through

---

[22] W. G. L. von Donop, *Historisch-geographische Beschreibung der Fürstlich Lippeschen Landen in Westphalen*, Lemgo, 1790, pp. 18–142.

[23] Staatsarchiv Detmold, D 71 no. 66. Archivarius Knoch, 'Status Ministerialis militaris et realis equestris lippiaci ordinis generalis', manuscript 1795–8, folios 8–28.

government and court service. Wulf and Münchhausen came and
went through money-lending against feudal land security. Old
families died out or moved their main seats into other territories, as did Wend, Mengersen, Westphal, Borch and
Schwartz.[24]

Between 1200 and 1800 some 300 noble families passed
through the books of the Lippe rulers. Although this represented a fairly high turnover of families dying out or moving on,
the number of fiefs that they vacated was very much more
restricted. Name and title often obscured material differences,
and the real problem is to discern the differences of wealth and
circumstance behind the uniformity of title and gentility.[25]

At the top of Lippe's modest noble pyramid were those who
held fiefs against knight service. In 1532 thirty knights with
their esquires participated in the siege of Lutheran Lippstadt.
Seven years later forty knights rode out to help the Count of
Hoya. Regular service was also seen under Philip of Hesse up
to 1547, and thereafter under the Guelphs and Maurice of
Saxony before the walls of Magdeburg old town, as directed by
Habsburg Commissar Schwendi in the early 1550s. At a grand
occasion in 1550 nineteen nobles who owed knight service
appeared with eighty-one horsemen in full military array, to
give company to the Elector of Cologne, who was also an
official regent and kinsman of the Lippe dynasty.[26]

Above all Lippe society was unremarkable here, except in
one point: it was remarkably archaic. As late as the mid-
sixteenth century the feudal levy was the essential feature of
Lippe's war-effort in the general contest unleashed by the
megalomania of Charles V. It was also on the strength of their
feudal military effort that the nobles obtained general tax-
evasion at the expense of the towns and countryside after the
1550s, thereby causing a split in the political co-operation of the
Estates which lasted into the nineteenth century.[27]

Lehentage or feudal assemblies were an important part of
fifteenth- and sixteenth-century Lippe society. They were quite
distinct from the *Landtage* or Estates' assemblies that began to

[24] Knoch, *op. cit.*, folios 28–33, 50–2.
[25] H. Schmidt, *Lippische Siedlungs- und Waldgeschichte*, Detmold, 1940, pp. 36–7.
H. Krawinkel, 'Die Grundherrschaft in Lippe', *Lippische Mitteilungen*, 15, 1935,
pp. 149–56. Knoch, *op. cit.*, folio 46.   [26] Knoch, *op. cit.*, folios 44–5.
[27] Staatsarchiv Detmold, L 9 vol. 1.

be called from the early sixteenth century onwards. To all intents and purposes the same people attended *Lehentage* and *Landtage*, but in different capacities. Whereas the latter flourished, the former did not survive beyond the sixteenth century. In the seventeenth and eighteenth centuries vassals made their own piecemeal arrangements with each new ruler and his chancellor. An attempt in the 1730s by Regent Dowager Wilhelmine to revive the *Lehentage* was an expedient to raise money. Her demand to the nobles to send in the original feudal contracts for renewal sounds naïve indeed in an age when the legal system had long since supported feudal property as the possessor's real estate.[28]

Rulers found increasing difficulty in preserving their feudal rights. The military effort in the mid-sixteenth century had been bought by allowing extensive tax-evasion to their vassals. In a council meeting of September 1625 it was agreed to hire mercenaries to defend the county against marauders. The nobles' feudal levy was no longer the reality it had still been in the previous civil war under Charles V.[29]

The feudal assembly as an institution did not go out with a whimper. It met for the last time in full pomp and circumstance to install Simon VI in 1579. In July Simon held an Estates' assembly where he outlined his plans of reform in church, police, law and federal taxation. He then went on procession through his towns and villages and finally held a carefully prepared feudal assembly on 15 September.[30]

Sixty-three feudal contracts were confirmed by the chancellery.[31] Of these only about twenty were granted to burghers and non-nobles. The nobility still seemed to have the upper hand, only their real position in this property market was less favourable, owing to sub-infeudation to their own non-noble financiers and creditors. There was thus a considerable discrepancy between the number of formal fiefs and the actual number of holdings.

Even so, Simon VI tried to make something more out of his feudal assembly than just a grand occasion at which holdings

[28] Order of 15 September 1735, Staatsarchiv Detmold, L 41a IV 207.

[29] 'There are hardly six noble families left who can equip themselves', Knoch, Repertoria L 9 and L 12.

[30] Staatsarchiv Detmold, L 9 vol. 3, folios 109–11; D 71 no. 19 (cited as *Mannbuch*). [31] *Mannbuch*, folios 318–403. Falkmann, *op. cit.*, 4, pp. 9–11.

were inventoried. To him the affair was an exchange of privileges whereby both sides should show the material confidence in each other that would be the basis of political co-operation during the coming reign. Simon thus called a feudal court together whilst his vassals were all suitably assembled. A detailed report of the proceedings has survived.[32]

The feudal court was held exclusively among the vassals themselves. They chose their own judge and assessors, who were duly approved by Simon himself. At the court meeting that followed, Simon sat in silence, whilst the elected judge sat next to him and conducted affairs. Rules of order and peace in court were issued and agreed to by those present. As his procurator Simon was allowed to have the Secretary of Lemgo town to safeguard his interests in the court. The vassals then in turn put their grievances in question form. Fourteen questions were put. The vassals wanted to know what punishments they or their colleagues would be open to if they did not renew their fiefs, which was above all a question of saving fees. Under what procedure would they be prosecuted? How long was the ruler intending to withhold enfeoffment of heirs? What rule of inheritance did Simon intend to follow in cases of family dispute? Would Simon hold to the practice of giving 'a year and a day' to the vassal before starting any proceedings? Under what conditions would Simon give out any fiefs again that fell into his hands?

Simon then got vassals, who were as likely as not to have been briefed before the meeting, to ask questions that would give him, as overlord, the chance to restrict the rights of the vassals if at all possible. So Hermann Schilder asked for the conditions, if any, under which vassals could burden, alienate or diminish their fiefs without the consent of the lord.[33] This was an identical point to one around which peasant-landlord relations revolved, and a question that has changed very little in its importance to landlordism in any age. Lemgo burgher and vassal Dietrich Cothman then asked *how* a vassal would lose his fief if he served with his lord's enemies. Also, what should a vassal do if he had more than one lord, and the lords were fighting each other? Vassal Bernd von der Lippe then asked the vital question, which court of appeal would stand above this feudal court? What appeals would be valid?

[32] *Mannbuch*, folios 405–10. [33] Question 9.

The last question was turned against Simon. The *Reichskammergericht* remained the only valid court of appeal in default of a Lippe *Hofgericht*. By the 1590s Simon had, however, remedied this defect. From then on the nobility came under internal jurisdiction for the first time. The new post of court judge became a sought-after office among the nobles.

Simon conceded that fiefs were divisible. He promised magnanimously not to prosecute any late-comers seeking renewals and to seek his rights against any vassal only in a court of the vassal's peers. All that Simon obtained in return was that the jurisdiction of a feudal court of peers was to be binding and that fiefs were inalienable in the first instance.[34] Thereafter the vassals took their oaths of loyalty.[35]

Simon had indeed achieved very little in this traditional way, but it is significant that at least an attempt had been made. If there was a policy towards vassals at all in the later sixteenth and the seventeenth centuries, then it came out in the system of assessment for the voluntary tax grants that the nobility made. If the ruler encouraged the assimilation of fiefs by outsiders, then he could tax them on their produce much more readily than if they were vociferous natives in the assembly. But then if fiefs were in the hands of natives, he could expect to be their patron and receive their credit. At all events Simon and his successors steered a halfway course in this, in an attempt to gain through both policies.

The book of Lippe vassals concluded with a fragment from 1632–5, when Count Simon Ludwig's officials made a last attempt to make an inventory of fiefs and their holders. Nobles and burghers were now segregated. Twenty-three nobles and only three burghers were listed. The 'out' faction of Donop and Grote refused to participate in a scheme that the 'in' leader, Landdrost Johann v. d. Borch, was first to support.[36] From then on the nobility formed their own curia with responsibility for running the appropriate lawsuits and collecting the voluntary tax grants that from time to time occurred.[37] Whilst the duties disappeared, feudal privilege remained for another 150 years.

---

[34] Falkmann, *op. cit.*, 4, p. 10.   [35] *Mannbuch*, folio 408.

[36] *Ibid.*, folios 430–9. H. Grote to L. von Donop, 18 November 1635, Staatsarchiv Detmold, L 10 Titel 1 no. 7.

[37] Staatsarchiv Detmold, L 10 Titel 2 nos. 15, 33; Titel 5 no. 2.

Over the burghers the rulers had no direct control. Burgher status was, like any other title, a commodity to be purchased or inherited. The loan of a sum of money against an annual rent would often facilitate such a process. The successful financier always had a chance to buy his way into the inner circle of town council families. From there he had the chance to represent his town at the assembly, to handle financial and judicial business, and to commend himself to his ruler. Thus the family of Tilhen rose from the Lemgo town treasury to prominence in the chancellery and as pensionaries of the ruler between 1550 and 1650. The patrician family of Wippermann likewise entered ruler's service but did not become nobles.[38]

As within the nobility, so within the burgher group the main difference was one of quality. Lemgo burghers included the chief financiers of Lippe. When the first bankruptcies came in the 1580s the craftsmen began to see their chance of a change in town leadership. The hopeless indebtedness of Lemgo during the transition from the debased mark-schilling currency to the hard taler-groschen system came in the first two decades of the seventeenth century. The town financed its own rebellion, and when that was concluded it had to face twenty years of imperialist troop occupation. But by the 1590s the surpluses upon which a sound economy and civic tradition had been based in the sixteenth century had already been replaced by annual borrowing to cover depressing deficits. The real problem was that after the mid-1620s credit was also hard to come by.[39]

By sporadic exploitation of the Lutheran mob against Calvinist rulers the common burghers had at times in the early seventeenth century been able to get the upper hand against the old town council families. Yet by far more skilful exploitation of superstition, a faction of the old oligarchy had always managed to get back into the saddle. Its opponents were hunted down as witches. The mob was enlisted and then cowed. The reign of terror extended to all layers of town society. It financed itself as ruler and town council shared the property of those who were

[38] Stadtarchiv Lemgo, Kämmereirechnungen 1557, 1584–9, 1599; Kr. 42, vol. 1, 'Gemeine Stadt Pensionarii (1621–7)'.

[39] Stadtarchiv Lemgo, Stadtobligationen und Renten, Repertorium der Urkunden und Abschriften, Kämmereirechnungen. The treasury records show that town income was supplemented by the sale of burgher status to newcomers and outsiders.

condemned. The name of Lemgo became a synonym for witch-hunting and torture in the seventeenth century.[40]

This served its purpose. The burgher oligarchy regained control and the town retained local autonomy. Despite its heavy indebtedness, the economic position improved in the early eighteenth century. Yet burgher bankruptcies continued at an average of one every two years all through the seventeenth and eighteenth centuries. Even so, nobles and rulers continued to build in the town, and to do their trading and financing through the town.[41] The big difference was that trade became local, as long-distance Hansa contacts folded up.

None of the other towns had such wealthy or independent burghers as Lemgo.[42] The next richest in the sixteenth century was Saltzuffeln. Here the salt masters certainly made enough to buy up surrounding land and to build substantially, but not in stone. The rulers retained control over the salt industry and farmed it so heavily that it became unprofitable during the seventeenth century.

Through their own town judges who were very much *ex officio* members of the town councils the rulers kept a strict eye on town council affairs in Blomberg, Horn and Detmold. The burghers in these towns were overwhelmingly craftsmen or small tradesmen and shopkeepers. Each town was also the centre of a rural district, with a castle within its walls where the ruler's *Amtmann* presided. The only thing that these small towns had in common with Lemgo was that they also sent their mayors to the assembly. Thus, although ruler's control was in-direct, the ruler had enough key appointments to local office to bring pressure to bear on all burghers except the rentiers of Lemgo. Pressure meant, above all, consent to taxation.

The last group with a degree of independence in the form of tax-freedom and freedom of movement were the officials. Until

---

[40] Meier, *Hexen, Henker und Tyranen, passim.*

[41] Stadtarchiv Lemgo, Repertorium, Konkurse. For a building enterprise, see the rulers' Lippehof, Meier, *Stadt Lemgo*, pp. 15, 30, 161, 237. For continued ecclesiastical patronage, Kittel, *Stift St Marien, passim.* Lemgo's financial difficulties influenced the credit situation of the whole county, especially government and nobility between 1620 and 1730. Staatsarchiv Detmold, L 28 K Section XI nos 1–3. In the seventeenth century the *Hofgericht* handled a case a year involving a Lemgo burgher in debt.

[42] Stadtarchiv Lemgo, Kämmerei. In 1585 Lemgo income was 32,102 marks. Detmold income in 1581 was only 7,245 marks, Staatsarchiv Detmold, L 111 C 1.

the seventeenth century these were chosen chiefly from the Estates. Although salaries were small, inherited wealth was often even smaller. [43] Nobles and burghers with only a name and some talent were keen to become councillors, secretaries, treasurers, local lieutenants (*Drosten*) or administrators (*Amtmänner*). Equally men without a name but with money to invest were attracted into office as security for their loans or in lieu of rents. [44]

The big expansion came first of all in the ruler's household. In the mid-sixteenth century Bernhard VIII built and expanded. His son, Simon VI, continued the grand style of living. Several castles had permanent staffs for the ruling family. Simon had his chamberlains, flunkeys, musicians, dwarfs and jesters like his better-endowed equals. When insolvency came at the end of his reign in 1610, his eldest son had to deal with the problem of financing a staff of over 200 on a residual income of well under 10,000 tlrs a year. By skilful management among the sons of Simon VI, household costs were reduced. Household numbers shrank during the regencies in the war period, especially in the later 1640s. They then stayed at well under 100 for the rest of the century. [45]

As the household stabilized in numbers, so the administrative side of the comital establishment continued to grow. Under Simon VI office in the administration had already become more important than office in the household. Increasing judicial and financial business meant that aspirants had to go into training in the law faculties of neighbouring universities and academies. [46]

[43] Staatsarchiv Detmold, L 92 A Titel 63 no. 81.

[44] Staatsarchiv Detmold, L 10 Titel 2 no. 11; L 4, K. Schwartz, on 27 March 1554 in a very modest noble family inheritance division included a noble who made a career in the administration and married rich.

[45] Staatsarchiv Detmold, L 63 B 12–I; L 16 A no. 2–1 O.N., Varia A; L 52 AP, A; L 92 A Titel 63 no. 63. In the early eighteenth century Elector George of Hanover had a household of 360. In England he retained 950, see *Niedersächsisches Jahrbuch*, 40, 1968, p. 190. In comparison the Count of Lippe kept about 70 (including central officials), still a disproportionately large number, Staatsarchiv Detmold, L 37 XVII no. 6.

[46] A. Schmidt, 'An welchen auswärtigen Schulen und Hochschulen haben Angehörige der Grafschaft Lippe bis zum Beginn des 19. Jahrhunderts ihre Ausbildung gesucht?', *Lippische Mitteilungen*, 15, 1935, pp. 233–302. Count Simon VI paid stipends to three sons of Lippe clergy to the value of 50 tlrs a year each for study at Calvinist academies and universities in the 1590s, Staatsarchiv Detmold, L 92 Z 1a, Kämmereirechnungen.

The Latin school of Lemgo flourished, and vicariates under elder kinsmen were eagerly sought wherever a saving on new investment in office could be made. Qualification was the least difficult task to accomplish. It was much harder to find a place.

In terms of the early modern concept of society, those who owned land and houses and had capital invested with rulers' and towns' treasuries were the only people with a claim to participate in politics and administration. They were the only ones with a recognized stake in the county. Everything and everyone was weighed in terms of 'quality', of status. Yet the whole system depended on an agricultural economy, and on the small-scale marketing and craftsmanship that went with it. The peasant machine kept everyone going.

In Lippe the peasant was a tenant-farmer. He was either a serf or a freeman, but that did not alter the fact that he was a tenant. From the sixteenth century onwards many serfs bought manumissions and in the war years in the 1630s and 1640s these were a firm item of treasury income.[47] Above all manumissions meant freedom of movement, as often as not from one tenant farm to another. In a society thus based on property and long-term investment, labour was cheap. The man on a wage was no match for the man on a fixed income. The family that toiled was no match for the family with a stake in the land. The question of the distribution of property was all-important, and wherever there were gross distortions, there a wasteful system of tenancy set in.

In the early seventeenth century new inventories of tenants, farms and the services due from them were drawn up. These were the *Salbücher*.[48] By this time there were about 5,500 farms in the county, which were divided into seven classes, according to age of settlement, size and quality of land. Well over a half of all farms carried serfdom with them, and less than 10 per cent of these serf-run farms were owned by others than members of the ruling dynasty in Lippe. Under one-third of all farms were run by free tenants. Lippe peasant society was thus basically static. Serfdom meant that each family was tied down to a specific farm for generation after generation. The most important fact of all was that 70 per cent of all tenant farms were rented

[47] Staatsarchiv Detmold, L 92 Z 1a; L 1 G XXXII–III.
[48] H. Stöwer and F. Verdenhalven (eds), *Salbücher der Grafschaft Lippe*, Münster, 1969.

directly from the ruling dynasty. The Estates, the church, those with exemptions of one kind or another and landowners living outside the county itself shared ownership of the remaining 30 per cent.[49]

The peasantry has found a place in the records that survive because its lords and administrators kept a record of rents and taxes, with a view to conserving property or increasing burdens. Thus in the second decade of the seventeenth century an attempt was made to keep registers of every tenant and every serf that came under the jurisdiction of the ruler's rural districts, in the *Bauerschaften* of the *Vogteien* and *Ämter*. Between 1614 and 1620 the peasants of 180 districts were recorded. Nearly 3,000 tenant-farmers had their cattle counted, their harvest assessed. Their rents in kind and in money, their labour services, their extraordinary tax quotas, debts and mortgages were recorded.[50] Lists of serfs and freemen were drawn up. An attempt was made to keep track of serfs who moved away.[51]

The early modern Lippe peasant was caught up in a strict administration that supervised his life. There was no record of dissent. No Lippe peasant rebelled, no one took part in the great movements that affected southern Germany or Austria.[52] The lone voice of serf Knickhencker survives among the documents. In 1593 he humbly appealed straight to Count Simon for tax reduction, claiming that he was only a labourer, helping his father to clean the dikes and fishponds, and that the Estates' tax commissioners had assessed him as if he were already a full serf tenant-farmer.[53] That a serf could presume to appeal straight to his ruler may have been the safety valve to peasant grievance which was not possible in less homely and primitive administrations.

One of the real problems that seventeenth-century govern-

[49] Krawinkel, *op. cit.*, pp. 143–8. W. Meyer, 'Guts- und Leibeigentum in Lippe', *Jahrbücher für Nationalökonomie und Statistik*, 12, 3rd series, 1896, pp. 801–837. The ruling dynasty was the largest landowner, and supported the tenantry in the courts against loss of lands, rights and contracts, for the tenants paid the bulk of the state's taxes in the form of land tax.

[50] Stöwer and Verdenhalven, *op. cit.*, pp. xv–xvi, xxx–xl, 31. Examples translated in Benecke, 'Labour relations and peasant society', *History*, October 1973.

[51] Stöwer and Verdenhalven, *op. cit.*, pp. 425–37.

[52] See G. Franz, *Der Deutsche Bauernkrieg*, Munich, 1965. Grüll, *op. cit.*, Benecke, *op. cit.*, Lippe peasants were conformists.

[53] Staatsarchiv Detmold, L 37 XVII no. 30.

ments in Lippe tried to face was how best to tax labourers and servants. Poll tax came in and employers were ordered to count heads. To make this attractive, decrees were published fixing wages at a level favourable to the employers. In the appropriate attempts to draw up registers, the common folk below the burghers and tenant-farmers for the first time entered recorded history. At the same time they were getting into the parish registers. The government began to see that all people who were not actually paupers were worth taxing, and they thus had to be kept track of.

To the farm labourers of Lippe the peasant was an enviable man. If the peasant was not the labourer's employer, then he was at least a person with responsibility, a manager. To the servants and artisans of the towns a burgher was also a grand person. He had bought town jurisdiction, he was in business. In 1656 the judge of Horn town sent to the chancellery a list of common people who had refused to be classified as servants, or to have their children classified as such. They opposed the new rules of wage maximum and taxation of wages which ruler and Estates had decreed in the previous year. The judge outlined the unrest that this new tax law had caused. He then briefly noted what each common person had actually been saying to him in order to avoid classification. All those who could stated that they would withdraw themselves or their children from service. Most invented a reason for keeping 'indoors'. This is one of the rare occasions when the basic stratum of society made its voice heard, and it spoke with truculence. The element of some form of strike activity should not be discounted here.[54]

The problem was solved two years later, at least for the time being, by increasing servants' wages by up to 50 per cent in a new taxation decree. Thus, in fact, the increase in taxation was borne by the employer rather than the employee, which after all made economic sense: for it was of little use to tax those who lived from hand to mouth. In 1655 servants' range of pay was 2–8 tlrs a year plus livery. In 1658 it was 3–11 tlrs a year plus livery.[55]

[54] Staatsarchiv Detmold, L 10 Titel 2 no. 7. Fifty-six heads of non-burgher households in Horn town were questioned for opposing the new domestic service tax, Benecke, *op. cit.*, for a complete translation of the document relating to this strike.

[55] *Lippische Landesverordnungen*, 1, Polizeiordnung 1620, Taxordnungen 1655,

In salaries alone, leading members of the government were getting between twenty and forty times as much as labourers and servants. A middling nobleman, who was assessed slightly above the average whenever the nobility granted a *don gratuit*, was worth 400 tlrs a year just before he was sold up for insolvency. He had been drawing up to 1,200 tlrs a year out of his estate and his creditors would no longer stand for it. Finally the Estates expected the ruler 'to live of his own' on a gross domain income of 42,000 tlrs a year.[56] With these relationships Lippe society turned its full circle in the middle of the seventeenth century. How could such a rigid small economy retain independence within the federal system?

[56] Staatsarchiv Detmold, L 63 A 12; L 92 A Titel 63 nos 63, 81; L 11 IV 5C; E. Kittel, H. Stöwer and K. Sundergeld, 'Die älteren Lippischen Landesgesetze und Ordnungen', *Lippische Mitteilungen*, 26, 1957, pp. 70–2.

1658. Staatsarchiv Detmold, L 10 Titel 5 no. 2 vol. 2. Cf. Huskens, 'Arbeitslohn in Münster im 16. Jahrhundert', *Westfälische Zeitschrift*, 58, I, 1900, pp. 231–5. Abel, *Massenarmut*, pp. 15, 17, 22–3, 25.

VIII

Rulers' Finances and Estates' Taxation

The territorial Estates' constitution in the county of Lippe is without doubt of such great age that one can no longer trace its real origin either in specific agreements and statutes or in the true exercise of rights stemming from them. Yet we do know that the nobility and towns were in the 13th century already closely bound together in government and administration.

Archivarius Knoch, 1775, Staatsarchiv Detmold,
Repertorium L 11

Public finance really developed between the 15th and 17th centuries. Former loans of ruling princes and towns at that time became the debts of the territorial Estates.

A. Manes, *Staatsbankrotte* (Berlin, 1918), p. 21

In Lippe a modest estate management developed into a state. The fifteenth century is a record of deeds, debts, land and tax registers. The sixteenth century provides government and Estates' assemblies. The towns retain their collective economic power: the nobility are the new success story and the ruling dynasty goes from strength to strength. The seventeenth century consolidates rulers, officials and nobles: the towns are entrenched. The county of Lippe becomes a fatherland to rulers and ruled, wealthy and poor. One-fivehundredth part of the Empire becomes a territory. The economic system, that no one at the time seems to have had a good word for, makes this possible.

What do the records tell us about this system?

181

By the thirteenth and fourteenth centuries the Lords of Lippe have entered the light of history and the records show an exchange of rents and duties, privileges and personal rights between rulers, knights, burghers and serfs.[1] Rulers live on direct profits from domain and jurisdiction. Extraordinary taxation is for rare emergencies only. The ruler is still exclusively a landlord or an overlord: he is not the embodiment of a government living from one ever more frequent tax grant to the next. Those who are in a subordinate but contractual relationship to him are still likely to bargain piecemeal for their own status and economy. He does the same to them as they do to their tenants. To consider himself a somebody, a man needs property and investments: to be accepted as a man of note he needs a pedigree as well. Social and economic life was still near the farmyard.

By the 1400s the pace of life was speeding up even in Lippe. There was more exchange and it brought more diversity and uncertainty, more venturesomeness and unpleasantness. Annuities and alienations began to determine men's relations with each other. High finance as yet remained outside the sphere of 'right': it was still a matter of honour or slander, self-help and private war. The law had still to evolve to contain but not destroy or markedly hinder capitalism in the interests of public peace and security.

Rulers' debts are scattered piecemeal through the fifteenth-century records. They give very little of a constructive pattern. In fifteen debt contracts between 1410 and 1499 the Lords of Lippe as debtors were given no special treatment as high nobles or territorial rulers. Of the 10,000 fl. involved in these contracts, over 60 per cent was borrowed from the rulers' own entourage, the *Ministerialen* or *Burgmänner*, soon to be emerging as families of the noble knights of Lippe, the early modern local nobility. The purpose of the documents was above all to get an admission in writing of a money-lending transaction. Four of the fifteen contracts were, on the face of it, direct alienations, mortgages of two degrees of unfavourableness to the debtor-owner.

First, for as long as the loan or any part of it plus acceptable interest or damages was outstanding, the creditor had the use

[1] H. Conrad, *Liegenschaftsübereignung und Grundbucheintragung in Köln während des Mittelalters*, Weimar, 1935.

and profit of specific property that the debtor had alienated to the creditor for this purpose. Redemption was then fixed for specific times—thus Easter in one year, or Michaelmas in twelve years' time, all dates notifiable six months in advance. Investments on these terms were naturally eagerly sought and Lippe noble families especially benefited by this form of extreme alienation, combining it with feudal tenure and high office.

The second degree of alienation was also profitable but the creditor received a fixed rent or annuity out of the debtor's income and property. As such it was an insurance: it secured the value of specific property in the event of its being lost by the debtor–owner. Only if the rent was in default could the creditor distrain on this piece of property that was especially designated for the purpose in the contract. There were infinite varieties of this procedure, depending on the reliability of the prospective borrower as a credit risk. Towns did better than rulers and high nobles: Lemgo better than its Lord of Lippe in this early period.

These fifteen samples show that in the fifteenth century in Lippe capitalists were often the future native nobility. It was their business skill in their rulers' affairs that helped them to establish themselves as the leading Estate. They did not get rich as his fighters or castellans, but as his creditors, and dealings were not in chivalry, armour and steel but in pigs, oats and *Goldgulden*. Rulers were made or broken on their policies of alienation. [2]

As chancellery and chamber did not emerge as government in Lippe until the later sixteenth century, the beginnings of rulers' finance have to be salvaged from what remains of rulers' private records. A colleague of Archivarius Knoch put these remnants in alphabetical order in 1785, scattering and burying the old among some of the newer financial records. [3] A number of paper

---

[2] Staatsarchiv Detmold, L 1 G XXXIVa, Schuldverschreibungen, 14 April 1410, 1411, 30 October 1414, 23 April 1427, 29 September 1446, 1455, 5 October 1456, 25 May 1458, 21 April 1471 (12 May 1416), 11 May 1477, 26 January 1490, 16 April 1497, 29 September 1499. *Lippische Regesten*, 2126, 2203, 2534, 2577, 2855. B. Kuske, 'Die Entstehung der Kreditwirtschaft', *Köln, der Rhein und das Reich*, Cologne, 1956, pp. 48–137. H. Planitz, *Das deutsche Grundpfandrecht*, Weimar, 1936, pp. 35–7, 104–28, 185–9, especially 'Substanz- und Nutzungspfand'.

[3] Staatsarchiv Detmold, Registrator Wasserfalls Repertorium der Cammerschulden Acten, 1785, Repositur L 92 X with nineteenth-century additions and twentieth-century clarifications. E. Kittel, *Lippische Mitteilungen*, 26, 1957, pp. 48–55.

drafts when parchments were drawn up regulating rulers' alienations and sales of rents against borrowed capital, and also some debts that remained on paper, have survived.[4] Here a third system of finance can also be seen at work. The borrower put up guarantors, usually from his noble and official entourage as well as from his town councillors, to secure his credit. The first and third systems of finance, namely *Verpfändung* and *Bürgschaft*, caused trouble and were as likely as not to have been a basic cause of *Fehde*, private war by ancient right of self-help in the fifteenth and early sixteenth centuries. Thereafter the development of imperial and territorial legislation provided more effective alternatives in civil courts, in *Kammer und Hofgerichte*.

In Lippe the emergence of a territorial assembly is a relatively late phenomenon. It was there by the 1530s, but earlier references to ruler-Estates bargaining are extremely rare. However, the names of later fifteenth- and earlier sixteenth-century guarantors, or *Bürgen*, to rulers' debts generally coincide with those that appear in the earliest territorial assembly and regency council lists from the later 1530s.[5]

Thus at an assembly in 1538 eighteen nobles appeared, all members of families that had been lending or guaranteeing rulers' debts since the 1450s. They were currently helping to finance dead Simon V's debts, thus keeping the regency administration going, and the county autonomous.[6] They prevented any loss of land or jurisdiction. It was the remarkable co-operation of a clique of noble and burgher families in politics and finance, as regency councillors, local satraps (*Drosten* in the emerging *Ämter*), and chief money-raisers in town and country

---

[4] Staatsarchiv Detmold, Schuldsachen 1463–1539, L 92 X no. II–71, cf. L 1 G XXXIV a–d.

[5] F. L. Carsten, *Princes and Parliaments in Germany*, London, 1959, describes territorial assemblies from the later fourteenth century onwards. Staatsarchiv Detmold, L 9 vol. 1; L 92 X no. II–71; L 1 G XXXIV a–d.

[6] Staatsarchiv Detmold, L 9 vol. 1 folio 41 verso, including Oeynhausen, Wend, Donop, Exter, Friesenhausen, Kerssenbrock, Werpup, Westfal, Offen, Barckhausen, Eichmann and Landwehr: L 1 G XXXIVa, 30 October 1414 (Megersen?), 25 May 1458 (Westfal), 21 April 1471 (von der Borch), 16 April 1497 (Barckhausen), 30 April 1514 (Wend, Westfal, Borch, Oeynhausen, Werpup, Schwarz, Exter as guarantors). Thereafter no *Bürgschaft* was completed without some local noble acting as surety. In a debt contract of 10 April 1531 there were even twenty-eight noble and burgher guarantors of whom twenty-six were Lippian or from the immediate vicinity. L 92 X no. II–71, 1479 (Zerssen), 1494–5 (Wend, Borch), 1530–1 (Haxthausen, Zerssen), 1539 (Mengersen, Kerssenbrock, Donop).

that kept Lippe together for the ruling dynasty in the first half of the sixteenth century.[7]

The sums that local nobles and patricians lent or secured for their rulers explain why these notables could consolidate their position institutionally in Lippe society and politics as the two Estates of nobles and towns in the early sixteenth century. They acted as controllers of the economy, in land, agriculture and towns' treasuries. Favourable tenures and offices made it permanently worthwhile for them to continue to support the ruling dynasty.

By the sixteenth century the best thing to achieve was still a fief, and a country seat now became a greater priority than a town mansion. Office as satrap or councillor better secured the holding and the social pre-eminence of the family that went with it. Speculation in alienations and land-tenures offset the hazardous duty of guaranteeing rulers' debts. In the last resort the families that exploited a ruler's wealth knew that they had to guarantee his debts or risk losing what they had gained from the domain. Ruler-Estates relations were determined by a complex of credits and debts, where the spectre of bankruptcy, disintegration and take-over by another territory was staved off only by the realization, by local creditor and debtor alike, that the existing system was the most mutually advantageous to both sides. At all costs, therefore, it had to be kept going. If this was achieved then only biological failure within the ruling dynasty could upset territorial autonomy. At all events the claim to participate in territorial politics and society depended on how much was invested in the government that could keep the ruling dynasty going. The sources of gain were extremely limited in Lippe's primitive agricultural economy. Economic ambitions had thus to be satisfied by cruder exploitation, violence and deprivation of others than is more apparent with systems operating nowadays that produce more, consume more and waste more.

At the beginning of the sixteenth century the Lippe rulers

[7] Of nobles, especially Mengersen, Wend, Kerssenbrock, Donop, Exter. Of burghers, Cothmann and Höcker. These were the inner circle of councillors available for consultation in Detmold or Lemgo as a committee or commission of the full territorial assembly of Estates (about thirty to forty noble families and the councils of six towns). Staatsarchiv Detmold, L 9 vol. 1 folios 42 verso, 45 verso, 61.

were probably worth well under 10,000 fl. a year.[8] Money came from a complex of sources, but not appreciably from extraordinary taxation. Domain administration was the most important sector of the Lippe economy. It was badly eroded by alienations of whole *Ämter* and jurisdictions, a policy that reached a crisis level under Bernhard VIII.

In the 1550s the Lippe Estates realized that alienations could only benefit a few individual members at the expense of county society as a whole and accordingly they all helped to buy out the Wends and increase domain revenue by redeeming the second largest *Amt* of Varenholz. Alienation increased extraordinary taxation for the whole body of members and the tenantry. However, each new financial method created a balance between the vested interests of the old and the advantages of trying the new. If the ruler could live fully on his domain revenue, then the Estates could be dispensed with in politics. If alienations were eliminated or not replaced by equally lucrative tax and rent farms and anticipations, then members of the Estates would no longer be able to finance rulers' debts. Thus rulers might look for support elsewhere, especially outside the county. This would destroy the social pre-eminence of the Estates, notably at court and in office, and would mean that they lost the benefits of patronage. To keep the economic *status quo* demanded a balance between old abuses and new expedients.[9]

Alienation was the counterpart of investment in government as much as extraordinary taxation the ancestor of regular taxation. Rulers and officials were the precursors of ministries and government departments, the Estates of private enterprise and big business. All combined to run their territory.

The money that Lippe rulers borrowed in the earlier sixteenth

[8] H. Kiewning, *Lippischer Geschichte*, Detmold, 1942, pp. 101, 104–5, 121–2, 134–40, 215–17. Staatsarchiv Detmold, L 92 Z 1a; L 10 Titel 2 no. 11; L 16 Varia 1; L 92 A Titel 63 no. 78; L 9 vol. 3, folios 136–41.

[9] The alienated Wend *Amt* of Varenholz which the Estates redeemed in the 1560s was the second largest source of income for Lippe, Staatsarchiv Detmold, L 92 Z 1a; L 63 A 12 B 12–I, II; L 92 A Titel 63 no. 3. Of 220,000 tlrs delivered by four *Ämter* (excluding *Amt* Detmold) between 1651–65 to the treasury, *Amt* Varenholz provided 130,000 tlrs. The policy that rulers should live of their own regular domain income was by no means totally unrealistic in Lippe. Staatsarchiv Detmold, L 37 XVII no. 6 and the *Landkasse* accounts (fragments from the 1690s, continuous from the 1740s). For economic theory, T. Mayer, *Handbuch der Finanzwissenschaft*, 1, Tübingen, 1926, pp. 239–43.

century tided them over the transition between living totally on domain revenue and being supported by Estates' tax grants. Yet nothing was substituted for a large domain income all through the early modern period, however eroded finances were by alienations and anticipations. The property situation demonstrated this. Of all tenant farms 67 per cent were domain. On total income from serfs the rulers claimed 55 per cent, on rents 47 per cent, on tithes 34 per cent of the territorial whole. Domain holdings even tended to increase at the expense of nobles, burghers, free peasants and 'foreign' landowners, according to statistics from the land registers of the fifteenth to eighteenth centuries.[10]

The rulers' economy was thus basically sound and it was this fact that may have ameliorated ruler-Estates relations, for despite recurrent conflicts over taxation and court expenditure, money from domain still outweighed money from Estates' grants when it came to the day-to-day financing of the territory.[11]

Between 1512 and 1570 thirty-five contracts were examined, involving the rulers in borrowing, guaranteeing or actually lending anything up to 7,000 fl. a time. Of 38,320 fl. and tlrs borrowed, 32,000 was secured by members of the territorial nobility. Of this the rulers immediately repaid 2,000 fl. and lent out a further 6,200 fl., the latter a bad debt, as it turned out, to the Guelphs. A further 7,000 fl. were guaranteed to near-bankrupt Count Gebhard of Mansfeld, possibly as part of a marriage agreement that saved the direct line of succession in Lippe. This money was also lost.[12]

Thus the Lippe nobility bore the brunt of rulers' finance, and it was they who, from the contracts examined, had to put up with the loss of over one-third of what they had lent to the dynasty. Their pre-eminence in Lippe politics and society was being paid for. That debts were liquidated, however, is shown

[10] H. Krawinkel, 'Die Grundherrschaft in Lippe', *Lippische Mitteilungen*, 15, 1935, pp. 146–8. W. Meyer, 'Guts- und Leibeigentum in Lippe', *Jahrbücher für Nationalökonomie und Statistik*, 3rd series, vol. 12, 1896, p. 803.

[11] Compare domain and tax income in the treasury accounts, Staatsarchiv Detmold, L 92 Z 1a, with the level of debt in the *Landkasse* accounts.

[12] Staatsarchiv Detmold, L 1 G XXXIVa, contracts from 29 September 1512 to Easter 1570, Knoch Repositur, L 1–G 1 folio 138. Mayer, *op. cit.*, pp. 214–32, especially p. 215, gives figures from the larger territories. E. Bamberger, *Zeitschrift für die gesamte Staatswissenschaft*, 77, for the medieval background.

by the cancellation of seals and cross-cutting of parchment in the contracts examined.

The worst upheavals were caused by the really large money contracts of the earlier sixteenth century. They were not based on property as security but merely on the good faith, the 'noble honour', of guarantors. At a time when a whole *Amt* was worth a mere 500 fl. against alienation, sums up to 7,000 fl. were being secured by rulers and their entourages on good faith alone.[13] This involved high and low nobles, patricians and burghers in a common activity that of necessity gave them a sense of unity as rulers, officials and Estates, especially when money was borrowed from outside Lippe. It made the idea of conflict in territorial politics between rulers and Estates an artificiality. It rather created local and native ties as rulers and Estates co-operated to perpetuate a common interest in a given area of land and jurisdiction. The idea of Lippe as a territory sprang from the achievement of rulers and Estates in keeping their economic independence.

In Lippe rulers and officials governed with the approval of local nobles and town councils at all times. What conflicts there were occurred as internal squabbles between rulers, officials and Estates. They led to no lasting breach. There was no absolutism, because the Estates provided enough finance to keep the territory solvent. Yet there was no official fear of an economic take-over by the Estates, because domain revenue still provided at all times the bulk of the money and provisions on which the state was run. Lippe could not afford absolutism because it needed Estates' consultations to help solve recurrent economic threats to independence from the 1530s onwards.[14] The privileges of the Estates were not feared by rulers and officials, because the domain was at all times in such a good shape as to make mean-

[13] Cf. *Amt* Enger alienated to Jülich, and the Saldern-Lüning loan to Count Simon V in 1531, Staatsarchiv Detmold, L 1 G XXXIVa. In 1458 Varenholz had been alienated for a mere 800 fl., L 1 G XXXIVa no. 4. *Lippische Regesten*, 2203.

[14] J. Heidemann, *Die Grafschaft Lippe unter der Regierung des Grafen Hermann Adolf und Simon Henrich 1652–97*, Göttingen, 1957, Appendix 3, lists 176 *Land- und Communicationstage* held by rulers and officials with the territorial Estates between 1614 and 1696. Knoch Repositur L 9 for the list of discussions with the Estates from the 1530s to 1790s. E. Kittel, *Geschichte des Landes Lippe*, Cologne, 1957, avoids the pitfall of the absolutist explanation. For the territorial assembly continued to meet, and sporadic attempts by the rulers to do without Estates' consultation sooner or later always failed for lack of money.

ingless the spectre of an Estates' take-over in politics. Instead threats came in the seventeenth and eighteenth centuries from the imperial military situation and from apanage demands within a quarrelsome ruling dynasty, which tended to guarantee the indispensability of the Estates.

The further credit operations of ageing Bernhard VII and Simon V that survive show sales of rents in kind (cereals) and even rents repayable in 'soft' currency (mark/schilling). Interest could be as low as $2\frac{1}{2}$ per cent, but even quite small loans demanded a considerable number of guarantors.[15] The range of money-lending varied from the safe to the disreputable. Motives were thus more complex than the purely economic sphere would warrant. A corn rent or low interest was attractive to nobles and burghers coming into rulers' service or already committed there. The security, let alone perquisites of office, would offer its own compensation. Alternatively an unfavourable investment may have been necessary to protect local interests from outsiders willing to buy their way into county society, like the Münchhausens (who succeeded), and the Lünings (who failed), or to consolidate the power of magnates, like Mengersen and Wend, who financed Lippe during the Regency of Bernhard VIII.[16]

On the other hand, outrageous interest or cheap alienations did provide a high return on capital, that because of the bad credit of the borrower was unlikely to be repaid. In that case the creditor had to make good the loss of his capital by a sufficiently high annual return whilst he still held the alienation. This was anything but good estate management and did nothing to husband resources.

Under Simon V Lippe was pressurized as a creditor by the bad debts of the Guelphs. The Guelph bankruptcy of 1533 left neighbouring Hoya so weakened that it was only a matter of time before that county followed suit.[17] Between 1510 and 1520

[15] Staatsarchiv Detmold, L 92 X no. II–71, 1470, sale of a *schilling* rent; 300 fl. loan of 1499 with eight guarantors including the Lippe nobles, Exter and Borch; 1530–1 Haxthausen receipt for 200 fl. interest on a 8,000 fl. loan. Guelph debts, L 42 no. 9–10.

[16] Staatsarchiv Detmold, L G 1 XXXIVa, 30 April 1514, 2 November 1531, 1 April 1532, 21 May 1535, 19 April 1568.

[17] Staatsarchiv Detmold, L 41a IV B 1. R. Wolf, 'Der Einfluss des Landgrafen Philipp etc. ...', *Jahrbuch des Vereins für Westfälische Kirchengeschichte*', 51–2, 1958–9, *passim*.

the rulers and kinsfolk of Schaumburg, Lippe, Hoya and Diepholz were complaining to the Guelphs of Lüneburg and Hildesheim about economic sanctions and alienations not honoured. It was the rise of Hesse and the equilibrium held by Jülich and its inheritors that prevented any one large neighbour from monopolizing the finances of any small county that lay in its path. There was no repetition of the way in which the Guelphs had tried to take over the middle Weser region at the beginning of the sixteenth century.[18]

It was the dangerous investment policy of Simon V that threatened Lippe with disintegration in the 1530s as much as had the failure of the dynasty to produce an heir in the 1510s. The latter problem was rectified by a second marriage, but the former was fought off only by an Estates' regency government that spared neither relative, friend nor foe in its fight to regain solvency.

The methods employed against defaulting debtors and guarantors were those of slander and libel. These were publicity campaigns that sought to drag those of status and honour into the mud in the crudest terms possible by means of obscenely illustrated verse and prose. The idea was to ruin the reputation and hence the further credit of reputable 'gentlefolk'. As such it was a form of self-help like *Fehde* and it took the most part of the sixteenth century before imperial legislation and territorial and imperial court procedures had evolved sufficiently to provide an effective misdemeanour of bankruptcy as an alternative to these libels, *Schandbriefe und Schmähungen*.

Thus unrecognized, repudiated and unpaid debt led to libel and from there to private war among *Reichsstände* and *Landstände* before the law of contract had caught up with advancing capital finance in the fifteenth and sixteenth centuries. Such a case early on had been the *Fehde* between Ludwig of Bavaria and Friedrich, Burggraf of Nuremberg, over 23,000 fl. lent to Emperor Sigismund for which Friedrich had acted as guarantor. The *Reichsabschiede* of 1530 and 1548 offered debtors some protection by forbidding pictorial libels, *gemalte Beschimpfungen*, yet the idea of *Schimpf und Beleidigung* still predominates in the German language, crudely used to destroy 'face' and dignity.

---

[18] Staatsarchiv Detmold, L 92 X no. II–71; L 42 Reichsstände, Mansfeld, Hoya, and Guelph debts to Lippe.

The 1532 imperial decree of law court procedure ordered corporal punishment for detected anonymous libels (§110). Finally the *Reichspolizeiordnung* of 1577 forbade all libels whether signed or anonymous, printed, written, drawn or painted.[19]

The Lippe cases of libel came mainly as a result of Simon V's financial operations, showing what a close connection there was between the world of usury and libel in the early sixteenth century, which could frighten the more sensitive and soft-headed nobles and burghers (those who feared to lose the honour and status they were born with) out of the world of finance. The libels surviving in Staatsarchiv Detmold include farmyard perversions which the noble, burgher or otherwise respectable and Christian defaulter is depicted and named as committing. It is implied that his seal on the dishonoured debt contract is not worth its wax but that a more suitable material would have been dung. The defaulter is then shown as a common criminal on the rack, in the stocks or hanging from a gibbet.[20]

Libel was thus a highly developed and destructive weapon in society and economics especially in Westphalia and Lower Saxony around 1500. It is significant that the hey-day of libel still coincided with that of *Fehde* and *Feme*, collusive law courts and procedures. It came at a time when local nobilities were the chief financiers of territories, and the ease with which it attacked a family's honour and status made nobles seek protection of office and service with rulers, or even give up high finance for fear of losing the social pre-eminence that normally made life so easy and credit operations so gentlemanly.[21] Which noble

---

[19] O. Hupp, *Schmähbriefe und Schandbilder*, Munich, 1930, *passim*.

[20] *Ibid.*, p. 8. Out of Hupp's forty selected cases, five come from Lippe alone and the Guelphs have 'a veritable rat's tail of cases to their name'. I. L. Klüber, *De pictura contumeliosa*, Erlangen, 1787, pp. iii, xxv–xxviii. *Lippische Regesten*, 3187. Staatsarchiv Detmold, L 9 vol. 1 folio 37, 'die Scheldbrieffe auff Graff Gebhard zu Mansfeld sollen vorhero der Landschaft vorgelesen werden', Landtag Cappel 1538 nach Exaudi. Personalia in C. Spangenberg, *Mansfeldische Chronik*, Eisleben, 1572.

[21] Debt occupied an awkward position in medieval criminal justice. The 'reception' lawyers made it a civil matter. H. Mitteis and H. Lieberich, *Deutsche Rechtsgeschichte*, 9th ed., Munich, 1965, paragraphs 38, 40. R. Schröder and E. von Künssberg, *Lehrbuch der deutschen Rechtsgeschichte*, 6th ed., Leipzig, 1919–22, pp. 834–6, 853. H. Planitz, *Grundzüge des deutschen Privatrechts*, Berlin, 1931, pp. 81–4, 85, 94; *Das deutsche Grundpfandrecht*, pp. 104–28, 176–90. A. Manes, *Staatsbankrotte*, Berlin, 1918, pp. 19–24.

or burgher would dare to sacrifice his birthright or, worse still, that of his children, to dabble in high finance and money-lending when the penalties of failure were so severe? The children of Mayor Cruwel in Lemgo were sold up: economically destroyed, they were then socially stamped out. They disappeared into poverty. At the other end of the scale the territorial rulers of Mansfeld lost their territory in the sixteenth century to pay their debts. Although they retained their social status, this was because of their success as adventurers on the battlefield and in the marriage market.[22]

Before debt guarantee could lead to libel, certain conditions had to be satisfied. When the debtor defaulted, the creditor cited the guarantors to a pre-specified town or inn to reside there at the debtor's expense until he had paid up. The guarantor became a hostage. By the sixteenth century this had become a formality and guarantors sent their servants or hired hostages and horses to the appropriate places to stay there till the debts had been paid (system of *Einlager*). The hostage system helped neither debtor nor creditor to pay or recover money more quickly. It merely added extra expense which the debtor could not pay, only making his indebtedness more hopeless.[23]

After hostages had been tried, another way was to notify the surrounding territories and courts of the ignobility of the debtor in question, thereby doing neighbouring authorities a service, but in effect making it even more difficult for the debtor to raise the money to repay his tormentor. Lippe sent such circulars in despair over the Mansfeld debt.[24] It had still to be realized that in any transaction the creditor had to preserve his

---

[22] On the bankruptcy and subsequent disintegration of the state of Mansfeld in the 1570s, *Territorien Ploetz*, 1, Würzburg, 1964, pp. 118, 516–17, and articles on Mansfeld and Eisleben in *Neuer Brockhaus*.

Especially among the nobility honour and status in the form of a signet or privy seal was used to command business confidence and credit worthiness, Hupp, *op. cit.*, p. 8.

[23] The system of *Einlager* was abolished by *Reichspolizeiordnung* of 1577 but it was of little use as creditors could often not be found under any other system. Yet enforcement of *Einlager* became increasingly dangerous. In 1536 the Lippe regency councillors kept an *Einlager* at Herford in lieu of their guarantee on Guelph debts to the Obergs, but broke it off after it had cost them 300 fl., Hupp, *op. cit.*, pp. 43–4.

[24] Staatsarchiv Detmold, L 45 M–N 2–8b; L 9 vol. 1 folio 233; D 71 no. 471; L 1 G XVI 1–32. *Lippische Regesten*, 3159, 3213. By 1545 Lippe was demanding debt repayment of 25,864 fl. in capital and accumulated interest from Mansfeld.

debtor's business reputation rather than rigidly insist on his 'pound of flesh' if he wanted to see his money again. Equally, crude libels were not effective. In Lippe they seem to have acted as a popular amusement for the crowd that saw these lampoons and drawings in public places, rather than as an inducement to debtors to pay. Libel thus led to a rupture of business confidence and set creditor and debtor at each other's throats when they should have continued to negotiate with one another.[25]

Just as creditors used the weapon of libel, so debtors used the accusation of usury. Both led to a crisis in business confidence, and as financiers, rulers, nobles and burghers were both debtors and creditors, it affected one and all unfavourably. The Guelph insolvency and usury accusations of 1533 foreshadowed the imperial decree of outlawry on Jobst of Hoya for failure to pay debts. It gave the Lippe regency trouble among other things, as Hoya's guarantors, on which they themselves defaulted.[26] At a territorial assembly in Cappel in 1547 this problem came up:[27]

Our gracious Lord of Lippe has pledged himself on behalf of the Count of Hoya against Hoya's creditors in front of the common country. One of these debts runs to 50,000 fl. It has been notified for redemption by the creditor, who has declared his hostility towards all the Lippe [Regency] representatives. Accordingly the common country has been informed because no compensation is forthcoming from Hoya.

They conclude that they know not how to counsel my gracious Lord of Lippe. His Grace has not the fortune with which to pay such debt either totally or in part, wherefore they are also inclined to do nothing, other than that one enquires of Hoya, notably on the opening of Count Erich's will, that the debt be secured by a sufficient alienation to Lippe, such as [*Ämter*] Stoltenau and Stegerbach. What has then to be repaid if Stoltenau and Stegerbach are not alienated, that will have to be further debated.

Ten years previously the Lippians had not spared their young ruler's grandfather, nor his guarantors in Thüringia.[28] In a

---

[25] Staatsarchiv Detmold, L 45 M–N 2–8b. For nearly a century Lippe tried to recover Gebhard von Mansfeld's loan.
[26] Staatsarchiv Detmold, L 41a IV B 1, Charles V's *Achterklärung* against Jobst, 'so-called Count of Hoya', issued by the *Reichskammergericht* trying him for debt, L 41a IV E 9 folios 36–7.[27] Staatsarchiv Detmold, L 9 vol. 1 folio 191.
[28] The picture of spendthrift, dressy and rapacious east German relatives that the plodding backwoods Westphalian gentry conjured up is amusingly sketched by

printed circular they made known that they had had to advance 7,000 fl. interest and compensation to creditor Albrecht v. Münchhausen because of Count Gebhard of Mansfeld's failure to pay and hold his promise. His Thüringian guarantors had then failed to compensate the Lippians, thereby forgetting their knightly and noble good status with their fraudulent seals and churlish behaviour.[29] Money came before family charity. The regency councillors in Lippe knew that the dynasty could not afford to lend money to bankrupt relatives. What rankled here was that the Mansfeld creditor was a member of a neighbouring noble family only recently established in Lippe, who could thus further consolidate his holdings in the county.[30]

The territorial assembly in Lippe continued to hear about libels arising out of their ruler's debts, credits and guarantees.[31] Here ruler and Estates were united in preserving Lippian business confidence. The problem was how to dissociate from kinsfolk in neighbouring or like counties. Thus during the 1530s Lippe had to break free from insolvent Mansfeld, in the 1540s from insolvent Hoya and in the 1550s from Schaumburg, temporarily in difficulty. However, Schaumburg was to experience the rule of a financial genius which enabled relative Simon VI of Lippe to plunge his county further into debt than ever before in the early seventeenth century. To a large extent, therefore, the counties associated with Lippe in the sixteenth century found mutual support, cemented by dynastic ties of kinship and marriage. Yet survival was not thereby guaranteed. In Mansfeld and Hoya the dynasties survived but their territories were sold up. In Schaumburg the dynasty failed and a county which was far richer than Lippe was partitioned.

Finance thus brought rulers and Estates together to preserve territorial independence, for economics did not favour mercantilism in splinter territories, that had to cover increasing

[29] Staatsarchiv Detmold, L 45 M–N 2–8b, 1538.

[30] From the Guelph middle Weser region—Münchhausen, holders of the Lippe water-castle of Wendlinghausen.

[31] Staatsarchiv Detmold, L 9 vol. 1 folio 214, 1550. In connection with a Schaumburg debt Lippe was involved in a demand for 6,000 fl. on an amount originally only half that sum—a choice between libel or blackmail.

Annette von Droste-Hülshoff, 'Der Edelmann aus der Lausitz und das Land seiner Vorfahren', *Bei uns zu Lande auf dem Lande, Ausgewählte Werke* (ed. F. Droop), Berlin, 1925, pp. 233ff.

administrative, military and legal costs at federal, circle and local level. In 1548 councillors and Estates of Lippe in their rôle as landlords discussed ways of fixing the wages and keep of labourers and living-in servants which in the absence of rules of contract legally binding at territorial level increased the burden for landlords in the number of mouths they had to feed. They thus clamoured for limited responsibility towards the poor.[32] The same plea was made in the 1570s and it found expression in the work and wage structure of 1620.[33] From now on Lippe landlords could not only insist that only those who offered to work could feed and shelter, but that only those for whom there actually was sufficient work could lay claim to the right to keep body and soul together. Without such draconian methods and diminished responsibilities Lippe could not have developed into an independent territory with an autonomous economy, paying out of domain, rents, and extraordinary taxation the increasing costs of government, court and dynasty, the imperial military, litigations of the propertied and the increasing burden of territorial debt.

Lippe politics thus became a battle of nerves between creditors and debtors. The extreme luxury of conflict between rulers, officials and Estates over principles, liberties, rights and policies that were not wholly money matters did not come into Lippe affairs. Hence the difficulty, despite substantial records of territorial assemblies, ruler's council meetings and committee reports of describing the constitution of Lippe. Here there was no dualism or dichotomy of government between rulers and Estates in the sixteenth century which by the eighteenth century could have led up to the defeat of the latter by absolutist rulers and their privy councillors. Just as the split between Lutherans, Calvinists and Catholics hardly altered the structure of early modern society as a whole, so squabbles between rulers and Estates were internal matters of finance and office that left status and society fundamentally the same. As always there were scapegoats. In religion it was the sectarians, in finance the Jews, in society the new rich.

The misdemeanour of bankruptcy became established in Lippe

---

[32] Staatsarchiv Detmold, L 9 vol. 1 folio 196, Landtag in Blomberg, esto mihi, 1548.

[33] *Lippische Landesverordnungen*, Polizeiordnung 1620.

from the 1590s as a regular court procedure, overshadowed by the *RKG* as a court of appeal for nobles and burghers.[34] Even so, as late as 1593, the von Saldern brothers circulated to surrounding territorial courts a printed denial of lampoons recited behind their backs. A servant of the Münchhausens had sung them a defamatory song, claiming to have heard it from a nobleman whose name he refused to disclose. The Salderns threatened to litigate in the imperial courts if the territorial authorities refused to help put an end to such embarrassments. To their aid they called the imperial constitutions (laws), especially the police decrees and procedures. They condemned all slanderers,[35] and prepared to litigate to defend their honour and good name.[36] Why all this bother? Saldern and Münchhausen had both been Lippe financier families earlier in the century. Their obsession with honour is inexplicable without reference to the business confidence it had to inspire. If the Salderns protected their name, they protected their credit. Hence their threat to litigate against all and sundry. At least the Salderns no longer took up arms immediately, for there were now sufficient laws for them to resort to first.[37]

It was inevitable that protection of debtors should have been desired over and above satisfaction of the creditor when the chief debtors in the sixteenth century were the rulers in the Empire and territories. What these politicians wanted was, however, contradictory: continued credit (hence creditor protection from usury laws) and limited liability for themselves as the chief debtors (hence debtor protection from libel or violence). The solution was found by increased civil legislation and judicial administration in Empire and territory. The way was opened for the move from *Fehde* and libel to forms of law, like bankruptcy (*Konkurs*), and actions, like distraint (*Exekution*). From the later sixteenth century the law had an

[34] Stadtarchiv Lemgo, Konkurse. Cf. Staatsarchiv Detmold, Hofgerichtsakten.

[35] Staatsarchiv Detmold, D 71 no. 471 (double folio, printed notice, signet sealed), slanderers were called 'Ehrlose/Verlogene Meuchlische Verleumbder und Ehrendiebe'.

[36] 'For the sake of our honour and good name, which we cherish more highly than all the world's wealth.'

[37] Similarly the libel of 1563, Schwartz versus Knipping, which led to a *Reichskammergericht* case in 1572. It involved a debt of 1,000 fl. and was settled out of court by arbitration of Count Simon VI after 1587, Hupp, *op. cit.*, pp. 81–2. Staatsarchiv Detmold, L 82.

interest in controlling individual debt for public security. As such law was in the hands of territorial authorities, it further guaranteed the existence of territorial units. Law as well as finance now operated more and more at this level. At lower levels of administration territorial authorities condescended, at levels above they gave their consent. Territories became indispensable to law and order, economy and finance. And this goes to explain why a county like Lippe could develop into a state within the federal Empire, an absurdity in another day and age.[38]

In the notifications for debt redemption by creditors of the regency of young Simon VI of Lippe notice was given biannually.[39] Thus the councillors in Detmold were faced with recurrent financial crises at Easter and Michaelmas when payments fell due. Out of nine notifications in November 1566, two came from Lippe nobles, one from a Lippe burgher and one from a Lippe official. Two more came from neighbouring Bielefeld. For Easter 1567 seven creditors presented themselves, of which only two were outsiders. At Easter 1568 there were five creditors, again with two from outside Lippe. Demands continued annually with the Lippe nobility in the lead as creditors of the ruling dynasty, followed by the town councils of Lemgo and Lippstadt and individual burghers. Sums varied from the 200 fl. credit of Bielefeld burgher Pott (1566), 1,000 fl. from local noble Westphal (1571), to 9,000 fl. from local noble Haxthausen (1576).[40]

Each demand by creditors had to be approved by the Regent, Count Hermann Simon in Pyrmont, before it could go through the treasury in Detmold. The councillors in Detmold kept a record of their transactions. As their ruler was a minor, they were preparing for audit when the time came to hand over to him.[41] Just as the previous regency of Bernhard VIII had led to

[38] The early modern material in Staatsarchiv Detmold would be decimated if all records of litigation for recovery of debt and inheritances were removed. It seems almost that early modern prominence was measured in terms of property, and no family could survive without litigating for its conservation. Where the sword had formerly protected status, the early modern lawyer now had to do likewise.

[39] Staatsarchiv Detmold, L 92 X II no. 63–I, *Losekündigungen* 1566–76/7.

[40] Regent Hermann Simon of Pyrmont and Spiegelberg exploited the resources of his ward and nephew in Lippe, using Lippe as guarantor for his debts, Staatsarchiv Detmold, L 1 G XXXIV a–d.

[41] Cf. Landdrost Schwartz, *Abrechnung* in 1579 for the years 1566–70 in *Amt* Detmold, Staatsarchiv Detmold, L 9 vol. 3 folios 136–41.

the recording of territorial assemblies and committee meetings for the first time, so the regency of Simon VI led to an attempt to record the dynasty's debt liabilities. Simon VI further encouraged this development. By the 1590s the first treasury accounts were being produced under the control of a Hessian Calvinist accountant with the first elegantly rather than honestly balanced account of Michaelmas 1594.[42]

Notifications for debt redemption again survive for the ruling dynasty between 1588 and 1615.[43] Until 1609 Simon VI managed to find sufficient credit in Lippe and the immediate vicinity, notably Minden, Ravensberg and Schaumburg. He first relied on Lippe nobles and Lippe town councils to provide the bulk of his credit. As his territorial Estates, Lippe nobles and towns had, however, to continue to guarantee his debts from outsiders, for their own resources were insufficient to finance Simon's demands by themselves. Between 1599 and 1612 the territorial Estates of Lippe pledged themselves for 215,000 tlrs of ruler's borrowing.[44] Simon VI was now having to borrow up to 30,000 tlrs a time, a sum as large as his regular annual income.[45] At this rate no members of the Lippe Estates could retain the hold that their predecessors had had over rulers' finance. Of territorial nobles the Westphals in neighbouring Paderborn could alone still compete, and they provided credit of 20-35,000 tlrs. No Lippe nobles or town councils came near to such a figure. Treasury official Hesberg provided something under 5,000 tlrs and the Wulffs, an outside family, could buy

[42] Staatsarchiv Detmold, L 92 Z 1a, Hessberg's accounts for Michaelmas 1593-4: income 6,428 tlrs, expenditure 6,458 tlrs, deficit 30 tlrs (hiding a real deficit of nearly 1,500 tlrs). A Hessberg had already been a Lippe creditor in 1569 (see L 92 X II no. 63-I). Johann Hessberg was appointed Lippe treasury scribe by Count Simon VI in 1592. By 1596 he was Simon's secretary and also socially accepted, having officiated as a sworn brother in a Mengersen marriage (middle Weser nobles and financiers). By 1606 Hessberg was a *Rentschreiber* and styled with the noble prefix. In 1608 his family married into the established Lippe nobility (von Exter). Staatsarchiv Detmold, Bestallungsrevers L 16 Appendix F III 5; Repositur L 16 and L 52, AP; D 1a.

[43] Staatsarchiv Detmold, L 92 X II no. 63-II.

[44] Staatsarchiv Detmold, L 92 X II no. 40, Ritterschaft und Städte, Schadlosverschreibungen (21 from 1599-1612).

[45] Cf. earlier borrowing, Staatsarchiv Detmold, L 1 G XXXIVa. 1497-1536 Simon V made twelve loans (four at 5 per cent, four at 6 per cent, and four in kind) totalling 20,000 fl. 1548-58 Bernhard VIII made thirteen loans (twelve for money rents, eleven at 5 per cent, one at 6 per cent, one in kind) with property and revenue as security.

their way into the Lippe nobility with loans of 25,000 tlrs for which they purchased a fief.

By 1608–9 the Estates of Lippe were as hard-pressed as their ruler to find further credit. Those who called the tune were now a scattering of foreign territorial rulers, nobles, chapters and burghers, notably Count Ernst of Schaumburg (50,000 tlrs), Count Anton Günther of Oldenburg (15,000 tlrs), various ecclesiastics, nobles and burghers in Minden and Hildesheim[46] and the Hansa town of Lübeck (22,000 tlrs).

When the crash came finally at Easter 1610, it showed that the Estates had failed along with their ruler.[47] Outstanding debt repayments in that year were over 130,000 tlrs to seventeen main creditors. Only six of these were Lippians. Including the Westphals, money owing for immediate repayment by the treasury in that year to Lippians themselves was as little as one-third of the total needed. At this rate the county was being bought up by outsiders, notably Simon VI's kinsman Erich of Schaumburg, whose demands on his father-in-law's treasury in Detmold in 1610 were greater than that of the Lippian investors put together.[48]

The treasury accounts for 1610 showed an Estates' tax grant of nearly 21,000 tlrs paid above all by the tenantry, but this was offset by newly borrowed capital of over 38,000 tlrs. Against this the treasurer could only find another 2,000 tlrs from regular revenues to plough into debt reduction. The whole sum of nearly 61,000 tlrs was used to pay interest and repay capital. Interest payment alone took over 40 per cent of this sum.[49]

Even so the Estates of Lippe made sure in their extraordinary tax grant of 1610 that native creditors were satisfied first. Thereby ruler and Estates conserved the specie circulating in the county for as long as possible. Even this skilful operation to save the pockets of Lippian creditors and give taxpayers the

[46] In 1610 the *Wechselherren* in Hildesheim took 7,500 tlrs plus 900 tlrs interest, Staatsarchiv Detmold, L 92 X II no. 63–II.

[47] For the causes of this financial crash, see Chapters XI, XIII and XIV. Simon VI's support of federal policies and taxes at circle, imperial court and imperial assembly was too expensive for his modest state to bear. Cf. G. Benecke, 'Relations between the Holy Roman Empire and the Counts of Lippe as an example of early modern German federalism', *Westfälische Forschungen*, 1972.

[48] 50,000 as against 48,000 tlrs, Staatsarchiv Detmold, L 92 X II no. 63–II; no. 40.

[49] Staatsarchiv Detmold, L 92 Z 1a.

chance to pay once again before satisfying any outsiders, produced a deficit of 25 per cent, despite the comparative modesty of the sum involved.[50]

This in turn led to a panic among leading Lippian financiers and by Easter 1611 Westphal and Münchhausen alone wanted back nearly 20,000 tlrs.[51] As county society no longer had confidence in its own treasury, it was folly to expect outsiders to continue as, let alone become, Lippian investors.

By 1614 Lippian insolvency had turned into a federal matter. Emperor Matthias consented to a commission under Count Christian of Waldeck and Cologne town to examine the debts of Simon VI, notably for arrears from his Westphalian circle leadership. The 1599 circle expedition still left Lippe liable for over 40,000 fl. Lippe was suspected of appropriating circle funds in the absence of coherent accounts for circle arrears from member territories. Imperial debt demands were repeated by Ferdinand II in April 1623. By November 1635 Lippe was still trying to clear herself by claiming non-payment of circle taxes from various territories affected by the earlier Spanish-Dutch war with Liège leading these at over 30,000 fl. in arrears. The county accepted no responsibility. Finally in 1641 Ferdinand III dropped these demands in return for Lippian support for his peace plans at Regensburg.[52]

The willingness of Simon VI to play a part in federal politics showed that unless finance and administration were drastically improved at all levels, his children and his subjects would be the losers through the financial burdens that such grand ambitions imposed on their county. Successor Simon VII improved the financial situation by withdrawing federal support with the wholehearted approval of the Estates, and the immediate political situation allowed him to do this. The coming of war to Lippe in 1623 was to impose its own special conditions.[53]

---

[50] Tax grant of 1610, nobles' *don gratuit* 2,000 tlrs
tax on drink 2,500
tax from tenantry 10,270
arrears charge 611

15,381 tlrs
notified debt redemption 21,600 tlrs
(especially to Lippian and local notables, Donop, Westphal, Münchhausen, Mengersen, Tovall, Gevekott), Staatsarchiv Detmold, L 92 X II no. 63–II.
[51] *Ibid.*   [52] *Ibid.*   [53] See Chapter X.

In 1593 the treasury (*Kammer*) started to pull in and supervise as much income and expenditure from the localities as possible.[54] By 1597 it had succeeded in gaining virtual control of all Simon VI's revenues and finance. Turnover increased from under 6,500 tlrs in 1593-4 to over 34,000 tlrs in 1597. During 1610-22 it functioned as the main department through which Simon VII managed to control his father's debts and ward off imperial and circle demands left over from the 1590s when Simon VI had played his grandest rôle in federal affairs.[55] Under the supervision of the Busch family the treasury also managed to manipulate Lippe through the 1640s to 1660s, as well as to collect Estates' grants successfully. This good management still saw Lippe safely through to the 1670s. From then on the treasury went into eclipse as it lost control over comital finance through lack of direction from the ruler himself until the partial recovery of 1709 and the total recovery after 1750.

Under Count Simon Henrich officials went back to accounting, if at all, at local level only. From this period (1675-82, 1688-1708) no treasury accounts are available, and although these could have been lost, the sheer bulk and incoherence of financial records that do survive from this period, when compared with what had gone before and what was to come after, show that there was a genuine lack of direction which allowed local and central officials to do as they pleased in the absence of audit. The period is characterized by the rise and methods of the former *Vogt* of Schötmar, Christoff Leineweber.[56]

As the financial records of 1680-1750 give an insight into administrative muddle it is easy but false to assume from them that there was overall economic chaos in the county. The use of these fragmentary financial records to condemn the whole Lippe economy around 1700 is an unwarranted interpretation of the archive materials that remain in Detmold.[57] Although Lippe

[54] The *Kammer* and *Hofgericht* functioned as departments distinct from the chancellery from the 1590s onwards, but because the state was so small, councillors from all three departments remained interchangeable.

[55] Staatsarchiv Detmold, L 92 Z 1a.

[56] Staatsarchiv Detmold, L 63 A 12; Repositur L 16 and L 52. H. Contzen, *Die lippische Landkasse*, Münster, 1910; 'Von den lippischen Finanzen im 18. Jahrhundert', *Lippische Mitteilungen*, 9, 1911, pp. 85-132.

[57] For contrary views, see Contzen, 'Von den lippischen Finanzen . . .', Heidemann, *op. cit.*

was once again on the brink of bankruptcy in the 1730s with a very real imperial commission of inquiry headed off only by the injection of a loan of 100,000 tlrs from Hanover against the alienation of *Amt* Sternberg, this situation was due to short-term conflicts between rulers, officials and Estates, which withdrew the support of the latter from financing the county and drove the former to expensive credit and financial dishonesty.[58] The sums that the *Hoffaktoren* or court financiers handled were insignificant when compared with the whole of county finance, but sufficiently concentrated at court to arouse prejudice.[59] As Simon VII and the Busch family had shown, the economy of Lippe was basically sufficient for running an independent territorial administration, whenever it was well directed by officials who had the confidence of the Estates in their economic policies. And this Simon August's officials were to show once again after 1750, just as had the regency councillors of Bernhard VIII after 1536.

One of the basic features of the early modern Lippe economy was the large part still played by fixed rents, and salaries paid in kind to landlord and official.[60] As the grandest landlords of them all, the rulers were able to keep open house at their castle in Detmold. The dining registers from court and castle kitchens have survived to give a picture of the Lippe establishment at work. For a twelve-month period in 1570–1 over 50,000 guests from neighbouring rulers down to beggars were offered hospitality at court. They accounted for over 12,000 loaves from the comital ovens. In the following twelve months over 25,000 received hospitality and the number of main meals served between Easter and Michaelmas 1574 was well over 28,000. One may assume, therefore, that the Detmold court comprised

[58] For the constitutional crisis of 1698, Staatsarchiv Detmold, L 8 K Section VII no. 7; Knoch Repositur L 9 folios 743, 745–6, 753–4, and a cautious levy of taxes by decree, L 37 XVII no. 2. 'Gravamina' (complaints by the Estates) were sometimes very constructive, see 'Vier Städte Gravamina, 1649', L 10 Titel 2 no. 1. By 1731 treasury income estimates were 77,000 tlrs, expenditure 200,000 tlrs, an impossible situation, L 63 A 12.

[59] Staatsarchiv Detmold, L 63 B 12–II. Simon Henrich had sixty-eight chief creditors between 1647–87, at 100 to 20,000 tlrs each, in all 250,000 tlrs. Most creditors were officials, nobles and burghers as well as relatives of the ruler. Jewish lending was a mere 10–30,000 tlrs, only 10 per cent of the whole, but what made it so conspicuous was that it usually came in the form of one lump sum.

[60] Staatsarchiv Detmold, L 92 A Titel 63 no. 81. H. Stöwer and F. Verdenhalven, *Salbücher der Grafschaft Lippe*, Münster, 1969, Introduction.

between 75 and 150 persons in any one day in the early 1570s, and this at a time of regency government when the ruler, being still a minor, had as yet no wife and family of his own.[61]

By 1617 Simon VII had reduced Detmold castle hospitality, but it was still lavish when it is considered that he probably had only about 30,000 subjects. The court kitchen still fed between 90 and 135 regularly every day. This included the actual members of the ruling family. The extraordinary food bill had, however, been cut to include between five and fifty meals a day. It had been over 150 a day in 1570 and may well reflect the diminished responsibility felt for the poor by Calvinist landlords like the Lippian counts. The third group to be fed at court were the household staff, lower officials and servants, who took between twenty and forty meals a day. Even so, at times of festivity over 1,200 meals were prepared at Detmold castle in one day alone.

By 1645 Detmold castle food bills were reckoned at a unit cost of 6–8 *Groschen*, according to whether meals were with or without soup. Between May and Michaelmas of that year the kitchen claimed only 270 tlrs expenditure on 1,400 meals, a drastic reduction by the standards prevailing under Simon VII. Detmold was momentarily deserted by its dynasty as the regency dispute of 1636 between Dowager Catharina and Count Johann Bernhard reached its last, disreputable phase with the wilful neglect of young Simon Ludwig.[62] From Michaelmas 1647 to Michaelmas 1648 Detmold castle still served only 12,000 meals but at a cost of nearly 2,500 tlrs, showing that although numbers receiving hospitality had been reduced by over 75 per cent since 1570, the simplicity of bread had given way to the sophistication of courses even introduced by soup. This was in modest keeping with the fashion of the day which catered for really spectacular gluttony that mollified allied Swedish and imperial military organizers in the peace dinners of 1648–9.[63] By the 1640s a free meal had become a

[61] Staatsarchiv Detmold, L 92 P Titel 19 B 1.

[62] Treasury payment for keeping Simon Ludwig and his brother was a few hundred talers only, pitiful when contrasted with what father and uncles obtained for themselves, Staatsarchiv Detmold, L 92 Z 1a; L 63 A 12, itemized accounts.

[63] H. von Zwiedineck-Südenhorst, *Deutsche Geschichte im Zeitraum der Gründung des Preussischen Königtums*, Stuttgart, 1894, 1, pp. 85–7, vividly describes a 'peace' dinner.

lavish treat for the important few. For two generations now the beggar was no longer welcome at the ruler's kitchen.[64]

Turning from rulers' hospitality to the investment that made it, among other things, possible, the pension lists from the earliest treasury accounts of 1593–4 have been examined with the help of a biographical register of Lippe's early modern officials, nobles and substantial burghers.[65] The debt charge at Michaelmas 1593 was just over 1,500 tlrs to forty creditors, and at Easter 1594 3,700 tlrs to seventy creditors, implying a capital debt liability of something over 100,000 tlrs. Each investor averaged an income of slightly under 50 tlrs and there were about 100 of them. Such a sum was hardly enough for anyone of status to live on, except perhaps a clergyman. It indicates that investment with rulers provided a supplementary income for most of those who indulged in it. This showed a lasting feature of Lippe rulers' finance, namely that support came from many small investors rather than a powerful and threatening few. Only a tycoon like Count Erich of Schaumburg temporarily upset this state of affairs.[66] The other point was that wealthy Lippians numerically dominated the pension lists, a natural sign of native support for the county. It is this level of native investment, indicated by the pension payments of the treasury, that really speaks for the overall support of the propertied for their rulers in early modern Lippe. It showed that although nobles and burghers might squabble in territorial assemblies and on committees among themselves and with rulers' officials, they remained committed to their rulers' administration to ensure that the pensions on their family investments were paid.

How much treasury expenditure was repayment of borrowed capital?[67] In the crisis year 1610 it was just over 50 per cent of the total income that the treasury had received. Yet 65 per cent of this total income of nearly 61,000 tlrs was newly bor-

[64] Staatsarchiv Detmold, L 92 P Titel B 1–8, Hofstaatsrechnungen 1558–1799. Accounts from the palaces survive from Blomberg (1563–1603, 1639, 1664–97), Schieder (1597–8, 1658–92), Brake (1595–1658), Barntrup (1583), Varnholz (1599–1650), Oesterholz (1626–32).

[65] Staatsarchiv Detmold, L 92 Z 1a; Repositur L 16 and L 52.

[66] Staatsarchiv Detmold, L 92 Z 1a; L 63 B 12–II; L 92 X II no. 63–II; no. 40.

[67] Staatsarchiv Detmold, L 92 Z 1a; L 63 A 12; B 12–I; II. The financial records have been dispersed and it is very likely that many more important account-books exist tucked away in a mass of local, antiquarian and genealogical material.

rowed capital. This was the outcome of having repaid no capital debt at all through the treasury since accounts began in 1593. It was only in 1617 that newly borrowed capital fell below the level of repaid capital debt. In that year total income was 41,000 tlrs, 25 per cent of it newly borrowed capital. Against this, capital debt repayment ran at 60 per cent of total income. By now Simon VII was using the treasury almost exclusively to repay debt and interest, or pensions, as interest on investments was called.

Between 1617 and 1622 Simon VII's treasury handled an income of 454,000 tlrs. Again 25 per cent of this was newly borrowed. Estates' tax grants brought in 36,000 tlrs, which shows how much more important were domain and regular revenues than Estates' tax grants. In this six-year period just before Lippe was first occupied by Tilly's troops, treasury income from domain and regular revenues amounted to over 60 per cent of the total. By contrast income from Estates' tax grants accounted for only 8 per cent of the whole. In none of the accounts from 1617 to 1622 was there an overall deficit. With 40 per cent of his total treasury income Simon VII repaid capital debts. Forty per cent also went to pay interest, the so-called pensions. Thus between 1617 and 1622 interest or pension payments ran at over 28,000 tlrs a year, indicating that Simon VII honoured capital debts of nearly 600,000 tlrs.

By comparison, in the first years of peace, 1648–52, the treasury accounted for an income of 115,000 tlrs, of which only 6 per cent was newly borrowed money. Estates' tax grants now made up nearly 25 per cent of the total treasury income. Under 15 per cent was repaid capital debt, but 30 per cent was paid as interest. Again there were handsome surpluses (15 per cent), left as working capital in the treasury. Between 1648 and 1652 interest payments were a mere 5,500 tlrs a year, showing that Lippe honoured capital debts of 110,000 tlrs, one-sixth of the 1622 pre-war total. In the six-year period 1652–7 Lippe honoured 300,000 tlrs of debt. In 1670–4, the last five-year period before chaos set in at the treasury, Lippe honoured 180,000 tlrs of debt.

Yet this reduction in interest payments was due to the repayment of over 300,000 tlrs capital debt between 1648 and 1674, whilst only 70,000 tlrs of new debt was contracted. This was

achieved by obtaining Estates' tax grants averaging well over
15,000 a year (net to the treasury). This was 33 per cent of
total treasury income for the period. Once more it shows how
the bulk of rulers' revenue continued to come from domain and
regular sources. Estates' grants had just increased to cut down
the previous impossibly high level of their borrowing. The war
years 1623–48 had indeed raised Estates' tax grants so that they
no longer supplied a mere 8 per cent but instead up to 33 per
cent of treasury income. This rise demonstrated that the
Estates were in general agreement with rulers' economic
policies after 1648, but as such it was still a small contribution
and it did not give the Estates of Lippe much leverage against
their rulers and councillors in any policy disputes that arose nor
did it give the Estates the right to the most say in financial
administration as a whole. Basically seventeenth-century Lippe
rulers still actually did live 'of their own'. Where individual
members of the Estates as well as skilful rulers' officials could
exercise power was as individual investors and pensionaries of
the rulers. Their piecemeal role here was more significant than
en bloc in Estates' assemblies or committees. The Estates' threat
to withhold tax grants was far less sinister to rulers and councillors than conspiracies among individual members to withhold
further credit or insist on capital repayment. Indeed the two
things went hand in hand. Estates' grants were specifically
made to repay rulers' debts and outstanding interest or pensions:
this was what was meant by Estates 'taking over' rulers' debts.

For 1648–74 treasury income in Lippe was just short of
1,200,000 tlrs. Towards this the Estates of Lippe granted over
400,000 tlrs in taxes paid to the treasury. In the same period
the treasury repaid over 300,000 tlrs of capital debt and 270,000
tlrs in pensions. This meant that for three decades after the war
Lippe continued to honour an average 200,000 tlrs of debt.
This was a very reasonable sum indeed and shows how little the
war had continued to affect rulers' finances in the years that
immediately followed 1648.

Debt reduction on the lines that had been worked out under
Simon VII was thus continued after the break of the war years
1623–48 with the intensified participation of the Estates. What
had been an honoured treasury debt of 600,000 tlrs in 1622 had
thus been reduced to under 200,000 tlrs by 1674. This process

the war period merely seemed to hold up. The overall position was not worsened by the war years, nor did the Lippe treasury after 1648 have to change its financial policy because of the war years. The system of borrowing and lending that the Estates ran for the benefit of their rulers, to help ends meet where domain and regular income were not enough to cover expenditure, was interrupted by the years of troop occupation, only to be taken up again exactly where it had been broken off.

In Lippe Estates' grants were not used to pay for the everyday function of government or court. They were not intended for this, for which purposes regular revenues above all from the rulers' domain tenantry in the *Ämter* were sufficient.[68] Estates' tax grants were for unexpected costs such as dynastic festivities and territorial, circle and imperial defence and of course treasury debt funding and reduction. Naturally one ruler or regent managed financially better than another, and this decided whether the Estates would have to grant more or less taxes, depending on the level of debt that the investors would tolerate.

By 1610 this level had clearly risen too high, as annual revenues could no longer cover all Simon VI's commitments. By 1617 Simon VII had pinned the debt down to something over 600,000 tlrs and it was now just a question of time as to how much the Estates would increase their tax grants to reduce or fund the debt, depending on how seriously they thought that the pensions of individual members were being threatened through lack of treasury revenue.

When Tilly occupied Lippe in 1623 this mutual system just froze. When it was taken up again after 1648 the way in which the Estates helped to reduce total treasury debt liability by two-thirds in under thirty years shows that they considered debt reduction essential to reduce the previous high level of interest and pension payment. Thus with their tax grants they accelerated the policy of Simon VII, so rudely interrupted by the troops in 1623. As far as Lippe finance was concerned, the war period was just a moratorium on debt, a nuisance that only accelerated a return to the policy of Simon VII after it was all over. As for the myth of huge new debts supposedly incurred during the war years, of this there is no sign in Lippe,[69] for the

[68] Staatsarchiv Detmold, L 92 A Titel 63 no. 3.
[69] Staatsarchiv Detmold, L 92 Z 1a; L 63 A 12; B I; II.

county could find no new investors as substantial as those before 1623 and after 1648. The problem was how to honour the back-lash of unpaid interest on old debt contracted before 1623, and this the Westphalian peace and imperial assemblies of 1654 and 1663 took care of by reducing the liabilities of territorial treasuries in imperial decrees consented to by territorial rulers and their delegates.[70]

After 1674 the economic situation deteriorated under the incapable Count Simon Henrich. This increased the bargaining position of the Estates and by 1685 they had achieved what seemed on the face of it a victory over the ruler's treasury. The Estates recognized a duty to take over rulers' debts and to fund them or repay them out of taxes that they themselves granted. This operation would be taken out of the hands of the treasury and placed in the hands of a new debt-reducing author-ity, the *Landkasse*, whose competence and membership was not, however, fully clarified until the 1740s. There were good reasons for this. From 1685 onwards there was a genuine con-flict of interest between treasury officials (and hence local *Amt* officials who accounted to the treasury) and the Estates. The fight for control of the new *Landkasse* developed with both sides claiming to dominate it. Thus if the treasury gained control the Estates would be less willing to grant taxes or provide invest-ments. If the Estates gained control the treasury would try to saddle the *Landkasse* with as much debt as possible, and to use the treasury solvency that was thereby gained to run into debt once more.[71]

The division of power between treasury and *Landkasse*, from

---

[70] Staatsarchiv Detmold, L 41a IV B no. 3.

[71] 'Remonstratio Status des Hochgräfl. Lipp. Hausses und Cammer zu Dett-molden', Staatsarchiv Detmold, L 63 B 12–II, 1674–87:

old capital owing	320,600 tlrs
old interest arrears	100,000
new interest arrears	144,170
transferred capital and interest	173,000
new capital owing	48,570
owing to Bückeburg	20,000
anticipated on cereals	29,000
	——————
	662,340 tlrs
paid off, about	380,000
arrears, about	280,000

(Note the inaccurate arithmetic.)

1685 to 1744, was enough in itself to drive rulers' finances out of order, for this system created two mutually hostile bodies. The *Kammer*, with responsibility for regular revenues and the running of the administration, and with the power to make new debts, pushed all responsibility for repayment on to the *Landkasse*. The *Landkasse* was assured of Estates' tax grants which previously had gone to the *Kammer*, but it exercised no control over the rate of new borrowing, just being held responsible for funding and repaying such new debt whenever the *Kammer* had over-borrowed.[72] Hence the unwillingness of the Estates to make the *Landkasse* work, for the *Kammer* could always raid the *Landkasse* by indiscriminate new borrowing which the *Landkasse* was bound to honour. The negotiations that led to the establishment of a *Landkasse* in the 1680s were thus disastrous, for they saddled the Estates with financial burdens without their being able to control the level of debt that the *Kammer* could still contract. It was thus only the ruler who could put his own house in order. Only he could control the level of new *Kammer* borrowing. Simon August was the first ruler capable of cutting his own standard of living, thus taking the sting out of the well-meaning but irresponsible division of financial powers that had taken place in 1685.

Examples of how the *Landkasse* actually fulfilled its task of funding and paying discarded treasury debts are hard to find before 1744 when regular accounts begin.[73] In an undated proposal of the 1690s the *Landkasse* was assigned debts of about 9,000 tlrs with which to satisfy eighty-six creditors. It was advised not to try to pay out of this sum the interest on 20,000 tlrs lent by Landdrost Donop. Simon Henrich had fallen out with his chief official, who had still combined territorial noble status and Estates' assembly participation with high office under the ruler in the sixteenth-century tradition.[74] In 1697 the *Landkasse* paid 13,000 tlrs of extraordinary treasury debts, including

[72] The *Landkasse* was set up to fund rulers' debts as state debts, but it was raided to pay officials' salaries among other illicit practices. Thus the *Landcasse* of 1686 had to be refunded with a new Estates' loan of 120,000 tlrs in 1712, Contzen, 'Von den lippischen Finanzen . . .', p. 26. Stadtarchiv Lemgo, Landkasse. Staatsarchiv Detmold, L 10 Titel 2 no. 23 vols. 1–2; L 10 Titel 2 no. 18; no. 20.

[73] Landkasse Revisionen 1687–90, 'Notanda bey der Cassa Rechnung des Amtmann Buschen', Staatsarchiv Detmold, L 10 Titel 2 no. 23 vol. 1 folios 127–35.

[74] Share-out of 9,000 tlrs interest in the *Casse* ('till'), Staatsarchiv Detmold, L 10 Titel 2 no. 20.

interest, capital, promissory notes of the ruler, his wife and relatives, salaries, food and travelling expenses, circle payments and *Armierte* bribes. This showed the Estates' fears about how the treasury would misuse the *Landkasse*. In 1697 the money had been provided by an Estates' three-year grant levied on the towns, which one of the Busch dynasty of Lippe finance officials accounted for. Here Lemgo actually paid up fully in two years a sum of over 4,000 tlrs, and all six towns provided the 13,000 tlrs that the *Landkasse* spent.[75] After the *Landkasse* was reorganized in 1712 it was given a list of pensions for regular payment which ran to 9,000 tlrs. It was thus expected to take on rulers' debts of 180,000 tlrs.[76] In the first systematic accounts from 1744 onwards the *Landkasse* took in 24,000 tlrs and spent nearly 15,000 tlrs.[77] It was now funding rulers' debts of 300,000 tlrs (gross), but at the same time building up a surplus, indicating a more realistic treasury policy that found more favour with the Estates.[78] This figure also compares realistically with the amount of debt that the Busch family had coped with from the treasury almost one hundred years previously.

The moneys variously accounted for in the *Kammer-, Amts-* and *Landkasse* accounts between 1593 and 1744 that have here been examined do, however, provide no coverage of the actual units of currency used, other than that these were *Talers* or *Reichstalers, Groschen* and *Pfennige*. Yet this was money of account at imperial bullion prices with regional and territorial variations which did seem to retain a reasonably constant value as a whole between the second half of the sixteenth century and the eighteenth. For the Lippe accounts as a whole reflect this. They show no steady rise in the level of funded debt, although domain revenue fluctuated wildly and Estates' tax revenues rose steeply.

In the early seventeenth century it seems that Lippe had to cope with a level of rulers' debt of well over half a million talers

[75] *Kasse* payments of 1697, Staatsarchiv Detmold, L 10 Titel 2 no. 23 vol 2. Even a bribe to the Bishop of Münster was higher than repayment to the *Hoffaktor* (2,000 as against 1,832 tlrs), showing that Jewish contributions to Lippe finance were only about 15 per cent of total finance for that year.

[76] Staatsarchiv Detmold, L 10 Titel 2 no. 23 vol. 2.

[77] Staatsarchiv Detmold, L 10 Titel 4 no. 1 vol. 1.

[78] The *Landkasse* received regular taxes granted by the Estates and paid by the localities, in all 20,000 tlrs a year, which included regular late payment of about 40 per cent and accounted for domain treasury embezzlement of a further 20 per cent.

of imperial account, and this level of debt was likely to have been reached again in the earlier eighteenth century under Simon Henrich Adolf, after having been down to one-third of this in the early 1670s. Thus rulers' officials and members of the Estates of Lippe did successfully finance the county despite administrative muddle and lack of direction from rulers who were as often as not unsuitable as heads of state. There were no long-term crises in early modern Lippe, whose society and economy were in overall harmony.[79] Except for the war years, 1623–48, treasury income ran at between 30,000 and 90,000 tlrs a year and annual debt charges at between 10,000 and 30,000 tlrs. This was burdensome as such, for it meant that approximately one-third of treasury income was pledged in advance in an average year. But because much of this money went to members of the Estates, officials and courtiers who had invested with the rulers in return for pensions, jobs and status, it helped to stabilize society and minimize any real opposition that would have threatened not only the dynasty and its administration but also the Estates and all those who had money and office in the county.

In 1698 a real crisis did occur as ruler and Estates clashed on military affairs. After the Peace of Ryswick the Lippe Estates naturally expected a reduction in circle and imperial military costs, and hence a reduction in tax demands by the ruler to the Estates' assembly. Instead the new ruler Friedrich Adolf had undertaken to raise a Lippe troop to help garrison Cologne town in return for Habsburg support against the demands of the *Armierte,* circle directors Münster and Brandenburg, whose troops had scoured Lippe frequently in the name of imperial war efforts in the previous reign. On 3 April 1698 the Estates sent Friedrich Adolf a decisive 'no' to his demands for increased taxation. He wished to introduce a so-called *Herren-Monat,* an adaptation of previous monthly levies on the tenantry, backed up by *dons gratuits* from nobles and towns to satisfy the demands of the *Armierte* troops, to set up a new Lippe militia of his own in direct imperial Habsburg service. This may have been compatible with the political situation in Europe on

[79] See footnote 8. Lippe practice bears out contemporary economic theory, Mayer, *Handbuch der Finanzwissenschaft,* 1, p. 23 (on Bodin 1577), p. 240 (on Kaspar Klock 1608).

the eve of the War of the Spanish Succession, but all that the Estates could see in 1698 was that after the recent peace the ruler was demanding a higher level of taxation than they had allowed even in the previous war years. He was making nonsense of the peace by a massive armaments policy instead of allowing the county to recuperate. They wanted a genuine, cheap peace policy. To them peace still meant no army taxes.

Since the inroads of the *Armierte*, Friedrich Adolf no longer thought the same way. He expected Lippe to survive as an independent territory in the Empire only if it fulfilled its own military obligations, and the billets of Münster and Brandenburg troops in Lippe had shown him that the county would never be able fully to control its own affairs if it did not also have its own federal military contingent. He was thus incensed when his Estates, encouraged by his cousin, apanage Count Casimir of Lippe-Brake, and the town councils, refused to make the money available. The Estates remonstrated. 'It is of course almost unnecessary to obediently continue to point out to your Grace the bad condition of the Fatherland, because your Grace yourself knows that without reminder from us. Thus the Estates in no way think to refuse that assistance which is possible but only obediently wish to point out that . . .'[80] In the tortured language of the German baroque the recent ruler was being taught a lesson by his elder, self-appointed counsellors as well as being given a 'no'.

This he refused to take for an answer. In his reply Friedrich Adolf denied that the territorial assembly had the right to interfere in military policy. This was a prerogative of imperial and circle assemblies. The Lippe Estates' decision was prejudicial to Friedrich Adolf's powers as a member of these imperial and circle assemblies, since these assemblies had left him alone with the right to decide whether to provide a Lippian military contingent or whether to pay subsidies. The Lippe estates were sabotaging his decision. This point the nobility had grasped and they were now on his side, but the apanage counts especially were not happy to see their ruling elder cousin so tangibly increase his power.[81]

[80] 'Statuum unterthäniges Memorial', 3 April 1698, Staatsarchiv Detmold, 8 K Section VII no. 7; Knoch Repositur L 9 folios 145–6, 753–4.

[81] Replicatorische Resolutio', Staatsarchiv Detmold, L 8 K Section VII no. 7.

There was no question here of Friedrich Adolf desiring a standing army to suppress his territorial assembly. In February 1698 the last demand for subsidy had come from Brandenburg, for 12,000 tlrs of arrears on previous war costs, threatening the county with distraint if it did not pay.[82] Friedrich Adolf's armaments policy was thus realistic in the face of continued threats of payment or billet from armed neighbours and unwanted allies. Whether peace or war, their demands were continuous. Lippe thus needed a troop of its own with which to win Habsburg support and secure its constitutional liberties as far as possible against the still real power of Münster and Hesse and the rising stars of Guelph and Hohenzollern.

On 26 April 1698 after weeks of fruitless talking with territorial assemblies Friedrich Adolf's chancellery ordered its local officials to collect taxes for Lippe's own imperial and circle troop contingent despite the refusal of the Estates to make such a grant. The matter was put in the hands of *Voigt* Leineweber and the *Ämter* tenantry were now assessed by decree of the ruler, without the consent of the Estates. This was the naked truth despite the caution with which the chancellery worded its illegal taxation decree. 'Because considerable difficulties have been encountered, the territorial assembly has since had to be somewhat delayed and that is why the tax assessment for this year has already had to be delayed by four months—but unavoidable necessity demands none the less that an assessed quantity of tax be raised.' The taxes required for the year came to no less than 42,000 tlrs.[83]

By the next year Friedrich Adolf had got his way. When the next tax assessment was made in February 1699 it was based on an Estates' committee grant of 25,920 tlrs.[84] This the chancellery stepped up arbitrarily by 30 per cent, by raising the basic tax assessment unit of one *Herren-Monat* from 540 tlrs, as allowed by the Estates, to 600 tlrs, and the number of units to be levied in the year from forty-eight to fifty-seven.[85] Two

[82] Staatsarchiv Detmold, Knoch Repositur L 9 folio 743, Communicationstag 14 February 1698.

[83] 'Ausschreiben an sämtl. beamte und respective Vögte', 26 April 1698, Staatsarchiv Detmold, L 37 XVII no. 2.

[84] '48 Simpla Herren-Monate jedes zu 810 fl. oder 540 tlr.'

[85] 'Ausschreiben über die bewilligten und angelegten Extra-ordinari Gelder über das 1699te Jahr', 23 February, Staatsarchiv Detmold, L 37 XVII no. 2.

days before this illegal increase the chancellery had been satisfied with an arbitrary 10 per cent increase in the Estates' grant and the money was to be used to pay interest on 140,000 tlrs debt, to help the regular account by 12,000 tlrs, to pay the ruler's mistress her pocket money, and still to repay *Armierte* arrears to Münster of 4,000 tlrs. The further increase by 20 per cent on this already illegally high tax assessment may account for the profit that local officials and tax-farmers were expected to take, for the Estates granted their taxes net, and the chancellery thus showed that it was determined to get this sum in full.[86]

The treasury accounts show that Estates tax grants were still a minor item of ruler's income as a whole in the seventeenth century, although steadily growing from less than 10 per cent under Simon VII to about one-third of the whole by the early years of Simon Henrich's reign. At times specific tax grants were higher than domain revenue for any one year, but tax grants remained sporadic until the War of the Spanish Succession which saw Lippe running its own standing army for the first time.[87] What contribution, then, did the various orders of society, nobles, burghers and peasantry make to this steadily rising tax demand, and how did each profit or lose by it?

It is a misconception to think that the nobility paid no taxes at all, or that the burghers paid very great amounts. Both paid very modest amounts compared with their actual wealth. But then they were a minority of the families that comprised the whole of Lippe society. By how much could this small number of households have increased tax totals, had they paid realistic taxes? How much of the whole territorial wealth did they alone consume? Some of the Estates' tax records have survived, owing in part to the zeal of one of the nobles' legal agents in the later eighteenth century, who desired to reorganize their records in order to prevent the further loss of lawsuits.[88] These records can be examined in relationship to the tax quotas levied on the lower orders of society, the tenantry, labourers and servants.

---

[86] 'Specificatio der bewilligten Extraordinari Anlagen auff das 1699te Jahr', Detmold ad cancellarium, 21 February 1699, *ibid.*

[87] Staatsarchiv Detmold, L 37 XVII no. 6, Extraordinary tax registers from 1704–7, averaging 25,000 tlrs a year.

[88] Translated from Staatsarchiv Detmold, L 10 Titel 2 no. 15, 'one works in the dark and often has to concede something very prejudicial, which our ancestors would have found good grounds to oppose' (von Blomberg, 1778).

The earliest tax grant in Lippe dates from 1511. It is an agreement between rulers, nobles and burghers to exchange a cattle tax on serfs for fixed labour services from tenants. The Estates thus exchanged an extraordinary tax for redefined services of twelve days a year for free tenants and eight for serfs.[89] This benefited the regular incomes of all landlords, and was intended to make the cattle tax unnecessary by increasing domain revenue, as the ruler was the chief landlord. It was thus considered a better policy to rely on regular services than on taxation.

Early sixteenth-century demands of the Emperors and Empire to pay for federal administration and federal war, as well as of territorial rulers to fund their debts and secure their courts, sent Lippe into the ranks of territories with their own Estates' assemblies. In 1538 alone there were seven full assemblies and ten meetings of the large and small committees of regency with the Estates of the county.[90] This was a mere five years after the first records of Estates' participation in politics had begun to be kept, although consultations with bodies of notables go back at least to the *Pactum Unionis* of the 1360s.[91] The problem of how to keep the dynasty and county together was never a new one. If the dynasty got into trouble, it had to be helped back on to its feet by its most notable subjects.

In the early sixteenth century new pressures of taxation consolidated the orders of society in Lippe. Thus the towns accepted responsibility for paying the Emperor's taxes in return for trading monopolies. When these were not enforced sufficiently, the towns handed on half their tax burden to the peasantry who were evading the towns' markets. When the *Reichskammergericht* collapsed in the 1680s the towns saw themselves further justified in their refusal to continue paying the county's *Zieler*, payments which for a century and a half they alone in Lippe had made via their rulers. The federal campaign against

[89] Staatsarchiv Detmold, D 71 no. 16, Wendisches Copialbuch, 3, *Amt* Varenholz, folio 312, mid-sixteenth-century copy.

[90] Staatsarchiv Detmold, Knoch Repositur L 9.

[91] Staatsarchiv Detmold, L 9 vol. 1 opens with an early sixteenth-century transcript of the document which allowed vassals and towns to choose a ruler from the dynasty in case of disputed succession in order to keep the county united. The final decision was to be with the mayors of Lippstadt and Lemgo, i.e. burghers and not nobles. As it turned out, these provisions never had to be put into practice. H. Kiewning, *Lippische Geschichte*, Detmold, 1942, Appendix.

the Turks, which saw Lippian troops at the siege of Budapest in 1542–3, brought extraordinary taxes levied equally on nobles, towns and rulers' tenantry in the rural districts. With the defeat of the Smalkaldic League in 1547 Lippe also received her quota of fines imposed by Charles V's commissars. It was now that the nobles contracted out of compulsory taxation and substituted a voluntary system of *dons gratuits* for themselves.

In the federal civil war of 1547–53 some of the Lippe nobility saw active military service. It was realistic for them to claim tax exemption in lieu of knight service. At a territorial assembly in 1551 Bernhard VIII's councillors asked for new federal tax grants in response to demands from Charles V and Ferdinand I. In their replies the nobility insisted on exemption for themselves, 'like others of the nobility in the surrounding principalities and territories who are not burdened with such imperial tax demands'. The towns refused to recognize that the nobility had a right to exemption.[92] The councillors supported the nobles and offered the towns greater economic control over the countryside in return for a grant sufficient to cover federal demands. The assembly broke up, with the towns insisting on taxation of the nobility at the same rate of one-third of the total as they themselves were responsible for, as a condition of their own further payments, to the displeasure of the ruler.[93]

The towns had made a blunder by direct opposition. Under Bernhard VII they had taken on tax burdens in return for economic concessions. Why should Bernhard VIII be treated less favourably by them? The answer was that a tax, once paid, produced a prescriptive duty to always pay, whilst a monopoly on commerce could always be withdrawn or naturally undermined. Even if it was not withdrawn but renewed, as was the Lippe towns' seventy-year privilege on trade and manufacture, it was as difficult to enforce an economic concession as it was to get rid of the tax burden that was its *quid pro quo*.

At the same time the rulers were claiming their own tax exemption, but, as domain revenue from the *Ämter* was by far the largest single item of territorial income, it was inevitable that the Estates should seek to hand on tax burdens to the tenantry in the rulers' *Ämter* or rural districts. This involved the

[92] Staatsarchiv Detmold, L 10 Titel 2 no. 11; L 11 IV no. 1; L 11 V 4.
[93] Staatsarchiv Detmold, L 9 vol. 1 folio 217.

rulers' officials who had every concern to keep extraordinary tax demands away from the tenantry, whose ability to pay rents, services and mortgages would thereby be jeopardized. In 1553 Chancellor Bernhard v.d. Lippe replied to a question posed by the neighbouring ruler, Count Otto of Schaumburg, on how Lippe was setting about collecting the fines imposed by Brunswick and Brandenburg-Franconian troops. In Lippe the ruler's subjects had taken on the whole tax burden and the ruler went tax-free. This was a question of averting military danger that affected all the middle Weser territories at the time: a classic example of emergency and extraordinary taxation. Chancellor Bernhard outlined the arrangements the Lippians had made. Without especial fuss the ruler was relieved of all responsibility in the matter. This information reached Count Otto just three days before he confronted his Estates in Schaumburg. Chancellor Bernhard had written to him:[94]

Well-born and noble Count, I have today received your letter about the Brunswick and other tax-demands. I do not desire to withhold from you that these demands have not called forth any especial arrangements. The nobles and towns have merely agreed to contribute a sum of money, each according to his wealth. The clergy and common householders will also be taxed, each according to his wealth and circumstances, which have everywhere been ascertained by the local officials. The sum will be raised from all Estates [*Stände*] without exception and according to the income and circumstances of each. This is now in progress. The [Lippe] subjects have thus taken responsibility for the whole tax burden. They have thereby exempted my gracious Lord of Lippe. This your Grace should not withhold from your [Schaumburg] subjects that have not helped you.

Yet the rural tenantry were no longer exclusively reserved for exploitation by rulers' officials for domain revenue purposes. This the Estates did not allow. From the 1550s the nobility withdrew from granting their own quotas openly. They now negotiated voluntary subsidies secretly with their rulers and gave the towns a permanent grievance. It enabled the towns to cut down their own quotas from the traditional one-third as operated in the 1540s. The *Ämter* tenantry had thus to pay more than their traditional one-third. Thus although nobles and

94 Staatsarchiv Detmold, L 37 XVII no. 8b. A receipt of taxes paid by a Lippe noble to this Brunswick troop demand is in L 11 IV no. 1.

217

towns no longer paid the lion's share of extraordinary taxes themselves, their right to continue to grant such taxes was in practice continued, and with it they dissipated any popular support in the territory: they, if anyone, were now the unrepresentative few, far more so than the ruler or his domain officials.

It was now time for nobles and towns to make deals with rulers' officials over quotas. By 1553 local treasurer Cato received already 22,500 fl. from the *Ämter* tenantry as against a mere 6,400 fl. from the nobles and towns in a grant that the nobles and towns as territorial Estates had specifically made. The nobles paid 7 per cent of the whole grant and the towns 11 per cent. The *Ämter* raised 75 per cent. At this stage the clergy were still separately assessed and they paid another 7 per cent of the whole. They were later merged with the nobility. Of this Cato embezzled as much as the whole nobility paid. Further, the nobles and towns had paid only 65 per cent of what they had themselves originally promised. It seems that in objecting to the nobles' unrealistic tax-payments, the burghers were being hypocritical: no doubt from their point of view it was only because the nobles paid so little that they did likewise. It was the tenantry and labouring population that lost by it, for they had to pay more.[95]

The tax granted in 1573 to pay the dowry of a Lippe countess was placed on the rural tenantry. Local officials were now operating as executive tax-collectors where formerly they had been domain officials or rent-collectors. The *Amtmeier*, chief peasants, paid cattle tax. As they did not have sufficient cattle, their labourers were also poll-taxed in order not to prejudice the poorer householders and farmers. Such taxes were raised in two instalments in the autumn and winter of 1574. Two nobles and two mayors as members of the Estates supervised tax collection for the regency government of the day. The money went from the *Vögte* in the *Ämter* to the *Amtmann* in Detmold, who accounted to regency councillors and Estates for it.[96] This happened in the following spring, 1575. The money was then used not for the dowry but to pay debts owing to the Münchhausens, members of the local nobility.[97]

[95] Staatsarchiv Detmold, L 11 IV no. 1.
[96] Staatsarchiv Detmold, L 9 vol. 3 folio 84.
[97] *Ibid.*, folios 102–5; L 1 G XXXIV–3.

These accounts give the receipts of eleven local officials who provided 7,200 tlrs with negligible arrears (less than 1 per cent). This shows up well against the arrears made by nobles and towns in 1553.[98] In the 1560s the Estates had already agreed to take on 17,000 fl. of rulers' debts which was then immediately passed on as a land and poll tax on the peasants and labourers, with local officials as executive tax-collectors and an Estates' committee as controllers. The actual money raised was over 20,000 tlrs. There was no mention of arrears and the Estates fulfilled their obligations to the ruler, taking a 17 per cent profit from the common people in the process.[99]

The Estates were always keen to grant a tax provided they did not themselves have to pay it, and provided they could help in supervising it. Already in 1536 local magnate Simon de Wend wrote to Count Simon V agreeing to follow orders in his *Amt* at Varenholz and levy a land tax on the tenantry. Simon V then gave permission for 700 fl. to be raised to pay debts owing to the Münchhausens in Minden, for which Simon de Wend had also acted as surety.[100]

The demand by Bernhard VIII for a 1 per cent capital tax to pay for the *Fehde* with Rietberg in 1557, which was granted at territorial assembly, was a unique event in Lippe. It showed how serious this local war really had been, and the Estates were acting far more generously than they did in other emergencies, by digging realistically into their own pockets, rather than leaving all to another land tax on the tenantry.[101]

More in keeping with Estates' methods was the tax-farm which a leading Lippe noble and official bought in 1599 in return for the right to exploit the source plus a return of 6 per cent on his capital outlay. He was allowed to take his profit notwithstanding *toti mali Laesionis usuarii contractus* in an attempt to nullify imperial legislation against usury.[102]

The Estates themselves were important as financiers in the

---

[98] Staatsarchiv Detmold, L 9 vol. 3 folios 102–5.

[99] *Ibid.*, folios 2–27d; A. Falkmann, *Beiträge zur Geschichte des Fürstentums Lippe*, Lemgo and Detmold, 1857–1902, 3, p. 165.

[100] Staatsarchiv Detmold, L 11 IV 5a.

[101] *Ibid.*, eighteenth-century copy. A 1 per cent capital tax was a 20 per cent income tax at the lowest current rate of 5 per cent, a rate twice as high as that proposed in the imperial tax assessment guide of 1542.

[102] Staatsarchiv Detmold, L 114 A, von Donop no. 73; L 9 vol. 4 folios 88–90.

county rather than as actual taxpayers. Their power to grant taxes was used to co-operate with rulers and officials at the expense of the common people. They funded and paid debts that threatened dynasty and territory alike. As such, nobles and town councillors were like *ad hoc* rulers' officials themselves, taking their own work and profit from the inadequacies of comital financial administration. This is shown in the following extract from Estates' assembly minutes.[103]

Consider the territorial assembly held at Barntrup, Thursday, 12th July 1561, where nobles and towns [*Ritter und Landtschafft*] granted a double whole land-tax to pay the federal tax and settle numerous other demands and debts of the ruler. The same has been borrowed because of the speed with which the money is needed, and will be paid back from the tax and proceeds.

Because of the increase in government duties and because the debts on the domain remain at the former level, which it seems the ruler has even considerably increased, the nobles and towns have suggested that a number of them should be delegated to deal with this.

Item that the ruler put his housekeeping in just order and thereby rid himself of unnecessary expenditure.

Fourthly that the ruler incorporate Varenholz into his domain.

The nobility did, however, pay *dons gratuits* to the rulers all through the period. For this the accounts as well as scattered receipts to individual nobles for money paid into the treasury or into their own curia have survived.[104] The Lippe nobility were not exempted from paying taxes out of their own family incomes. Equally they paid their quotas reasonably well. In 1553 they had 35 per cent arrears, the same as the towns. In 1628–9 they had arrears of under 10 per cent on an all-time high, war-time *don gratuit* of 4,000 tlrs. These arrears were the subject of threats of distraint by the chancellery which led to distortion of the picture of the size of real arrears compared with the actual amount paid. Like the federal authorities, the territorial authorities demanded 100 per cent tax payment, *pour encourager les autres*. This distorted the real picture as tax arrears are found to be small when it is possible to check them against the original quota and the actual payment received.[105]

---

[103] Staatsarchiv Detmold, L 10 Titel 2 no. 11.

[104] Staatsarchiv Detmold, L 11 IV no. 1–5d, Adlige Rittersteuer; receipts in L 10 Titel 5 no. 2 vol. 1.

[105] Staatsarchiv Detmold, L 11 IV no. 5a; see Chapters XI and XII.

In 1632 noble Friesenhausen paid 52 tlrs of taxes to the nobles' own receiver, for which Secretary Strop at the *Hofgericht* issued a receipt. This court exercised direct jurisdiction over the nobility and also employed a procurator-fiscal to litigate for tax arrears.[106] The salary for a male servant at that time was between five and eight talers a year plus livery. Friesenhausen's cash payment was thus not a paltry sum, but it is unlikely that he paid so much every year. The year 1632 was, after all, an active war year.

It is perhaps unfair to expect that, had nobles' *dons gratuits* been realistic, nobles would have contributed a very large proportion of all taxes themselves. Their numbers were too small for that, notwithstanding their probable wealth relative to the rest of the population.[107] The same seems to be true of the burghers and officials. But this is not to deny that the nobles especially paid unrealistically small amounts of their income in voluntary taxes by 10 per cent imperial income tax guide-lines ($\frac{1}{2}$ per cent capital tax) operative at that time.[108]

In 1658 Count Hermann Adolf acknowledged a tax grant from his Estates to pay his pressing debts. The nobility were to pay 1,000 tlrs (3 per cent), the towns 3,000 tlrs (8 per cent) and the common people 32,000 tlrs (89 per cent). This was followed by a monthly tax on the *Ämter* population with an annual increase there of $12\frac{1}{2}$ per cent as officials and financiers took their commission.[109] At this rate neither nobles' nor towns' tax payments were realistic, but something they did at least pay. It is significant that the town councils were in practice as successful as the nobles when it came to evading realistic tax payments.

Landdrost Donop left notes on the taxes which the Lippe nobility granted out of their own pockets between 1647 and 1695. They paid a total of 30,000 tlrs in fifty years, partly to finance their own curia, pay their own *syndici* and receivers, and

[106] Staatsarchiv Detmold, L 10 Titel 5 no. 2 vol. 1; L 10 Titel 2 no. 11; Repositur L 16 and L 52.

[107] Up to sixty-eight establishments according to a model assessment signed by twelve nobles in 1630, Staatsarchiv Detmold, L 10 Titel 5 no. 2.

[108] Staatsarchiv Detmold, L 11 IV 5c; L 92 Z 1a, 'Specificatio der gewilligten Rittergelder, 1643–58' totalled 8,700 tlrs. During the same period the treasury received 158,000 tlrs in taxes from Estates' grants. Nobles themselves thus paid an equivalent of 6 per cent of the extraordinary tax bill, whilst an overwhelming 94 per cent was paid by the burghers and peasants.

[109] Staatsarchiv Detmold, L 10 Titel 1 no. 10.

run their own social club.[110] For the rest presents were made to the rulers and festive occasions were subscribed to, including a ruler's visit to the imperial assembly.[111] Contributions were also made towards Lippe's federal and *Armierte* costs in 1663, 1673, 1675, 1680, 1687 and 1690. The later-seventeenth-century nobility were thus paying on average well under 600 tlrs a year in voluntary taxes, just about the cost of a week's session of the territorial assembly of that time. This was an average of under 10 tlrs a year per noble or exempted establishment. It meant an average annual income tax of 1–3 per cent assuming an average modest income of 500 tlrs a year per noble family. They were thus paying charity to the Lippe government, not realistic taxes.[112] The level of the 1542 imperial tax guide had been a 10 per cent income tax. Nobles were thus evading realistic taxes and paying voluntary sums that were a quarter of the size that they should have paid by the standards of the time.

After 1550 nobles, exempted and towns together, paid well under 20 per cent of all taxes which they themselves had granted. The common people, peasantry, labourers and servants paid the overwhelming rest. They were indeed well over 75 per cent of the population, but nobles, officials and burghers were expected to earn vastly more than peasants, let alone the labourers and servants they employed. The Estates were more important as financiers and rulers' *ad hoc* financial officials than as actual taxpayers. As a clique of tax-granters they ran just another tax-system comparable with the domain system alongside the local and central officials. The Estates were dependent on their rulers for further financial commissions and could not become legislators or watchdogs of any collection of liberties, because they had not themselves paid for them. They had got the common people to pay and these obtained no privileges for their money. The Estates, whether burghers or nobles, could never be a threat to rulers' power on these terms.

Lippe's economic crises were of a superficial or, if more prolonged by external situations such as the Thirty Years' War period, of a temporarily serious nature. Basically rulers' and

---

[110] 'Specificatio der Rittersteuer so ab anno 1647 inclusiv angeleget', Staatsarchiv Detmold, L 10 Titel 2 no. 33.

[111] In 1653 nobles gave 2,800 tlrs to their ruler to attend the imperial assembly.

[112] Table compiled from L 10 Titel 5 no. 2.

Estates' economy and society were well attuned, and this is why Lippe could develop into a territory with an unwritten, uninterrupted constitution of rulers, officials and Estates controlling a docile tenantry. There are no records of peasant revolt in Lippe and mob violence was endemic only in Lemgo and perhaps Lippstadt, notably in the 1530s. The religious rather than economic reasons given for it in Lemgo, anti-papal in the 1530s, anti-Calvinist and establishment in the early seventeenth century and manipulated through fear of witchcraft and the black arts all through that century, do not explain the whole story. Yet Lemgo rebellion only contrasted all the more vividly with the docility of the rest of town and country in Lippe.

Lippe was dependent on the ability of its ruling dynasty to control fluctuations in its territorial economy. The Estates as regency advisers kept the county together after the death of Simon V. Bernhard VIII seems to have been gifted enough to retain his regency councillors and their relatives with whom he did not interfere. Simon VI was a strong personal ruler who was at one and the same time an innovator and a notorious spendthrift. He turned Lippe into an effective administrative unit. Simon VII saved the county from bankruptcy whilst at the same time preventing the new administration from falling foul of partition treaties within the ruling dynasty. Hermann Adolf again supported a sound economic policy after the war years, whilst his successor Simon Henrich seems to have been the real disaster of the Lippe dynasty. Like Simon VI, Simon Henrich was a spendthrift, but, unlike his ancestor, he had no qualities of leadership or talent in administration. By the 1680s the treasury system established under Simon VI had disintegrated. By the 1690s the co-operation of rulers and Estates set up in the last years of Simon V's reign had also broken down.

It was left to Friedrich Adolf to attempt to pick up the pieces of constitutional practice evolved between 1530 and 1680 and destroyed by his father in the last decades of the seventeenth century. He did it, not by placating the Estates with an inward-looking peace policy, but by entering federal affairs in the grand style of his ancestor Simon VI. His pro-Habsburg policy worked and rid Lippe of *Armierte*, circle directors' control. Joseph I and Charles VI were better masters to Lippe rulers than had been Rudolf II and Matthias. Yet although internal affairs were suspended in the face of federal successes scored by both Friedrich Adolf and Simon Henrich Adolf, the economic situation was not improved. The arbitrary methods of Simon Henrich's days in *Amt* and *Kammer* were only sporadically overcome. Neither the new *Landkasse* nor the treasury (*Kammer*) were placed on a sound footing during this time. Central control and audit was still the exception, and the disorganization and secrecy that followed attracted the hostility of the Estates, who showed their disapproval by increasing indifference to their ancestral responsibilities as the chief politicians and financiers of the territory.

This, then, was the period of 'absolutism' in Lippe, a failure on the part of rulers between 1680 and 1750 to convince the territorial Estates, the moneyed and propertied subjects of Lippe, of the sufficient soundness of government and economy for them to wish to join in and invest in it as fully as their ancestors had done. There was no question of the Estates not pledging support when insolvency threatened the independence of the county, or when granting taxes and taking on of rulers' debts could still provide a profitable rent or farm. But suspicious 'foreigners' and social inferiors were no longer kept out nor were they readily or easily accepted into county society. There was no question of sacrificing the dynasty and hence the whole territory to bankruptcy, disintegration or oblivion. There was no question of exchanging the Lippe dynasty for some neighbouring, more substantially endowed ruler. By 1700 no Lippian of note who stayed at home was likely to have wanted to become a provincial subject of the Hohenzollerns, Guelphs, Wittelsbachs or Hessians. To this extent Lippe rulers with bad economic policies could find enough passive support from their important subjects to keep the county independent. But support was kept to a bare minimum, leaving the door open to more disreputable officials and financiers whose operations were, however, insignificant in the overall long-term financing of the county.

When after 1750 Count Simon August's officials produced a realistic economic policy once more, the Estates were prepared to give up their opposition and socially merge with officialdom in a plethora of privilege, property and profit. This was the beginning of the end for the early modern constitution in Lippe, a generation, but hardly more, before the final crash under

Napoleon. Although Lippe survived 1803–15 with ruling dynasty and frontiers at all times intact, the real casualties of the Napoleonic upheaval were the territorial Estates, who emerged in the 1820s and after 1848 reconstituted and enlarged by a peasant Estate, not as a result of their own internal reforming zeal, but by the will of arbitrary rulers and their nineteenth-century ministers. With the destruction of the early modern Estates, constitutions and unwritten customs of the Holy Roman Empire, privileged subjects' techniques of conserving liberty for themselves had been destroyed in favour of extending the very idea of liberty from rulers to ruled, but with the rulers and their officials dictating the terms.[113]

Lippe developed not because of the lack of anything foreign to the German federal system, such as centralization from one capital, but because of the amount of expertise and strength in local county society which could provide the men and women capable of understanding and operating the imperial and territorial system. The Lippe archives show that the Holy Roman Empire worked at small territorial level, guaranteeing a larger number of liberties to a greater number of persons than possibly any other system in early modern Europe. In an age of unquestioned inequality, before the birth of natural rights, the greater the diffusion of power and scattering of individual liberties, the more the number of persons who could wield their own power and take responsibility for their own affairs, however small a minority of the whole population they still undoubtedly were. The imperial system was no safeguard against petty tyranny but it did deny the rise to overall power of grand absolutists, just as it allowed the flowering of precocious paternalist planners among its more enlightened despots. The sporadic delinquencies of the largest territories do not satisfactorily direct attention away from the small states that were successfully working within the imperial federal constitution.

[113] Illustrated by the political conflict between Clostermeier and Antze under Regent Pauline which went to the federal *Bundesrat* in Frankfurt-am-Main after 1817. Antze tried, but failed to resurrect the early modern constitution, the political Estates of nobles and town councils. New liberties of the nineteenth-century 'liberal' era were not built around old privileges.

IX

✦✧✦✧✦✧✦✧✦✧✦✧✦✧✦✧✦✧✦✧✦✧✦✧✦

Lippe during the Thirty Years' War

✦✧✦✧✦✧✦✧✦✧✦✧✦✧✦✧✦✧✦✧✦✧✦✧✦

> The war from the outside is dangerous to us, yet the dis-
> sensions at home take precedence.
>
> Henrich Grote to Levin von Donop, 18 November 1635[1]

THERE was of course literally no Thirty Years' War, and no
disarming simplification of German history in the first half of
the seventeenth century is possible. The imperial constitution
was not in abeyance, but between 1614 and 1645 no imperial
assembly and no *ad hoc* gathering of territories was as fully
representative as any during the previous or following years.
The federal system was run by factions that were mutually
hostile and excluded each other at the conference table. Federal
bodies of arbitration were captured as Ferdinand II, following
in the footsteps of his ancestor Charles V, abandoned the path
of equity and justice to destroy a revolutionary minority,
abandoning himself and the majority of territories to the
consequences of war.

When Charles V broke the Smalkaldic League in 1547, he
enjoyed the military services of Maurice of Saxony, who
emerged with the electoral title of his elder cousins as his
reward. Maurice then rounded on the Emperor and put an end
to the civil war in 1552. When Ferdinand II broke the Union
in 1620, he enjoyed the military services of Maximilian of
Bavaria who also emerged with the electoral title of his elder
cousins as his reward. But Maximilian did not round on his
cousin the Emperor, and this civil war became only a part of a
general European war. In 1547 the Habsburg lands had not

[1] Staatsarchiv Detmold, L 10 Titel 1 no. 7.

been threatened by revolutionary Calvinists. In 1618–19 it was no longer only a question of teaching German Protestant militants a lesson, a matter which the League could cope with, but of retrieving Bohemia for the Habsburgs. The jealousies of junior and senior branches of Wettin and Wittelsbach were given full outlet by the events of 1547 and 1620. In both cases the Habsburg supporter won. But in 1620 this was not enough to stop the war.

As federal concord cracked, small territories were buffeted this way and that, as armies dictated their own terms from campaigning season to billet. In 1547 Lippe was caught arming in support of the Hessians by Charles V's forces and accordingly fined. To the end of that war the county remained unwillingly imperialist and more willingly neutral. In 1618 the county was neutral and it remained so. It provided troops for no one and thus hospitality to all who could command it. In 1623 the first imperialist troop occupation took place in Lippe. In the 1630s the Swedes mounted raids into the county as it remained in the imperialist zone of influence and occupation. Only one garrison was stationed in the county for any length of time—an imperialist force in Lemgo. It did not prevent the comital administration from paying monthly tribute to both sides. After 1648 Lippe paid its share towards the demobilization of both sides.

What was the trouble? Did politicians lose their power to the troops who then misbehaved and caused all the traditional horrors of war? What happened on one of the fronts, the middle Weser front: what do the records in Lippe, in backwoods eastern Westphalia, say about the war years?

The Lippe records become bulky in the 1630s. Day-to-day correspondence survives between the local and central officials, Estates and notables of court, town and country, concerned with borrowing, lending, supply and victualling. There are no horror stories in these papers, despite day-to-day correspondence, as the civil administration of the county continued in control under its own native rulers, officials and notables.[2]

In some years there was a greater burst of activity than in

[2] Staatsarchiv Detmold, Knoch L 56–60. A similar wealth of material (day-to-day official and semi-official correspondence) is in Stadtarchiv Lemgo. Cf. Ingomar Bog, *Die bäuerliche Wirtschaft im dreissigjährigen Krieg*, Coburg, 1952, pp. 165, 142–54.

others as billeting and marauding increased or decreased according to policies and tactics beyond the scope and control of
Lippe.[3] Thus in August 1630 the imperialists imposed curfew
and censorship on Protestant Lippe. It was decreed no man's
business to speculate and pamphleteer on religion nor by
implication on Gustav Adolf's chances after the Mecklenburg
landings. An inquisition was to enforce these views with exemplary punishments on life and limb.[4] At the same time Lippe
regency councillors were coping with the material threat of
Ferdinand II's Edict of Restitution. Too many Lippe rulers,
nobles and burghers had committed themselves to non-Catholic
ways. Any religious threat implied a change in property and
landownership. Thus any conflict would involve far larger
sectors of the economy than those directly claimed by the Roman
Church when it demanded the restitution of church lands.
In August 1629 Hofrichter v. Schwartz advised Landdrost v.d.
Borch to pay lip-service to the Edict:[5]

I have received certain information from Minden that the Emperor's
Commissar, Hein, has arrived in person in Minden, and is especially
ordered to deal with the County of Lippe: namely to repossess the
ecclesiastical lands and properties sequestered after the Passau agreement [of 1552], and to reconvert people in the County of Lippe to
Roman Catholicism or to the Augsburg Confession and law, which
latter, thank God, we now also have the choice of—note well, all according to the choice and decision of the Detmold government.

This Commissar was in County Schaumburg the last weeks, and he
demanded the restitution of all the ecclsiastical lands and property of
the University there.[6] The Schaumburg councillors raised considerable
objections upon which the Commissar soon went to His Excellency,
Tilly. Thus one fears he will ask for military reprisals.

The Emperor's Edict is ordered to be carried out in County
Schaumburg. I suggest that one do likewise here in Lippe. If the
Commissar should come and not find that this has been done, it is to be
expected that the same will happen here.

This subterfuge was accordingly carried out. The landing of
Gustav Adolf then altered the balance of power, so that,

[3] Thus 1635 was a calm year in Lippe, but 1636 saw the heaviest marauding by
the Swedes and their allies. [4] Staatsarchiv Detmold, L 41a IV F no. 2 vol. 1.
[5] The University at Rinteln was founded by Calvinist ruler Ernst von Schaumburg in 1619 with a patent from the Elector Palatine acting as imperial viceroy
during the interregnum. [6] Staatsarchiv Detmold, L 41a IV 207.

although remaining within the imperialist army zone, Lippe could take part in Saxony's peace conference from 1631, notwithstanding the opposition of Ferdinand II.[7]

Any ideological conflict was thus minimized as territorial governments remained in control, profiting from the blunders of their neighbours, as in the case of the Lippians here learning from the Schaumburgers' lack of duplicity. As long as the territorial government kept a pace ahead of the imperial commissar, then it stood a chance of protecting itself from retaliation. Thus Detmold published the Edict of Restitution in early 1630, keeping within the letter of imperial law as Ferdinand II had made it, yet by no means entering into the spirit of the thing. In playing successfully for time, Lippe remained Calvinist, as an unarmed, if possible 'neutral', supporter or passive host to the imperialists. As such the county may have fared better than if, by chance geography, it had been within the Swedish zone, for the *Reichskammergericht* at least remained open to Lippe dynasts and subjects who accordingly made increasing use of it from the 1630s.[8] In the regency dispute of 1636–40, Swedish supporter Count Johann Bernhard was ousted by Dowager Catharina who armed herself with *Reichskammergericht* (and Emperor's) mandates and cultivated the local imperialist troops to carry her to power.[9]

A conference and audit of March 1630 shows how the territorial government in Detmold remained in control, acting as the real channel through which Tilly's officers' demands on the county populace had to go. It shows the considerable power of the native and civilian regency councillors and Estates over their foreign, military guests. At Detmold castle Tilly's general commissars met and agreed with apanage Count Otto of Lippe, Landdrost v.d. Borch for the government and the nobility and three burghers for the towns. The minutes were taken by an army scribe.[10]

Tribute paid to Tilly's personal establishment was audited and passed. The county would continue to pay at Tilly's

[7] Staatsarchiv Detmold, chancellery note of 22 April 1630; L 41a A no. 16; L 41a IV F no. 1; L 41a IV no. 2 vol. 1.

[8] See Chapter XI.

[9] K. Meier, *Die Standhafte Katarine*, Detmold, 1935.

[10] 'Kürtzer protocollarischer Abscheidt', Staatsarchiv Detmold, L 37 XVII no. 9a, the twelve points of which are outlined and discussed as follows here in the text.

pleasure, but he would be petitioned for exemption or at least reduction in payments to alleviate the 'extreme exhaustion of the poor subjects' of the county of Lippe.

Count Otto of Lippe-Brake agreed to pay for the continued upkeep of Tilly's adjutant and horse-troop in the county but only at the existing rate and in return for protection from the claims of all other officers and men.

Otto was buying protection from Tilly. Yet to do this Otto had pledged the support of the Estates and regency government, and that he did not fully have. The nobility objected outright, and the regency councillors in Detmold insisted that they refer back to the official regent, the Count of Waldeck. Otto was the dynasty's young uncle behind the throne. The Estates refused to accept his decision. Yet the towns, who really had most to lose if an agreement with Tilly over troop billets was not immediately reached, agreed provisionally to Otto's undertaking, and only formally reserved their rights and those of the official regent in the matter. When dealing directly with troops it was best not to refer back and procrastinate as could be done with a Turk tax or a ruler's debt.

Otto and the towns further agreed to help bear the cost of all future, unavoidable imperialist troop movements through the county, on the same basis as in the past, notably that Otto and the towns be reimbursed for what they had given in food, money and money equivalents, but not for any other damages (i.e. war damage, 'enemy' operations).

This clause indicates that some kind of troop occupation insurance was in existence, whereby the army received tribute from its civilian hosts, and had to live on it through barter and trade, which enabled the civilians to get their money back for the next round of tax payments to the army. The troops in Lippe therefore negotiated peaceful methods: in return for order and protection the civilians paid—in return for money and accommodation the army bought, and did not plunder, what they needed from the civilians. Thus as long as the civilians produced enough for their own and their military guests' needs, the system of tribute–barter–tribute could go on peacefully and indefinitely. Only there was the problem of rival commanders and rival armies. In drawing up their agreement with Lippe in 1630, Tilly's commissars refused to reimburse for acts of war, accepting responsibility only for their soldiers' behaviour in the market-place.

The towns agreed to continue to help support the cost of the troops, but insisted on a cut of excess levies, demanding that quotas be kept. The towns would pay for minor overnight stays of troops marching through the county. They would not be able to deduct these costs from their quotas of tribute. Yet if half or a whole regiment demanded hospitality then it must notify its hosts in advance and work out costs per head before arriving.

Survival depended on planning the needs of troops as far as possible in advance. Here the towns wished to pay incoming troops a fixed amount of spending-money. It was then up to the townsmen to get it back before the contingent moved on by charging the highest prices they could without provoking the soldiers into rioting. This minimized the idea that the soldier was entitled to something for nothing for lack of pay. The town thus preserved civic order and still had the chance of planning its economy to cover the cost of troop incursions.[11]

The towns refused to support a Lippian home guard as they already had to defend their own walls. Equally the home guard had not found territorial assembly approval. What would in future be granted at assembly, the towns would bind themselves to uphold, just as they agreed to support the hue and cry. The regency government in Detmold, however, remained committed to a home guard.

Costs of distraint were to be shouldered evenly by all debtors actually involved. Travelling expenses, messengers and miscellaneous costs would be examined on their merits against receipts. Thereupon the accounts were closed and signed by all parties. The haggling continued, however, between Otto, the regency government, the nobles and the towns.

The payment of interest and pensions was to be open to further discussion, with priority given according to the uses to which the borrowed capital was put. Yet the return of expropriated money was to follow according to due process of law. No decisions would be taken whereby anyone was deprived of his just

---

[11] Staatsarchiv Detmold, L 10 Titel 2 no. 2, complaint of Saltzuffeln against Lemgo's profiteering from its billeted troops; 'dahe alles der Soldatescha auffs theuerste vorkaufft wirtt'.

deserts. As regards the payment of servants, the towns agreed to pass the accounts rendered, with a proviso that a further investigation be carried out. Otto then demanded that Lippstadt pay its arrears. The regency government delayed its decision. Not to lose what had already been gained, the matter was dropped from the agenda with a demand for further information.

Otto then insisted that tribute be levied uniformly in the whole territory, and that subjects be relieved of one-sixth of their quotas, which Otto would provide from subjects in his own apanage Brake. Thereby Otto obtained his own tax powers separate from the jurisdiction of the Detmold regency government. This was the beginning of that freak state within a tiny state, the seventeenth-century apanage of Brake within Lippe.

Otto's self-interest as a junior member of the dynasty dominates this agreement. It was this and not the war activities of outsiders in Lippe that really upset Lippe politics and finance. For once Otto had been silenced, another regency occurred within four years, and with it came a new young uncle behind the throne of a minor, Count Johann Bernhard of Lippe. Whereas Otto had been intent on immediate agreement with the imperialists, Johann Bernhard was much more pro-Swedish. The Swedish raids of 1636 had put Otto in a near-suicidal frame of mind. Gone was that enthusiasm for federal politics that had seen Otto in service under Mansfeld in 1619 and making amends in Munich and Vienna in 1624–6.[12] But the Swedes loosened the imperialist hold on the county until 1640 when Johann Bernhard and his brothers retired to await their return to power from the comparative safety of Swedish Minden and Rinteln.

In the meantime faction fights went on among the Estates, who took their cue from the dissensions among the ruling dynasty. With nobles Schwartz and Borch as the 'in' group, Donop and Grote had to bide their time. In November 1635 Grote was deploring the number of yes-men in the noble curia who passively made one *don gratuit* after another whilst nothing ever got better and no real safety was purchased.[13] Yet two years later as one of a group of *Landräte* Grote was threatening his fellow nobles with military reprisals if they did not pay their

---

[12] W. Süvern (ed.), 'Letzter Wille und Lebenslauf des Grafen Otto zur Lippe-Brake vom Jahre 1636', *Lippische Mitteilungen*, 30, 1961, pp. 134–44.
[13] Staatsarchiv Detmold, L 10 Titel 1 no. 7.

overdue taxes within eight days.[14] It was easier for Grote to be in opposition. When to this home situation the Swedish raids of 1636 are added, then the Lippe picture looks black indeed. But only for a very short time. The horrors remained distant or controllable by astute territorial civil government. With squabbles at home the situation temporarily got out of hand. It was, as Grote said in November 1635, 'the war from outside is dangerous to us, yet the dissensions at home take precedence'.[15]

What, then, of the financial situation according to the accounts and bribes of Lippe authorities in this period? They show one consistent point; everyone claimed to be paying too much themselves, whereas their colleagues, neighbours and equals were not paying enough. No one claimed to have a penny and so there had to be dearth everywhere to prove this claim. Yet large payments were made regularly and even larger damages were as equally regularly alleged. Persons operated within the letter of the law and jealously denounced their neighbours. There was a lack of consistency and even of detail and thus a lack of truth in the outrageous demands for damages made by the towns as each vied with the other to obtain quota reduction before the next round of taxation. Under such conditions no straightforward picture emerges from the Lippe records of the war and occupation years, unless the naïve view prevails and every time a general plea for exhaustion and dearth is made in order to avoid further taxes, it is taken at its face value and ascribed to war horrors on the lines of the simpleton's bestseller, 'Simplicissimus'.[16]

After 1638 Lemgo town, on the strength of having to support the only permanent garrison of foreign troops in the county, managed to obtain tax exemption from the monthly war-levies that the Lippe government had to send to the Swedes and imperialists. Above all the imperialist garrison in Lemgo objected to the town being taxed by the Lippe government to help pay their enemies the Swedes in Minden. The remaining towns objected to having to take on Lemgo's quota of monthly war tax. In the resulting contest each town tried to prove that

[14] Staatsarchiv Detmold, L 10 Titel 2 no. 11.
[15] Staatsarchiv Detmold, L 10 Titel 1 no. 7.
[16] Cf. G. Benecke, 'The problem of death and destruction in Germany during the Thirty Years' War', *European Studies Review*, 2, 1972, pp. 239–53.

it was incapable of bearing any tax increase. Instead each town demanded reduction by showing how much it had already been forced to pay since the opening of hostilities. Between 1640 and 1642 the towns sent in their 'accounts' to the Lippe chancellery.[17]

Between 1623 and 1639 Lemgo claimed total war costs to its inhabitants at just over 1 million tlrs. This included over 70,000 tlrs weekly war taxes up to 1632, presumably as a multiple of a much smaller fixed sum of money circulated between towns' tradesmen and soldiers in a tribute–barter–tribute pattern that prevented soldiers from demanding something for nothing, and regulated their appetites by making them town-council wage-earners.

The actual billeting costs of the imperialists' garrison in Lemgo was 1,550 tlrs a month. Between July 1625 and September 1627 Lemgo paid nearly 31,000 tlrs of this. The town thus had arrears of only 20 per cent which it induced the surrounding villages as well as apanage Brake to pay. From the monthly rate here it is feasible to assume that a sum of well under 2,000 tlrs in actual coin was sufficient to keep the troops paid, provided the supply of produce was sufficient for the burghers to recoup by the end of every month what they had paid the troops in tribute at the beginning of that month.[18] This would account for an inflated reckoning as so often occurs in financial records from the war years. The same amount of specie seems to have circulated at a much faster rate in order to adapt a barter economy to the conditions of a consumer system in wartime.

Up to 1632 nearly half of Lemgo's war claims were even in multiples of weekly war-tribute. Thereafter another 320,000 tlrs was claimed as property damage in the two Swedish raids on the town in 1636–7. Yet no compensation for deaths was ever claimed, though the accounts were searched for such 'human' items: damages were asked for things, not for people. By 1650 Lemgo had raised its claims to nearly 1,400,000 tlrs, and this even excluded alleged plunder of another million. A typically dubious item showed not war horrors, but merely how unrealistic the town's attitude was to war, for,[19]

[17] Staatsarchiv Detmold, L 10 Titel 2 no. 2.
[18] Staatsarchiv Detmold, L 10 Titel 2 no. 11.
[19] Stadtarchiv Lemgo, Kr 57, 'Kosten und Krieges Beschwerden der Stadt Lemgo, 1622–50'.

What otherwise in this town with deterioration of the prisons, towers and gates, buildings, also burghers' houses and otherwise the inhabitants with their fields and gardens, fruits, with harvesting of burghers' meadows and fields, restriction of burghers' livelihood through perpetual watch-keeping, mustering, cost of repairs to buildings, decimation of the oaks and beech woods, have had to suffer in damage, also what through nocturnal insolences between 1640–48 has been pressed out of the poor burghers, as well as what both secretly and openly has been stolen and taken away, is almost impossible to assess in money and can at the very least be reckoned at 60,000 tlrs.

Such an unrealistic attitude to wartime has to be reckoned with in Lippe war 'accounts'. At this rate Lemgo could claim in all that she had average war costs of 30,000 tlrs a year between 1622 and 1650.[20] Yet how credible is this?

In 1621 Lemgo had a civic debt of about 100,000 tlrs. It thus needed to raise 5,000 tlrs a year just to pay pensions in the period immediately prior to the coming of foreign troops to the county.[21] After demobilization in the 1650s another survey of civic debt showed about 140,000 tlrs owing. This included 85,000 tlrs to non-Lippians. To cover this the town needed at least 7,000 tlrs revenue a year. By 1655–9 there were about 130 main creditors who claimed an average of 50 tlrs pension a year each.[22] But although foreign investment was higher than Lippian in the 1650s, total civic debt had increased by only 40,000 tlrs during the whole war period. This was just at a time when Lemgo burghers claimed nearly 1,400,000 tlrs war damages. Did they have that much property to damage in the first place? Why was only 140,000 tlrs borrowed on it? The whole war period had increased Lemgo indebtedness by a mere two-fifths of its pre-war figure. If there was exhaustion of credit, then it set in very early in the war, with the war years making little improvement but causing little deterioration because basically by 1620 Lemgo seemed already to have reached its optimum level of debt, war or no war.

Lemgo's heaviest borrowing was between 1605 and 1624, and its lowest periods of borrowing were 1625–7, 1631–8 and

[20] Stadtarchiv Lemgo, Kr 57, cf. Kammerbelege, Kriegsunkosten, notably from 1632.
[21] Stadtarchiv Lemgo, Kr 42 vol. 1 1621, Gemeine Stadt pensionarii.
[22] Stadtarchiv Lemgo, Kr 54, Summarisches Verzeichnis der Stadt Lemgo Schulden 1655–9.

1651–4. Between 1605 and 1624 civic borrowing was about 110,000 tlrs. Between 1625 and 1654 it was about 18,000 tlrs. It was this that hit civic respectability hardest. Yet the bad debt situation was not due to the war but had been created before the war. However easy it was for town councils to lay the blame on war, town finance had been ruined by dissensions within the town and county before the foreign troops came to Lippe and dried up the sources of credit. The economic squabbles between town councils and town mob, the civil war between Calvinist counts and Lutheran Lemgoers in the first two decades of the seventeenth century had had to be paid for by increased borrowing prior to the war.

To make matters worse, the occupying troops in Lemgo after 1625 were no great investors in town pensions and the slow recovery of credit after 1648 equally tended to give plausibility to the argument that somehow it was all due to the war. Between 1648 and 1660 Lemgo borrowed only about 16,000 tlrs. However, this was at a time when new borrowing was officially frowned upon, as deflation continued as the economic religion.[23]

What then was town income? In the first full year of occupation, 1624–5, Lemgo town chamber took in about 25,000 tlrs and spent about 27,000 tlrs.[24] With a minimum debt charge of 5,000 tlrs set against this, town finance looked very realistic indeed.[25] Yet the imperialist troops billeted in the town officially took over 18,000 tlrs of this, but spent it weekly and monthly in the town again in order to live.[26] In theory the town council was left with 5,000 tlrs for day-to-day costs and for reducing or refunding capital debt. The town could spend less than 20 per cent of its annual income on itself. Yet a real annual income of 25,000 tlrs is unbelievable when contrasted with the income of the peace years. In 1622, just before the occupation, town administrative costs had been a mere 1,440 tlrs.[27] As late as

[23] Staatsarchiv Detmold, Repertorium Stadtarchiv Lemgo 1952, Verzeichnis der Urkunden und Abschriften, Stadtobligationen und Renten (extracted sources for 1605–60). [24] Stadtarchiv Lemgo, Kr 42 vol. N–84.
[25] Stadtarchiv Lemgo, Kr 42 vol. 1.
[26] Staatsarchiv Detmold, L 10 Titel 2 no. 11. The items 'wöchentliche- und monatliche Contribution' were multiples of fixed weekly or monthly tributes, levied by troops on burghers and peasants. Thus under monthly contribution every one taler collected appeared twelve times in the annual accounts.
[27] Stadtarchiv Lemgo, Kr vol. 12 (1622), giving total expenditure at seven pay-days.

1599 the town chamber still accounted in debased marks. In that year income had been about 30,000 marks. This included new borrowing of about 15,000 marks and about 10,000 marks paid by new families for the legal right of becoming Lemgo burghers. Regular taxation was therefore minimal in Lemgo town before the troop billets altered the system and made this impossible after 1623.[28]

From 1585 the Lemgo mark ran at eighteen to the taler. Regular income was thus extremely low and even a possible 5,000 tlrs residual income from the war-billet year of 1624–5 shows a fourfold increase for the town chamber on pre-war income. It shows equally that pre-war Lemgo income was already hopelessly inadequate to cover existing debts. Lemgo was not doing too badly by the war. The huge war damage claims have to be taken for what they were, attempts to get tax-relief. They were dishonest, but in the case at least of Lemgo after 1638 reasonably effective, as the town got exemption from county war taxation in general.

Lemgo now paid no taxes to the regency government. This infuriated Horn town, which accordingly in March 1640 made its own attempt at tax reduction by claiming war damages of 190,000 tlrs for 1623–40. It included property damage of 16,000 tlrs and an arithmetical error of nearly 12,000 tlrs for good measure. The town's ambition seems to have been to get to the 200,000 tlrs damage mark. A second claim in January 1642 nearly two war years later eliminated the arithmetical error and even so was reduced to 175,000 tlrs. There is thus reason to believe that such material was laughed at by the military and territorial authorities of the day. Detmold town claimed 21,000 tlrs damages for 1633–40.[29] Saltzuffeln claimed nearly 270,000 tlrs for 1634–9. This spectacular figure, that even outdid Lemgo, included alleged plunder to the value of 185,000 tlrs.[30] Who could believe that?

Saltzuffeln claimed that by having permanent troops of occupation Lemgo could make a profit out of the trade they brought, which the other towns could not do. Instead they had

[28] Stadtarchiv Lemgo, Kr vol. 8 (1599).

[29] At the rate of 2,500 tlrs a year. Yet town treasury income in those years of peacetime for which figures still survive was a mere 345 tlrs (1585), 537 tlrs (1662–3), 693 tlrs (1668), 1,483 tlrs (1680–1), Staatsarchiv Detmold, L III C 1.

[30] Staatsarchiv Detmold, L 10 Titel 2 no. 2.

to pay marauders and troops spending the night within their walls and then marching on with the townsmen's money unspent within the walls. Saltzuffeln declared to the Lippe government:[31]

We can see how the poor small towns, and further among them this town of Saltzuffeln is mightily burdened, compared to which Lemgo town is hardly affected, for although Lemgo has for several years now had a regular garrison [which Saltzuffeln never had], so not only is a considerable sum contributed towards this garrison, but the Lemgo burghers also get a good livelihood out of it, as everything is sold to the troops at the dearest price. This is why we object to the Lemgoers being allowed to have freedom from all tax-burdens, from the [Swedish] contribution to Minden, as well as from their own [imperialists'] contribution.

Saltzuffeln then claimed that with its own war damages of 270,000 tlrs in six years it should undoubtedly have tax exemptions and that Lemgo should pay in full.

Here was the truth of the matter. A war damage claim was an unscrupulous attempt to get tax reduction from the territorial authorities irrespective of neighbours' problems. It was not a credible account of actual war damage.

If the Lippe towns had not fallen out with each other over Lemgo exemptions this civic approach to war would not have come out. The war years gave vigorous scope for local dishonesty, in enterprise that had no feelings, that failed to obey the moral principles underlying any organization of the marketplace. This indeed was the war 'horror', but one of the conscience. It was not the mere brutality of camp life that degraded Mother Courage, but the way that she put barter and the market above everything, including the life of her last son. The moral of Grimmelshausen and of Brecht is one of warning against degradation, as deaf-mute Katrin's sacrifice of her own life to save yet another town from secret night attack tries to show. It is not that of jobbing, self-pitying Mother Courage, who conforms ever to a way of life that slowly strips her of all her humanity.

Expediency smothers any true picture of war damage to property and human life. Property was made much fuss of in the records, but loss of life was ignored. To loss of life local and

---

[31] *Ibid.*

territorial government papers of the period remain indifferent. They just pay lip-service 'to these clouded and troubled times'. They uncover no horrors of war at this local level in this area. What then of recent arithmetic on wartime population loss in Lippe?[32]

These estimates were based on the counting of names in contemporary tax and rent registers, stiffened by a multiple of so many per register name, for each name is assumed to be a head of a household. With the desire to escape taxation as strong as it was in the towns of 1640 Lippe, any total of population gleaned from tax and rent registers becomes highly suspect. The Lippe war evidence is far too ambiguous for any credibility to be given to Kuhlmann's assertion that Lippe population was reduced by 35 per cent from 40,220 to 26,000 between 1618 and 1648.[33] This view does not detract at all from the great value and importance of the demography that Kuhlmann produced.[34] From such study, however, a conclusion about population loss cannot be drawn. Yet one cannot assume that there were no war losses. The documents do not tell us anything as fundamental as overall wartime population loss. In this case any assessment of war damage remains guess-work.

As nobleman Grote implied, whilst in political opposition in 1635, internal dissensions came before the horrors of war in the county. In fact by the 1640s the Lippe regency government had settled down to raising regular monthly taxes which it then paid to the imperialists in Lemgo, inside the county where the money could easily be recouped, and to the Swedes in Minden, where an increase in Lippe-Weser trade across the army fronts had to bridge the monetary gap. Right at the end

[32] M. Kuhlmann, *Bevölkerungsgeographie des Landes Lippe*, Remagen, 1954, pp. 2–3, 38–44, and statistical tables and maps. The method was to find the number of farms presumed as mentioned in the land tax and poll tax lists of the local districts, to collect any subsequent local population census figures, then to divide the number of farms culled from the estate records into the number of population and arrive at an average figure for the number of people per farm for the county, with the tax lists standing for heads of households and acting as a crude kind of 'control group'. Accepted by G. Franz, *Der dreissigjährige Krieg und das Deutsche Volk*, 3rd ed., Stuttgart, 1961, pp. 12–13, cited in H. Kamen, 'The economic consequences of the Thirty Years' War', *Past and Present*, 39, 1969, p. 49.

[33] Kuhlmann, *op. cit.*, pp. 40–1, 92.

[34] Reviews by W. Muller-Wille, *Westfälische Forschungen*, 9, 1956, pp. 20–1; Pittelkow, *Lippische Mitteilungen*, 24, 1955, p. 293.

in 1647 and 1649 both Swedes and imperialists were receiving
4–5,000 tlrs a month each from Lippe. This implied an annual
tax bill of about 100,000 tlrs, but in reality a monthly turnover
of about 10,000 tlrs in coin, showing the efficiency with which
the tribute–barter–tribute system worked.[35]

Finally, the comital treasury accounts show that the ruling
family was also having to pay its share of the war by suffering
a massive decrease in rents and revenues. At Easter and
Michaelmas 1627 treasury income from the *Ämter* was still
33,700 tlrs. With this sum debt and pension payments of
19,000 tlrs were made. Total arrears were now only 35,000
tlrs.

By 1632 *Ämter* income was at an all-time low of 16,000 tlrs.[36]
Pension arrears alone were 53,000 tlrs in 1630. If the ruling
dynasty as the leading landlord in Lippe suffered loss of regular
income, then presumably all Lippe's landlords did so too.[37]
This would also help account for the decrease in the number of
names on rent and tax registers as the war brought its own
temporary economic system to Lippe. To calculate population
from these registers would produce no total of Lippe inhabitants,
but only a total of those still caught up in the residual *Ämter*
finance system, not fully revived until some time after the troops
had gone.

These factors, then, upset Lippe most. Its ruling groups found
no more credit to finance already very serious pre-war debts.
In the tribute–barter–tribute system they had to accept decreases
in rent as the soldiers now needed what the tenantry produced.
What better than to retaliate by blaming the war for everything
and computing high losses in the hope of reducing taxes or
avoiding them altogether? Who in any age can be expected to
take a cut in his standard of living? Thirty-Years'-War Lippe
landlords could not be expected to do that without showing
serious unrest.

County government and society retaliated in the only possible
way—by claiming huge war damages. There is no reliable
record of its economy, merely evidence of tortuous expediency.

[35] Staatsarchiv Detmold, L 58 XXII nos II–III; L 59 XXVII nos 1–IIa; L 60
XXIX nos 1–IIIa; L 60 XXX nos IIa–d, IIIa.

[36] Cf. estimates between 1650 and 1701, putting total *Ämter* income to the
treasury at 42–51,000 tlrs. Staatsarchiv Detmold, L 92 A Titel 63 no. 63.

[37] Staatsarchiv Detmold, L 63 B 12–I.

What does emerge, however, is that native civilian authorities retained control of society, economics and politics in the territory, and co-operated with regular occupation troops. Natives kept control of taxation. Military distraint for taxes was not found: it was rare enough for collecting serious arrears,[38] but more common as a threat of Lippe's own chancellery and *Hofgericht*.[39] This civilian control was the real achievement of Lippe, for despite internal rivalry, as regency followed regency, Lippian politicians survived with territorial power intact. There could indeed have been martial law and war horrors if the politicians had blundered here. They did not, and Lippe's hard-luck stories from this period could not be substantiated from the financial records that were examined.

[38] Staatsarchiv Detmold, L 63 A 12, *Scharfe Execution* in 1683. See the Fiscal's returns in the treasury accounts of the Thirty Years' War, L 92 Z 1a.

[39] Threats of distraint, Staatsarchiv Detmold, L 10 Titel 2 no. 1 (towns 1649), no. 11 (nobles 1637); L 11 IVa–Va (nobles 1624).

Part Four

<hr>

Relations between State and Federation: Lippe and the Empire

<hr>

X

Lippe and the Emperors

THE Habsburg imperial administration caught up with Lippe in the fifteenth century. Geographical remoteness, smallness and lack of direct feudal ties with the Emperors all helped Lippe to remain federally undetected. Although Lippe was assessed for pikes and lances in earlier fifteenth-century imperial assembly lists, notably to help fight the Hussites, it was not permanently caught up in demands from federal military, judicial and financial registers until the reign of Maximilian I.[1]

At Christmas 1470 Emperor Frederick III's chancellery in Graz sent a writ to the Lord of Lippe to come to an imperial assembly in the following month of April at Regensburg. Frederick promised to be there in person. Together with the Pope and the German princes, counts, lords and towns the protection of the Christian faith against the Turks was to be the subject of discussion. Lippe was exhorted to appear because of a 'duty' to the Christian faith, and to the Roman Emperor, and in accordance with a provision from the previous assembly to continue federal discussion of the Turkish invasions. No further threat, no real compulsion was exercised. It is not known what

---

[1] *Reichstagsakten*, old series, 2nd ed., Göttingen, 1956ff., 6, pp. 7, 9, 73; 8, p. 159; 9, pp. 176, 530. In the 1420s Lippe assessments varied from 2 to 5 units of lances and 10 marksmen. By 1489–91 Lippe's imperial assembly assessment was 4 horse, 8 foot and 20 fl. This changed to 5 horse, 4 foot and 150 fl. in 1507, stabilizing in 1521 at 4 foot, 18 horse and 60 fl. Koch, Senckenberg and Schmauss (eds.), *Sammlung der Reichsabschiede*, 1, II, Frankfurt-am-Main, 1747. By 1527–30 Lippe was paying substantial Turk taxes, 240 fl. in lieu of horsemen, and 135 fl. in lieu of footsoldiers' pay for half a year. Receipt from Frankfurt-am-Main, *Reichstagsakten*, new series, Gotha, 1893ff., 8, p. 1094.

Bernhard VII decided.[2] A beginning had been made, but Lippe was not forced at one go into federal politics.

Three years later Frederick cited Bernhard to another imperial assembly. His chancellery was now operating from outside Vienna. The tone of the writ was much harsher. Frederick deplored the fact that the previous Regensburg assembly had been fruitless. A new assembly was called to Augsburg to deal with the Turks. Bernhard was warned to appear and give aid on pain of losing all grace and favour, his fiefs, privileges, freedoms, rights and jurisdictions, which he was duty bound to owe to the Holy Empire and to the Emperor himself. This clause was new and important. Despite the fact that Bernhard had no ties with the Habsburgs whatsoever, and no feudal tie with the office of Emperor, a legal bond of sorts had been forged. From now on writs from imperial chancelleries to full assemblies demanded Lippe's participation in federal affairs because of a general and unspecified duty that the lordship owed to the concept of the Empire, to the *Reich*, as well as to the person of the Emperor as head of this federal concept.[3]

In 1474 Bernhard by an open imperial order was warned not to give aid to an outlaw. Frederick was trying to enforce his imperial land-peace. Bandit von Hanstein had continued his feud with a town under the jurisdiction of Archbishop Adolf of Mainz. As Mainz was then in the service of Frederick, managing the current assembly at Augsburg, the Emperor felt particularly sensitive about this infringement of his peace. The principle of federal peace-keeping, as well as the practice, seemed to be at stake and it is this that may have induced the chancellery to include Bernhard in the public circular. Also, Bernhard was a notorious local bandit himself. The world of *Fehde* was his own true *métier*, although it is unlikely that Bernhard's sphere of operations ever extended to the other side of Hesse. Even so, Frederick was taking no chances, and he justified his declaration of outlawry by appeal to the Golden Bull, his own *kunigkliche Reformacion* and his four-year land-peace.[4]

By 1479 a tone of disillusionment had set in. From Graz Frederick now asked Bernhard to come to an *ad hoc* gathering of princes to deal with the current, *twenty-third* invasion of his

---

[2] Staatsarchiv Detmold, L 37 XVII no. 6. *Lippische Regesten*, no. 2395.
[3] Staatsarchiv Detmold, L 41a IV E 9 vol. 1. [4] *Ibid.*

lands by the Turks. The idea of an organized imperial assembly had been given up. The Bavarians would be at the next meeting in Freising, to run affairs on imperial commission. The writ again made a strong appeal to religious fervour, yet there was no telling compulsion to it.[5]

From the scanty evidence that survives, the first federal contacts with Lippe were made under Frederick III and the subjects were the Turk menace and the land-peace. Two pillars of German federalism had been erected. Turks on the frontier and bandits at home remained the backbone of federal politics from the fifteenth century to the eighteenth, whether the delinquents were spectacular like Markgraf Albrecht or Frederick II of Prussia, or local nuisances like Hanstein or Grumbach.

The next period of federal demands on Lippe came after 1505 when there was a relatively short-lived general enthusiasm for swashbuckling Emperor Maximilian I after the death of his political opponent Berthold of Henneberg. Although still only in a temporary form, it was in this period, especially at the imperial assembly in Konstanz in 1507, that real advances were made in establishing a federal executive. Tax registers for military purposes and for financing a supreme court of appeal were drawn up and taxes were granted, using these registers on a sliding scale according to current needs.[6]

Between 1507 and 1511 ageing Bernhard VII of Lippe was caught up in Maximilian's demands. Following imperial assembly grants, Maximilian's chancellery issued printed formulas demanding troops and money. The form was more than just a demand, however, for it contained a long preamble, outlining Maximilian's military plans. It was his skill to put territorial rulers into the picture, to give the impression that he was taking them into his confidence. On 3 August 1507 two orders were sent from Konstanz to Lippe.[7]

Elector Frederick of Saxony was declared viceroy whilst Maximilian went off to war against the Venetians. Territorial rulers were asked to show him obedience and four regions were delineated to deal with internal security. The other order

---

[5] Staatsarchiv Detmold, L 41a IV 207. See W. Neumann, 'Die Türkeneinfälle nach Kärnten', *Festgabe H. Steinacker*, Munich, 1955, pp. 84–8.

[6] L. von Ranke, *Deutsche Geschichte im Zeitalter der Reformation*, popular ed., 1, Munich, 1914, pp. 152–97.

[7] Staatsarchiv Detmold, L 41a IV E 9 vol. 1; L 37 XVII no. 7.

warned Lippe to provide five horsemen and four footsoldiers for the coming Italian campaign. Detailed instructions about the type of equipment were given. Maximilian outlined his grand designs against the French and Venetians. He warned that the French king desired to exclude the German nation for all eternity from Italy and to make himself hereditary Emperor.[8] Maximilian repeated the Konstanz assembly grants. He expected 120,000 fl. with which to hire mercenaries for a six-month campaign.[9] He notified the restarting of a *Reichskammergericht* in Regensburg.

Bernhard VII paid his due quota. In March 1508 he obtained a receipt for 240 fl. from Maximilian's treasury secretary, his marshal and treasurer. Bernhard had paid money in lieu of troops as agreed upon at the assembly in Cologne.[10] Payment had, however, been made only after threat of legal proceedings for the recovery of debt. It is significant that tax-grant arrears were already being treated as debts recoverable by legal action. Treasury jurisdiction under the guidance of the Emperor's own procurator fiscal was the most important development of federalism as far as the Emperor was concerned. The *Reichskammergericht* was above all a court for enforcing the payment of tax arrears, and Lippe felt this for the first time in 1507-8.[11]

In August 1507 Lippe had been notified that the *Reichskammergericht* was open again.[12] Lippe had little benefit from the fact. Instead the court issued orders, threats and fines to Lippe in attempts to get the lordship to pay taxes for the Court's upkeep and to erase imperial assembly tax arrears. The court was a useful weapon of the Emperor and his financiers.

---

[8] 'Die teutsch nation in ewig zeyt auss ytalien zuvertilgen vnd sich selbs erblichen kaiser zu machen.'

[9] In an order from Bozen, February 1508, Maximilian noted that of 12,000 troops promised, several hundred only had appeared, and only one-third of the money had been paid. The French had 7,000 troops in the field and the Venetians 12,000.

[10] Staatsarchiv Detmold, L 37 XVII no. 7.

[11] Orders from Konstanz, 3 August 1507; Bozen, 8 February 1508; Konstanz, 26 June 1508, Staatsarchiv Detmold, L 37 XVII no. 7, 'wolten auch nichts destminder vnserm künigklichen Cammerprokurator Fiscal gestatten / mit den obbestimbten penen, straffen vnd püssen / darumb gegen euch on auffhalten / für zunemen vnd zugefaren / darnach wisset Euch zu richten'. The threat worked at least partly for the last order was endorsed in Lippe chancellery hand, 'de van d. Lippe vifftig gulden hyr to vthgedoin. De van Lemgo, Horn, Blomberg, Detmold und Vffeln gegeven hyrto twehundert rinsche gulden.' Lippe's federal taxes had been paid by the towns. [12] Staatsarchiv Detmold, L 37 XVII no. 24a.

It as yet played no rôle in upholding the liberties of small
territories like Lippe.

In 1509 demands for unpaid taxes took a more strenuous
turn. Lippe fell into the hands of Maximilian's procurator fiscal.
Lemgo town had been given a separate assessment and Bernhard
was suddenly expected to pay 786 fl. of arrears. In January
Bernhard was cited before the *Reichskammergericht* at Regensburg and threatened with a sentence and gold fine whether he
appeared to plead or not. Two months later Bernhard wrote to
Maximilian's commissars on the Lower Rhine.[13]

We would have you know that we have indeed often been assessed for
a sum of money that is too large for our circumstances, and impossible
for us to give. Even though we have sent and paid our due money to
Cologne this year, which was achieved with the assistance of our
subjects [*lantschup*] and for which we did obtain receipts, so now we
have been warned by Imperial order to pay 786 fl. tax arrears from
grants made at Konstanz and Cologne as well as 25 fl. fees to the
fiscal and 24 fl. to the assessors of the Court at Regensburg. Equally,
although our town of Lemgo is subject to us and duty bound to assist
us, yet it has also been cited to pay Imperial taxes. We find all this
impossible to carry out. *For it has previously never been our custom to give
the Emperor money* [my italics]. Yet we will talk with our subjects
[*lantschup*], neighbouring rulers, friends and kinsfolk to obtain their
views on your demands, and we will similarly follow what our neighbours have done in this matter.

Maximilian's foreign wars were a failure and this drastically
influenced his chances of obtaining further imperial assembly
grants. He had to fall back on other expedients. In 1511
the Jews of Lippe paid an imperial tax.[14] In 1513 Simon V of
Lippe obtained a receipt for 80 fl. paid in lieu of troops. In fact
Simon himself never paid up. This debt was the subject of a
Reichskammergericht case, brought against Simon in the 1520s
by a Brunswick noble who had actually paid the tax.[15]

Maximilian fell back on the expedient of selling expectancies.
In 1517 the Guelphs bought such an expectancy on Lippe,
although they had no feudal rights over the lordship, in the case
of Simon V dying without heirs, which seemed to be very likely

[13] Palm Sunday 1509, Staatsarchiv Detmold, L 37 XVII no. 7.
[14] *Ibid.*, receipt of 6 February 1511.
[15] Staatsarchiv Detmold, L 82 (H 20) no. 310, Appendices.

at that time.[16] It is this branch of imperial power that Charles V continued to build up and exploit in return for money. Lippe now entered the field, seeking confirmations, appointments, rights and privileges in a modest way, whenever necessary and when it could afford it.[17]

In 1520 Charles V sold Simon V the appointment of imperial councillor and household servant under the great seal and Spanish counter-seal from Brussels. There were no specific duties or grants in the patent and Charles probably never even saw it. It was a purely formal prestige document, and it is not known why Simon should have wanted to identify himself with the Habsburgs in this way.[18]

The indication is, however, that Simon V wanted to get out of the clutches of the Guelphs. A year later he bought another patent from Charles V. If Simon was to die without direct heirs then he was to be allowed by imperial privilege to have the heir that he had nominated in his will upheld as his rightful successor. The towns of Lippstadt and Lemgo were to uphold this choice in accordance with the 1368 treaty of indivisibility, which had given them the right to choose a successor from the ruling dynasty in case of disputed succession. Above all the expectancies which Maximilian had sold to the Guelphs were to be confounded.[19] Lippe had entered the field in search of imperial privileges. But as late as 1521 the ruler of Lippe still turned to his towns and not to his feudal following of nobles and knights for guaranteeing his dynasty's undivided succession to the lordship.

In the 1520s federal legislation began to percolate through to Lippe. A proposal by the *Reichsregiment* in 1521 to get rid of *Fehde* by the age-old expedient of *ad hoc* courts of peerage and arbitration, where the aggrieved chose one of a number of impartial social equals to judge the case, was mooted in Lippe. Traditional methods were being used to enforce the perpetual land-peace. In cases where this did not work, the matter was to go before a commissar nominated by the Emperor, or the council of nine, the short-lived *Reichsrat* in Worms. Only those

[16] *Lippische Regesten*, no. 3051, 3051a.

[17] Imperial privilege could also attempt to work against Lippe. In 1541 Charles V sold the wardship over Bernhard VIII to Count William of Nassau. The regency councillors in Detmold ignored this after consultation with the Estates. Staatsarchiv Detmold, L 9 vol. 1 folios 102b, 190, Appendix folio 2.

[18] Staatsarchiv Detmold, L 1 A personalia 2.   [19] *Lippische Regesten*, no. 3091.

with no overlord other than the Emperor were to have recourse to this; all others were to appeal to their territorial rulers in the first instance. In the case of Lippe there were as yet no legal facilities to deal with such cases beyond the local, disciplinary courts that were in any case unable to deal with nobles, officials or wealthy burghers. Yet the Empire was attempting to provide the legal machinery to destroy a vicious system of self-help. It was asking territorial rulers of all ranks for support by expecting them to increase their own territorial legal powers.[20]

As Lemgo town was included in the federal tax register of 1521, the Emperor's officials and lawyers tried to force Lippe to pay separate taxes for the town. This would have doubled Lippe's federal tax-bill. The matter led to sporadic lawsuits and complaints until the early eighteenth century.[21]

A favourable interpretation of the rules for Turk tax laid down by the imperial assembly of Speyer in 1542 allowed rulers and nobles to assess themselves according to their own Christian conscience, whilst burghers and peasants were publicly assessed. Circle director Jülich was ordered by the Emperor and his brother Ferdinand to play an executive rôle in arranging for Turk tax collection. Jülich was also responsible for the organization of the Westphalian circle contingents of member territories campaigning in Hungary in 1543. In return the first general rules of federal currency regulation and military employment reached Lippe under the seal of King Ferdinand.[22]

Personal involvement with Emperor Charles V came for Lippe in 1547 as a result of the failure of the Smalkaldic League. Young Bernhard VIII and his brother Hermann Simon fell into disgrace for allowing their councillors to support Philip of Hesse. Regent Count Jobst of Hoya had already been outlawed as a notorious bankrupt in 1541. After his convenient death in 1545 Lippe found an excellent regent in the religiously conservative coadjutor and future Elector of Cologne, Adolf of Schaumburg. As a count, neighbour and kinsman by birth and upbringing Adolf was able to protect the young rulers from Charles V's more rapacious officials and military commanders.

[20] Staatsarchiv Detmold, L 41a IV E9 vol. 1.
[21] F. Copei, 'Lemgo und das Reich', *Lippische Mitteilungen*, 15, 1935, pp. 163–88. Staatsarchiv Detmold, L 28 C Section II no. 1; L 28 L Section VII; L 41a IV B 1; L 42 9–10; L 45 2–8a–c; L 1 G XXXIV a–d; L 9 vol. 1.
[22] Staatsarchiv Detmold, L 37 XVII no. 2, 6, 24a; L 9 vol. 1 folio 220 verso.

He smoothed the way for the transfer of feudal lordship over Lippe from Hesse to the Emperor. Bernhard's councillors were, however, not so cowed that they did not register a strong protest against Charles V's treatment of the county at the imperial assembly of 1548.[23]

Repeated demands by Charles V that Bernhard should come and plead for mercy and seek enfeoffment for the former Hesse fiefs in person at Charles' court were turned down by the councillors at Detmold. Instead Hermann Simon was sent, and he appeared only in the safe entourage of Elector Adolf.

Just as Lippe played for time in the feudal issue, so there was a marked policy of delay as regards the carrying out of the terms of the 1548 Augsburg Interim in religion. The bishopric of Paderborn had been commissioned by Charles to see to the recatholicization of Lippe. This worked at least *pro forma* with rulers and nobles for as long as Charles had control of the military situation in the north-west in the period up to 1552. But notably Lemgo town refused on the ground that the town council would not be able to guarantee law and order among the burghers if popish priests came back within its walls. Bernhard had to abandon his town to the mercies of imperial commissars as he refused to lay himself open to any further imperial fines because of religion.[24]

In the outcome the religious issue ran into the sand as Charles V lost control of the war effort. Lippe was partly plundered by Markgraf Albrecht and his mercenaries in the summer of 1553 just before the battle of Sievershausen that ruined Charles' political reputation and left the Protestants victorious but without their natural leader. The fact that Charles had at one time supported the notorious Albrecht was enough to plunge the reputation of the Habsburg Emperor to a depth that was not plumbed again by another Emperor until the 1620s.[25]

It was Ferdinand I who saved the situation by presiding over negotiations that gave two generations of peace and internal security. Lippe had her own representative at the Peace of Augsburg in 1555. She received copies of the new federal security measures involving a circle and *Reichskammergericht*

[23] Staatsarchiv Detmold, L 6 no. 14; L 41a IV E 9 vol. 1.
[24] Staatsarchiv Detmold, L 29 B Section II; L 9 vol. 1 folios 198–201, 207, 210–11. [25] Staatsarchiv Detmold, L 41 vol. 1; L 41a IV E 9 vol. 1.

system to enforce internal peace. She became a part of the new currency area which tried to enforce monetary unity by regulating the price of precious metals and checking the value of coin. The achievements of the period 1555–9 under Ferdinand I were thus the real outcome of a policy of federal co-operation started by Berthold of Henneberg two generations previously.

In the 1550s and 1560s the Empire was left with the problem of demobilization. Hardened mercenaries and their followings, such as those of Markgraf Albrecht, Grumbach and the Mansfelds, were dispersed only by armies raised on federal taxes made available by the territories after imperial assemblies. These armies in turn caused further demobilization problems. The foreign war issue also continued as the Turkish frontier became static and federal taxes were needed to help fortify it on a more permanent basis. As ever, the Turkish issue provided the real mainspring for further imperial assemblies. It was around this issue that Habsburgs and territorial rulers could centre their bargaining and sink their differences.[26]

The circles now began to play their part as regional executives. In Westphalia Circle Director Jülich called regular, almost annual, meetings of the territories within the circle to discuss ways and means of complying with federal tax demands, the monetary situation, the visitation and appointment of regional assessors to the *Reichskammergericht*, with a view to carrying out federal decisions or at least achieving something by direct local threat.[27]

So Bernhard VIII was caught up as an auxiliary officer in the circle administration, whilst Lippe suffered from a breach of the peace caused by a neighbour of hers, the Count of Rietberg in 1557. The matter was settled by a circle army that borrowed Bernhard's guns and pounded Rietberg out of his castle.[28]

Again Lippe got into tax arrears, both genuine and alleged, because of this circle campaign and the persistence with which federal chancellery officials insisted on keeping Lemgo at a reduced rate in the tax registers. Demand notes poured into Detmold from Emperors' chancelleries, their treasurers and

[26] *Ibid.*   [27] Staatsarchiv Detmold, L 41 vols 1–2; L 37 XIII 1–2b; L 28 C II–1.
[28] Staatsarchiv Detmold, L 9 vol. 1 folio 223; L 11 IV no. 5a, L 11 V no. 1. P. Casser, 'Der Niederrheinisch Westfälische Reichskreis 1500–1806', *Der Raum Westfalen*, II, 2, Münster, 1934, p. 46.

roving commissars, from procurators fiscal at the *Reichskammergericht*, and from the Westphalian circle treasury under Cologne town council and seconded Jülich officials. Certain accounts were paid and consultations with the Estates of Lippe were held. Yet the majority of these demands were handed on to legal agents to plead at the *Reichskammergericht*.

Some arrears were undoubtedly fictional. Even rises in taxation, such as the extra two-thirds for the assessors at the *Reichskammergericht* in the 1570s, were decided without the participation and consent of small-fry like Lippe. The county thus refused to pay the increase with the result that within a few years there were substantial 'arrears' in the court's treasury accounts. Like claims for war damage, claims for arrears, especially from federal sources, have to be examined with extreme caution. No tax official ever operated without claiming arrears and no taxpayer ever contributed for long without asking for reduction or compensation of some sort. This was the system and the Lippe records show it clearly at work.[29]

Above all, however, the system of Ferdinand I worked, and the second half of the sixteenth century was a period of federalism *par excellence*. Lippe undoubtedly benefited from the internal peace and security that followed, the more so after Simon VI took over in 1579. He made a name for himself in the service of Rudolf II and tried to prevent the Spanish-Dutch wars and the Palatinate-Calvinist issue from wrecking the 1555 system in his part of the world.

Simon VI believed in the federal system of his day. At his first territorial assembly in July 1579 he pursued a firm policy of prompt federal tax payment, and he stuck to this for the rest of his reign. His Estates were admonished to make suitable arrangements well in advance. Thus Turk taxes were generally paid with borrowed money and recouped from the taxpayer with the appropriate commission later.[30] The federal debts of Rietberg were also paid along with Lippe's quotas during the short time that Simon ruled there, during his first, childless marriage with Rietberg's co-heiress. Many of the federal tax receipts that survive date from Simon VI's reign.[31]

[29] Staatsarchiv Dettold, L 37 XVII nos 6–7; L 11 IV no. 1.
[30] Staatsarchiv Detmold, L 9 vol. 3 folios 109–11; L 114 A, von Donop, no. 73, for a Turk tax farmed out to the nobility.
[31] Staatsarchiv Detmold, L 28 C II zu 1; L 41a IV E 9 vols 1–2; L 37 XVII no. 6.

In 1582 Count Simon VI attended the imperial assembly in person. He was the first Lippe ruler to do so. From now on federal politics began to take up more and more of his time. He took on his father's old post as an auxiliary officer in the Westphalian circle. He sought contacts in Prague and the 1590s saw him making a career for himself under Emperor Rudolf II. In return Rudolf confirmed Simon's right to mint his own coins in 1592. A year later Simon's new *Hofgericht* was given power to decide definitively all cases involving 200 fl. or less. Only amounts above this sum still carried the right of appeal to the imperial courts. At the same time Rudolf confirmed three family treaties and wills that Simon from time to time altered as he began to face the problem of how to endow his younger sons and yet keep the county from being split up. Finally on 9 August 1598 Simon was confirmed in his appointment to Rudolf's *Reichshofrat* in Prague.[32]

With the growing debility of the Jülich-Cleves dynasty and the bishopric of Münster in absentee Wittelsbach hands, there was a vacuum in the Westphalian circle directorate which threatened the effectiveness of the circle as a federal executive. Simon kept the circle going. With the support of Rudolf, Simon became circle leader, although with Lippe he had not the territorial resources to fully exercise the responsibility that such a post entailed. Simon tried to find a way of upholding the neutrality of his circle against the raids of the Dutch and Spaniards on the Lower Rhine in the 1590s. He organized a circle army which campaigned in 1599. It was a singular failure. Thereafter Rudolf confined Simon more and more to the task of Turk tax arrears collector in the region around Lippe. The resulting debts and alleged arrears that Simon had made in imperial and circle service were borne by the county. Lippe became insolvent in 1610. Imperial treasury demands on Simon's heirs continued until 1641 when the alleged debts were written off by decree of Ferdinand III.[33]

What induced Simon to go into Rudolf's and the circle's

[32] Staatsarchiv Detmold, L 1 A; L 1 C; L 41a IV B 3. The Simon-Rudolf relationship has been fully described by A. Falkmann, *Beiträge zur Geschichte des Fürstentums Lippe*, Lemgo and Detmold, 1857–1902.

[33] Staatsarchiv Detmold, Repositur L 41; L 41a IV 207; L 92 X 11 no. 61. A. H. Loebl, 'Eine ausserordentliche Reichshilfe', *Sitzungberichte der phil.-hist. Klasse d. kais. Akad. d. Wiss.*, 153, Vienna, 1906, pp. 97–8.

service? For a start he probably did not reckon with the financial outcome. Simon was a spendthrift at home as well as abroad and it was his eldest son who with considerable success tidied up the mess after 1610. The promptness with which Simon paid all his Turk taxes, until the Lemgo rebellion made him go into arrears after 1607, shows that he was a keen supporter of Rudolf's war against the Turks. His efforts both military and diplomatic to end or at least confine the Spanish-Dutch wars within the Burgundian Netherlands show that he was in accordance with the views of Rudolf, that the Turkish campaigns must take priority over any other conflicts in the Empire. He tried to improve the Westphalian circle's Turk tax payments accordingly.[34]

That Simon had considerable skill in diplomacy and that he liked the round of social calls, banquets, discussions and exchange of formalities is brought out by the report of a secret peace mission which he conducted for Rudolf at The Hague in 1592. Acting on a verbal arrangement made by Rudolf and himself in an audience which he was granted with the Emperor whilst visiting Prague in 1591, Simon travelled without real instructions and certainly with no offers to make to the Estates General. Even so he met Maurice and Ernst von Nassau and discussed with Barnefelt the possibilities of Rudolf's place in a Spanish-Dutch peace. Simon hinted at the delicate position of Rudolf but assured the Dutch that the Emperor wanted peace in order to continue his Turk war with the resources of the whole Empire. The Dutch even offered their support and loyalty to the imperial cause if Rudolf would make his position clear. In this way the Dutch had made their gesture towards Rudolf, and Simon, having no powers to negotiate, was given a banquet, was voted the appropriate silver-ware worth 2,000 fl. (which he noted that he had declined to accept), and sent back to Lippe to write his report.[35]

Although this mission looks amateurish, and although it proved to be an expensive journey for him, costing 2,400 fl., yet Simon did see the Dutch leaders and he accurately concluded that the Dutch were prepared to wait until their demands for

[34] Staatsarchiv Detmold, L 41a IV E 9 vol. 2, arrears lists of January 1602, imperial tax demands sent to Simon to deliver to his neighbours.
[35] Staatsarchiv Detmold, L 41a IV E 9 vol. 1.

full independence from Spain were met.[36] Over the issue of loyalty to Emperor and Empire they were still prepared to bargain, if Rudolf was prepared to show an independent line within the Habsburg network. Yet basically Simon with his Westphalian interest and ambition to serve his Emperor was stepping into a hornets' nest. As Rudolf's councillor he was not more than an occasional servant: he remained an insignificant territorial ruler. And yet Simon was the only ruler who in his part of the world played a rôle in federal affairs, and on the strength of this he ranks as the great man of Lippe politics.[37]

By 1586 Simon was getting news-letters about the state of the European Protestant movement. At the same time he was going Calvinist himself. The Calvinists in the Empire kept him supplied with copies of their grievances. Simon's attitude was twofold. At the level of the imperial assembly he did not declare for the Palatinate extremists, whilst yet continuing to keep himself informed on the progress of their cause. On the other hand Simon had no time for the new line of Habsburg Wittelsbach intolerance advocated by the new generation. He clung to the demand for unity in the Empire to fight the Turks. This policy became more and more difficult to support as the conduct of Rudolf's war administration came under heavy fire from Catholics and Protestants alike at imperial assemblies after 1608.[38]

The matter started when a commission of audit set up by the territories became dissatisfied with the Turk tax accounts of Treasurer Geitzkoffler between 1594 and 1603. The matter came to a head after the death of Rudolf, whose officials had partly cleared and protected Geitzkoffler, and it bedevilled the first imperial assembly of Matthias in 1613. Simon also lived just long enough to receive a report of the affair, which

[36] Simon reported on the Dutch, 'so befinde ich aber, das die antwort nit affimativa noch negativa ist, ausserhalb das sie anmelden, wegen hiebevor ergangener handlung, vnd darunter gesuchte practicken vnd erfolgten beschwernus sie nichts (das ist soviel zusagen kain subiect) sehen, wie mit frucht solche handlung zubefurdern sey'.

[37] Cf. L. Schmitz-Kallenberg, 'Des Grafen Simon VI Gesandschaftsreise', *Lippische Mitteilungen*, 4, 1906, pp. 44–82.

[38] Staatsarchiv Detmold, 'Zeitungen aus Halberstadt, Frankreich und Polen', Repositur L 41; L 41a IV E 9 vols. 1–2.

discredited an administration in which he had also sunk his life's work and money.

Three Regensburg imperial assemblies in 1594, 1598 and 1603 granted a total of 226 *Römermonate* at a *simplum* of about 60,000 fl. This gave a tax grant of 13½ million for the territories. Geitzkoffler alleged 2 million of arrears, so in fact between 1594 and 1603 85 per cent of all Turk taxes were paid. Of the 11½ million that Geitzkoffler actually received, auditor Hemerl claimed that he had misappropriated about half a million. By the standards and practices of the time an actual payment of 85 per cent of the theoretical total granted, as well as another 5 per cent loss in misappropriation by the Receiver, was a by no means dissatisfying record.[39]

Yet Hemerl, as auditor for the territories, was not satisfied. Even though Geitzkoffler was able to fight for and in 1617 obtain acquittal in the imperial courts, the blow to confidence in the federal system of the day was mortal. This in its turn played into the hands of the religious extremists, as it was now no longer possible to freeze internal differences by appeal to a united administration conducting a foreign war against the Turks that Christians of all denominations in the Empire could agree to support. It must have further rankled with the territorial rulers that Geitzkoffler had bought himself the title and appropriate splinter territory of a Swabian imperial knight, where he built himself a mansion in the latest Italian style.[40] Geitzkoffler's defence in 1613 was also suspect, for he refused to discuss technicalities arising out of the accounts. He claimed innocence because his methods had worked. The troops were always paid on time and he could not take responsibility for every single item of expenditure, especially those of his subordinates.[41]

Undoubtedly Geitzkoffler's problems were genuine. He

---

[39] Staatsarchiv Detmold, L 41a IV E 9 vol. 2. The Geitzkoffler affair found its apologist in J. Müller, *Zacharias Geitzkoffler 1560–1617*, Vienna, 1938; 'Das Steuer und Finanzwesen des Reichs im 16. Jahrhundert', *Neue Jahrbücher für das klassische Altertum, Geschichte und Deutsche Literatur*, 9, 1902, pp. 652–78; 'Die Verdienste Zacharias Geitzkofflers um die Beschaffung der Geldmittel für den Türkenkrieg Kaiser Rudolfs II', *Mitteilungen des Instituts für österreichische Geschichtsforschung*, 21, 1900, pp. 251–304. For an explanation of *Römermonate* see Chapter XII.

[40] *Neue Deutsche Biographie*, article on Geitzkoffler.

[41] Staatsarchiv Detmold, L 41a IV E 9 vol. 2, from a report dictated by the Mainz arch-chancellery to the territories at the imperial assembly of 1613.

worked with a system of anticipation of revenue because of the slowness of tax payments. He had to contend with the pilfering of Rudolf, his brothers, nephews and courtiers, and he had genuine arrears. Thus it was not a question of right, but a question of non-confidence in the Habsburg running of the military machine which the territories expressed after 1608, and which after 1613 left very little room for manœuvre against the rising tide of religion.[42]

Simon's handling of religion at home was also mistimed. In the Lemgo rebellion he hoped to counter the town's appeals to the *Reichskammergericht* with a decision in his favour from his colleagues on the *Reichshofrat*. Yet when his commissioner reached Prague in 1611, Rudolf and his *Reichshofrat* were no longer in control. Some councillors were in prison and the rest were waiting for decisions from Matthias and the Bohemian Estates. A firmer line on religious matters was expected in the Empire and the Lippe suit had no chance of finding a hearing. Even so Simon did not give up trying to get a verdict on the strength of his record of service with Rudolf in an administration that had begun to by-pass Rudolf and leave him without any real power. In terms of the 1555 peace Simon's case as a Calvinist had little chance of success. Although he had the right of declaring religious uniformity as a territorial ruler over his subjects, this could hardly have extended to Calvinism in strict terms of constitutional law before 1648.[43]

Simon's obsession with federalism clearly failed for reasons beyond his own power to control, but not perhaps beyond his own power, as ruler of Lippe, to have foreseen. When he died in 1614, he left a large family to be provided for as social status demanded, a bankrupt domain administration and a territory split by a civil war that neither side could afford to wage. It was no wonder that his successor, Simon VII, found support from his Estates only in a further policy that shook off all federal responsibilities and dealings. Simon VI found no one to follow in his footsteps, and through him Lippe had learnt her lesson to keep as much as possible out of imperial and Habsburg service. Yet had Rudolf and his administration not become so discredited, the outcome might well have been more positive. As it was,

---

[42] Staatsarchiv Detmold, L 41a IV E 9 vol. 2.
[43] Staatsarchiv Detmold, L 41a IV C 6–7.

the reign served to warn Lippe rulers to cultivate their own gardens and not be captivated by imperial assemblies and courts.

The seventeenth century saw a marked increase in litigation of a constitutional and dynastic nature. Some of this now went to the *Reichshofrat* although the towns and their burghers continued to use the *Reichskammergericht*. Lippe received a copy of the 1626 *Reichshofratsordnung*, but did not take an interest in this court's decisions as precedents to be followed at home until the later eighteenth century. It became standard practice, however, to obtain the Emperor's sanction for appointment to regencies on the accession of minors. He was also then approached to confirm attainment of the age of responsibility in the appropriate cases. Regencies within the ruling family were confirmed by imperial patent in 1627, 1637–9, 1668, 1704–12, 1735, 1749, 1791 and 1802. This included diverse branches of the ruling family, which had been remarkably compact in the sixteenth century and had split and multiplied only after Simon VI. Thus the seventeenth and eighteenth centuries saw the late flowering of wardship and inheritance as an essential ingredient of Lippe politics and dynasticism. In the contests that ensued Emperor and imperial courts, above all the *Reichshofrat*, played an important rôle in the affairs of the Lippe dynasty. This court claimed jurisdiction over all cases involving conflict among *Reichsunmittelbare* themselves, because of the feudal overlordship of the Emperor who still presided in theory over the court. It was partly due to the loss of one case after the other to the Lippe-Schaumburgers that Archivarius Knoch was appointed in the mid-eighteenth century to Detmold to tidy up the archives and prevent further losses to hated relatives. To Knoch the preservation and study of documents was essential in order to uphold and extend the rights and jurisdictions of his rulers in an age that believed above all in litigation.[44]

The Emperors also began to have a say in the system of government by proclamation and decree which in Lippe reached its peak in the later seventeenth and earlier eighteenth centuries. Between 1630 and 1759 there were at least thirty-two such decrees published in Lippe. They had one thing in common: they nearly all contained military instructions in the ebb and

[44] H. Kiewning, 'Das Lippische Landesarchiv in Detmold', *Archivalische Zeitschrift*, 42–3, 1934, pp. 295, 296–314. Staatsarchiv Detmold, L 1 A.

flow of demobilization and escalation, which became the main preoccupation of federal politics after Ferdinand II had reintroduced civil war in the 1620s.[45]

It was the preoccupation with war that pushed the Emperor's desires to the forefront even in Lippe in the 1620s. There was a reversion to the days of 1547–53, as voluntary co-operation gave way to one of military threat and coercion once more. It was not that the federal system as it had still worked in the days of Rudolf II totally broke down, but rather that the Emperor took sides. Thus at federal level there was no real appeal or arbitration but only attempted enforcement of preconceived ideas and policies.[46]

The Estates of Lippe just in the Thirty Years' War period made especially telling use of the *Reichskammergericht*.[47] After the religious issue, which Ferdinand II especially had exploited at federal level, had been finally regulated in the Empire in 1648, Vienna reverted to the Turks and then the French as the traditional enemies on the frontiers, around which to build up federal co-operation and leadership. Coercion of the small-fry like Lippe was no longer by direct military methods as practised by Tilly or Wallenstein, but indirectly through circle directors and powers with large standing armies. From the 1660s to the 1690s Lippe had no direct military contribution of her own to make to the federal war effort. Leopold I thus assigned her to the tender mercies of the *Armierte*, Münster and Brandenburg. As regards Lippe this policy was reversed by Count Friedrich Adolf in 1698, who provided his own troops and thereby achieved a greater degree of independence from his overpowerful neighbours than had been customary in the previous reign.[48]

Demands for *Römermonate* for the federal war effort reached their peak in Lippe under the Emperors Leopold I, Joseph I and Charles VI. Foreign wars were pursued with general success

---

[45] W. Sellert, *Über die Zuständigkeitsabgrenzung von Reichshofrat und Reichskammergericht*, Aalen, 1965, pp. 37–45. Staatsarchiv Detmold, L 41a IV A no. 16. Imperial proclamations were either counter-sealed by the Lippe chancellery or reprinted with the name of the Lippe ruler to lend weight to the Emperor's demand. Cf. *Lippische Landesverordnungen*, 1–2.

[46] Staatsarchiv Detmold, L 41a IV 207; L 41a IV F no. 2 vol. 1.

[47] Staatsarchiv Detmold, L 11 V no. 1.

[48] Staatsarchiv Detmold, L 37 XVII no. 6–9a, 22. See Chapter XIII.

and they were the unifying force behind this second flowering of federalism in the Empire.

As far as Lippe was concerned, the Emperor acted as a war-lord and as the guarantor of a system which settled dynastic squabbles and shortcomings within the ruling family of Lippe. He lent his name to imperial assembly legislation and to the decisions of the *Reichskammergericht*, especially in the recovery of federal tax arrears. Except during the civil wars of Charles V and Ferdinand II, the Emperor's powers were more remote and presidial as far as Lippe was concerned. For this reason they have not been examined before, as if they were cog-wheels in a piece of machinery that people once knew about and have since forgotten.

XI

Lippe, *Kammerzieler* and *Reichskammergericht*

LIPPE paid taxes for the upkeep of the *Reichskammergericht* before its rulers and Estates began to use the facilities of the court to put their own cases. Equally this was the court that above all hunted Lippe for tax arrears, the *Zieler*, so called because they were fixed biannual assessments which paid for the operation of the court itself, and the *Römermonate* which paid for the federal war machine. In March 1508 Bernhard VII wrote to Maximilian's commanders in Cologne that he had paid his federal war taxes. The money had been levied from his towns and he demanded a stop to the threat of a case against him at the *Kammergericht*. He had no arrears and they must recognize this fact. Nevertheless a case was brought and decided against Bernhard, although he categorically refused to pay. The court was undermining federal authority by trying to enforce an unfair tax demand.[1]

The earliest surviving record of Lippe actually paying *Kammerzieler*, the taxes for the upkeep of the court itself, dates from 1531. Count Simon V sent 12½ fl. to the town of Frankfurt, whose town council generally received Lippe's federal

---

[1] R. Schröder and E. von Künssberg, *Lehrbuch der deutschen Rechtsgeschichte*, 6th ed., Leipzig, 1919–22, pp. 914–19, 923. R. Smend, *Reichskammergericht*, *Geschichte und Verfassung*, 1, Aalen, 1965, p. 311. Staatsarchiv Detmold, L 37 XVII no. 7. Federal documents from this period have been lost. There is no record that the Lippe administration ever kept separate registers, files or chests for these materials. The remnants were classified by Archivarius Knoch in the eighteenth century in Repertorium 37, where the material is incomplete and unsorted.

taxes over the next century. This was the system of *Legstädte*, places of deposit, which made federal administration cheaper and more regional, and which benefited the places of deposit themselves, notably Frankfurt-am-Main, Augsburg, Ulm, Nuremberg and Leipzig. In the case of the *Zieler*, they were assessed according to the basic 1521 Worms *Matrikel*. Lippe recognized a half-yearly assessment of 25 fl.[2] Yet before 1556 the court was still only a sporadic affair, dependent on direct imperial assembly grants from year to year for its existence. Simon's letter accompanying his small payment in 1531 also showed the need for a more efficient system of record in Lippe to prevent falling foul of excessive federal demands. Simon wrote in December:[3]

We have hereby ordered on our behalf a merchant to pay you the first instalment of the new three-year Imperial assessment for the upkeep of the Court in Speyer to date from this last autumn fair by order of Imperial decree. We thought that payment had already been made but now find that this was apparently not so. We send you therefore 12½ fl. in fat pennies to conform with the requirements of the decree and ask you to send us a satisfactory receipt.

A year later Johann Helfmann, Lippe's agent at Speyer, wrote to Simon V warning him that the Fiscal was starting proceedings against Lippe for recovery of the third *Ziel* which had not been paid. This letter was dated from September 1532, and the third tax instalment had been due only that autumn. This illustrates a feature that was to be met time and again in federal tax demands on Lippe—the speed with which the court threatened to litigate for the recovery of arrears. The system of decree was one of persistent nagging: arrears were speedily assessed, especially when they concerned the court officials' own emoluments. Helfmann wrote:[4]

Today the Emperor's Fiscal demanded payment of the third instalment of the three-year upkeep of the Court as granted at the last Imperial

[2] 'Anslag zuw vnderhaldung des keyserlichen Camergerichts', giving a total *Ziel* of 25,400 fl. with Lippe assessed at 25 fl. The court at Speyer was running on 50,000 fl. a year. Another *Matrikel* from 1548 put Lippe's *Ziel* at 25 fl. and gave Lemgo a separate one of 30 fl., which the county refused to accept. Staatsarchiv Detmold, L 41a IV E 9 vol. 1. *Reichstagsakten*, new series, Gotha, 1893ff., 2, pp. 138, 442 for Lippe and Lemgo in the Worms 1521 *Matrikel* (see also below, Appendix 2).   [3] Staatsarchiv Detmold, L 28 C II–1.
[4] Staatsarchiv Detmold, L 37 XVII no. 24a.

assembly in Augsburg. Although I pleaded for another month's time in order to inform you of his demand, he did not grant me this, in view of the fact that the Emperor's Judge and assessors have not been paid yet. You should therefore make payment and avoid the extra costs and damages that Fiscal's proceedings entail.

The development of fiscal jurisdiction at *Kammer* or treasury level was a basic ingredient in the growth of government, especially at federal level. There were *Reichsfiscalprocuratoren* already in 1427. Under Ferdinand I fiscalism went forging ahead, especially in the Habsburg territories, and it produced real solutions to the legal problems of tax arrears. Taxes were determined at law according to grant and precedent. The question of right, of property, was by-passed. In the interests of peace and security fiscal procedures could be extended to the whole field of debt. This proved to be the sixteenth-century administrative revolution that found alternatives to *Fehde* and self-help. The court at Speyer was moving towards the control of debt in a very real way. [5]

Ten years later Helfmann was again there to come to the rescue, this time of the regency councillors of Bernhard VIII who had got into arrears. In 1542 Lippe tried to stop the Fiscal from starting proceedings for the recovery of *Zieler* arrears by claiming that the county had been over-assessed and that it had therefore no arrears. The councillors notified that they would continue payment of what they regarded as a legitimate amount within the next month. It seems that they had delayed all payment in an attempt to draw attention to the unfair assessment of Lemgo which they were trying to get erased from the *Matrikel*. [6]

In November 1542 Helfmann was writing that the majority of the Protestants had stopped their payments until their demands for reform of the court had been met. [7] Helfmann was

[5] E. Rosenthal, 'Die Behördenorganisation Kaiser Ferdinands I', *Archiv für österreichische Geschichte*, 69, 1887, pp. 215–23. Schröder and Künssberg, *op. cit.*, pp. 600–2, 953. H. Brunner, *Grundzüge der deutschen Rechtsgeschichte*, Leipzig, 1905, pp. 255–9. C. von Schwerin, *Deutsche Rechtsgeschichte*, Leipzig, 1912, pp. 62–80. W. Endemann, 'Von dem alten Reichskammergericht', *Zeitschrift für deutschen Civilprozess*, 18, 1893, pp. 177–8.

[6] Staatsarchiv Detmold, L 37 XVII no. 24a.

[7] 'Dieweil aber der mherer theil der protestirandem stende obengemelt erst theil bezahlt, aber nichts weither zu dem Cammergericht erlegen, noch dasselb erkennen wollen, es sei dan zuvor reformiert.'

Hesse's spokesman in Speyer and by using him Lippe was moving into the Protestant extreme group which included other small-fry like Hoya and Mansfeld, Lippe's kinsfolk. Even so, the first instalment of *Zieler* in 1542 had been paid. Lippe had sent 25 fl. to Frankfurt and had demanded that the town council backdate the payment to fall within the time limit set by the imperial decree that had threatened Lippe with legal proceedings and a fine for non-payment after a fixed time-lag. This was no question of taking the matter lightly.[8]

In the spring of 1543 Lippe paid two *Zieler* at one go to Frankfurt in accordance with the current three-year imperial assembly grant. The county even agreed to pay more if the imperial Estates reached agreement on enlarging the third *Ziel*. A year later Lippe was paying a residual sixth instalment and thereby claiming to have fully paid up all its *Zieler*. The blow came, however, in 1545, when the Fiscal claimed that Lemgo had paid tax twice according to its separate *Matrikel* assessment, thereby establishing precedents for its inclusion as a federal taxpayer separate from the rest of Lippe. The Fiscal denied that he had received sufficient evidence to the contrary. Lemgo could not be exempted and must pay its arrears.[9]

Above all, records about *Zieler* have survived whenever there was conflict. At other times one may assume that Lippe paid smoothly and on time, for when at last there were interim reports on who had paid up over a longer period of time the county showed up very well indeed.[10] Yet the problem of Lemgo continued to bedevil Lippe-*Reichskammergericht* relations.

The Emperor's Fiscal relied on the 1521 Worms *Matrikel*, despite evidence that proved Lemgo's status as a territorial and not imperial town. No one seemed to question how it was that Lemgo could ever have been included in the *Matrikel* in the first place, and it is not known who put the town there. In 1537 Lemgo was let off taxes *pro tunc*, yet by 1542 the town was being assessed once more.[11] To help Helfmann at the court in Speyer, Simon V appointed Beckmann, another lawyer, to

[8] Staatsarchiv Detmold, L 37 XVII no. 24a. Cf. R. Wolf, 'Der Einfluss des Landgrafen Phillip etc. . . . .', *Jahrbuch des Vereins für Westfälische Kirchengeschichte*, 51–2, 1958–9, *passim*.

[9] Staatsarchiv Detmold, L 37 XVII no. 24a, Helfmann to the regency councillors 3 April 1545. [10] Staatsarchiv Detmold, L 41a II D vols 1–4; L 41a IV 207. [11] Staatsarchiv Detmold, Knoch Repertorium L 28 folio 269.

try to put the Lemgo case at imperial assemblies, as well as to join the general scramble for assessment moderation and reduction which broke out in the 1540s. The result was that the Lemgo assessment remained but at a much reduced rate. This Lippe still did not recognize and between 1527 and 1577 the county sent eighteen deputations to lobby imperial assemblies and committees on the matter.[12] One wonders if travelling and legal costs did not actually prove more expensive than payment of the federal demands for the town would have been. However, it was a question of jurisdiction for the Counts who could not afford to see their chief town go imperial. It is doubtful if the county could have survived such a financial loss in the sixteenth century.[13]

In December 1535 Lippe received a solemn condemnation under Charles V's seal, signed by the Speyer Judge himself. Simon V had not paid his taxes for the upkeep of the *Reichsregiment* or *Reichskammergericht* for the years 1524, 1526 and 1529. The last year had since been paid but the others were still outstanding. Simon was by no means cowed and wrote to Helfmann to fight the judgment. Lippe had paid all its *Zieler* and had the receipts to prove it. It saw no reason why it should pay for Lemgo. Simon wrote:[14]

You will know how much in every way we feel that we are being pestered. We have been assessed far above our wealth in this and other taxes of the Empire, and have petitioned with greatest diligence for relief. Yet until now we have paid our due taxes, notably the two instalments [of 1524 and 1526] for which we obtained receipts, the copies of which we send to you.

The demands for *Zieler* from Lemgo were of course minute compared with the simultaneous demands for *Römermonate* for the Turk wars. In October 1542 Speyer was litigating for 10 horse and 55 foot from Lemgo alone, claiming that this was the assessment that the Westphalian circle had made. This was despite the fact that Helfmann had obtained the support of a procurator at the court and that Lippe Stathalter Hermann von

---

[12] Staatsarchiv Detmold, L 28 C Section II 1–4b.

[13] Cf. F. Copei, 'Lemgo und das Reich', *Lippische Mitteilungen*, 15, 1935.

[14] Staatsarchiv Detmold, L 28 C Section II–1, 'Mandatum Caroli V Imperatoris, Lemgo contra Fiscal', Speyer, 13 December 1535, and the reply of Count Simon V to Helfmann, Easter 1536.

Mengersen had obtained from the Chancellors of Hesse, Münster and Paderborn a promise of support for Lippe's case in the coming imperial negotiations for moderation. In 1546 Lippe even sent copies of treaties between the rulers and their town of Lemgo from 1245 to 1511 to Speyer, to really prove the town's territorial status. The Hessian advocacy further put Lippe out of favour with the imperial authorities after 1547, and even in better times, as under Simon VI, Lemgo could not be erased from the *Matrikel*. By 1582 the Fiscal was demanding 1,880 fl. in arrears from the town. This was more than the town council had in revenue during the whole year.[15]

The continuation of litigation meant that no orders of actual distraint were ever served on Lemgo. Yet the Speyer court hung on to its demands. In August 1542 it deemed that Lippe must still pay in full for what it had been assessed before moderation could be considered. If it paid in full, however, then Lemgo would remain liable for taxes because of precedent, which in fact the Fiscal alleged by 1545. When Lemgo approached the imperial assembly in July 1545, it was told to be satisfied with a reduction from 10 horse and 55 foot to 2 horse and 12 foot. Equally the imperial Estates' commission replied that as the *Reichskammergericht* had taken up the case originally, it could now go before no other imperial body until that court had reached its verdict. The only success came in 1544–5 when Lippe eased Lemgo out of the circle *Matrikel*. At Speyer the matter was kept pending, decade after decade. This prevented real distraint or outlawry, the *Acht* or *Exekution* that small-fry like Lippe always had to fear. In practice Lemgo paid along with Lippe and there the effective assessment was 4 horse and 18 foot for the whole county upon which the sliding scale of federal tax was operated.[16]

Yet Lemgo continued to be plagued by demands for federal taxes. In 1602 an imperial order demanded payment of 13 *Römermonate* or 936 fl.[17] Writs continued to demand its presence at imperial assemblies until Ferdinand II hamstrung the con-

---

[15] Staatsarchiv Detmold, L 28 C II–1. Stadtarchiv Lemgo, Kämmerei, half-year revenue in 1582 was 12,000 marks (about 1,200 fl.).

[16] Staatsarchiv Detmold, L 28 C II–1.

[17] Alleged *Matrikel*, 2 horse and 12 foot with money commutation at 12 fl. per horse and 4 fl. per footsoldier per *Römermonat* at 13 such months = $(2 \times 12 \times 13) + (12 \times 4 \times 13) = 936$ fl. Schröder and Künssberg, *op. cit.*, p. 920.

stitution. In the 1630s when Lippe got behind on its *Zieler* Lemgo was again cited to pay a separate quota. In the 1660s when Leopold I was trying to increase federal aid and battling against a *Matrikel* that was designed for peacetime after 1648, Lemgo again came under fire. The final demand came in the 1720s, but this time the matter brought an apology from Charles VI himself.[18] The Lemgo affair, 1508–1722, illustrates a fiscal and legal side to Lippe–Empire affairs, running like a thread throughout the period. It shows the resilience and persistence with which federal taxation was demanded, even when the authorities were manifestly in the wrong.

After 1556 the *Reichskammergericht*'s finances were put on a regular footing. The *Zieler* became permanent biannual levies on the territories and no longer subject to short-term imperial assembly grant. The tax could thus be counted up in numbers of *Zieler*, progressing at the rate of two a year. Thus in 1569 the Procurator demanded payment of the thirty-fifth to fortieth *Ziele* from Lippe. In 1583 he even got as far as to give Paderborn the right of distraint in order to recover Lippe's debts to the court, and this led to complaints from farmers in Lippe between 1586 and 1588 as payments had been forced. In 1589 when the Procurator again demanded arrears, Lippe paid and the receipt for the eightieth *Ziel* has been preserved. The imperial assembly had consented in 1570 to raise the number of *Reichskammergericht* assessors to forty-one, and this meant a *Zieler* increase of two-thirds. The arrears conflicts that arose out of this, especially from the 1580s, continued into the seventeenth century, as the rulers in Lippe found it extremely difficult to raise the quotas of the Lippe towns, which traditionally paid the *Zieler* in the sixteenth and seventeenth centuries to the comital treasury, which then passed them on to Frankfurt.[19]

Seventeenth-century *Zieler* payments in Lippe show how a system of taxation by fits and starts was operated at federal level. Various bodies threatened Lippe to pay up, according very much to the political and military situation. Then right at the end of the century, as the court got under way again in its last

---

[18] Staatsarchiv Detmold, L 37 XVII no. 6; L 28 ad C II, C II 2, 4.
[19] Staatsarchiv Detmold, Knoch Repertorium L 37; L 37 XVII 24a; L 41a II D no. 1 vols 2–3, J. H. von Harpprecht, *Bericht des Unterhaltungswerk des Kayserlichen und Reichskammergerichts*, Frankfurt-am-Main, 1768, chapter 14.

home, in Wetzlar, Lippe came under a more orderly system watched over by the Westphalian College of Counts, in which pool Lippe was very much a big fish.

In 1611 the Procurator Fiscal demanded *Zieler* straight from the towns and started proceedings against Simon VI and his son. They were paying federal taxes into their own pockets, and the *Reichskammergericht* replied by threatening to by-pass the Counts, a threat to their powers of taxation over their subjects. This illustrated a real problem of all federal taxation. In a two-tiered system, rulers granted taxes, but only if their subjects actually paid them. By 1600 a tax like the *Zieler* had become a regular one, territorial subjects paid it: in the case of Lippe, the burghers. The fight then broke out as to who would spend it, the rulers or the federal body to whom it was due. This case came up again in the military field, where Lippe governments arbitrarily increased federal grants, in order to live on the surplus. This was vital in the Thirty Years' War period, when the presence of troops meant that the government could not afford to keep any taxes that were earmarked for federal or outside purposes, as could much more easily be done in peacetime.[20]

Yet the two-tiered federal tax system could also work in favour of the territorial subjects that were actually paying. When the comital administration made its *Zieler* accounts for the period 1641–74, it found that the six towns had paid 920 fl., but that the administration had handed on 1,200 fl. to the *Reichskammergericht*, which was now no longer operating via *Legstädte* but receiving taxes directly through its own treasurer. The comital administration therefore started proceedings in its own *Hofgericht* for recovery of the deficit from its towns.[21]

Receipts of *Zieler* that Lippe paid remain for 1612–16, 1620, 1623–4, 1626–34, 1642 and 1650–1. In between these dates the Procurator issued threats, notwithstanding the pleas for delay as Lippe complained more and more of war commitments and inability to contribute. By the later 1630s the Westphalian circle had taken the matter in hand, and by 1646 the Emperor had enlisted the support of the circle directors in his demands for

[20] Staatsarchiv Detmold, L 41a IV D 1; Knoch Repertorium L 37; L 37 XVII 24a, zu 24a, 24b.
[21] Staatsarchiv Detmold, L 37 XVII no. 24b, six parcels, 1671–4.

Zieler arrears as well as meeting the demands for *Reichskammergericht* reform. Lippe in the Thirty Years' War period had been under the imperialists and its continued payments to the *Reichskammergericht* show its general obedience to the Catholic-imperial party. A change came in the 1650s as Lippe refused to pay its *Zieler*, despite warnings from the court, the Emperors and circle. In 1655 a threat to serve an order of distraint on the county for non-payment of *Zieler* arrears was ignored. In 1654 the *Reichskammergericht* had been reconstituted to take in the provisions of 1648, but a corresponding liquidation of outstanding tax arrears had to wait until 1657. Although the court invited the refiling of old suits as well as new cases, it had to admit defeat on its arrears, some of which were now a hundred and more years old. Liquidation accounts with Lippe covered the period 1641–74, as the towns continued to pay for the whole county. After 1676 their payments lapsed, and when the reconstituted *Reichskammergericht* eventually emerged out of its difficulties in the 1710s it brought with it a new system of accounts. The county now paid *Zieler* as a matter of course out of its revenues. The tax was too small to continue to be separated: it meant that the burghers got off the old tax, a small but regular relief to the town treasuries.[22]

As far as Lippe was concerned, *Reichskammergericht* financing became really businesslike after 1712. *Zieler* continued, numbered in series. Genuine arrears were reckoned in old and new series, and taxes were already notified as arrears on the last day on which they were currently due or as soon as possible thereafter. *Zieler* were increased by reckoning them in sixteenth-century coin, which included higher rates for 'old' arrears, that is those from the 1650s to 1680s, partly liquidated arrears from before that, and new ones for the current Wetzlar court.[23]

An imperial commission issued its findings to the territories in 1719. The matter went from Wetzlar via Regensburg and the Mainz arch-chancellery, showing the increased interest and power of the territories at the permanent imperial assembly in the court. An apology was given for the shortcomings of the

[22] Staatsarchiv Detmold, L 37 XVII no. 24b.
[23] Staatsarchiv Detmold, L 37 XVII zu 24a, 'Höchst-gemüssigte Vorstellung des Kayserl. und Reichs Cammergerichts Unterhaltung betreffend', Wetzlar, 1712. Endemann, *op. cit.*, pp. 217–27.

court. This was due to the French disruptions in the 1670s and 1680s. A half-hearted restart at Wetzlar in the 1690s then gave way to internal conflict, as the court demanded more money and more attention from Emperor and territories. The way the *Matrikel* was manipulated without showing a direct increase in rates was a masterpiece of federal tax-bargaining. Thus the court's treasury reckoned Lippe at a traditional 20 tlrs per *Ziel*, but this currency was to be at 1555 coinage value. So in 1719 a conversion to more debased current rates of coin was thoughtfully provided. In 1720 the biannual *Zieler* rate was increased so that each *Ziel* was levied $3\frac{1}{2}$ times a year.[24] The *Ziel-Reichsthaler* was valued at the very high rate of 90 *Kreutzer*. What this all amounted to was that Lippe's original 50 fl. a year was now 212 tlrs a year in *Zieler* tax. The eighteenth-century Wetzlar court was assessing the territories for 50,000 tlrs in upkeep a year, rising to just short of 80,000 tlrs by the 1740s. This was still remarkably cheap, for the Wetzlar court was undoubtedly the more independent even if the slower of the two imperial judicatures, and it was costing the territories hardly more to run than by comparison the small county of Lippe needed to run itself as an independent territory within the federation.[25]

In the accounts which the court's own treasury in Wetzlar regularly printed and circulated, it is possible to follow *Zieler* payments in full detail. The accounts followed the latest *Matrikeln* and divided the territories by circles. Debt, arrears and payments were recorded year by year, territory by territory, circle by circle, and the totals for the Empire summarized. Thus in 1721 Lippe paid 53 tlrs and appeared as owing 212 tlrs. This was the current assessment for the year, which already appeared as arrears. In that year total territorial payment had been 21,000 tlrs. Alleged total debt stabilized at around half a million after 1720. This included a claim for arrears of 105,000 tlrs from before 1654 and of arrears from that date to 1714 of 130,000 tlrs. In the notification of 1720 Lippe had no arrears from before 1718, and it is more important when looking at arrears lists to see who was not in them and to compare what was actually paid with what was claimed as owing. In this

[24] Not approved at Regensburg until 1732, Staatsarchiv Detmold, L 41a IV 207.
[25] Staatsarchiv Detmold, L 41a II D 2; L 41a IV 207; L 92 Z 1a.

earlier part of the eighteenth century, of Lippe's neighbours Paderborn had practically no arrears, and Münster had arrears only in new *Zieler*. Of the heavyweights, Saxony was paid up, and Brandenburg as yet still had far less arrears than Austria. The position of 1707–12, when there were 90,000 tlrs of arrears in lawyers' pay and a total alleged debt of 880,000 tlrs, had substantially improved ten years later.[26]

In 1732 total debt was down to 404,000 tlrs, which still included 87,000 tlrs of arrears from before 1654. Lippe was owing only the current *Ziel* once again, and the year's total territorial payment had been 25,000 tlrs.[27] The question was thus not one of how dreadfully slow payment was, which is indeed what the Wetzlar treasury tried to allege in its arrears policy, but in fact how tenacious the court was in hanging on to arrears that were ancient history, real or fictitious, in terms of financial administration. The barrage of currency rates, *Ziel* raising and liquidation proposals that had gone on since 1570 was enough to confound any registrar or archivist who tried to put his territory straight and argue the case with Wetzlar by the eighteenth century. Even Lippe, with its reasonable record of payment, left much of the general scrutiny of accounts to the Westphalian College of Counts, whose archives are deposited in Detmold. This meant above all running the policy of moderation and tax-relief, as well as keeping an eye on what neighbours paid and cutting one's own cloth accordingly. This showed one of the basic principles of all federal taxation. The territories demanded lists of all tax payments, to compare payments with assessments and the *Matrikeln* upon which they were based, and thus satisfy themselves of the fairness of the whole process. In such a system arrears were over-emphasized. That the majority should pay up did not satisfy anyone; the yearning was for perfection or 100 per cent payment, something that was impossible to achieve reasonably. Yet the publicists and finance officials did their job well. Their arrears policies have generally been believed literally and have given federal taxation especially a bad press.

When a Regensburg territorial commission audited the

[26] Staatsarchiv Detmold, L 41a IV 207; L 37 XVII no. zu 24a; L 41a IV D 2.
[27] Arrears list no. 2, Wetzlar, 1733, Staatsarchiv Detmold, L 37 XVII no. zu 24a.

Wetzlar accounts in the 1770s, covering the period back to 1713, it produced several thousand folios of memoranda and several hundred chapters of complaint and reform. The striving was for perfection, an inevitable administrative weakness in a federal system where responsibility was shared and where co-operation was not commanded so much as invited by argument which sought to convince. Wetzlar operated on a system of ideals which no centralized system could emulate, and it is this that has always to be taken into account in any criticism of the early modern Empire.[28]

The Emperor and territories, in their audits, desired also to check the venality of office in eighteenth-century Wetzlar. *Reichskammergericht* sessions 407–703 were examined to find out how much work had actually been done and by whom. In 1759 accounts were also audited, as the court itself tried to keep some order in its own treasury. The matter was tied up in a legal jargon that carries conviction at least in terms of its earnestness. Like any court, Wetzlar was aware of expense and time, factors that threaten to overwhelm legal systems in any age.[29]

Right at the end of the period in 1795–7, Wetzlar income exceeded expenditure by up to 25 per cent. The annual assessment the territories paid to the tune of 83 per cent in 1795, 78 per cent in 1796 and 76 per cent in 1797. The court did not stress this point. It claimed arrears of 300,000 tlrs and claimed that the territories, circle by circle, were between one and twelve years in arrears. Lippe had no arrears at all. The circle that came off with least arrears included the territory of Brandenburg.[30] Annual accounts for 1742–70 verify this general picture. With an annual demand of about 80,000 tlrs from the territories, Wetzlar conceded that it actually received between 52,000 and 93,000 tlrs a year. By the 1780s the territories were managing to pay 90,000 tlrs and by the 1790s just over the 100,000 tlrs

<hr>

[28] Staatsarchiv Detmold, L 41a II D 1 vols 1–4; D 2 vols 1–5; L 41a IV D 5, 'Baden-Durlachische Relation über der Kayserl. und Reichs Kammergericht Pfennig Meisterey Rechnungen', decision of *RKG* session 703, 17 May 1773.

[29] Staatsarchiv Detmold, L 41a, IV D 5.

[30] *Neuer Usual Matrikel*, Wetzlar, 1795, Staatsarchiv Detmold, L 41a II D 2 vol. 5, giving arrears by territory and circle at current *Zieler* per annum, including demands that were by then over one hundred years old. Yet in more recent years the majority of *Zieler* had been paid, and the current financial position was good.

a year. These figures are more realistic than the arrears demands.[31]

In *Zieler* payments over nearly three centuries Lippe had its initial difficulties, owing to the way in which its towns were assessed for the tax internally, the Lemgo *Matrikel* affair and the inconsistencies and muddles of the comital administration, that seemed to keep no separate files on federal taxation at any time. In the eighteenth century, however, Lippe emerged in an exemplary way, and its only arrears were current ones, caused by regular late payment of a few months at the most. Although *Zieler* were small, they were paid regularly, and, as far as Lippe was concerned, payment shows that the *Reichskammergericht* was effectively financed until well into the 1790s.

The first agent that the county of Lippe kept at the *Reichskammergericht* was Dr Helfmann. He was appointed procurator in 1544 but was already serving Simon V in the 1520s. He was followed by three others up to Lic. Bennon who was paid 20 tlrs a year to look after Lippe's affairs at Speyer in 1590. In that decade Simon VI had four different agents, and between 1622 and 1627 his son kept just as many. From the 1580s onwards hardly a year went past without correspondence between the comital administration and its agents on litigation at Speyer. This continued through the Thirty Years' War period. In the eighteenth century business at Wetzlar became popular as appeals moved from Lippe's courts to the imperial courts. The *Reichshofrat* also increased its business but the *Reichskammergericht* remained the more popular of the two, because Wetzlar was closer to Lippe than Vienna, because Wetzlar was cheaper though slower, but also because Wetzlar specialized in appeal according to due process of law concerning territorial subjects. Vienna dealt more equitably with cases of a dangerous political, social and constitutional nature, yet decisions there had a Habsburg bias.

Between 1732 and 1763 Lippe employed Procurator Meckel at Wetzlar. He dealt with 154 Lippe cases, concerning above all the ruling dynasty, in his thirty years of office. These were appeals from Lippe courts and cases against Lippe rulers by native nobles and burghers, as well as by other territorial

[31] Staatsarchiv Detmold L 41a II D 1 vols 1–4, Wetzlar, annual printed accounts, numbered in series for the scrutiny of the College Directory, Westphalian Counts.

rulers and subjects, notably for debt, trespass and breach of the peace. Very common were hunting on someone else's land and felling of trees in neighbouring woods, with the damage to rights and jurisdictions that these entailed. Officials, their dependants and lawyers also litigated for debt, overdue salaries, rents and fees. Whenever the territorial system could not cope, the *Reichskammergericht* was there to take the matter on. It was not so important for a decision to be reached; rather the court provided an outlet for peaceful and due process of law, when territories themselves could no longer cope with the matter without leaving themselves open to violence.[32]

There was no doubt about the popularity of Speyer and Wetzlar. Much has been made of the sporadic functioning of the *Reichskammergericht*. The split in religion did much to hamstring it, and when this was removed the aggressions of the French disrupted the court. Finally it had to put up with spasmodic delinquencies of the heavyweight territories; the Hohenzollerns, Wittelsbachs and Guelphs were not the easiest of its customers. But to small-fry like Lippe the court was of real importance.[33]

Between 1522 and 1806 the Detmold Archive has about 1,100 cases involving over 2,000 rulers, officials and subjects of Lippe as plaintiffs or defendants at the *Reichskammergericht*. In all these cases either plaintiff or defendant or both were Lippians. There are what we today might call 'private' and 'public' cases between Lippians themselves and between Lippians and other territorials. The dynasty and its administration also provided a solid block of cases. There were a total of 203 cases against Lippe rulers and their officials, 17 in the sixteenth century, 80 in the seventeenth century and 106 in the eighteenth century. There were

[32] Staatsarchiv Detmold, Repertorium L 74, also 'Registratura und Repertorium der Cammergerichts Procurator Judicial Protocollen das Regierende Haus Lippe betr. von Dr. Meckel' (Knoch).

[33] *Reichskammergericht* cases were arbitrarily sent to territories of origin when the Prussians dismantled the Wetzlar archives after 1815 in the *Deutsche Bund* era. In 1852 Lippe received 'her' quota of cases, and they are in Repositur L 82, Staatsarchiv Detmold. Cases found elsewhere are now being added to this. Archives are beginning to make their imperial court cases more easily available as these begin to be appreciated as the essence of a federal system that tried to run law and war on a supra-territorial basis. G. Aders and H. Richtering, *Das Staatsarchiv Münster und seine Bestände*, Münster, 1966–8, nos 3225–35, lists cases now in Staatsarchiv Münster where the Counts of Lippe were plaintiffs in the primary instance at Speyer between 1557 and 1672, and p. 473 for cases where the Counts were defendants.

no cases between members of the ruling dynasty in the sixteenth century, but as the family branched out thereafter it produced 65 cases between 1613 and 1783. The vast majority of cases were, however, between territorial subjects themselves. The Detmold Archive has records of 833 of these from Lippe subjects alone from the period 1544–1806. This also included cases of Lippe subjects against neighbouring territorial rulers and officials, notably against the bishops of Paderborn with whom the Lippe rulers shared local condominium. These cases also increased in number over the centuries. Thus there were 42 of them in the sixteenth century, 280 in the seventeenth century and 510 in the eighteenth century.[34]

Who had access to the *Reichskammergericht* in practice? The propertied undoubtedly had a monopoly here. The Lippe subjects who appear in the court's files were the nobles, officials, burghers and richer, exempted farmers. The town councils appeared as corporations and right at the end of the period even a peasant district, a *Bauerschaft*, used the court's facilities. Yet the court at Speyer and Wetzlar was undoubtedly made most use of by members of the Estates, the 'gentry' of Lippe. Peasants and artisans did not appear in these lists, basically because they owned no property which would warrant the costs of an action at the *Reichskammergericht*. As anywhere else at the time, law was a business, almost a pastime, for those of substance, education and leisure. Yet it comes as a surprise to see that, after the comital administration, the town councils of Lippe were involved in the greatest number of cases. The leading burgher families of Lemgo were even keener on litigation than the nobility in Lippe. Lemgo led with sixty-five cases, and all together the towns produced almost twice as many cases as the ruling dynasty alone. Not only were the burghers paying Lippe's *Kammer-Zieler* in the sixteenth and seventeenth centuries but they were appropriately making most use of what they paid for. Lippe's leading noble family, the Donops, however, were not far behind. They alone opened twenty-nine cases at the court. An examination of the social status of Lippe subjects using the *Reichskammergericht* shows that the burghers made by

---

[34] Figures are from two alphabetical registers, one ordered according to plaintiffs, the other according to defendants. There is no chronology. Staatsarchiv Detmold, L 82.

far the most of the court's facilities, followed by the nobles. Members of the Lippe dynasty came in third place, partly because their main outlet, as peers, for family litigation was the *Reichshofrat*. In the eighteenth century an increasing number of officials sought their rights at Wetzlar, as well as a very few adventuresome peasants in the last years of the court's existence. From the 1590s onwards Simon VI's *Hofgericht* was operating in Lippe. From then on Lippe subjects' cases went up to the *Reichskammergericht* as appeals. Before that the territorial nobility had had direct access to Speyer. Burghers and the rest only ever had appeal access as they had always been under the jurisdiction of town and country courts. However, after the 1590s all subjects including nobles had access only by appeal. That this was made much use of is shown by the figures. All *Reichsunmittelbare* had, however, direct access to both *Reichskammergericht* and *Reichshofrat*, as the system of peerage operated. For them it was a matter of tactics which court they chose. Once the choice had been made the decision had to be stuck to, at least until the final verdict was produced. In their rules of procedure all imperial bodies tried to prevent federal subjects from playing the one off against the other, and no simultaneous actions could be brought in different imperial courts.[35]

What actually were the cases about? The following is a survey of sixteenth-century Lippe cases. The first case of all was lodged in 1522 to try and compel Simon V to repay 80 fl. which had been advanced by a territorial noble family in fulfilment of a 5 footsoldier, 4 *Römermonate* tax levy on the county. The case thus arose out of federal taxation, and it went on until 1544. It remained inconclusive as far as the court was concerned, but this did not leave out the possibility of settlement out of court, which was perhaps at the back of the plaintiff's mind all along in such a case of debt. But by 1544 both parties had died and the matter was in the hands of their heirs. The original prosecutor, Dr Hess, was still alive and it was he who revived the case at times with the help of a deputy in 1523, 1524, 1527, 1536 and 1544.[36]

[35] W. Sellert, *Über die Zuständigkeitsabgrenzung von Reichshofrat und Reichskammergericht*, Aalen, 1965, *passim*. Staatsarchiv Detmold, L 84, Hofgericht, I, Prozesse, 16.–18. Jahrhundert. L 83, Justizkanzlei.

[36] Staatsarchiv Detmold, L 82 (H 20) no. 310.

In 1544 Dr Hess had at last found out that Simon V was dead and had sent a question to the chancellery, asking for the names of the new rulers in Lippe. The answer came back swiftly, regency for Bernhard and Simon under Landdrost Christof Donop and Simon de Wend. Hess had looked through his register of clients and was testing his chances of further fees on the case.

In the 1520s this case was defended for Simon V by Philip of Hesse's chancellor, Lic. Hitzhofer, and he was able to draw the matter out by procrastinating and staying away when he could, bringing in points of procedure when pressed. The court thus handled this case in seventeen different sessions. At one point in August 1524 it seemed that it would be decided, but then Hitzhofer retired. After his death the court demanded a new defending counsel to be sworn in and fully empowered. It never got this far again.

At this early stage of federal legal development the *Reichskammergericht* had taken on a matter of tax liability and tax debt, which it had tried to prove as a question of right.[37] It was courageous of the plaintiff to throw good money after bad by going to court, especially in an age where slander, libel and self-help were still very much in use.[38] It helped little that he produced the original receipt of payment from 1513, nor was the decree of the *Reichsregiment* from July 1521, ordering Simon V to pay within three weeks on pain of a fine of 20 gold marks, effective. One further reason why Simon did not pay up may have been the change that was taking place in Lippe politics, as the county moved over from Guelph to Hessian support. The plaintiff had served under the Guelphs and was one of their vassals. The rising star of Hessian influence came out with Lippe getting the services of Helfmann and Hitzhofer, Hessian protection at federal level. This illustrates the political as well as experimental legal quality of the case.

---

[37] '19 Augusti 1524, zwischen Bertholden von der Heiden gegen Herrn Simon, Graven von der Lypp, ist der Bescheid das Doctor Hess der Copien angetzogener quittung am funfften tag Octobris negstverschinen (1523) eingepracht original vnd Licentiat Christoff Hitzover seinem gethanen bestand nach gnuegsamen gwalt mit rectification geubter handlung einpringen sollen. Ferrer in der sachen zugescheen was Recht ist.'

[38] See the libels in O. Hupp, *Schmähbriefe und Schandbilder*, Munich, 1930, *passim*. Staatsarchiv Detmold, L 45 M–N, 2–8b; L 9 vol. 1 folio 233; D 71 no. 471.

In Minden the Cathedral Chapter family of Halle opened cases against Count Jobst of Hoya and his kinsman, Simon V of Lippe, for dispossession of lands and jurisdictions in Minden and Schaumburg. Simon V had taken violent possession of alleged Halle lands using the services of his Varenholz *Amtmann*. The case ran at the *Reichskammergericht* from 1536 to 1552. In March 1536 Halle got an imperial criminal order against Simon V. Halle insisted that he had a right to the disputed lands by virtue of possession over the last 'ten, twenty, thirty, forty, fifty and longer years'. Simon V empowered Helfmann to defend him. The first delay was achieved by notifying Simon's death. The Lippe regents were now saddled with the case. Helfmann then produced an order from Landgrave Philip of Hesse demanding that the case be transferred to his court as Lippe's feudal overlord. In March 1537 Philip wrote to Helfmann:[39]

Equally our faithful Simon of Lippe has been cited to the *Kammergericht* on the matter of the Minden Dean's lands. As you will appreciate from enclosed evidence, the very lands over which they are squabbling are owned by us and are his [i.e. Simon's] fief. Thus such a matter should come before us. Please see to it that this is carried out and demand that the case be sent to us for trial.

This was successful. Once more Lippe had won through the defence of Hesse.

After the Smalkaldic War Hesse was in eclipse and Lippe was forced to become a fief of the Empire. The Halle family then took the matter up again in 1551 at the *Reichskammergericht*. Another imperial criminal order was issued, this time against Bernhard VIII. The case petered out in 1552 with an account by Halle of how he had ridden over with the protection of Minden Chapter to Detmold and confronted Bernhard and his noble councillor Schwartz with the Order. In the reconstituted Speyer court after 1555 the case no longer appeared and after 1562 the fief reverted to Hesse.

In 1549 the Emperor's Fiscal opened a case against Bernhard VIII and Lemgo town council, claiming that Lemgo was an imperial and not a territorial town. A year later the de Wend family used the court against Bernhard VIII, alleging that he,

[39] Staatsarchiv Detmold, L 82 (H3) no. 293.

their ruler, had deprived the family of serfs, forests, rents and movables. Above all the kidnapping of serfs seemed to rankle. In the reconstituted Speyer court in 1558 the Wends asked for protection in possession against further inroads by Bernhard and his officials. The matter reflected internal politics, where, on the death of Simon de Wend, ruler and Estates in Lippe had redeemed the Wend-administered *Amt* of Varenholz in a very successful plan to get the Count and his officials to live off domain revenue and save the Estates' own pockets.[40]

In 1576 the ruler of Münster accused the Lipperode Drost under the Simon VI regency of armed robbery in the Münster *Amt* of Stromberg, a serious case of breach of the land-peace which in earlier times would have led to *Fehde*.[41]

A Lemgo burgher took his case against his ruler, Simon VI, direct to Speyer in 1581, when he demanded that the Count should stop maintaining a tenant-farmer and return the property. From now on cases against Simon VI by subjects and neighbouring nobles and burghers came up frequently. Between 1585 and 1599 there were nine such cases, which does not speak so highly of Simon's fairness as a ruler or 'good' neighbour. On the other hand it did mean a sharp rise in the popularity and legal techniques of the court in Speyer.[42]

The record against Simon was diverse, showing the *Reichskammergericht* to be very much a jack-of-all-trades. The von Landens in Minden demanded the return of two farms in Schaumburg. The wards of the Amelunxens demanded repayment of 2,500 fl. accumulated on a sum of 1,525 fl. lent without land security. The Bishop of Paderborn and the monks of Falkenhagen appealed against the force that Simon VI's officials had used when trying to gain access with a Protestant commission of reform. These the monks had expelled. The ensuing religious conflict was worked out in terms of trespass and ownership which provided the Speyer and Wetzlar court with revenue until the Jesuits were abolished in 1773. This corner of Lippe, however, remained Catholic, to the displeasure of Calvinist Lippe rulers and consistories.

The von Nagels demanded that Simon VI honour his promise to alienate revenues from one of his *Ämter* to cover a 4,000 fl.

[40] *Ibid.*, F 20, W 4, 5, 8.   [41] *Ibid.*, M 41.
[42] *Ibid.*, S 54, L 5, A 6, P 1–2, N 1. G 18, Q 1, S 1, C 32–3.

loan of theirs. A Lemgo family disputed Simon's handling of their inheritance conflict. Another case concerned two Lippe enfeoffments in the bishopric of Minden, a matter that should strictly have gone to the feudal court, had Simon VI been truly able to implement his 1579 feudal assembly proposals. Two Hildesheim vassals complained of unjust imprisonment in Lippe, and in a bankruptcy case the Lemgo family that had been sold up complained of unfair tax assessments and sequestrations.

This matter concerned the Lemgo town council family of Cruwel. In May 1589 the Speyer court had ordered Simon VI in the name of the Emperor to stop all action in the Lippe courts against the Cruwels for bankruptcy and to send all the materials relative to the case to Speyer for a decision.[43] The language was indeed strong; Lemgo town and Simon were accused of having denied justice by due process of law to Dr Johannes Cruwel. The accused were ordered to deal through Speyer on pain of 10 gold marks fine, half of which Cruwel should pocket and the other half of which the court would collect. The order was served by court messengers on Simon VI on 13 August 1589.

Here was a clear case where the *Reichskammergericht* was interfering with a ruler's jurisdiction. As it happened, the court chose its case badly. Johannes Cruwel's father had been mayor of Lemgo. On his death in 1582, the heirs disputed heavily over the inheritance, and the creditors lost faith and demanded repayment. The Cruwels went bankrupt. Their kinsmen, the Cothmanns, bought their magnificent Lemgo residence when it came under the hammer in 1600. Several Cruwels were imprisoned for debt and for violent resistance to distraint for debt. Johannes Cruwel shot a bailiff in 1592. A brother of his came under sentence of death for defamation of Lemgo council, and was finally whipped out of town. Thus a burgher family moved out of the world of gentility. The *Reichskammergericht* could not stop them going.[44]

Another ruler came under fine from the *Reichskammergericht* in 1634 as a result of a conflict over taxation that broke out anew between the towns and nobles of Lippe. Troop exactions had, according to the towns, widened to an unbearable extent the gap between the taxes that they were forced to pay and those the

---

[43] Staatsarchiv Detmold, L 41a IV E 9 vol. 1; L 82 C 38-9.
[44] K. Meier, *Geschichte der Stadt Lemgo*, Lemgo, 1962, pp. 84, 92-4.

nobility actually got away with by private arrangement. To bring this point home, the towns had refused to pay taxes to Simon Ludwig's officials until the nobility paid the same total amounts as the towns, that is one-third of all Estates' grants. The comital administration had replied by collecting burghers' taxes by force through bailiffs after legal action brought by the Lippe Fiscal at the *Hofgericht* in true emulation of *Reichskammergericht* fiscal procedure. [45] The towns had appealed to Speyer, which had replied by ordering the Lippe government to immediately stop collecting taxes without consent from the burghers. It ordered the nobility to stop evading taxes, but left Simon Ludwig free to appeal against the decisions. [46]

The towns had given up seeking redress through the Estates' assembly, through the chancellery and *Hofgericht* in Lippe. They had gone straight to Speyer where the *Reichskammergericht* was quite willing to support their case of unjust taxation in order to stress the fact that even territorial rulers were under the federal law. [47] Taxation without consent was stressed as illegal and inequitable. The court claimed that unfair distribution of tax burdens in these times when the imperialists' troops, the *kayserliche Soldatesca*, had to be provided for was further untenable. It was unjust for the government to protect its nobles especially after decisions obtained from the law faculties of Heidelberg and Leipzig, where the matter had gone for arbitration to the experts in 1631. [48] Simon Ludwig was threatened with a commission of inquiry, and then even with summary force to carry out the Universities' decisions. The language was offensive. [49] Simon Ludwig was condemned because of the evil councillors whom he had not stopped in their activities against the towns. [50] He and they had broken the golden rule to settle the matter in

[45] These moneys were itemized in the treasury accounts, Staatsarchiv Detmold, L 63 B 12 I–II.

[46] Staatsarchiv Detmold, L 11 V no. 1, Speyer, 3 October 1634.

[47] 'Des hayl. Reichs Abschieden vnd Verfassungen, vnd der Natürlichen billigkait.'

[48] 'Also dass die von der Ritterschaft vnd andere so bis dahero ledig aussgangen, nach Jhrem vermögen belagt werden, vnd sich angraiffen müsten, acceptiret.'

[49] 'Das Judex a quo DU, beklagter Jetziger Grafe, mit vnaussstelliger execution verfahren sollen.'

[50] 'Due, Graff, ahn seithen der supplicanten erschöpfter stätte mit sattem bestendigen grundt notorie erwiesen, dass solche einwendungen ahn sich selbsten nicht von dir, Grafen, sondern dero Rhäten, alss mitbeklagten vnd condemnirten herührendt.'

discussions where no one should be compelled against his own free will. The nobility were included in the condemnation for having taken part in the 'game' which made it seem that they had agreed to pay fair taxes whilst in fact having produced no real evidence of doing so.[51]

The court upheld the towns' claim that they had since paid 100,000 tlrs in arbitrary, weekly military taxes, whereas the ruler, his officials and the nobility had not made any realistic contributions at all. The *Reichskammergericht* was taking up a constitutional issue and trying to defend the burghers against the establishment in Lippe, a combination of dynasty, councillors and nobles. It came forth with remarkably 'liberal' concepts: territorial taxation should be run on the lines of consent, free will and fair assessment according to real wealth; and this in the middle of the Thirty Years' War period, coming as it did from the supreme federal court, was indeed the language of *teutsche Libertätt*.[52]

Simon Ludwig and his councillors replied by sending a lawyer to Speyer to defend themselves and to appeal against the court's decision of October 1634 in favour of the Lippe towns. The Count claimed that the nobles had indeed paid their fair share of war taxes, and that taxing them by force was unnecessary. In March 1635 he told the Speyer judge that 'the nobility of the County of Lippe in these hard times has suffered and withstood many troop occupations just like the rest of the territory and they have paid and are still paying about 10,000 tlrs in money towards these war costs'.[53] All reference to arbitrary taxation collected by force from the burghers was avoided.

Much *Reichskammergericht* business was, however, of a direct legal and technical nature which helped the modest and often hopelessly unschooled Lippe legal administration to cope with awkward cases. There were thus many cases between Lippe subjects which went on appeal from town and country courts as well as from the *Hofgericht*. The earliest surviving case between territorial subjects was brought in 1544, when two noble

---

[51] 'Auch mit einem geringschätzigen vnachtlichem zueschuss, so sich von der Ritterschaft mehr zue einer ludification wohlabgesprochener vrtheil, alss güetlicher composition ansehen lasse.'

[52] Above all the concept, 'zuer güetlichen composition, warzue Niemandt wieder seinen freyen willen zue compelliren'.

[53] Staatsarchiv Detmold, L 11 V 1, 15 March 1635.

families referred to Speyer to settle a conflict over the interpretation of an agreement by which money had been lent, which had led to sequestration of lands, goods, tithes and serfs. The matter went deep because in the background was the ruling dynasty which had condoned the sequestrations. The nobles who had suffered, the Westphals, had in quite another deal traded away Lippe rulers' rights alienated to them in the bishopric of Paderborn. The Westphals had called in the *Reichskammergericht* for protection as the Lippe government retaliated. Speyer moved in on an Augean stable, the *Verpfändung* system of late medieval Lippe.[54]

In 1560 the richest Lippe noble family, the Kerssenbrocks, disputed a will among themselves at Speyer. Two prospective vassals disputed a Lippe fief in the bishopric of Paderborn in an appeal from a special comital commission, convened to settle the matter. Non-noble officials fought over a mortgage of 100 tlrs, after they were dissatisfied with the decision of the Detmold *Gogericht*. In 1572 two Lippe *Droste* fought a libel in which the county's chief official, Landdrost Schwartz, questioned the honour and name of a colleague for unpaid debts and unredeemed sureties, a matter that would in an earlier age have led to violence and *Fehde*. Lemgo treasurer Tilhen questioned the right of a tenant-farmer to build a new mill, and this brought a counter-demand from the miller for protection in possession. A Ravensberg noble claimed possession of a farm in Lippe, expressing dissatisfaction with the commission that had dealt with the matter at Saltzuffeln. The Elector of Cologne demanded redress for an armed raid from Lippstadt into the neighbouring duchy of Westphalia. An appeal came against a judgment of the comital chancellery concerning a conflict over the inheritance of one-third of a Lippe fief.[55]

In the 1580s a Saltzuffeln burgher appealed against the sale of fourteen pieces of land because there was a mortgage on them. He expressed no great faith in his town council over the matter. A burgher was dissatisfied with a local court decision on his claim for 200 tlrs from another burgher. A Westphal demanded

---

[54] Staatsarchiv Detmold, L 82 W 12, Westphal in Paderborn against Donop in Detmold, Horn and Schwalenberg. Cf. Estates' assembly dealings from the early 1540s in L 9 vol. 1.

[55] Staatsarchiv Detmold, L 82 K 11, H 18, S 30, K 38, T 6, H 41, nach C 36, B 41.

protection in possession of land against other members of his family. A dealer in the Lippe-Pyrmont trade demanded damages for non-delivery of cereals worth 500 tlrs. Saltzuffeln burghers disputed possession of half a salt-well. A widow in the town was taken to court in Speyer for building a pigsty on the defendant's land. The Westphals again demanded protection in possession of lands, and the Cruwels of Lemgo fought over their inheritance as bankruptcy closed in on them.[56]

In the 1590s the Cruwel case continued as one leading family after the other was involved. The Lemgo Cothmanns fought the Wippermanns, their kinsfolk, over ownership of a farm. A Blomberg burgher alleged a case of perjury. Saltzuffeln burghers demanded recovery of 365 tlrs of lent capital. A Lemgo burgher claimed damages from the *Amtmann* of Blomberg for unjust imprisonment. The town council of Lemgo fought back against Johannes Cruwel, who had denied that the council had the right to decide matters of debt. Christian Cruwel asked for help in the recovery of merchandise that his creditors had removed, after the town council had found against him. He then tried to dispute the bankruptcy order served on him. The century ended with Osnabrück patricians trying to recover an annual rent of 2 fl. from a Saltzuffeln burgher.[57] As the figures show, business increased in the seventeenth and eighteenth centuries. The world of *Serenissimus* in Lippe was a sham, for no Count provided a sovereign legal system of his own.

Although the *Reichskammergericht* did not deprive Lippe rulers of their powers at any time, it did take up matters of alleged injustice in Lippe. It did not fight shy of injunctions against rulers, neither did territorial subjects fight shy of litigation because of any threats from their rulers. Apart from dealing with matters that were beyond the scope and legal capacity of the Lippe administration, the *Reichskammergericht* acted as the watchdog of early modern Lippe constitution and society. Above all it served individual territorial subjects, their families and corporations, without becoming the irrevocable enemy of their territorial rulers and governments.

Rulers, officials, nobles and burghers of Lippe made vigorous use of the court in Speyer and Wetzlar. All the leading families

---

[56] *Ibid.*, G 10, S 44, W 20, S 14, K 10, K 9, W 13, K 51, G 17.
[57] *Ibid.*, C 37–9, S 21, S 61, N 6, L 10, C 31, C 30, G 19.

in the county took cases there between the sixteenth and eighteenth centuries. This shows how popular the federal legal system was. It was not until the early nineteenth century that appreciation of this fact was destroyed as the Wetzlar archives were dismantled. Then, no one was interested any longer in understanding or preserving the unity of a federal legal system that had ceased to exist. Instead the opposite trend towards territorial independence was accentuated as a rump of territories which included Lippe gained *de jure* sovereignty in Metternich's *Deutscher Bund*.[58]

Lippe paid its share of *Reichskammergericht* costs and really did make use of what it thereby bought. The court was used by *Reichsstände* and *Landstände* alike. Here they all came into one melting-pot, as the court decided cases by due process of law as much as political and financial pressures on it from interested parties would allow, in this grand age of European venality. If the court did not reach a decision, it did at least register the case and bring it to public notice outside the territory and locality in which it occurred. It encouraged mutual agreement. The important point was always that the case in question had been brought in the first place for federal scrutiny, not whether it could be decided at all. In this way *Reichskammergericht* procedure helped to take the violence and furtiveness out of everyday life. It provided alternatives to self-help and *Fehde*. It helped the territories to organize themselves more effectively in the running of law and order. It took care of inter-territorial problems and in the case of Lippe kept a firm eye on the territorial administration.

[58] F. Hertz, 'Die Rechtsprechung der höchsten Reichsgerichte', *Mitteilungen des Instituts für österreichische Geschichtsforschung*, 69, 1961, *passim*, does much to rectify this. See also the recent *Repertoria* of *Reichskammergericht* sources compiled by Looz-Corswarem and Scheidt in Staatsarchiv Koblenz, and by Aders and Richtering in Staatsarchiv Münster.

XII

◇◇

Lippe, *Römermonate* and *Türkensteuer*

◇◇

LIPPE's earliest tax grants were made to pay for imperial war efforts. The fifteenth-century federal tax system had provided the methods that were basically adhered to until the eighteenth century. Military taxes were granted at imperial assemblies, with all rulers listed according to their status in the Empire and as from the later sixteenth century according to circle membership. Assessment was according to number of pikes during the Hussite Wars and by the end of Frederick III's reign was divided according to horse and footsoldiers and their war pay. It stood at this until the War of the Spanish Succession when horsemen were commuted to footsoldiers as eighteenth-century armies found less use for cavalry. Assessments were for the campaigning month. It was understood that a horseman cost 12 fl. per campaigning month and a footsoldier 4 fl. Territories could be expected to provide their assessed troop numbers themselves for a given number of months and on top of this pay their troops' campaigning salaries. Thus at worst an imperial troop tax could entail recruitment, equipment and salary payments for the whole time that a territorial contingent was campaigning. Less burdensome was the system where territories only paid salaries in lieu of troops and left the matter to *condottieri*. Other territories were equally willing to supply mercenaries and attract the money of the less militaristic.

All imperial war taxes were granted at imperial assemblies with the current Emperor as chief war-lord. With the development of the circle system in the later sixteenth century Emperors' commissars scoured the countryside asking for aid from individual territories and circles without resort to imperial assemblies.[1] Under Leopold I this system of blackmail flourished once more as the Emperor gave powers of billet and assigned badly paid imperial war taxes to the large, armed territories. They were the circle directors, who used these powers to treat the smaller, unarmed territories as they more or less pleased. The standing armies which this policy furthered were created not because of the dreams of absolutists wishing to destroy their Estates by finance and by force, but rather because of a desire for small dynasties to survive as independent rulers by providing their own militias in the federal war effort. They had to see to their own defence, internal and strategic security, in order to deny the big territories any chance of being able to swallow up small-fry by monopolizing the imperial, federal military system. During the period of Louis XIV's wars the large territories were fighting for control of the imperial military machine in Germany. The small territories survived by providing their own armies, thereby frustrating the aims of the largest territories.

The advantage of the system of military assessment was that it was flexible to operate. Demands for men could be converted to money and vice versa without undue paper work and negotiation. The assessment was thus the mainstay of cheap federal government. It was called the *Matrikel*. Like the problem of arrears, the problem of assessments was a matter of perpetual litigation and arbitration for all the territories. A ruler's status depended on his inclusion in the imperial assessment and it equally provided the basic point around which his federal politics were conducted. The smaller the territory, the more important at some time or other its imperial assessment. For the small state was too small to lobby effectively at the imperial assembly where tax grants were made, too vulnerable to risk ignoring payment, and generally too financially unstable to make payment without concessions to its nobles and burghers as its chief financiers.

In Lippe *Römermonate* and *Türkensteuer* were basic factors in the development of ruler-Estates finance and politics in the sixteenth century. They provided much of the impetus for the constitutional development of Lippe into a territory and a state,

---

[1] See A. H. Loebl, 'Eine ausserordentliche Reichshilfe', *Sitzungsberichte der phil-hist. Klasse d. kais. Akad. d. Wiss*, 153, Vienna, 1906.

from being a loose collection of jurisdictions and domains up to the fifteenth century. A *Römermonat* was a month's campaign of a territorial contingent on the assessment. *Türkensteuer* was basically the same thing, only the campaign was specifically to be against the Turks. Size of contingent, money equivalent and number of campaigning months were alterable on a sliding scale as the basic assessment remained constant and applicable to all territories at one and the same time. The proportions that territories paid towards any total agreed upon at the imperial assembly remained constant as the *Matrikel simplum*. The system was thus infinitely adaptable, and above all it could produce the threat of an army of practically unlimited size not by command of the Emperor but by consent of the member territories of the Empire. It was this system that enabled the Empire to cope above all with the Turks, but also with any other enemies from within and without, though with less long-term success than against the Turks.

Lippe's first imperial war taxes were paid in 1507-9. Maximilian was using a *Matrikel* drawn up with the consent of the territories at the imperial assembly of Konstanz in 1507. There is no record that any Lippian attended this assembly, or indeed any of Maximilian's later assemblies. However, Bernhard VII was on the *Matrikel* with an assessment at this early stage of 5 horse and 4 footsoldiers. Bernhard chose to pay money in lieu of troops. This suited Maximilian who as a *condottiere par excellence* recruited his own *Landsknechte*. Bernhard, however, paid far less than was demanded from him. On the 1507 *Matrikel* he should have paid something over 800 fl. for the six months' campaign granted for 1508. In actual fact he handed over 240 fl., saying that even this sum was a free gift and that his predecessors had never paid the Emperor taxes before. In retaliation the Emperor's financiers had tried to increase Lippe's taxes by putting Lemgo into the *Matrikel*. Bernhard was already complaining about this in 1509. In studying the *Matrikel*, however, it does seem that from the size of Lippe compared with the estimated imperial whole, the county was under-assessed without Lemgo, and over-assessed with Lemgo. The town's Hanseatic background gave it an extra allure to federal tax officials.[2]

[2] H. Conrad (ed.), *Recht und Verfassung des Reichs in der Zeit Maria Theresias*, Cologne, 1964, pp. 517-21. Staatsarchiv Detmold, L 37 XVII nos 6-7.

The money that Bernhard did pay came from his towns.[3] Bernhard had the same difficulty getting it as Maximilian's officials had in getting Bernhard to hand it on. In 1507 Lippstadt town council refused to pay and claimed that its other co-ruler, Cleves, was getting the town's imperial war tax contribution instead. In February 1508 Lippstadt claimed further exemption. It had paid its share of the costs of sending Cleves to attend Maximilian's court at Worms. Next day Bernhard threatened Lippstadt with distraint. The town then paid 50 fl. Bernhard was acting on the threats of the Emperor's orders to him to pay up. The federal system was working.[4]

On 4 February 1508 Bernhard and his sons with three councillors discussed federal tax demands with the mayors of his towns. The meeting was held in the presence of a *Notar*, a lawyer versed in Roman and Canon law.[5] The rulers wanted money to pay Maximilian. The mayors wanted trading concessions, a 'redress of grievances', meaning an economic policy favourable not to the peasants but to the burghers. Bernhard demanded that the towns help him to satisfy the Emperor's orders. They should supply troops and money for imperial purposes, otherwise he would denounce his towns to Maximilian. The presence of the lawyer meant that Bernhard was effectively threatening the towns with litigation. The mayors referred back home and then returned to Detmold on 13 February with their replies.

The towns stressed how much they had helped Bernhard in his private wars in the past fifty years and what heavy debts they still had to pay. They complained that craftsmen were active in the villages, against the towns' monopoly, and that markets were being held outside the towns. Customs barriers were destroying the free movement of towns' trade. It was not their duty to pay imperial taxes. Why could not they also be exempted from paying imperial taxes, as were the nobility? After all, they held nothing from Maximilian.[6]

Bernhard replied that his private wars had been waged for the good of the whole county. It was a case of self-defence and

---

[3] Staatsarchiv Detmold, L 37 XVII no. 4. [4] Ibid., nos 4, 7.
[5] *Ibid.*, no. 4, Notariatsinstrument. *Lippische Regesten*, 2946.
[6] 'Sie hätten auch nichts vom Röm. Könige, gleich der Ritterschaft, welche mit der Steuer verschont würde.'

necessitas. He knew of no craftsmen operating outside the towns, and towns were free of customs duties. Markets were forbidden outside the towns. Bernhard was stonewalling. He then complained of the towns' intractability and disobedience. He would complain to Maximilian.

The outcome was that the towns got their trade monopolies extended over the villages and Bernhard got his imperial tax. This established a precedent, and boded ill for the future of the burghers as they were now firmly branded as taxpayers. The towns had recognized a duty to pay taxation. They paid, and the precedent established the principle that burghers always paid taxes. In return they got trade concessions. The nobility never let themselves in for this. They too paid in emergencies, but they made voluntary contributions. They negotiated behind closed doors. They let no official or outsider look into their incomes or dictate to them quotas and assessments that they had not worked out themselves.

The great step in constitutional development, however, had been taken under Bernhard VII, and the impetus had come from Emperor and imperial assembly. The towns of Lippe had established a precedent by paying imperial taxes to their ruler. Bernhard VII had established a precedent by handing at least some of the money on, in obedience to the Emperor's orders and imperial assembly grants. The February 1508 meetings in Lippe were the first recorded ruler-Estates discussions about taxation, and the taxation demanded was imperial. Lippe was modernizing in order to meet the demands of a federal system that was extending its hold over Germany.

Maximilian's wars were unsuccessful. This was not so much because of lack of federal support, as he claimed. He really never got this far, for his policies were unrealistic and his campaigns were rushed. Alone in fighting the Venetians, he tried to rely on the Swiss, the traditional enemies of the Habsburgs. *Römermonate* thus became a sham and the system lapsed for lack of success in the wars and in the diplomacy that they were meant to finance. The last payment that Lippe made to the Emperor in 1513, Simon V induced an outsider to settle, who was never repaid.[7]

The revival of *Römermonate* and the *Matrikel* upon which to

[7] Staatsarchiv Detmold, L 82 (H 20) no. 310, Appendix.

base them in the 1520s was due to the dynastic fortune of the Habsburgs and the overweight of Turkish power in the southeast. The 1521 Worms *Matrikel* rekindled federal militarism under the direction of a new war-lord. *Reichsregiment* and *Reichskammergericht* established the principle of constitutional government. A share of government in the name of the Emperor was also taken by territorial rulers and not always by privy councillors and secretaries behind the Habsburg throne. Again it was the conflict of personalities that destroyed the working of any federal system at home. Just as Maximilian and Berthold of Henneberg had not been able to get on with each other, so Charles V sacrificed his constitutional powers and his personal reputation to humiliate Elector Johann Friedrich of Ernestine Saxony and his kinsman, Landgrave Philip of Hesse.[8] Whereas Maximilian had refused to recognize the futility of foreign war, Charles refused to see that he had not the resources to act like a despot within the German federal system.

What was left for federalism as home affairs became more and more deadlocked in the 1530s? The fight against the Turks staved off civil war for a time. The Empire nourished itself on foreign war and ideological conflict with the infidel on its doorstep. With this the federal system was once again strong enough to dig down as deep as Lippe with its military demands. *Türkensteuer* had come to cure the ills of federalism.

In the Worms *Matrikel* of 1521 Lippe was assessed for 4 horse and 18 footsoldiers, an increase in money terms of two-thirds on the 1507 assessment. Between 1521 and 1545 the demands on Lemgo were, however, an extra 10 horse and 55 footsoldiers.[9] Troops and money were regularly demanded. Records survive for Lemgo partly because all assessments were disputed and the evidence was thus needed for litigation. For the rulers themselves, one may surmise that many federal

---

[8] L. von Ranke, *Deutsche Geschichte* (popular ed.), Munich, 1914, 4, pp. 565–575. G. Turba, 'Verhaftung und Gefangenschaft des Landgrafen Philip von Hessen 1547–50', *Archiv für österreichische Geschichte*, 82, 1895, pp. 205, 213, 219, 225.

[9] Kayserliche Mandate, Speyer, November 1541; April, October, December 1542; January, June 1543. Staatsarchiv Detmold, L 28 C Section II 1–4b. K. Zeumer, *Quellensammlung zur Geschichte der deutschen Reichsverfassung*, 2nd ed., Tübingen, 1913, *Reichstagsakten*, new series, Gotha, 1893 ff., 2, pp. 438, 442, for the Worms *Matrikel* of 1521. See Appendix 2 below. The lords of Lippe at 4 horse, 18 foot and 60 fl.; Lemgo at 4 horse, 22 foot and 60 fl.

records were lost because there was no immediate legal purpose to be served in preserving them. Thus in their allegation of despotism against Charles V which was presented to the territories at the Augsburg assembly of 1548, the Lippe regency councillors were careful to point out that Lippe rulers and their governments had always contributed in full to imperial grants for men and money.[10]

Whilst Simon V had called his first *Landtag* for which records remain to discuss religion in 1531, his second specific territorial assembly was called a year later to discuss imperial Turk taxes. After a *Landtag* in the village of Lage the towns sent a letter of promise to the chancellery to pay 500 fl. Turk tax to a committee of twelve nobles and burghers. The money was to pay salaries to troops in the field by next St Bartholomew. Lemgo alone promised 300 fl. Furthermore the towns promised to send troops of their own.[11]

Thus by the 1530s only the Lippe towns were paying Turk tax in accordance with the 1508 precedent. *Landtag* consultations had, however, become a necessity to induce them to grant payment. The nobility were also now involved in consultations as well as in the collection of taxes. Yet they were not paying Turk tax along with the towns. The peasants and common people still remained to be drawn into the tax system, and this the towns achieved in the next decade.

By 1541 the bargaining position of the Lippe towns as the effective Turk tax payers was hardening. Led by Lemgo, they agreed to pay only half of the county's Turk taxes, and then only in return for more effective trading and manufacturing concessions. The other half they granted to the regency councillors to be levied on the tenantry and common people. The towns were now exercising power as Estates to grant taxes that the politically unprivileged population would have to pay. This was not because of any prescriptive right; it was the burghers' retaliation against clandestine trade and manufacture in the villages and on the farms. If the towns' monopolies were not to be enforced, then the culprits would have to share in tax burdens that the towns had taken on only in return for sole

[10] Staatsarchiv Detmold, L 41a IV E 9 vol. 1.
[11] Staatsarchiv Detmold, L 37 XVII no. 6. Cf. L 29 B Section 1 vol. 1. *Lippische Regesten*, 3207.

rights in trade and manufacture. The towns wrote to the regency councillors:[12]

After you had shown us His Majesty's demands for tax and contribution against the Turks at the recent territorial assembly held in Cappel village, we called a meeting of all the towns and have agreed to the following.

Although Lippstadt did not appear at Cappel we have communicated the Roman King's demands in accordance with Imperial practice, and the town has joined us in protesting that we have frequently been taxed too heavily, as you undoubtedly will know. We made this clear to the last Count that no livelihood was to be found in the Lippe towns as the common craftsmen have moved to the villages to the detriment of all the guilds, with whose wealth we are supposed to render arbitrarily high and frequent services and taxes to our rulers.

We demand redress so that we can make payment. We have so far noticed no change for the better. There is no control over buying and selling in the countryside, yet we are expected to pay our taxes all the same.

We thus demand with the support of Lippstadt that the common countryside take over and pay one-half of the outstanding Turk taxes and we will pay the other half, each town according to its size and wealth.

The imperial war tax system reached its first climax in 1542–1543. Under the direction of Ferdinand I the territories granted and actually provided the men, equipment and money to field an army that besieged the Turks in Budapest. The military outcome was of lesser importance compared with the advances in federal administration that this entailed. At the imperial assembly in Speyer rules of taxation were laid down for the territories to follow, in assessing rentiers and territorial Estates for federal Turk taxes. These were guidelines upon which territories could base their own administrative development in taxation, for which they hereby obtained sanction by *Reichsabschied*.

Lippe possessed its own copy of these guidelines.[13] All rulers, nobles, corporations and towns that lived on rents and interest were to pay a $\frac{1}{2}$ per cent capital tax, reckoned at interest rates of 5 per cent, which meant an annual income tax of 10 per cent. In return movables were to be tax-free. Equally the war equipment of rulers, nobles and knights was to be exempt from

[12] Staatsarchiv Detmold, L 37 XVII no. 6. [13] *Ibid.*, no. 2.

taxation. This encouraged capital investment in war material, which would then ideally be used against the Turks. The Church was equally to pay a 10 per cent income tax, and the Teutonic Knights and Knights of St John were also to contribute. As the arrangements were for war against the infidel, they were not allowed to claim tax exemption as religious military organizations. It was easier for ordinary nobles and knights to do this, for the tax exemption of military equipment provided the warrior class, above all the nobility as military entrepreneurs, with the loophole through which to slip out of all realistic taxation in the following decade.

Church jewels and treasures were not as yet to be sold, but if the war went badly the right to sell them was reserved. The key to the whole system was that it now divided taxpayers into two classes, those who taxed themselves and those who were assessed by the territorial authorities. The axe fell not between territorial rulers and their subjects, as would have been fairest, but between rulers, nobles and officials taxing themselves, and burghers, tenantry and common folk being assessed mainly by the former group. This decision was of revolutionary importance. In Lippe it meant a split between nobles and towns over taxation quotas which lasted into the nineteenth century. Being allowed to assess themselves, the nobility paid only nominal taxes. Above all they paid in secret and they stressed that their payments were voluntary. The towns, however, had a fixed assessment, which meant that they paid the same proportion of whatever tax total was at any one time granted.[14]

With this arrangement the federalists were attempting to cut across territorial development. A fundamental obstacle was put in the path of nobles-towns consolidation in politics as territorial Estates. The nobles, as also the officials, went with their rulers; the towns were left in an unfavourable position along with the tenantry. It helped rulers of the size of Lippe to divide and rule, mainly with the help of their nobility.

Yet there was a sign in the guidelines pointing towards

[14] 'Dwile aver etzliche beswerunge tragen muchten, sych Jres vermogens apenbar zumachen, so soll eyn Jder Churfurst, furst, geistlicher oder weltlicher, prelaet, prelatynne, graffe, frieher, herre, vnd van adel, fursten Rhede, vnd dergleichen personen, auch de frie vnd Reichsstedt sych selbst erinnern syne geborende anlage van allen vnd Jdern habe vnd gutern, bewechlich vnd vnbewechlich allene an den orde da er gesessen ist entrichten lassen.'

territorial consolidation under the rulers. The propertied were to pay Turk taxes for all their holdings only to those territorial authorities within whose jurisdiction they had their chief residence. This made taxation of 'foreign' landowners illegal at least for imperial purposes. Hence propertied families were encouraged by territorial rulers to group within territories. In Lippe those of substance were encouraged to be Lippians and to lay claim to a place in court and assembly in the county.[15]

All territorial authorities were to draw up tax registers of their peasants, their tenant-farmers. Records should be kept of what each man paid in order to punish those who did not pay fully. Towns were to let their councils have a free hand in taxing all corporate wealth under their jurisdiction at a standard 10 per cent on income from capital. However, towns' treasury income was also to be taxed as if it were capital. Furthermore the small men, burghers, peasants and common subjects, were to pay 10 per cent income tax. The basic rate was for 6 kreutzer tax on every 20 fl. capital.[16] Capital under 20 fl. was charged at a flat rate of 4 kreutzer. All Jews, whether rich or poor, were poll-taxed at 1 fl. Apart from this discrimination, which put all Jews at the equivalent of a Christian with 200 fl. capital, the Turk tax was directed against the small investor, the common peasant and the common tradesman in the towns. This after all made economic sense for it was no good taxing the rich because they could exploit any existing system to their own advantage as the chief financiers, collectors and administrators of any federal tax, and it was no good taxing the labouring poor as they had no resources whatsoever.

In each territory the profit as well as duty of tax administration was to go to a consortium of four, one official, one cleric, one noble and one burgher. They were to operate on oath to ruler and country (*Herr und Landschaft*). They were to keep a locked treasury chest in a fortified place and hand their territorial quotas over to the circle treasuries by a fixed date.

Circle treasuries were federal executives at regional level.

---

[15] 'Das eyn Jder allen an den orde da er gesessen syne anlage zu diser beharligen turkenhilfe gebe, van allen synen haben vnd gutern, so er allenthalben hat, vnverhindert wo de syn ader ligen.'

[16] 20 fl. = 16½ tlrs; 1 tlr = 72 kreutzer. Standard interest rate 5 per cent. Annual interest on 20 fl. = 60 kr. 10 per cent tax on this interest for the Turk war = 6 kr.

They operated when two basic conditions were satisfied, namely when the biggest territories were interested in the duties of being circle directors, and when they could effectively threaten or, better still, gain the consent of member territories within their circles to pay imperial war grants. In 1542 this worked to some extent even in the Westphalian circle despite the fact that director Jülich-Cleves was in dynastic and armed conflict with the Habsburgs over Gelderland. The Turk war effort thus engaged federal, regional and territorial authorities.

At the imperial assembly of Nuremberg in 1542 Ferdinand I and Charles V's Commissar, Bishop Christian of Augsburg, negotiated the Turk aid. Elector Joachim of Brandenburg was made commander-in-chief of the federal army. This time the war effort would not just be a tax grant to pay for Habsburg mercenaries; men and horses with equipment and pay were to ride out of their territories to the succour of Emperor and Christendom. It was attractive to look for a solution to reformation heresy at home on the battlefield against the infidel abroad. Once again the Empire launched into a policy where the enemy on the frontier should solve internal dissension on the home front. The enthusiasm percolated through to Lippe.

A Lippe agent went to Nuremberg in 1542 to get fairer assessment in the planned Turk army establishment. At circle level the regency councillors negotiated with co-director Münster, and in the county itself an Estates' committee of two nobles and two mayors was set up to administer Turk aid.[17] Collection was to follow according to the Emperor's orders and the conclusions of the common country (all the territorial subjects).[18] These conclusions had at last drawn the Lippe nobility into the net of imperial taxation.

In May 1542 nobles and country (*gemene Ritter vnd Landesschupp*) met in Lippe to grant Turk tax.[19] Because the Roman

[17] Writs to Donop, Kerssenbrock, Cothmann and Warnecke, 'de Turcken schattunge intoforderende', Staatsarchiv Detmold, L 41a IV E 9 vol. 1.

[18] Staatsarchiv Detmold, L 37 XVII 24a. Cf. R. Borgmann, 'Die Türkensteuerliste des Märkischen Amtes Bochum vom Jahre 1542', *Westfalen*, 21, 1936, pp. 13–32.

[19] Although the term *Landtag* is frequently used in the earliest minutes, it is not exclusively used to describe Estates' assemblies. The members of the Estates were individually important as negotiators with specific legal status, and their assembly was at first just a meeting of these individuals, becoming institutionalized in the seventeenth century.

king's instructions were not so exact as to where and how taxes should be collected and paid out, the Estates put up a committee of three nobles and three mayors to take responsibility for the tax, making their own arrangements without waiting for the Westphalian circle assembly in Essen to take the matter in hand. Pensions, incomes, stores, goods and possessions were to be valued forthwith in Lippe by the Turk tax committee. The Estates then agreed to an advanced payment of 1,200 fl. to pay the Lippe troops for three months and dispatch them to the front as soon as possible. The Estates would recoup the loan, 400 fl., from each of three groups, namely the towns, the nobility and the ruler's peasants. What was new here was that twenty nobles were named and assessed at between 40 and 10 fl. each. The peasants were to pay according to rural district, *Amt* by *Amt*. Fr *Ämter* ouwere given quotas in these negotiations.[20]

Three months' pay was quite insufficient. In August the Lippe Estates met again to discuss their Turk war effort. They granted a further three months' pay, and even discussed *Kammerzieler* as part of the federal issue. The money forthcoming from the country (*Landesschupp*) was now divided as follows. The ruler's peasants and with them the clergy would provide 200 fl. Seventeen nobles contributed 10–60 fl. each, and the towns were expected to provide 500 fl. The towns refused and offered 250 fl. This was accepted, and the Lippe troops in the field were cut down to half-pay, as it was the winter season when there was supposed to be no campaigning. Troops' pay was thus cut just when they had most leisure to spend it in camp, because of tax conflict back at home between nobles and officials on the one hand and the towns on the other.[21]

An official from Detmold travelled with the money to Austria to pay the Lippe troops under Johann Bose, using the Westphalian circle's line of communication under instructions from Cologne town council. This suspicion of the circle treasury on the part of Lippe led to regional conflict, as the circle authorities demanded proof that Lippe had made its own Turk war arrangements. To fight the circle's 'arrears' policies, Lippe furnished itself with receipts. The most notable of these was the attestation of Commander-in-Chief Joachim of Brandenburg from

[20] Staatsarchiv Detmold, L 37 XVII no. 2; Knoch Repertorium L 9 folio 31.
[21] Staatsarchiv Detmold, L 37 XVII no. 2; L 9 vol. 1 folio 130.

October 1543 that the Lippe contingent had done full and faithful service in the field against the Turks.[22]

The circle came off badly as Lippe fulfilled its war duties to the Empire by paying her field troops directly from the Lippe treasury. Lippe placed no trust in the circle treasury in 1542, not because it wanted to evade federal taxation, but because it wished to make sure that its efforts did not run into the sand at regional circle level. The 1542 Turk war episode showed that federalism could work, and it also immeasurably furthered the scope and powers of territorial taxation.

Even whilst territorial contingents were campaigning together in Hungary, home affairs began to close this chapter of federal co-operation in foreign wars. In 1542 Philip of Hesse was demanding feudal knights' levy from Lippe as the Protestants dealt sharply with the Guelphs and protected their co-religionists in Brunswick and Goslar.[23] After 1555, however, the way was once more clear for federal co-operation against the Turks, but not before the question of Turk tax had in 1553 been used as the vehicle for manoeuvring the nobility out of the tax lists in Lippe.

At the end of 1553 Charles V made a last demand for Turk aid, a demand that came to Lippe via the Westphalian circle assembly in Essen. It was admitted that previous Turk tax had been used for other purposes by the Emperor and that the money could not be returned, a bleak reference to the civil war. Lippe thus had arrears of 4,500 fl. To this the Lippe government claimed that in negotiations held with the Estates at Blomberg the nobles and clergy had been assessed for contribution as they had not paid their previous Turk taxes. The Estates granted a common, whole *Landschatz*. This was a basic unit of payment to be made by peasants and tenant-farmers who were listed in the current tax registers in the rural districts. The towns were also to pay their quota, a third of the total (1,500 fl.). The towns refused but offered to refer back home. They were withholding their grant until the nobles declared themselves willing to take on the same amount as them. The nobility snubbed the towns by claiming to have made their own separate

[22] Staatsarchiv Detmold, L 37 XVII no. 2; L 9 vol. 1 folio 132; L 41 vol. 1.
[23] Ranke, *op. cit.*, 4, pp. 273–304. Staatsarchiv Detmold, L 9 vol. 1 folio 128 verso.

tax arrangements already with the ruler.[24] Nobles and towns thus became deadlocked on an imperial war tax issue, to the detriment of their mutual co-operation as Estates in territorial affairs. The federal tax guidelines of 1542 had reaped their crop of dissension; nobles were in one tax class and the burghers in another.

From the later 1560s until the first decade of the seventeenth century Turk taxes were paid by Lippe. Despite the regional disruption caused by the Spanish-Dutch wars the system still worked well in Lippe after 1580 because of the convinced federalism of Simon VI. The Turkish frontier was stabilized and fortified. This was reflected in federal tax grants for building and fortification. When hostilities broke out anew in the 1590s large federal war taxes were forthcoming and for a brief period under Zacharias Geitzkoffler the office of federal tax receiver or *Reichspfennigmeister* was one of supreme importance in keeping the war effort going. Thereafter the Turk war lost its urgency and allure as a federal policy, only to be revived again in the 1660s and fought to a successful military conclusion by the 1730s. Thus it was vital for German federalism to have the Turks hammering at the gates of the Empire, because this danger from without was really the only issue upon which all the territories could unite and follow a common policy by consent.

It was now possible to see who was paying Turk taxes in Lippe and how well total quotas were met. In June 1571 the Lippe regency councillors sent their fourth and last instalment of 1,440 fl. Turk tax to Frankfurt-am-Main in accordance with an Augsburg imperial assembly grant of 1566. They wrote:[25]

Since our young ruler, Simon, Count and noble Lord of Lippe, has been warned by His Majesty to pay to you immediately in return for a satisfactory receipt the still outstanding fourth part of the Turk aid granted at Augsburg in 1566 which was allocated and demanded at Regensburg in the year following, so we have done this and send you 1,440 fl. at 15 *Batzen* per fl.

Up to 1605 this is how Lippe paid its Turk taxes, by merchant banker to the *Legstädte* in return for a receipt. Receipts are scattered but remain in substantial numbers, especially for

[24] Staatsarchiv Detmold, L 9 vol. 1 folio 220 verso.
[25] Staatsarchiv Detmold, L 37 XVII no. 6.

the 1590s. They vary in size of payment from 600 to 3,600 fl. By comparison this represented anything up to an equivalent of 10 per cent of the ruler's annual gross income upon which he was expected to run the dynasty and administration of Lippe and was thus fairly well in accord with the Speyer guidelines of 1542. For a generation Turk tax found a regular place in Lippe finance, the more so as year after year this money was being raised by direct taxation with the full participation and consent of the Estates.[26] In 1602 Simon VI had even paid Turk tax arrears from eight years previously and made the appropriate compensation to Geitzkoffler.[27]

Receipts were as much in demand at territorial as at federal level, and they provide the surest proof of the importance of imperial war tax. In 1604 Simon VI acknowledged receipt of Turk tax from his towns, actually mentioning the original imperial assembly grant. As territorial subjects were thus clearly footing the imperial tax bill, they were as vitally interested in federal affairs as their rulers, if only to make sure that they were not paying too much and to satisfy themselves that money was really needed. The confirmation was in no uncertain terms.[28]

We Simon etc. herewith recognize that our nobles and towns have granted at the most recent territorial assembly that the common imperial assembly grant of 86 months against the Turks, the hereditary enemy of the Holy Name, made at Regensburg last year, has been fixed according to a common assessment at 3,720 fl. which just this once has been raised to 3,720 tlrs for paying the first 31 months of the imperial grant.

We confirm that on behalf of all our towns the mayors and town council of Lemgo have paid us 1,240 tlrs to be quit of the above imperial tax instalment.

Turk taxes were, however, not only paid by the towns in Lippe. All three tax groups in the county made contribution at

[26] Receipts in Staatsarchiv Detmold, L 28 C II zu 1; L 37 XVII no. 6 ; L 41; L 41a IV E 9 vols 1–2; L 92 Z 1a; negotiations in L 9; L 12.

[27] Staatsarchiv Detmold, L 37 XVII no. 6.

[28] Staatsarchiv Detmold, L 11 IV no. 3. Lippe's *Reichsmatrikel* assessment was still 4 horse and 18 foot under Emperor Rudolf II, the same as in 1521. This gave a *simplum* of $(4 \times 12) + (18 \times 4) = 120$ fl. 31 *Römermonate* were to be paid of the 86 granted at the 1603 imperial assembly, thus $120 \times 31 = 3,720$ fl. This was

some time or other. Above all imperial taxes were carefully negotiated at territorial assemblies between rulers and Estates. The Turk tax quotas brought forward at the territorial assembly of Cappel, in April 1577, put the towns down for 2,000 tlrs in four instalments. Lemgo paid 666 tlrs, Lippstadt and Saltzuffeln 333 tlrs each, and Horn, Blomberg and Detmold each something over 200 tlrs.[29] As the treasury income of Lemgo for 1577 was only about 1,000 tlrs it was hardly conceivable that imperial taxes could have been paid without increased local taxation or increased town council borrowing. In Lemgo the latter, more short-sighted, course was chosen. What this does show is that imperial taxation could seriously affect the towns' finances.[30]

The peasants and tenant-farmers under the jurisdiction of the ruler's rural district officials were also paying Turk tax according to special registers drawn up in the *Ämter*. A badly damaged register just for Turk tax survives from *Amt* Detmold from 1579. Here the rural population were paying between $2\frac{1}{2}$ groschen and $2\frac{1}{2}$ tlrs Turk tax each.[31] From imperial assembly right down to territorial peasant the imperial war tax system was now linked up. That the money was getting through to the federal tax receiver is shown by the receipts at imperial and territorial level.

Another register from *Amt* Sternberg from 1584 listed Turk tax payment from Lippe peasants, name by name, village by village. A total of 407 tlrs $16\frac{1}{2}$ gr. was collected from the tenant farms here, with the maximum single payment as high as 4 tlrs and a minimum of $\frac{1}{2}$ Ort ($4\frac{1}{2}$ gr.). Further increases in rates are shown by the Turk tax registers of parish Detmold from 1598 at the height of the federal war effort. In this one parish alone the villages raised 470 fl. of Turk tax in 1598. Single payments varied from 3 gr. to 8 fl.[32] This demonstrates the huge discrepancy between peasant wealth in each locality. If it is dangerous to group nobles together because they have similar titles

---

[29] Staatsarchiv Detmold, L 37 XVII no. 6.
[30] Stadtarchiv Lemgo, Kämmerei, Kr; Urk. Regest. no. 820. 16,226 marks at the debased rate of $16\frac{1}{2}$ marks to the taler.
[31] Staatsarchiv Detmold, L 37 XVII no. 6.   [32] *Ibid.*

---

raised to talers. In Lippe the towns traditionally paid one-third of all tax grants, here therefore 1,240 tlrs, which Count Simon duly received.

and social contact, it is far more misleading to think of the peasants as one group in the light of these differences in taxation.

On the Speyer guidelines of 1542 a Turk tax assessment range of 3 gr. to 8 fl. at 10 per cent of annual income meant a taxable capital wealth of 16–1,600 fl. per common rural inhabitant, *Amtsuntertan*, in this part of late-sixteenth-century Lippe. Huge economic differences within a group that had the same social and legal status and duties were thus part and parcel of village life. 'Peasant' could thus mean anything in terms of social economics, and this is brought out by tax registers that were devised not only for territorial purposes but specifically for federal war tax.

The nobility appeared in the Turk tax records of Lippe above all in arrears. In the 1570s an arrears list included eleven native nobles, a monastery and market towns. Only one town had arrears of 20 tlrs. The nobles owed 235½ tlrs. Foreign land-owners in Lippe had further arrears of 346½ tlrs, but these were more legitimate as the Speyer tax guidelines of 1542 had allowed the propertied the right to pay federal taxes only to the authorities where they had their main seat of residence. Once again arrears claims of a dubious nature were being made, this time by a government at territorial level.[33]

What relationship had arrears to the full grants? How far were taxes under-subscribed? No arrears policy argued this way during the early modern period in Lippe and it leaves the suspicion that taxes were relatively well paid. Comparative figures are, however, available for the Turk tax of 1594 which was collected from the nobility and their tax-privileged equals in 1598. It is noteworthy that this was for a federal tax where the money would be going out of the county, thus an unpalatable tax to finance at territorial level. Yet up to 90 per cent of the total demand was collected. Twenty-seven noble families should have provided 777 tlrs and actually paid 686 tlrs. Five ecclesiastical foundations should have paid 265 tlrs and rendered 257 tlrs. Four market towns were assessed for 244 tlrs and handed over 216 tlrs. Five *Vögte* even paid one taler more than their modest assessment of 29 tlrs.[34] On the Speyer guidelines of 1542 this meant that the average Lippe noble establishment was rated at a capital wealth of 5,730 tlrs (7,640 fl.), not much

[33] *Ibid.* [34] *Ibid.*

more than four times the wealth of the richest peasants, the serfs and free tenant-farmers.[35]

That Turk tax collecting was by no means unprofitable is shown by a seventeenth-century copy of a Turk tax granted at an assembly in Lippe in 1583, which shows quotas and actual payments by all three tax classes. The peasantry were paying two-thirds of the total grant and the towns and nobles together were paying the residue. Even so, the towns were having to pay three times as much as the nobles. Thus the nobles were heavily tax-evading, the towns moderately so, and the extra was being pushed on to the peasantry. On top of the original grant the tax collectors were making an extra levy, in this case of 16 per cent, which the peasantry were again chiefly expected to pay. Thus of a net grant of 5,800 tlrs in 1583 the peasantry were actually paying 4,000 tlrs as the collectors' margin of profit pushed the total tax-bill up to 6,760 tlrs.[36] It seems unlikely therefore that the Speyer guidelines of 1542 of an all-round 10 per cent income tax were being equitably adhered to in taxing all income groups.

There were striking differences between Lippe's Turk tax payments in 1508, when only the towns paid, and in 1542 when towns, nobles and peasants paid one-third each. In 1583 the nobles were paying less than 10 per cent and the towns had fallen to around the 20 per cent mark. The rest was shouldered by the rural districts, who had no voice in the finance and politics of the county. They were not in the Estates, therefore they could be made to pay.

Tax collection even of federal grants was thus well worth the effort.[37] In the 1540s the towns still had equal representation on tax committees, but under Simon VI the nobility came to the fore. In 1594 Turk taxes came under a committee of territorial nobles. The towns were excluded. Simon wrote to six of his nobles:[38]

As all our faithful nobles have unanimously agreed in the most recent territorial assembly to make a substantial sum available out of their

[35] For capital taxes and tax theory that included the nobility, T. Mayer, *Handbuch der Finanzwissenschaft*, 1, Tübingen, 1926, pp. 234–5, 239–40.

[36] Staatsarchiv Detmold, L 10 Titel 5 no. 2 vol. 3.

[37] Staatsarchiv Detmold, L 114 A, von Donop no. 73; L 9 vol. 4 folios 88–90, Landdrost Oeynhausen's tax-farm of 1599.

[38] Staatsarchiv Detmold, L 11 IV nos. 1–5d.

own resources and to ask you to collect this money from the nobility as well as from the other common subjects living in the countryside, so we graciously ask you to come here next Wednesday and make the necessary arrangements.

A group of nobles thus co-operated with Simon VI's local officials over Turk tax collection. The market of Varenholz was given a receipt by two nobles calling themselves delegated tax collectors in July 1598 for paying 14 tlrs 9 gr. Turk taxes. The nobles were using Lemgo as their base.[39] A month later Simon VI ordered his local officials to collect Turk taxes from the rural tenantry in accordance with a grant made by the Estates. The order shows a well-developed system of grant, assessment and collection of imperial war tax at work in rural Lippe.[40]

Simon etc. To all local officials [*Amtleute*] about collection of Turk tax.

Since the common Estates of our County have recently obediently granted us numerous Turk, Imperial and other taxes, and since these must now be paid, so we graciously herewith order you and your colleagues [*Amtsverwandten*] to collect from the existing land-tax register one double Land-tax to pay off these grants between Whitsun and this coming Michaelmas.

In order that the people may have cognizance of this, we will see that they are informed from the pulpits in your district by the Clergy.

Two things of importance were shown in this order. The local officials were being given far too little time in which to do their assessing and collecting. The order came at the beginning of August, it was backdated to Whitsun, and final payment was expected by the end of September. As late as August the people who were actually going to have to find the money had not even been told. The other point was that imperial federal taxes were now mixed together with other taxes of a territorial, but, to the local officials, unspecified nature. What the actual sums granted at imperial or even territorial level were, was not communicated to the localities. Indeed their quotas would be fixed from above, but the local official could not really tell the people who were paying what the taxes were for. There was thus an element of furtiveness and secrecy about taxation that did little to encourage the common people to pay with a will.

[39] Staatsarchiv Detmold, L 11 IV 5a.
[40] Staatsarchiv Detmold, L 37 XVII no. 6.

This was even true of taxation at imperial assembly level. Despite its reputation of being an assembly that made all its business public via the dictation room of the Mainz archchancellery or via an authorized printer, actual numbers of *Römermonate* granted were kept from the public. It was thus in the particular interest of a small territory like Lippe to attend imperial assemblies and have first-hand knowledge of grant discussions in the *Fürstenrat*, for on this point the official account gave little away. And at second hand, as from a circle codirector like Bishop Christof Bernhard Galen of Münster, no trustworthy account could be expected.[41] Taxation had brought with it a new development in administration and law. It worked only with a substantial amount of consent, and in this *Reich*, circle and territory in the sixteenth century were no exception. The actual receipts of imperial war tax paid by Lippe tell more of the truth than imperial assembly discussions and Emperor's writs, which provided the public relations rather than the direction of a federal war effort to which the people of Lippe in their turn dutifully contributed.[42]

From the 1560s the Westphalian circle began to play a rôle of increasing importance in the organization of imperial war taxes within its region. The circle was dealing with matters of security rather than just the Turk war. Thus the 1566 imperial assembly Turk tax grant for the following three years was to be paid by the territories directly to the *Legstädte* at 12 *Römermonate* per annum. This by-passed the circle authorities.[43] The circle, however, did organize the collection of *Römermonate*

[41] True also of seventeenth- and eighteenth-century compendia keeping the form but rarely giving the content of financial negotiations, see *Aller des H.R.R. Reichstage, Abschiede und Satzungen*, Frankfurt-am-Main, 1720. Also publicized *Abschiede* brought back by Lippe rulers and agents at imperial assemblies of the later sixteenth and seventeenth centuries in Staatsarchiv Detmold, L 41a IV B no. 3, *Reichsabschied*, published officially by Mainz in 1582, folios 2–3, binding the territories to pay an unspecified sum of Turk tax for the next four years. K. Rauch (ed.), *Traktat über den Reichstag im 16. Jahrhundert. Eine offiziöse Darstellung aus der Kurmainzer Kanzlei*, Leipzig, 1905, shows that contemporaries avoided this reality in their publicity. See also W. Fürnrohr, *Der immerwährende Reichstag zu Regensburg*, Regensburg, 1963, pp. 19–21 and illustrations.

[42] Staatsarchiv Detmold, L 41a IV E 9 vol. 1, Emperor Rudolf II's writ to the imperial assembly of 23 August 1597 sent to Count Simon VI as an example of publicity, also L 41a IV 207.

[43] Staatsarchiv Detmold, L 37 XVII no. 7, Maximilian II's Turk tax demands 1566–7.

granted by the imperial assembly to deal with internal rebellion and bandits, notably in the Gotha affair. Specific imperial and circle aids in troops and money were forthcoming to put down the last remnants of the *condottieri* called into being originally by Charles V's civil war effort, in 1546–53, and never properly demobilized. Thus between 1565 and 1571 the circle demanded Gotha grant arrears of 700–800 tlrs from the regency councillors in Lippe.[44] In July 1567 Dietrich Muntz, Westphalian circle treasurer, sent an extract of Lippe's circle tax accounts to Detmold. This shows an elaborate system at work, as the circles under the direction of Elector August of Saxony, Director of the Upper-Saxon circle, dealt with the last *condottiere* in Gotha.

Lippe owed 4 *Römermonate* of imperial tax on the Gotha war costs and 2 *Römermonate* of circle tax, granted in February 1567 at circle and not imperial level as a special reserve fund for the circle's own disposal. By April of that year Lippe had paid one-half of these two demands. On 1 August 1567 the circle paid supporting sums to the Upper-Saxon circle which had actually undertaken the military measures against Grumbach. On this Lippe was charged another 3 *Römermonate* with an outstanding *Römermonat* to come. Thus between February and August 1567 Westphalian circle demands on Lippe were 10 *Römermonate* of which 3 had been paid in April 1567.[45] Again the demand came a month in advance but already sounded like an arrears threat. By August Lippe had paid another 3 *Römermonate*. The county was thus 60 per cent paid up.[46]

Two years previously the regency councillors in Lippe had already been leaving taxation to a committee of the Estates, which was giving orders to the local officials, fixing dates of collection. Either taxes were not being passed on by the Estates, or they were not being collected or the demands of Empire and circle were capricious and levied at very short notice.[47] Lippe admitted only one-half of the arrears which the circle claimed, and then over a much longer period from 1564 to 1568. Threats now came in from circle director Jülich and from

[44] Staatsarchiv Detmold, L 37 XVII no. 7.
[45] Receipt of Anna Muntz, the circle treasurer's wife, Düsseldorf, 2 August 1567, Staatsarchiv Detmold, L 37 XVII no. 7.
[46] 'Ein überschmickter Auszug', 8 July 1567, L 37 XVII no. 7.
[47] Committee note of 25 February 1565, L 37 XVII no. 7.

the Emperor's Procurator Fiscal in Speyer. Lippe should pay 240 fl. and 120 fl. towards the 1,500 horses granted in 1564 and the 1,200 horses granted in 1566. 360 fl. were still demanded for payment to the circle. This frightened Lippe into reviewing its own calculations. The regency councillors now claimed to have been assessed at circle and imperial level for 2,318 tlrs and to have actually paid 1,484 tlrs.[48] The muddle was caused by Lippe first finding the money with which to pay federal taxes and only secondly recouping it from taxation granted by the Estates. This was a wasteful and laborious system. Thus on the above grants the towns seem to have been overlooked until the threats from Speyer came in. Then they were asked to pay their customary one-third, and finally by October 1568 Lemgo did something to ease the situation by paying 775 tlrs of circle and imperial tax to the regency councillors.[49]

Lippe's tax system was in a mess, but this was partly due to the suddenness with which demands were made on the territory from the federal bodies. Just as the territorial central government gave its local officials very little time in tax matters, so the federal bodies seemed to do the same to the territorial central government when the state was of the size of Lippe. The system of demand, arrears calculation and threat from circle director and *Reichskammergericht* as well as Emperor's court was used on Lippe with considerable effect. The federal tax system worked at least by bullying the smallest.

The Gotha affair tax arrears continued to be pursued in 1568–1569. The circle directors co-operated, so Elector August of Saxony made his demands to the Duke of Jülich and five circle officials put pressure on Lippe. The matter eventually came before a circle assembly at Münster in March 1569. Lippe still had alleged arrears of 814 fl. Further demands for increasing the Westphalian circle reserve came in July 1568 and April and August 1569. Again they demonstrated the flexibility of the federal *Matrikel simplum* tax system. Instead of increasing the number of *Römermonate* outright, the *simplum* was doubled. In 1568 the circle demanded two 'plain' *Römermonate*, in the

<hr />

[48] There were also separate Turk tax grants of 2,880 fl., showing the division in federal tax administration between *Legstädte* for foreign war money, and the circles for internal security and local troop recruitment during the 1560s. 'Lippische Turckenhulfe Anno 1566', Staatsarchiv Detmold, L 37 XVII no. 6.
[49] Staatsarchiv Detmold, L 37 XVII no. 7.

year following it demanded not four 'plain' *Römermonate* but two 'double' *Römermonate*. In a world of precedent and equity this shows how fiscalism advanced at federal level.[50]

By 1599 circle leader Simon had begun to apply some of these federal methods of taxation even to his own territorial nobles and exempted establishments. Thus the latter were given one week only within which to pay their quota of the Westphalian circle campaign against the Spaniards and Dutch which Simon had organized, 'for the need of our fatherland's fair defence, the now pending Imperial armament'.[51]

The run-down of the Turkish war and the Spanish-Dutch truce left both Empire and circles without a common policy with which to distract the territories from religious dissension. The military bond forged to keep a real semblance of unity in the federal system was also broken by the discrediting of Rudolf's government over the conduct of the Turk war at imperial assembly level in the first decade of the seventeenth century. The Geitzkoffler scandal gave territories very good grounds for refusing supply before redress of grievances. It was not only the religious issue that counted, and not only the Protestant militants that had grievances. The attack on the Turk tax accounts was supported by Bavaria who supplied the chief accountant who fought Rudolf's former federal war-tax receiver.[52]

At home Lippe had its own problems. The Lemgo rebellion prevented Lippe from paying any more federal war taxes after 1605. By 1609 Simon was appealing directly to Rudolf for time to pay, but by this time the Habsburg government that Simon had so faithfully backed in federal affairs was no longer in a position of control to help Lippe, even if it had wanted to do so.[53] On the other hand the Fiscal could not get his demands for arrears distraint carried out as Calvinist Lippe benefited from the religious split in the federal constitution. The outcome was not by any means as Simon VI would have wanted it. The system of concord at home by foreign war on the frontiers with the infidel had failed. Federal taxation now became arbitrary as occupation armies collected it without reference to the imperial

---

[50] *Ibid.*   [51] Staatsarchiv Detmold, L 37 XVII nos 6–7.
[52] Staatsarchiv Detmold, L 41a IV E 9 vol. 2; L 41a IV E no. 1.
[53] Staatsarchiv Detmold, L 41a IV E 9 vol. 2.

constitution. It was the achievement of politicians in the 1640s to put the system of consultation and consent back on its feet by revitalizing a federal system that had broken down in 1608–13.

During the Thirty Years' War no *Römermonate* were granted, for no imperial assemblies were called. Federal taxation by consent as developed in Empire, circles and territories since the days of Maximilian I had given way to taxation by military exaction. In 1641 Emperor Ferdinand III had made an attempt to put back the system of consent under imperial, Habsburg direction. His imperial assembly failed because it was partisan. No grants were forthcoming from the territories that attended and in return the Emperor retained troop strength despite general dearth and his desire to stop the war.[54] The key Protestant minority had stayed away from this imperial assembly; the Guelphs, Palatine Wittelsbachs, Hesse-Kassel and Mecklenburg were holding out with the Swedes.[55] Yet war escalation had stopped and peace negotiations could get under way.[56]

After 1643 demobilization of Swedes and imperialists was at last financed from legitimate imperial tax payments. *Römermonate* were again consented to by a revived federal system as agreed to in the treaties of 1648. Germany returned to constitutional federalism, and the old problem of finding a common interest reappeared. The old methods and practices were again resorted to. Thus in 1650 Lippe paid its first *Römermonate* again, but directly to the imperialist troops, thus by-passing Westphalian circle co-director Christof Bernhard Galen, Bishop of Münster. In July, General Hatzfeld had demanded 6,000 tlrs. On 3 September this was down to 4,000 tlrs. On 27 September he accepted 3,000 tlrs to be quit of Lippe. By the terms of the Nuremberg demobilization interim of September 1649, circle director Christof Bernhard had a valid grievance against being by-passed. He got his revenge in the 1670s by billeting his troops in Lippe. The re-establishment of the federal constitution brought its own new difficulties. In internal affairs the big

[54] Staatsarchiv Detmold, L 41a IV B no. 3.

[55] List of territories present, 'Kayserliches Reichs Abschied', printed by Mainz in 1641. The Swedish allies were excluded by Emperor Ferdinand from Regensburg, see Staatsarchiv Detmold, L 41a IV B no. 3.

[56] F. Dickmann, *Der Westfälische Friede*, Münster, 1959, pp. 98–105.

territories to fear were once again those that acted as circle directors.[57]

The small territories in the Lippe region corresponded with each other in order to find out how their neighbours and social equals were coping with federal demands. Out of this grew the Westphalian College of Counts which acted as a consortium of small territories in the region in the post-war period and all through the eighteenth century. In March 1651 Nassau-Hadamar was already asking Lippe what the Count had done about meeting federal tax demands of 300 *Römermonate*. Had Lippe paid by assignat to the circle treasury under Galen in Münster? Johann Bernhard of Lippe replied that he had paid 3,000 tlrs but that two-thirds of the *Römermonate* that were already being demanded at circle level had not yet been granted by an imperial assembly. Payment would therefore be postponed.[58]

When the imperial assembly did meet in 1653–4 it even felt rich enough to make a really wholly unnecessary grant of four *Römermonate* to exiled Charles II of England. Even Lippe had followed the English situation and sympathy ran high for the royalists, so high in fact that Lippe was now expected to pay 320 tlrs charity grant to young Charles in Cologne. Charles had the support of the Count of Tecklenburg who had made payment and was thus asked to invite his fellow Westphalian counts to do likewise. Tecklenburg was informed by Hermann Adolf of Lippe that the Estates of Lippe had agreed to the grant to Charles II as it was an imperial assembly decision. He wrote to his apanage uncle in Brake that Charles should be paid and Brake must pay one-sixth of it like any other federal tax grant. Otto of Brake consented.[59]

If Lippe was capable of taking such a red herring of federal taxation seriously, the revived system of 1648 could indeed be expected to be working again. If money was forthcoming for

[57] Staatsarchiv Detmold, L 37 XVII no. 9b. H. von Zwiedineck-Südenhorst, *Deutsche Geschichte im Zeitraum der Gründung des Preussischen Königtums*, Stuttgart, 1894, 1, pp. 89–91, for the *Friedensexecutions-Hauptrecess* finally concluded 26 June 1650.

[58] H. Kesting, 'Geschichte und Verfassung des Niedersächsisch-Westfälischen Reichsgrafen-Kollegiums', *Westfälische Zeitschrift*, 106, 1956, pp. 176–84. Staatsarchiv Detmold, L 37 XVII no. 7.

[59] Staatsarchiv Detmold, L 8 K Section IV no. 2 C; L 37 XVII no. 7; L 41a IV E 9 vol. 7; L 9 vol. 11 folios 275–6.

the support of an exiled foreign ruler after all the complaints of Thirty Years' War damage and the heavy cost of demobilization then German rulers either lacked a sense of proportion or the economic situation was not really as bad as the debt reductions agreed upon at this imperial assembly implied. Above all it shows once again how adaptable the *Matrikel simplum* system of *Römermonate* was.

Just as attempts to obtain moderated assessments had been a real feature of territories' attitudes to the imperial *Matrikel* system in the later sixteenth century, so after 1648 the *Matrikel* had been revived at the 1521 rate. This satisfied most territories as it meant that the Empire was bent on a cheap policy of peace-keeping rather than expensive warmongering. The inadequacy of this revived *simplum* was shown when between 1681 and 1698 it was increased by stages to nine times its Westphalian Peace level, as Leopold I began to cope with the French and the Turks. Yet it was this low rating that caused such inflated *Römermonate* demands from the 1660s onwards, which, when they were not paid by the smaller territories, were collected by force from circle directors in the name of Emperor and imperial constitution. The big territories had gained control of the revived imperial war effort in their regions.[60]

The cheap military system envisaged in 1648 was upset by a new threat from the Turks on the south-eastern frontier. After a break of nearly half a century, Turk tax demands from imperial assemblies and Emperor's commissars were made again. To start with, Lippe tried to cope with these demands itself. Hermann Adolf tried to get some order into assessment and collection. The nobility were charged with the military effort, the towns and rural districts with payment of *Römermonate*. By 1660 the last remnants of illegal taxation by military exaction had disappeared in Lippe. A new territorial assessment had been worked out which took account of the dynastic fragmentation that the apanage system had brought with it since the 1610s. The towns were still quoted for one-third, the apanage of Brake was given one-sixth and the rural districts the rest. The nobility were on a private system of *dons gratuits*. Grants were subject once more to Estates' consent with apanage

[60] Zwiedineck-Südenhorst, *op. cit.*, 2, pp. 41–2. Staatsarchiv Detmold, L 37 XVII no. 2.

members of the dynasty acting as members of the Estates rather than of the ruling dynasty. It was thus extremely difficult for the ruler to obtain grants from assemblies that now contained such discordant elements as nobles, towns and members of his own family, jealous of his claims to primogeniture.

On top of this, Lippe had to contend with revived military pressure from the circle directors, Münster, Brandenburg and the Guelphs. To meet federal demands new forms of taxation were thought out in Lippe. In 1661 the territorial assembly granted a poll tax on all male householders. In December *Amtmann* Cappel was ordered by chancellor and councillors in Detmold to draw up poll-tax registers for a Turk tax granted at circle level.[61]

We herewith notify as has been agreed at the territorial assembly which was held here, that the Turk tax granted at the Circle assembly in Cologne be collected in the form of a poll-tax. We have agreed to this policy and order you herewith to draw up lists of all male householders in your local district, which should also include all shepherds and millers, and that you send these lists in as soon as possible in order that quotas may be allocated.

In January 1662 Hermann Adolf ordered his officials and servants at court and in the household to negotiate their own contributions to the Turk tax with the treasury secretary individually. The establishment was poll-taxed and a list was prepared that started with the *Landdrost* and Chancellor at the top and included the chimney-sweep at the bottom. Local officials were also included, as were judicial officials, clergy, churchwardens and authorized teachers. Assessments varied from 4 tlrs down to a quarter of a taler. The establishment contributed barely 300 tlrs to the Turk tax out of their own pockets. Compared with this, the rural district of Detmold alone was assessed for little short of 2,000 tlrs. Only twenty-seven *Römermonate* had been granted at federal level. This gave Lippe a bill of 2,160 tlrs, with estimated collection expenses of a further 300 tlrs. Yet the rural districts were assessed by the chancellery for an extra 2,000 tlrs. The ruler was adding his own profit to the federal tax. He allowed his tax farmers $12\frac{1}{2}$ per cent and took an extra 80 per cent for himself. The bill went up from 2,160 tlrs net to 4,460 tlrs gross.[62]

[61] Staatsarchiv Detmold, L 37 XVII no. 6.   [62] *Ibid.*

Once again the towns paid their quotas to the ruler in lump sums for which they received receipts.[63] A check was also kept on what the rural districts paid. Thus between 1657 and 1663 the apanage *Amt* of Sternberg paid an average of 60 tlrs a year in federal taxes to the ruler.[64] Finally the nobility were pressed for a *don gratuit*. Assessed at between 1,000 and 2,500 tlrs in 1647, 1653, 1658 and 1663, they fluctuated wildly on arrears from almost nothing to over 50 per cent. On the Turk tax the nobles still owed four months of assessment.[65] In his warnings to the nobles not to get into arrears on federal taxes the ruler was talking about imperial assessments of 230 *Römermonate* by March 1664, quite a different proposition from the twenty-seven *Römermonate* of 1661.[66] With such an increase in *Römermonate* Lippe could no longer afford to exempt anyone from taxation. Levies once again became monthly in reminiscence of the Thirty Years' War period. This applied especially to the rural districts which were paying on an average almost 100 tlrs a month each in Turk tax by the autumn of 1664.[67]

By 1664 it was clear that the ruler could no longer cope with increased demands for federal war tax. In the first four months of 1664 Brake apanage, all the towns, the markets and the nobility had paid practically nothing. Towns and nobles were prepared to levy income tax on their servants and employees but were withholding payment from their own pockets. The full weight of taxation now fell on the rural districts alone.[68] Although they were threatened by the use of force in order to speed up their payment of Turk tax arrears to the collectors, the tenantry had their rents and mortgages to pay. Ruler's officials had thus to be lenient with hard cases to prevent total ruin.[69]

Hermann Adolf failed above all to collect the towns' increased Turk tax quotas. It took him all the year to get Lippstadt to recognize a duty to pay in 1664. However keen he may have

---

[63] Staatsarchiv Detmold, L 10 Titel 2 no. 23 vol. 2, accounts of Secretary Busch were audited six-yearly, L 92 Z 1a.   [64] Staatsarchiv Detmold, L 37 XVII no. 6.
[65] *Ibid.*, no. 2.   [66] *Ibid.*, no. 7.
[67] Staatsarchiv Detmold, L 10 Titel 2 no. 23 parcel 11.
[68] 'Restanten vom 4 Monatzlichen Turckenschatz, 30 Junii 1664', with reminder to the towns of 30 July 1664, Staatsarchiv Detmold, L 37 XVII no. 6.
[69] 'Mandat an alle Beambte den Leuten biss zum newen Jhren schulds halber zu geben', 2 January 1664. Hermann Adolf ordered 'das mit den Leuten Condolentz getragen', Staatsarchiv Detmold, L 37 XVII no. 6.

been on poll taxes, his demands for them from the towns in 1664–5 remained fruitless. When in January 1666 the chancellery sent subpoenas to the towns to pay Turk tax arrears on pain of distraint the situation had already moved out of territorial control. The circle directors as armed powers had moved in to discipline the county. Distraint was now a federal matter.[70]

In the autumn of 1665 Brandenburg troops moved into Lippe to spend the winter. The county became a favourite stopping-off place on route marches. It was now no longer a question of *Römermonate* and Turk taxes to be paid to suitably distant circle and imperial treasurers. The big territories had moved into the county to collect federal taxes at source. Whereas the territory had paid military 'contribution' to Thirty Years' War troops a generation previously, it now paid the same thing as 'subsidy' to its armed neighbours, ostensibly as part of a legitimate war effort.[71]

In November 1665, faced with the presence of Brandenburg troops, the Lippe Estates granted 18,600 tlrs of federal troop subsidies to be paid to the armed powers, Brandenburg and Münster. The Lippe government gave immediate instructions to its local officials on how this was to be collected from the rural districts. Each official was to carry out the following five points.

Officials are encouraged to assess people according to wealth and availability of foodstuffs, and to consider getting help with payments from their creditors.

Retired peasants and families living-in shall also be taxed and not overlooked.

Village collectors shall be allowed a reduction of one-half on what they themselves would normally pay, had they not taken on the job of collector.

Those subjects who have been granted any years free of taxation will remain exempt only if they can produce relevant proof, whilst they should still be entered into the registers.

Each official must have sent his register in triplicate to the chancellery one day before he is finally due to deliver up the amount he has collected. He must appear at a given time in the chancellery with his local subordinates, the peasant judge and two leading men from each village.

One half of the money was to come in by December and the other half by January. In order to achieve this all those with

[70] *Ibid.*   [71] *Ibid.*, no. 22.

mortgages were to pay a tax of one-sixth out of their rents from the rural districts. Arrangements were made for commissioners to go from district to district, drawing up special mortgage registers. The threat against non-participation was loss of the mortgage, which could be established by comparison with peasant registers. In this way the Estates were being indirectly taxed, for they and those who had invested in land and agricultural produce were now being forced to pay a capital tax, as the subsidy took priority over all other claims to the rents and produce of the rural tenantry.[72]

The situation became urgent as the village of Schötmar alone claimed to have been forced to pay 1,000 tlrs in damages to Brandenburg troops. A commission drew up a register of every claim and a fruitless complaint was made to Elector Frederick William. By February 1666 Lippe was paying subsidies to Brandenburg troops of 1,200 tlrs a month, and the money was coming from the rural districts. Lippe itself claimed that it had a duty only to pay 205 tlrs a month in federal war tax. This did not save it from being forced to pay over five times that amount to Brandenburg alone.[73]

Correspondence with Elector Frederick William proved that any *pro forma* appeal on a ruler-to-ruler basis was fruitless. The split was final between the territories that were *Armierte* and those which were *Nichtarmierte*. Only Lippe could put the picture straight by offering the Emperor better terms as an *Armierter* itself, and this policy had to wait another thirty years for a more skilful ruler. In the meantime the best that Lippe could hope for was a guarantee from Elector Frederick William that Brandenburg troops coming through Lippe would keep the peace and behave in such a way that no insolence or excess was committed.[74]

This presumably worked as long as suitable food and lodgings

[72] *Ibid.*, no. 8a.   [73] *Ibid.*, no. 22.

[74] 'Wir haben vnsern darbey commandirenden Officiren ernstlich anbefohlen gute und scharfe ordre zu halten vnd die geringst insolentien oder excessen nicht zu verüben', Elector Frederick William to Count Hermann Adolf, Cleves, 13 January 1666. Cf. F. L. Carsten, *The Origins of Prussia*, London, 1954, p. 273. For previous pillaging Frederick William had demanded the names of the officers concerned. There was no talk of indemnifying Lippe, but only a desire to deduct from their official Prussian pay packets what the troops had wilfully taken. Frederick William to Hermann Adolf, Cleves, 22 December 1665. Staatsarchiv Detmold, L 37 XVII no. 22.

with presents were forthcoming. To ensure this the local officials were ordered to raise subsidies in full and above all on time. Soldiers would not and indeed could not wait for their money. The formula writ of February 1666 ran as follows:[75]

As the subjects of our district of N must contribute as from February 1st until further notice N tlrs monthly soldier tax for the upkeep of billeted Electoral Brandenburg cavalry, we herewith graciously command you to give the levying of such taxes first priority, and to really pay them in to us monthly in return for receipts.

In 1666 there was a change of ruler in Lippe. The new Count, Simon Henrich, tried to get out of the clutches of Brandenburg and Münster whilst still remaining a *Nichtarmierter*. He called in Guelph troops in the 1680s in the hope that they would expel the Brandenburg and Münster contingents. He attempted to play the *Armierte* off against each other, as his kinsmen in Schaumburg-Lippe were doing with considerable success. The plan misfired, and Lippe now had to pay contributions to the troops of three 'protectors' instead of two. Simon Henrich also tried to return to the traditional policy of payment to *Legstädte*, thereby ridding the county of the troops of distraining circle directors. His finances were not sufficiently orderly to carry this out. In 1670 when he tried to pay federal taxes directly to Frankfurt-am-Main, he had to issue an assignat to the imperial receiver for 500 tlrs to run on the revenues of his own Lippe treasury. It was clear from the weak financial situation in Lippe that federal war taxes would be forthcoming only if the policy of distraint by the circle *Armierte* continued. Hermann Adolf had been served well by the Busch family in the treasury and accounts had balanced. Under Simon Henrich officials resorted to living from hand to mouth and the accounting system broke down. Under these conditions federal war taxes continued to be collected by the troops of outsiders with imperial sanction.[76]

The Münster invasions of the 1670s, which were thought to have recaptured all the traditional horrors of the Thirty Years' War period of a generation previously, were troop billets by a

[75] Hermann Adolf to his local officials, 17 February 1666. Monthly quotas followed in appended documents. An attempt was made to get money from the towns as well, Staatsarchiv Detmold, L 37 XVII no. 22.
[76] Staatsarchiv Detmold, L 92 Z 1a.

circle director in lieu of unpaid federal war taxes from the county. Thus in August 1675 Münster demanded 16,000 tlrs from Lippe in return for calling off its troops. The county would agree to pay only 8,000 tlrs. Lippe had already been paying at the rate of 1,300 tlrs a month earlier in the year to Münster.[77]

Lippe had a weak ruler and chaotic finances. It was an easy prey to Münster and Brandenburg, who as circle directors had been given a free hand by Emperor and imperial assembly to distrain for arrears. Thus in January 1664 Emperor and imperial assembly had already ordered the circles to proceed against territories with Turk tax arrears. Lippe was informed: 'It has further been agreed that in this case of the Turkish expedition the Circle Directors [*ausschreibende Fürsten*] shall undertake to distrain those with arrears with a firm hand and by military methods.'[78] To get his federal war support Leopold I had abandoned Habsburg protectionist policies towards small-fry like Lippe. He continued to make deals with the bigger territories. He handed the circle system over to them in return for real support for his wars.[79]

During 1676–81 Lippe was unwilling host first to Münster and then to Lüneburg-Celle troops. In June 1678 Simon Henrich ordered his officials to pay subsidy to Celle troops only. He hoped thereby to force Münster out. In June 1679 towns and officials were ordered to pay victualling costs to Lüneburg troops on summer campaign. War reached Lippe. The villages of the north-west were exempted from taxes because of damage from French troops. Lemgo was ordered to make contribution and the Estates granted taxes to pay troop damages of 14,000 tlrs. Lüneburg troops stayed on in Lippe during the winter of 1679–80 and cost the inhabitants 4,000 tlrs a month. There had been a sharp rehearsal of the Thirty Years' War situation, only this time the outsiders demanded subsidies strictly within the terms of the imperial law and constitution and not illegal contributions. In 1680 the situation stabilized as Lippe engaged Celle to be its sole *Armierter* at a flat rate of 1,300 tlrs a month.

[77] A. Falkmann, *Beiträge zur Geschichte des Fürstentums Lippe*, Lemgo and Detmold, 1857–1902, 'Münstersche Invasion'. E. Stegemann, 'Die Grafschaft Lippe im dreissigjährigen Krieg', *Lippische Mitteilungen*, 3, 1905, Staatsarchiv Detmold, L 37 XVII nos 6, 22. [78] Staatsarchiv Detmold, L 41a IV 207.
[79] Staatsarchiv Detmold, L 41a IV B no. 4.

The troops that remained in occupation were ordered out of the towns and their monthly bill was settled by the proceeds from cattle tax. Thus the rural inhabitants continued to bear the brunt of war and taxation.[80]

In 1682 Lippe's quotas of federal war tax went up once again. This time the basic rate of assessment, the *Matrikel*, was increased to a new *simplum*, whereas in the 1660s and 1670s the increase had been in numbers of *Römermonate*. Rates were worked out from first principles. To all federal troop totals the Westphalian circle contributed one-tenth in men, equipment and money. Increases were in basic units of 20,000 at imperial level with Lippe going up in units of 80 tlrs (120 fl.) in money terms alone. This unit was computed from the 1521 *Matrikel* which still remained the basis upon which the Empire assessed its war efforts. As each imperial assembly grant varied in size, so the quotas all along the line from circle to territory, to Estates and common people in the territories had to be worked out afresh. The territories above all aimed at fairness at their level. Whatever the real total of each new federal demand, the Lippe chancellery shared the burden at a fixed rate of one-sixth Brake apanage, one-third the towns and one-half the *Ämter*. Assessments were diligently drawn up. One cannot say that the chaotic way in which federal tax records have survived is due to any chaotic way in which they may have been drawn up. The system of assessment and sharing out of local quotas was diligently followed and it produced a mound of paper work and calculation as each quota was worked out to the last fraction of a taler.[81]

Lippe got a respite from the demands of the *Armierte* in the mid-1680s. This was the period when ruler and Estates developed the *Landkasse*, which was an agreement to put certain debts into a fund over which the Estates had some degree of control in return for increased extraordinary tax grants. Ruler's officials threw up a barrage of figures in an attempt to keep the Estates out of their affairs. They lumped all taxes together into one monthly levy from the rural districts, on top of which the towns would pay their quota annually, according to how net figures of tax grant were fixed in territorial assembly. Federal

[80] Staatsarchiv Detmold, L 37 XVII nos 2, 22.
[81] 'Subrepartitiones matriculares', 'Städtische Contributions Desideria', Staatsarchiv Detmold, L 37 XVII nos 2, 4, 6.

taxes thus disappeared from view, as the lump sums that Lippe could raise from domain, Estates and tenantry were subjected to three great pressures. There were the external demands of the *Armierte* who were expected to keep their demands to within the limits set by the imperial assembly in the war effort against French and Turks, but which went in excess of Lippe's quotas whenever troops came into the county. There were internal expenses, as the dynasty failed year after year to live on its regular revenues. Finally, there was the financing of debts and rents from both internal and external sources.

The forming of the *Landkasse* in 1685 did not immediately improve the situation and the war demands of 1688–97 really threatened Lippe with disintegration, not so much because of a bankrupt situation, which was far worse in the 1730s, but because of bad leadership under a ruler who had no control over his officials and yet refused to co-operate with the Estates on financial matters. It was the county's good fortune that Simon Henrich died in 1697 and that he was followed by a ruler who, although he still refused to co-operate with the Estates, could control his officials, and who above all had a real flair for politics at imperial, federal level.[82]

Between 1689 and 1691 Leopold on the one hand and Simon Henrich on the other tried to keep the *Armierte* out of federal war tax collection in the county. In January 1689 Lippe paid Leopold's commissar Gödens, who was accredited to the Lower-Saxon and Westphalian circles, 4,200 tlrs as part of imperial assembly Turk tax grants.[83] When hostilities were reopened with France, however, Gödens, try as he would, could not get satisfaction from Lippe. As regards *Türkensteuer*, Lippe already owed 50 *Römermonate* by 1686. The claim went as high as 280 *Römermonate* by May 1688. This represented 33,600 fl. in real

[82] H. Contzen, *Die Lippische Landkasse*, Münster, 1910, *passim*. J. Heidemann, 'Das Lippische Wirtschaftsleben und Finanzwesen in der zweiten Hälfte des 17. Jahrhunderts', *Westfälische Forschungen*, 15, 1962, pp. 143–71. F. W. Schaer, 'Der Absolutismus in Lippe und Schaumburg-Lippe', *Lippische Mitteilungen*, 37, 1968. Staatsarchiv Detmold, L 37 XVII no. 2, 'Monatliche Contributionsgelder 1685–7'. In 1685 an annual total of 25,000 tlrs was expected from the rural districts in extraordinary tax in an attempt to break free from the *Armierte*. H. Kiewning, 'Der Lippische Fürstenbrief von 1720', *Lippische Mitteilungen*, 1, 1903, pp. 39–62.

[83] Receipts of Commissar Gödens to Count Simon Henrich, 28 January 1689, Staatsarchiv Detmold, L 37 XVII no. 7. Receipts at territorial level for Turk taxes paid by the towns of Saltzuffeln, Horn and Detmold in 1687, L 37 XVII no. 6.

terms, a sum that came near to one-half of the annual revenue of the county and was clearly impossible to meet. When payment of one-fifth of this sum was made to Gödens in January 1689 Simon Henrich was hoping for support from the Emperor for setting up his own Lippe army contingent. On this he failed to get the support of his territorial Estates and he was not strong enough to push the issue and levy taxes without consent, as did his son ten years later on the same policy. Lippe did, however, get rid of Brunswick troop billets, and threats of circle distraint were dropped. Leopold still believed that he could get enough money from Lippe without once again having to hand it over to the *Armierte*.[84] As in previous wars, Leopold's demands got out of hand. Once again Simon Henrich was shown to have no control over his finances and no support from his Estates. In May the Lippe Estates were informed that a 230 *Römermonate* demand from Gödens could be liquidated with 2,000 ducats paid immediately. In July a poll tax was levied on all inhabitants from the nobility down to the domestics. By October the towns were still being urged to pay their quotas. In December Lippe began to play for time by claiming to have been assessed at a higher rate than other territories. Gödens immediately stepped up his demands to 300 *Römermonate*. A deadlock ensued in 1690. The Habsburg commissar was now aided by demands from the circle authorities and Simon Henrich began to make an effort to pay circle troop costs of 450 tlrs a month as from February 1690. This was far less than Leopold had hoped for, and it necessitated a return to distraint by *Armierte*. In 1691 Lippe assessed its inhabitants for 2,400 tlrs to pay subsidies to Brandenburg and Münster at monthly rating. Finally by September 1692 Leopold lost patience and Gödens instructed Simon Henrich that 200 *Römermonate* of Lippe federal war tax arrears for the period November 1691 to October 1692 had been assigned to Brandenburg. Lippe had failed in the eyes of the Emperor to produce 24,000 fl. of war taxes in a year (about one-third of total comital revenue) and was thus not worth protecting from the *Armierte*.[85]

Even if Lippe had been efficiently governed, could she really

---

[84] *Ibid.*, no. 7.
[85] Gödens to Simon Henrich, 9 September 1692. In heavy baroque style Lippe was informed that Leopold had sold its federal war taxes to the Brandenburgers, *ibid.*, nos 7, 8a.

have paid such high federal war taxes as Leopold demanded? As it was, Simon Henrich's officials soldiered on and made their own threats of distraint at home in the county in last attempts to fend off the Brandenburgers. In November the government threatened the market of Schwalenberg with distraint if it did not pay Turk tax arrears from 1689–91 within eight days. In May 1692 officials informed the towns of Gödens' threats to distrain for federal war tax arrears with Brandenburg troops. The chancellery notified all those inhabitants with arrears that, if this happened, they would be held solely responsible and would be fined by their own authorities as well as being distrained by the outsiders.

Yet it was no longer just a question of arrears. Simon Henrich had never really had control of the internal financial situation and the federal authorities could no longer wait for payment. Although Gödens continued to claim for less and less *Römermonate* in the hope of some real payment in 1694–5, the matter was now in other hands. Equally the unrealistic attitude of Brake apanage did not help the situation. As late as July 1695 Cassimir of Lippe-Brake was writing to Simon Henrich, telling him that in future he would consent to no extraordinary taxes and certainly to none from the Emperor without much more time for prior consultation. Although federal tax demands were exorbitant at this time, it does seem that Lippe brought distraint upon itself by adopting an attitude of long delay with a view to final non-payment, which as a *Nichtarmierter* it could not realistically afford to do.[86]

After the 1660s Lippe had run down its own military commitments in a policy favourable to the Estates but unrealistic as regards the military situation in the Empire as a whole. Demands from the *Armierte* increased, no matter what Leopold's protectionist policies towards the small unarmed territories were. Thus the rural districts of Lippe actually paid a monthly 2,450 tlrs to Münster troops in the winter of 1690–1, at the height of Commissar Gödens' campaign against Lippe for federal arrears.[87] Inside the county the chancellery kept its

[86] Orders of distraint of 9 November 1691 and 19 May 1692. Gödens to Simon Henrich, 12 January 1693, sporadically to February 1695. Brake to Simon Henrich, July 1695. Staatsarchiv Detmold, L 37 XVII nos 6, 7.

[87] Registers of Münster officers and dragoons paid off by Lippian officials, *ibid.*, no. 8a.

own running account of arrears. The overall picture for 1691 was that the towns and markets still owed 4,000 tlrs and the rural districts 19,000 tlrs. By March 1692 the rural districts had paid 10 per cent of this. In another account the chancellery alleged that 24,000 tlrs had actually been paid to Brandenburg and Münster in 1690 with a further 17,333 tlrs in 1691. Even so there were arrears on top of this for 15,500 tlrs, which the chancellery hopefully claimed were still perhaps in hand in the treasury. Even these arrears were a figure arrived at after Münster and Brandenburg had remitted a further 8,000 tlrs.[88]

Thus in the two war years 1690–1 Lippe had been expected to contribute over 30,000 tlrs a year to the *Armierte*, a sum that was well over half the comital revenue from all sources. For two years the towns had made payment to the tune of over 60 per cent on their quotas. A further 12½ per cent had been remitted. Actual arrears were 25 per cent. The subsidy demands of the *Armierte* in the thirty years of the 1670s to 1690s were no less than the demands for contribution to the war effort in the thirty years of the 1620s to 1640s in Lippe. But Thirty Years' War demands were carried out in abrogation of the imperial constitution, whilst the demands of the 1670s to 1690s were made strictly within the form of law.[89]

As Lippe was paying so well, what induced the Brandenburgers to come into the county in the last days of the war in 1696? By 1694 the towns and rural districts had passed their peak in payments to the *Armierte*. In that year the towns had arrears of 60 per cent, having barely paid 2,200 tlrs of a 6,600 tlrs assessment. The rural districts were as bad with payments of 9,200 tlrs and arrears of 13,300 tlrs. In 1695 payments from town and country together were only 3,000 tlrs with 1,200 tlrs to follow as late payment. In 1696 the comital authorities could raise only 2,800 tlrs. Yet the overall picture was far better than this tailing off in the last war years implies. From 1688 to 1695 Lippe had paid Brandenburg alone 68,000 tlrs in lieu of federal war taxes. On top of this there was an arrears claim of 67,000 tlrs. The newly installed *Landkasse* had paid out a total of 23,700 tlrs to the *Armierte*, which included

[88] 'Noch unbezahlte Subsidien', *ibid.*, 8a.
[89] Cf. Chapter IX. Staatsarchiv Detmold, L 37 XVII 8a; Knoch L 56–60; L 41a IV E 9.

Münster as well as Brandenburg between 1689 and 1697. This shows that only about one-third of the war effort had been financed by the Estates and their money. The rest was borne by the domain and comital rural population.

Lippe had achieved federal war tax payments at an average 10,000 tlrs a year, but on a wildly fluctuating basis of 24,000 tlrs right down to 2,800 tlrs in any one war year. Demand had on an average been just twice that of actual supply with payment of 50 per cent and arrears of 50 per cent. Again the actual figures looked better at the beginning than at the end of the war. Looking at the overall picture, however, Lippe actually paid an annual war tax of about 20 per cent of gross comital income. It was the disappointing performance of the Estates that upset the picture. Here ruler-Estates relations played a vital part. Simon Henrich could not co-operate with his Estates, and the county paid the penalty. The problem was not with the officials, because from the figures of the *Kammer* relative to those of the *Landkasse*, the government, and therefore the ruler's peasantry (not the nobles and burghers), bore the brunt of war taxation and paid up well.[90]

Yet this is not what the Brandenburgers thought at the time. In October 1696 Elector Frederick III as a Westphalian circle director claimed the right to Lippe's imperial and circle taxes to help pay for the Brandenburg military effort against Louis XIV. Frederick's Ravensberg treasurer, Meinders, demanded all arrears from 1694–5, as he had long ago borrowed the money in anticipation of these taxes and was now hourly paying interest which he could not afford. The current taxes were collected by the troops themselves. The plea of Simon Henrich for tax exemption because of exhaustion of the county, which had paid war taxes to *Armierte* since 1672, was unsuccessful and perhaps unrealistic. Anyway, Brandenburg troops were on their march back from the Rhine to the north-east. The Ryswick Peace and demobilization or cold-storage of troops cost the Elector dear in any case, so a traditional policy of delay of payment would have been as fruitless for Lippe as the appeal for remittance based on a claim of impoverishment which Simon Henrich actually made. In the outcome Meinders stayed on hand with the troops in Paderborn-Lippe to supervise collection

[90] Cf. Chapter IX. Staatsarchiv Detmold, L 37 XVII no. 8a; Knoch L 9.

which, however, stuck to the principle of troop billet, until the last farthing of arrears had been paid.[91]

A new ruler brought a new policy with the short peace after Ryswick and before the death of the last Spanish Habsburg. Friedrich Adolf fought the Estates for an increase in taxation which his demand for a standing Lippe circle contingent entailed in the spring of 1698, and he won. Just when the Estates expected substantial war tax decreases because of the peace and consequent end to Brandenburg troop exactions, Friedrich Adolf increased the rates of extraordinary taxation, initially ignoring refusals of the Estates at territorial assemblies. He demanded 22,000 fl. alone to put Lippe's circle account straight, although accounted arrears in Cologne were only 4,400 tlrs for Lippe. He accepted garrison duties in Cologne town and laid the foundations of the Lippe army, which in six years was ready to play its part on the allied imperial side in the War of the Spanish Succession. A standing army had become a necessity for the survival of an independent Lippe, as the war of 1688–97 showed. The opposition of the Estates to a standing army lasted only for one year. By 1699 Friedrich Adolf was getting annual grants of supply, although never at the sum that he wanted, but this was tactics and not difference of policy between ruler and Estates. It thus seems that the failure of the county against the *Armierte* was caused by the weakness of Simon Henrich as a leader, for his son was strong enough to carry through an army policy that Simon Henrich had been toying with since the beginning of his reign, forty years previously, but which he could never finance or get through the territorial assembly.[92]

The transfer of federal war taxes from the *Armierte* to a Lippe army of its own, operating within the circle system, certainly meant no decrease in taxation to the towns and rural population. It did mean, however, that control of taxation remained with the ruler, his officials and to some extent the Estates within the county. The last word was once again with Lippians themselves, even if those with a stake in the county had to impose higher burdens on the common people to obtain this autonomy

[91] Correspondence between Elector Frederick and Count Simon Henrich, 13 to 27 October 1696. Meinders to Lippe Chancellery President, 26 October 1696, Staatsarchiv Detmold, L 37 XVII no. 8a.

[92] Staatsarchiv Detmold, L 9 vol. 22 folio 63ff.; Knoch L 9; L 8 K Section VII no. 7.

in the federal war tax system. Lippe now had its own recruiting, equipping, route-marching, salary and billeting costs. It went well above its minimum circle commitment of 270 men. Between 1705 and 1707 the military treasury took 13,000–35,000 tlrs from the rural districts to finance this war effort.[93]

At the same time money payment was made once again to *Legstadt* Frankfurt-am-Main with a small six *Römermonate* to fortify Philipsburg on the Rhine in 1704. This payment showed a revived direct federal tax system at work and also showed how Lippe made its arrangements within it. An official provided the money in advance, so payment to the Empire could be punctually made at Frankfurt. Frankfurt town council wrote out a receipt which was presented at the Lippe treasury and the official was duly paid. For this repayment the treasury got a receipt from the chancellery that had taken the original policy decision to make payment.[94]

Under Charles VI the federal tax system made a last sustained effort to keep the territories paying for a concerted, Habsburg-led imperial policy. On accession in 1712 Emperor Charles obtained a *don gratuit* from the territories. On this Lemgo objected to having to pay 666 tlrs but all the towns settled for 1,000 tlrs and Lemgo thus got away with one-half of the original assessment. The money was paid immediately and the West-phalian counts borrowed with a view to repaying out of the taxes levied in due course. The result was that although only four territories under the comital directorship of Friedrich Adolf defaulted, the wasteful exchange rate and high interest rates on the Frankfurt money market turned a 5 per cent arrears on the original *don gratuit* into an immediate 25 per cent deficit on the collection of the tax from the counts. A loan at 10 per cent was raised from Schaumburg-Lippe which was never repaid, despite claims that ran at 50 per cent of the total original grant by 1724. This shows that a federal body like the

---

[93] Staatsarchiv Detmold, L 37 XVII no. 6. See H. von Dewall, 'Kurzer Abriss der Lippischen Militärgeschichte, 1664–1804', *Lippische Mitteilungen*, 31, 1962, pp. 82, 106–9. The era of the *Armierte* came to an end in Lippe in 1697.

[94] Receipt of 21 May 1704, and correspondence, Staatsarchiv Detmold, L 37 XVII no. 7. Barge, *Lippische Mitteilungen*, 26, 1957, pp. 102ff. overdid the conflict between Friedrich Adolf and his Estates by looking for absolutism in the minutes of the territorial assembly, rather than checking in the financial records for the pecuniary weaknesses that any absolutist policy in Lippe ran up against.

Westphalian College of Counts did not necessarily fail because it had a host of defaulters in federal taxation but because it could not manage to pay its commitments without heavy capital loss, as its business methods were inefficient and took too little account of time.[95]

In 1713 the war in the west closed down for Lippe. It did not, however, disband its troops. They were billeted in the rural districts and the system of reduced pay and reserve was introduced. The necessary finance was found for the time being by exploitation of the arrears system. In the war there had been demands for *Römermonate*, *Kreismonate* and *Soldatenmonate* for war efforts at imperial, regional and territorial levels. The *Matrikel simpla* of each group, although all based on one common system, had got out of hand and a mass of individual assessments had been superimposed upon the original revived structure of the 1680s.[96]

With the end of the war in the west, attention in the Empire was once again drawn to the war with the Turks. Once again *Römermonate* were granted at imperial assembly and the territories were assessed as in the days of Ferdinand I. In 1717 Friedrich Adolf was ordered by the Vienna treasury to pay within six weeks 6,000 fl. of 50 *Römermonate* granted at Regensburg in the previous year.[97] In 1721 the Vienna treasury sent its accounts to Lippe and now demanded another 50 per cent because of Lemgo as an alleged imperial town. The outcome was a remarkable admission of the faithful way in which Friedrich Adolf had supported the Habsburgs with federal tax payments, a policy continued by his son Simon Henrich Adolf at the beginning of the reign. Emperor Charles VI wrote to the Count:[98]

You have fully paid your above mentioned Turk tax, which our treasury also found and dutifully informed us to be true, so we recognize the

[95] Staatsarchiv Detmold, L 41a IV no. 4; L 37 XVII no. 7; H. Kesting, *op. cit.*, pp. 191–2.

[96] Staatsarchiv Detmold, L 37 XVII nos 2, 4, 7, 22.

[97] Vienna Hofkammer to Lippe, 9 November 1717, Staatsarchiv Detmold, L 37 XVII no. 6.

[98] Staatsarchiv Detmold, L 37 XVII no. 6, Vienna, 31 August 1722, after a *Mandat* of 13 October 1721, and Simon Henrich Adolf's letter of complaint, 13 April 1722. Cf. A. Biederbick, *Der deutsche Reichstag zu Regensburg 1714–24*, Bonn, 1937, pp. 24–7.

case not only proved and correct, but also with gracious thanks that you were one of the first among those who fully paid their contingent of Turk tax to the honour of God, for the love of Us and the common need with patriotic good will and praiseworthy eagerness.

However, Lippe fell more and more behind in federal tax payments. Part of this may have been genuine muddle and lack of control over the officials, as the dynasty's economic difficulties at home in any case prevented the efficient payment of further federal taxes. In the total tax grant for 1726 from the territorial assembly, federal circle taxes were a mere 1,200 tlrs whilst the apanages alone were allowed nearly 13,000 tlrs. The ruler himself was cut down to 600 tlrs in pocket money, and his treasury was assigned only something under 4,000 tlrs for the running costs of government out of a total of over 51,000 tlrs. Debt finance took the lion's share. Yet Lippe was expected to provide a contingent of 118 foot and 54 horse in that year.[99] Imperial taxes had shrunk to a point of insignificance and they were now lumped with extraordinary taxes as a whole in the towns and markets as well as in the rural districts and in Brake apanage, which continued to be administered separately, despite the demise of its agnates, so as not to upset the tax quota system.

In the early 1740s attempts were made to find out when *Römermonate* had last been paid in Lippe. For a brief period in 1742–3 the Wittelsbach Emperor Charles VII was trying to get federal taxes but had to contend with a system where records as well as technical expertise were still in the hands of the very Habsburgs whom he was trying to oust from imperial leadership. Lippe was ordered to pay 12,000 fl. arrears from 1734 to 1743, but, on searches being made, the Lippe chancellery reckoned that it had paid all its commitments. Payment was claimed to have been carried out via the Bishop's exchange in Paderborn. The last recorded payment, probably the last that Lippe made that was in *bona fide Römermonate*, was 2,000 tlrs (3,000 fl.) in April 1743.[100] The year previously Lippe had been engaged in the Westphalian counts' troop contingent as the largest member with 61 men and 6 non-commissioned

[99] Staatsarchiv Detmold, L 37 XVII no. 2, 'Repartitio der bewilligten Gelder in die Ämbter, Flecken vnd Vögteyn dieser Graffschafft'.
[100] Staatsarchiv Detmold, L 37 XVII nos 4, 7.

officers out of 400 men and 45 non-commissioned officers.[101] Here the federal demand on Lippe was 3,632 tlrs which was covered by an Estates' grant of 5,439 tlrs payable by the rural districts, leaving a handsome profit of 50 per cent. This was to be left to the *Landkasse* for its own profit.[102]

Between 1747 and 1751 Emperor Franz's officials tried to collect money for federal defence and even for alleged arrears from the period of hiatus under Charles VII. Demands were also sent to the Westphalian College of Counts, an example of a late use of an *ad hoc* body for federal tax demands.[103] During the Seven Years' War Lippe was again asked for federal war taxes as part of the Westphalian College of Counts. The county paid a probable 2,400 tlrs in October 1757 but thereafter kept in arrears as Prussia was far too close to warrant a pro-Habsburg policy.[104] However, as late as 1795 the federal system of *Römermonate* remained active enough to petition Lippe, and as long as there was an Empire, *Römermonate*, just like *Kammerzieler*, were the fiscal part of its make-up.

Lippe was part of the *Römermonate* system from 1507 to 1795. The county made contribution in men either directly itself as in 1542 and after 1697, or through money payment in lieu of troops. Under Simon Henrich, between 1666 and 1697, the latter system even seriously threatened the further independent existence of the county, and excessive federal tax demands in this period played their part in undermining the county's finances until the restoration of credit in the 1750s. It was not only when the imperial constitution was hamstrung, as during the Smalkaldic War, the Thirty Years' War and the wars of Frederick II of Prussia, that Lippe was induced to make military contribution. During the long periods in between these spectacular failures of federal politics, during the times when the imperial constitution did operate by law and consent, the system was strong enough to obtain payment of war taxes from even the small inaccessible territory of Lippe with considerable success, owing to the tenacity and skill with which demands were made.

[101] Staatsarchiv Detmold, L 41a IV A no. 4.
[102] Staatsarchiv Detmold, L 37 XVII no. 2. [103] *Ibid.*, no. 7.
[104] Staatsarchiv Detmold, L 41a IV B no. 7, anti-Prussian war propaganda in L 41a IV 207. Contrast O. Weerth, *Die Grafschaft Lippe und der Siebenjährige Krieg*, Detmold, 1888.

In the case of Lippe the Empire may have been a 'monster': what is relevant, however, is that the Empire made commands and that these were carried out at territorial level. It was the federal military system by consent that kept Louis XIV at bay. It finally defeated the Turks in a campaign that lasted two centuries. The Lippe documents show not what went wrong with the Empire but where its strength lay. It was an effective military unit, and that was also its greatest weakness. For the Empire was not generally 'weak' but one-sided in its strength. When the Turks had ceased to be a menace after the early eighteenth century, what rôle was left for the Empire? It was not that the Empire had no power, but that its earlier strong military rôle needed adaptation in the eighteenth century to a new common policy as unifying as the Turkish and French threats had been in previous centuries, and this the Empire did not find. Affairs at the grass-roots in the county of Lippe show that this was at the heart of the German dilemma.

XIII

<><><><><><><><><><><><><><><><><><><><><><><><><><><><><><><><><><>

Lippe at Imperial Court, Assembly and Circle

<><><><><><><><><><><><><><><><><><><><><><><><><><><><><><><><><><><>

LIPPE'S size and geography dictated the rôle it could afford to play in the various bodies that made up the federal legislature. Above all its limited financial resources made it a major event for the county to send representatives to federal meetings at regional and imperial level. At the end of the period in the later seventeenth and eighteenth centuries a compromise was found by leading participation in the Westphalian College of Counts. At the same time the expense of litigation at the *Reichshofrat* in Vienna put that court in the same category as the *Reichstage* and *Kreistage* legislatures where Lippe had a natural place but where the county was far too small to lobby effectively on its own.[1]

The *Reichshofrat* functioned continuously from 1559 to 1806 with changes in composition from Emperor to Emperor. From the end of the seventeenth century, apart from the Wittelsbach interlude under Charles VII, it sat in Vienna. Before that it moved around with the Emperor. The *Reichshofratsordnung* of 1559 established it, and subsequent reforms did little to change this original structure. It was the Habsburg Emperor's own court of equity that persons of approved status could resort to, provided they wanted a decision with a Habsburg bias.[2]

---

[1] For a federal outline, S. E. Turner, *A Sketch of the Germanic Constitution*, New York, 1888, pp. 116–66. K. Rauch, *Traktat über den Reichstag im 16. Jahrhundert*, Leipzig, 1905. G. Granier, *Der deutsche Reichstag während des spanischen Erbfolgekrieges*, Bonn, 1954, pp. 2–6. J. J. Moser, *Grundriss der heutigen Staatsverfassung*, 7th ed., Tübingen, 1754.

[2] O. von Gschliesser, *Der Reichshofrat*, Vienna, 1942, pp. 514–22.

The *Reichshofrat* could move more swiftly in decisions necessary to uphold the *status quo* than could the *Reichskammergericht*. It therefore tended to take more serious cases of tyranny and revolt, as well as dynastic and feudal matters at territorial rulers' level. Its decisions were worked out on the merits of each case by a board of legal experts and Habsburg career politicians. The court paid the highest salaries in the legal profession and received bribes, so it could attract lawyers, administrators and diplomats of high social standing in the Empire and in the Austrian lands. This was essential, as the court could not function without some recognition of the concept of peerage in legal matters. Yet as a working court it was not over-staffed by honorary members. *Reichshofräte* worked their way and appointments were never wholly inappropriate sinecures.[3]

That Lippe got involved in the *Reichshofrat* of Rudolf II was purely due to the political ambitions of Simon VI. He had been on the *Reichshofrat* as an occasional member since 1591 and officially as from 1598. As Detmold was a long way from the court in Prague, Simon attended in person only when on a visit to Rudolf. In 1602 Simon even had the honour of chairing the court. It was not until the later eighteenth century that members of the Lippe dynasty once again became members of the court in Vienna. Here the Lippe-Biesterfelders were involved, and Count Karl Christian made a career in the law there, sitting between 1771 and 1791 in the *Reichshofrat*.[4]

Compared with the *Reichskammergericht*, very few Lippe cases went to the *Reichshofrat*. Lippe was not a territory with social unrest, nor were its rulers specifically criminal. It produced no scandals of the Hohenzollern-Hechingen, Schaumburg-Lippe, or Fürstlich Fürstenberg type, and thus did not attract *Reichshofrat* attention because of internal misgovernment.[5] Even so, it did bring its own few cases that were of sufficient importance to show that even this law-abiding, and, by the standards

---

[3] See F. Hertz, 'Die Rechtsprechung der höchsten Reichsgerichte', *Mitteilungen des Instituts für österreichische Geschichtsforschung*, 69, 1961. W. Sellert, *Über die Zuständigkeitsabgrenzung von Reichshofrat und Reichskammergericht*, Aalen, 1965. O. von Gschliesser, *Der Reichshofrat*, Vienna, 1942, frontispiece and pp. 515–18.

[4] Gschliesser, *op. cit.*, pp. 165, 180, 192, 233, 250, 483, 486–7, 500, 502, 506.

[5] See Hertz, *op. cit.*, and K. S. Bader, 'Die Rechtsprechung des Reichshofrats', *Zeitschrift der Savigny—Stiftung für Rechtsgeschichte*, 1947.

of the time, socially integrated county had problems which only the *Reichshofrat* could handle.

Certain counts were very keen to keep paid agents in Vienna, in a system of legal scrutiny rather similar to the agents kept at Speyer and Wetzlar. As a member of Rudolf's *Reichshofrat*, Simon VI appointed an agent who also had to see to *ex officio* matters as Simon was an absentee most of the time. A special agent came from Lippe to Prague in 1611 to try and get a *Reichshofrat* decision in Simon's favour against specific injunctions that rebellious Lemgo had obtained at the *Reichskammergericht*. But the matter was ill-timed. Simon's colleagues were no longer in power in Prague. This was the first case where a Lippe ruler had attempted to use the Habsburg court for help against his leading town in an internal territorial religious matter.[6]

Twenty years later the Lippe regency government again appointed an agent in Vienna. This time it was not to start litigation but to prevent it. In the 1630s the Lippe towns were fighting the government for distraint of taxes demanded without consent, and for protecting the nobility, who were contributing only one-tenth of the amount of war tax that the towns were paying. It was a case of the Lippe government attempting to prevent the nobility from appealing to the *Reichshofrat* against the towns on this internal tax issue in retaliation against the towns who had so far been successful in bringing their case to the notice of the *Reichskammergericht*. The government furnished itself with the latest *Reichshofratsordnung* from 1626.[7] Uncertainty in religious affairs equally induced the Lippe government to keep itself informed of *Reichshofrat* condemnations of Protestants between 1621 and 1649. The county followed the fate of the Austrian rebels, the problems of the Guelphs nearer at home and the position of the Protestants in Silesia. To be informed on federal affairs thus meant a general knowledge of *Reichshofrat* decisions at territorial level. This applied to Lippe.[8]

The agent appointed in 1638 by Lippe was already demanding arrears of pay five years later. It was a feature of the Thirty

---

[6] Staatsarchiv Detmold, L 74 A–1; L 41a IV E 9 vol. 2.
[7] Staatsarchiv Detmold, L 74 A–1; L 41a IV C no. 6.
[8] Staatsarchiv Detmold, L 74 A–2; L 41a IV C no. 7. *Merckwürdige Reichshofrats— Conclusa und Anschlags Protocolle*, Frankfurt-am-Main, 1726ff.

Years' War period that it increased litigation in Lippe as governments, nobles and towns fell out with each other over increased tax burdens. Cases went to the universities for expert advice and thereafter to the imperial courts. One of the tasks of territorial government was to cut down litigation which threatened the power and business of its own *Hofgericht* and also used up money that the territory could not afford to lose. In the 1620s and 1630s the rise in outside litigation shows that there was no shortage of money in Lippe.[9]

With the coming of peace in 1648 the Lippe government once more showed interest in the *Reichshofrat* as it began to face the problem of how to get the Jesuits out of the south-east of the county, where they had been installed by Catholic Paderborn in 1626, after the year of normalization, 1624. Paderborn kept its mission and pulled Catholic strings at federal level to do so. In 1653 Calvinist Hermann Adolf felt wealthy enough to try to buy the support of the *Reichshofrat* in an effort to get a favourable interpretation of the 1648 religious provision. He promised four members of the *Reichshofrat* 100 tlrs a year, its secretary 50 tlrs and a Lippe agent 70 tlrs provision annually. At the same time Paderborn retaliated by claiming that allodial lands in the county were really fiefs of the Bishop. Furthermore the Lippe dynasty within itself had started to contest apanages and inheritances as the original family of Simon VI multiplied and split up into separate lines, some of which in turn died out, leaving complicated and legally lucrative inheritances to new family complexes within the dynasty. Between 1653 and 1663 Hermann Adolf gambled with the law at the *Reichshofrat*. His first family case concerned the inheritance of Sternberg apanage. He also had to fight the Lemgo *Reichsmatrikel* which reappeared as the imperial constitution was restored after 1648. In the 1670s the Lippe government once more called a halt to *Reichshofrat* agency and litigation.[10]

The matter was revived in the 1690s. This time Lippe made headway in the feudal dispute with Paderborn. In 1692 Simon Henrich was confirmed in his claim that his land rights over Saltzuffeln and Barntrup were allodial, and not fiefs held from the Bishop of Paderborn. In a printed decree the *Reichshofrat*

---

[9] Staatsarchiv Detmold, L 82; L 74; L 11 V 1; L 10 Titel 2 no. 1 (26), no. 11.
[10] Staatsarchiv Detmold, L 74 A-1.

accused Paderborn of gross excess in this matter and the Bishop was ordered to keep the peace on pain of 60,000 tlrs fine.[11]

This encouraged Lippe to try its luck at Vienna once more in the legal field. Between 1695 and 1704 Imperial Knight v. Imbsen was retained as Lippe agent at 100 tlrs a year, and he was even sworn in as a councillor in Detmold. Between 1704 and 1720 Imbsen's nephew took on the agency at 500 tlrs a year for life. Thereafter the agents Fabricius, father and son, managed Lippe affairs in Vienna from the 1720s to the 1750s. On top of this, legal experts were hired for specific cases in Vienna as needed. Thus in 1705 a prosecutor was given a case for one year only at 100 tlrs to get it before the *Reichshofrat*. Like Simon VI before him, it was Friedrich Adolf who here displayed most Lippian interest in affairs at imperial Habsburg level.[12]

The appointment of full-time Lippe agents in the early eighteenth century naturally corresponded to a marked increase in Lippe litigation in Vienna. The fact that the *Reichskammergericht* was *de facto* out of action from 1683 to 1712 influenced the increase of Lippe business at the *Reichshofrat*. Members of the Lippe dynasty fought each other over inheritances. Thus Lippe-Schaumburg claimed the Lippe-Brake apanage which Lippe-Detmold had sequestered in 1707. In this contest Lippe-Schaumburg had the better of the case, as it won the battle by producing more telling documents in court, although retrospectively Lippe-Detmold, as the senior branch, had a better case, but a more badly organized archive and registry. These apanage cases came up in fifteen sessions of the *Reichshofrat* and were published in a law compendium of important *Reichshofrat* cases covering the decade 1715–25.[13]

The apanage problem further involved Hesse-Kassel as Lippe overlord for certain lands and fiefs since the fifteenth century. This involved wardships and meant that in family fights with Lippe-Schaumburg, Detmold had to take account of the bad blood between Lippe-Schaumburg and Hesse on the political

---

[11] Staatsarchiv Detmold, L 10 Titel 2 no. 33, 'dass Paderborn hierinfalls gröblich excedirt'.

[12] Staatsarchiv Detmold, L 74 A–1.

[13] *Merckwürdige Reichshofrats Conclusa*, I, p. 705; II, pp. 18, 618; V, pp. 468, 470–1, 473–5, 612; VI, p. 759; VIII, p. 101 (1729) and index.

front. In 1715 Detmold fought a wardship over Alverdissen apanage with Kassel at the *Reichshofrat*. The fight over Alverdissen then continued between the two Lippe houses.[14] Kassel retaliated with sequestration of a new coal-mine and with troop occupation, putting pressure on Schaumburg-Lippe from its stronghold on the middle Weser at Rinteln. The death of Friedrich Adolf called forth inheritance quarrels in 1718 with Detmold as embroiled with Kassel as she was with her kinsfolk in Bückeburg. Litigation at the *Reichshofrat* thus became highly technical, dynastic and feudal. It caused bad blood back at home in the middle Weser area, as all three capitals, Detmold, Bückeburg and Kassel, fell out with each other.[15]

Litigation was expensive. In one year alone the Detmold treasury paid out 4,000 tlrs to the *Reichshofrat*, representing 10 per cent of regular income. Lost cases to Schaumburg-Lippe put Detmold finances further out of balance, so that by the 1720s and 1730s under Simon Henrich Adolf and Johanette Wilhelmine regular expenditure outstripped income by as much as 100 per cent. Federal litigation had gone wild in the earlier eighteenth century and it seems that Detmold had to pay as much in law costs and lost inheritances as federal war taxes had swallowed up under Simon Henrich and the régime of the *Armierte*. The county had exchanged a weak war policy for a weak dynastic policy.[16]

Added to this were two cases of long standing that went up interminably for litigation at the imperial courts. Both cases were of a constitutional and political nature, the one affecting inter-territorial settlement of the 1648 religious peace, and the other internal territorial Estates' taxation levels. In neither case could the imperial courts be expected to reach a decision. In both cases they achieved stay of execution on the basis of the *status quo* at the start of litigation and thus prevented breach of the peace and local war. This was precisely what the *Reichskammergericht* and *Reichshofrat* were for: not to make decisions, at least not in constitutional conflicts, but to prevent violence from breaking out in the federation.

[14] *Ibid.*, V, p. 468.
[15] *Ibid.*, III, p. 395; V, pp. 467–9; VI, p. 760.
[16] Staatsarchiv Detmold, L 63 A 12; L 92 Z 1a. H. Kiewning, 'Der Lippische Fürstenbrief von 1720', *Lippische Mitteilungen*, 1, 1903, pp. 53, 56, 58–9, 60, 62.

In 1729 Simon Henrich Adolf sent his chief councillor Piderit to Vienna to confer with the two Lippe agents there and get the *Reichshofrat* to terminate a counter-appeal by the Lippe nobility against the Lippe towns in an original *Reichskammergericht* suit brought by the towns against the nobility for tax evasion. The Count asked for a compromise and was careful not to give the impression that he was taking sides. A case that had flared up already in Speyer in the 1630s was thus no nearer solution a century later. The question of nobles' tax evasion was a territorial matter which had already led to conflict between towns and nobles in the 1550s, when Bernhard VIII had taken the side of his nobles. In 1729 Piderit's mediation was successful and brought the nobles' counter-appeal to a temporary end. As late as 1766–72 the matter was given another airing in Vienna.[17] This shows that the imperial courts were expected to resolve a conflict between territorial Estates which territorial ruler and territorial *Hofgericht* had not been able to solve. It was not a question at the *Reichshofrat* in the eighteenth century of commanding each side to follow a court judgment, but of getting the interested parties together to find their own solution. The concept of *Austrag* remained an essential ingredient in the Holy Roman Empire's federalism.

The other matter became a *cause célèbre* in the Empire. After 1648 the Jesuits stayed on in Falkenhagen, in south-east Lippe, in contravention of the Westphalian Peace. After Hermann Adolf's attempt to take the matter into the Catholic camp by litigation in the *Reichshofrat* had proved futile and unnecessarily expensive in the 1650s and 1660s, the matter went in 1676 on appeal to the *Corpus Evangelicorum*, as an extremely delicate constitutional issue for the Protestant lobby at the Regensburg imperial assembly. Friedrich Adolf, however, tried once more to fight Paderborn on its own Catholic ground by making a counter-appeal at the *Reichshofrat* in 1717, in reply to the Jesuits' allegation of breach of the peace caused by commissioners from Calvinist Lippe in cases from 1701 to 1702 and 1717.[18]

---

[17] Staatsarchiv Detmold, L 11 V nos 4–5.

[18] *Merckwürdige Reichshofrats Conclusa*, I, pp. 284–5; V, p. 6, 'Jesuiter contra Lippe; Lippe-Detmold contra Paderbornische Jesuiter'. The matter found coverage also in Schauroth, *Sammlung aller Conclusorum . . . des Corporis Evangeliorum*; Faber's *Staatskanzlei*; Thucelii, *Reichstaats Acta*, and in the *Monatlicher Staats-Spiegel* from Augsburg.

Whilst Paderborn could rely on the Catholic majority at Regensburg and Jesuit confessors in Vienna to immobilize imperial assembly and imperial court in favour of the *status quo* at Falkenhagen since 1626, which was against the Westphalian Peace, Lippe had little chance of success in its appeals to *Reichskammergericht* and *Reichshofrat* against the Catholics. At imperial level appeal could always go from the courts to the assemblies, as established by the visitation and review of *Reichskammergericht* cases by decree of Emperor and territories in 1556, re-established in 1712 and never really given up in principle, despite the religious split in the original visitation commission since the 1580s. A way round this split had been achieved by tacitly allowing any territory to lobby at imperial assembly level if it thought it was being unfairly treated at imperial court level. The provisions of 1648 over redress of grievances in religion were still as imperfect as ever. The only advance was that it now became impracticable to use a religious issue to hamstring constitutional co-operation in all other affairs. Religious issues in fact became open questions. This did not prevent religious questions from threatening the 1648 constitution, as the suppression of Palatinate Protestants between 1690 and 1730 showed, but it did mean that territories did not move over the brink and jeopardize the imperial constitution for the sake of religion.[19] With the provision of a system of *itio in partes*, of mutual split on religion, so as to prevent all majority decisions from penalizing any constitutionally tolerated religious minority, the federal system had pioneered a way round further religious dissension by denying such dissension a position of major importance in politics. Although the formation of a *Corpus Evangelicorum* tended to reactivate religious issues, it provided a useful lobby and talking-point at imperial assembly level, where those conflicts due to religion which the imperial courts could not handle were given the chance to cool off peacefully. The case in point was Falkenhagen.

The monastery at Falkenhagen had been disbanded in 1596 and its wealth shared between Lippe and Paderborn, in accordance with the condominium between bishopric and county

---

[19] A. Biederbick, *Der deutsche Reichstag zu Regensburg 1714–24*, Bonn, 1937. Schauroth, *Sammlung aller Conclusorum ... des Corporis Evangelicorum*, 1–3, Regensburg, 1751.

over the rural district of Schwalenberg, where the monastery was situated. This arrangement had papal confirmation. In 1604 Paderborn gave its share to the Jesuits. In 1626 the Jesuits took over the whole monastery, its lands and revenues, with the military support of the Wittelsbach Archbishop of Cologne, who had driven the Calvinist Lippians out of their half.[20]

The Westphalian Peace gave Lippe a constitutional right to her half-share in the monastery. The county turned to the circle directors for support. In the Westphalian circle, the Catholic directors of Cologne, Münster and Pfalz-Neuburg were pro-Jesuit. Lippe turned to Brandenburg, Magdeburg and the Guelphs as Protestant circle co-directors in the Westphalian and Lower-Saxon circles. The Jesuits called in the *Reichshofrat*, and Lippe replied by lobbying the Protestant territories at imperial assembly level. Falkenhagen became a test case: could the revived imperial constitution of 1648 actually safeguard the rights of the Protestant minority of territories in the federation by peaceful means? In May 1649 Lippe asked the directors of the Lower-Saxon circle to guarantee the Count's repossession of his half of Falkenhagen, from which the Jesuits were expelled. In 1652 the Jesuits obtained a commission of inquiry from the *Reichshofrat* in an appeal against Lippe violence. In May 1654 the commissioners, Bishop Christof Bernhard of Münster and Count Anton Günther of Oldenburg, failed to agree. Oldenburg agreed with the Lower-Saxon circle that the Jesuits did not have a case.[21]

The problem was that force had been used to get the Jesuits out. Although the Jesuits broke the 1648 Peace by staying in the whole of the monastery, their Protestant opponents broke the Peace by using force to expel them. Both sides thus had legitimate grievances as religious concord in the Empire followed the letter and not the spirit of the law of 1648. At amnesty discussions in Württemberg in 1672, Lippe denied that the Jesuits had a legitimate grievance and appealed to the Emperor for protection against a new case at the *Reichshofrat*. This failed and a new commission was appointed with Christof Bernhard of

[20] E. Kittel, *Handbuch der Historischen Stätten Deutschlande*, 3, 1963, p. 197. Schauroth, *op. cit.*, I, pp. 628–30. In 1675 Lippe claimed to have been driven out of Falkenhagen 'von damaliger Chur-Fürstlicher Durchlaucht zu Cölln, als verordenten Commissario, mit militarischer Gewalt'. [21] Schauroth, *op. cit.*, pp. 628–30.

Münster and the Count of Tecklenburg in place of Anton Günther who had died. The commission failed to hear both sides. It reached a pro-Catholic verdict that the Protestants could not recognize. In 1678 the Jesuits got an execution order against Lippe from the Emperor acting on the recommendation of this commission.[22]

The Protestant territories at Regensburg now took the matter in hand. As a self-styled *Corpus Evangelicorum* led by Brandenburg, Saxony and Magdeburg as alternate chairmen, they collectively signed and then handed on appeals from Lippe to the Emperor. In January 1675 Simon Henrich appealed that he might continue to have half of Falkenhagen, which he would dutifully share with the Jesuits. At Nuremberg in 1672 Lippe had been confident, now it was on the defence. The 1675 appeal was repeated via Saxony in 1678. The Jesuits had now got their execution order, but could not carry it out. Another twenty years passed and then in December 1698 the Jesuits obtained a new commission of inquiry from Vienna. The commissioners were Westphalian circle directors Münster and the Palatinate, who acknowledged the *Reichshofrat* order, but pointed out the danger of denying full religious parity on the commission where Brandenburg as the only Protestant circle co-director would be in a minority position. Again the matter became a constitutional issue as the Protestant minority upheld its rights of religious equality at federal level.[23]

The Protestant lobby at Regensburg signed an appeal by Lippe via Saxony to the Emperor in July 1699, demanding the abolition of this latest commission. The signatures of representatives of two electors, seventeen ruling princes, three colleges of counts and four imperial towns were obtained. The Jesuits were condemned for contravening the 1648 Peace, a precedent that no Protestant territory could allow.[24] Even the Catholic-biased circle directorate in Westphalia cautioned the *Reichshofrat*, drawing attention to the Protestant complaint at Regensburg.[25] By February 1700 the Protestants had begun to

---

[22] *Ibid.*, I, pp. 628–46, 'Falkenhagische Closter Restitutions—Sache'.

[23] *Ibid.*, documents I–IV, *Falkenhagische Sache*.

[24] *Ibid.*, document III, citing the Peace of Osnabrück, Art. IV, and claiming that 'kein Evangelischer Stand des Reichs seiner aus dem Westphälischen Frieden erlangter restitution wider der Catholischen oder der gesitlichen Orden ansprüchen mehr gesichert seyn könte', I, pp. 635–7, 641   [25] *Ibid.*, document IV.

use threats to protect Lippe against the Catholic Westphalian circle directors. The directorate of the Lower-Saxon circle warned that if the Protestant appeal was ignored, and the Palatinate and Münster carried out the execution order to put the Jesuits in possession of Falkenhagen monastery with the use of force, then it would not stop short of opposing force with force in order to protect the Count of Lippe in possession.[26]

Encouraged by this, Lippe in a sealed statement to the Emperor via Regensburg stressed that, having enjoyed possession of Falkenhagen for fifty years, the Count would in future ignore all orders issued on behalf of the Jesuits by the *Reichshofrat*. The Protestants continued to press for a final settlement in their favour. In 1702 the Lower-Saxon circle repeated its guarantee of military support to Lippe. In that year the Protestant lobby at Regensburg included the Falkenhagen case in its plea for support from the English government. After obtaining the moral support of England, the Protestant territories held a special conference and asked the English to use their good offices at the Catholic courts where they had diplomatic representation to clear up outstanding religious conflicts between the German territories.[27] It was none too soon to clear the way for a common front against the Bourbons and to patch up the rift in the allied ranks caused by the Ryswick Peace.[28] At Regensburg, Resident Whitworth promised his government's support in March 1703. The Falkenhagen case had led to a general accusation against the illegal activities of the *Reichshofrat*. The Emperor was ordered to keep to his election-oath (*Wahlkapitulation*) and specifically guarantee not to use his *Reichshofrat* to threaten territorial rulers with summary execution.[29]

This did not prevent the Jesuits from asking Vienna for yet another commission of inquiry in 1710 which the directors of the Lower-Saxon circle once more blocked by threatening to oppose force with force. Even so, as during the Thirty Years' War period, in 1720 the Jesuits took over the whole of the monastery.

[26] *Ibid.*, document V, section III. [27] *Ibid.*, documents VI–IX.

[28] *Ibid.*, II, pp. 534–7. W. Fürnrohr, *Der immerwährende Reichstag zu Regensburg*, Regensburg, 1963, p. 27. H. W. von Bülow, *Gegenwärtiger Reichstag*, 1792, I, p. 234n. P. Hiltebrandt, *Die Römische Kurie und die Protestanten*, Rome, 1910, pp. 134, 138–45, 195–6.

[29] English guarantee, Schauroth, *op. cit.*, II, pp. 536–7; request to Leopold I, document VIII, 'Falckenhagische Sache'.

In 1773 Lippe took it back as the Jesuits were disbanded, but from 1794 undertook to observe the privileges of the Catholic parish there.[30]

The Falkenhagen matter shows how alive Empire and territories still were to religious affairs in federal politics. Indeed if the Peace of 1648 had been obeyed in its spirit and not merely to the letter, then there would have been no need for a Protestant lobby, the self-styled *Corpus Evangelicorum*. Yet this body was used against the *Reichshofrat* even when the case in point was not necessarily a Protestant-Catholic conflict. In 1665–6 Lippe was already using the Protestant lobby under Brandenburg at Regensburg to draw its complaints about a contested will between Lippe and Emperor Leopold's chief finance minister Count Georg Ludwig Sinzendorff to the notice of Archchancellor Mainz and the imperial assembly.[31]

In 1708 Count Friedrich Adolf used the *Corpus Evangelicorum* to try to prevent his subjects from resorting to the *Reichshofrat* against him. The case in point was the presentation of lay nuns to livings in Lemgo convent. The dynasty had presented one nun too many, and the precedent would threaten the livelihood of the others if allowed to pass. It was a purely internal territorial and Protestant conflict. No Catholic was involved. The nuns appealed to the *Reichshofrat* on a legal point; the dynasty had overstepped its *ius conferendi beneficia et providendi*, its *ius primariarum precum*. Friedrich Adolf turned to Regensburg and claimed that Vienna was interfering with his ecclesiastical jurisdiction as a Protestant ruler as guaranteed in 1648. No imperial court should interfere in conflicts between territorial rulers and their territorial ecclesiastical establishments. Finally no territorial subjects should fight lawsuits of this sort against their ruler at the imperial courts.[32]

The religious content of this case was, however, very tenuous. It showed that religious bodies had the same non-religious problems as any other institution or person of status, but that the provisions of 1648, which put religion in a special category of constitutional law, could be exploited to the disadvantage of

---

[30] *Ibid.*, document X. Kittel, *op. cit.*, 3, p. 197.

[31] Schauroth, *op. cit.*, II, pp. 108–9, 183–4; *Allgemeine Deutsche Biographie*, 34, p. 409. Lippe demanded a hearing at Regensburg.

[32] Peace of Osnabrück, V, paragraphs 1, 48; VIII, paragraph 1. Schauroth, *op. cit.*, II, pp. 100–3.

religious bodies in civil law at federal level. The *Reichshofrat* suffered perhaps more than it should have done through the activities of a *Corpus Evangelicorum*. The latter, after all, protected the interests only of Protestant rulers, whilst the former had a more general interest also in territorial subjects. The Habsburg was Emperor and the territorial rulers in the *Corpus Evangelicorum* were after all only members, even if the leading members, of a federal system of law that at least included all territorial subjects of independent means and status.[33]

The *Corpus Evangelicorum* was a lobby of members of the imperial assembly. Lippe was on this as part of the collective vote that the College of Westphalian Counts exercised. This itself was the Protestant half of a vote that had been accepted as valid in the Council of Ruling Princes (*Fürstenrat*) in 1654. Lippe never had a vote of its own at the imperial assembly, but always had a seat in the *Fürstenrat*. In this it was like other territorial counties and lordships and similar to the prelates, who were all grouped so as not to swamp the larger territories when debating and voting.[34]

Between 1495 and 1654 there were forty-one separate imperial assemblies which were followed in the 1660s by a permanent conference of representatives from the territories that stayed in being all through the eighteenth century at Regensburg. The Emperors generally appeared in person at the sporadic assemblies and this added an inducement for a fluctuating minority of territorial rulers to do likewise. After the 1660s this personal element disappeared as the Emperor was represented by commissars and the territorial rulers by envoys and agents. Regensburg became the third federal capital along with Vienna and Speyer-Wetzlar.[35]

Whilst imperial assemblies were still sporadic, they were held mainly in south German towns but in 1512 the assembly came as far north as Cologne. The key cities for meetings were, however, Augsburg, Nuremberg, Speyer, Worms, Frankfurt-

[33] Schauroth, *op. cit.*, I, pp. 365–75; II, p. 102. H. W. von Bülow, *Über Geschichte und Verfassung des Corporis Evangelicorum*, 1795.

[34] H. Kesting, *Geschichte und Verfassung des Niedersächsisch-westfälischen Grafen-kollegiums, mit einem Beitrag zur Entwicklung der Kuriatstimmen*, Münster, 1916 (printed extract), and another extract, *Westfälische Zeitschrift*, 106, 1956, pp. 175–246. [35] Fürnrohr, *op. cit.*, pp. 23–5, 78.

am-Main and above all Regensburg, the latter accessible by boat from Vienna. A survey shows that twenty-four leading dynastic principalities at the first forty imperial assemblies after the reforms of 1495 put in a much higher attendance than actual votes given in subscription to the conclusions of these assemblies show. Thus in 1495 these leading princes took twenty-nine seats in the *Fürstenrat* but cast only ten votes. Three years later abstentions were over twice as numerous as votes among this group. Under Charles V performance improved and by 1541 there were only eight abstentions to twenty-three votes. There was a sharp relapse until the later 1550s when the qualities of Ferdinand I as a leader in internal affairs began to show through in voting patterns. An all-time peak was reached in 1570 when the group took thirty-five seats in the *Fürstenrat* and cast the same number of votes. By 1641 this had eroded to half, as abstentions were once more almost as frequent as votes. Yet, in the troubled assembly of 1613 there had been twenty-eight votes to only four abstentions. As the group included only dynastic ruling princes, this was a significant achievement for Habsburg imperial policy over a century and a half when these territories were the vital factor in federal politics. [36]

Collective votes in the *Fürstenrat* were more difficult to exercise because they depended on prior meetings of at least a substantial number of those counts and lords and their representatives who had a share in such a vote. Although ruling counts and lords were called individually to imperial assemblies, where they and their kinsfolk could find access to the *Fürstenrat* and take part in the social activities of the assembly as their status warranted, they had no vote except via their collective or curial representative. In 1495 the Wetterau and Swabian counts exercised collective votes in the *Fürstenrat*. The Franconian and Westphalian counts and lords followed in 1607 and 1654. [37]

Imperial knights never succeeded in getting their own seats or votes in the imperial assembly. The cantons, formed chiefly in the sixteenth century, operated within the imperial constitution and were covered by the Peace of 1648, but were never a

---

[36] W. Dohmke, *Die Viril-Stimmen im Reichsfürstenrath 1495–1654*, Breslau, 1882, voting table and pp. 1–25, 120–34. Turner, *op. cit.*, pp. 183–5.

[37] Kesting, *op. cit.*, pp. 8, 21.

constituent part of the imperial assembly.[38] Even the counts and lords had to fight for their collective hold in the *Fürstenrat*. In 1576 the princes tried to exclude the counts from taking seats with a view to excluding all except their actual two to four representatives who would exercise the counts' collective votes. This induced the Wetterau and Swabian counts to canvass the support of all counts and lords in the Empire. They obtained the support of young Rudolf II and their union in 1579 led to greater participation in politics at imperial assemblies. Simon VI of Lippe is an example of this. The Wetterau counts from 1586 onwards took in a number of Westphalian counts as a prelude to the formation of a new and separate curial vote.[39]

The first lord of Lippe to attend the imperial assembly was probably Simon V at Worms in 1521.[40] The next was young Hermann Simon in the entourage of his kinsman, Adolf of Schaumburg, Elector-designate of Cologne in 1548. In 1582 Simon VI appeared at Rudolf II's first assembly and he retained a personal interest in assemblies, dying on his way to his last one in 1613. Hermann Adolf went to the last traditional assembly in 1653–4.

These Lippe rulers obtained access to imperial assemblies because of their status. They had a right to a seat in the assembly, although no right to a vote of their own. This facilitated the presentation of petitions and gave access to the society of better-endowed social equals. It meant that some degree of federal patronage that extended beyond the bounds of kinship was available to members of the Lippe dynasty. It also gave acquaintance with methods of negotiation and procedure which could be applied modestly at home, at territorial assembly level. It provided access to *Fürstenrat* debates and to all binding

---

[38] See H. Rössler (ed.), *Deutscher Adel 1430–1555*, Darmstadt, 1965. R. Fellner, *Die Fränkische Ritterschaft* 1495–1524, Berlin, 1904. R. von Collenberg, 'Die deutsche Reichsritterschaft', *Genealogisches Handbuch des Adels*, 13, Glücksburg, 1956, pp. xxxff. The place of the *Ritterkreise und Kantone* in the early modern German federal system has still to be worked out.

[39] Kesting, *op. cit.*, pp. 2–21; 'Geschichte und Verfassung des Niedersächsisch-Westfälischen Reichsgrafen-Kollegiums', *Westfälische Zeitschrift*, 106, 1956, p. 176. R. Wolf, 'Der Einfluss des Landgrafen Philipp etc. . . .', *Jahrbuch des Vereins für Westfälische Kirchengeschichte*, 51–2, 1958–9.

[40] *Reichstagsakten*, new series, Gotha, 1893ff., 2, p. 438 and index. A Lord of Lippe had already attended a royal meeting at Koblenz in 1414, *Reichstagsakten*, old series, 2nd ed., Göttingen, 1956ff., 7, p. 201.

decisions which were useful to hear at first hand rather than through neighbours, kinsfolk or circle directors.[41]

To this extent, even if Lippe rulers or members of the ruling dynasty could not attend, then representatives, lawyers and councillors were empowered to sit in the *Fürstenrat* instead. It meant that although the counts were a tiny voice when it came to debating and voting at imperial assemblies, they were a strong lobby that listened to *Fürstenrat* discussions, sitting in the chamber and in the Arch-chancellor's dictation room and not as petitioners on the steps outside. The counts also asserted a place for themselves on committees and deputations of the princes. They were in fact minor princes themselves.

The Counts of Lippe sent representatives of their own to imperial assemblies. The letter of credence of Simon V's representative to the assembly of 1527 has survived. He was sent 'like those representatives of others who like us hold no fiefs directly from the Empire'. Even so, what this representative agreed to, Simon V promised to carry out 'on pain of alienating all our lands and goods which we now hold or will in future take over'.[42]

Simon V was interested in reducing Lippe's quotas of war tax and tax for upholding *Reichskammergericht* and *Reichsregiment*. He joined in a petition for federal tax reduction in 1522, barely one year after the promulgation of the basic Worms *Matrikel*.[43] Seven years later he achieved a reduction on *Reichskammergericht* payments of 10 fl. per *Ziel*.[44]

In this period imperial assembly legislation also began to affect Lippe, as far as the surviving records go, for the first time. Arrangements for legal arbitration on a voluntary basis were accepted from the *Reichsregiment* in 1521, and in the 1540s Lippe regency councillors tried to implement them in settling a nobles' vendetta over land in which Erich v. Donop was

---

[41] Kesting, *Geschichte und Verfassung*, p. 20, believed that the cost of imperial assembly attendance was prohibitive for the majority of counts and lords. Even so the *Abschiede* of sixteenth- and seventeenth-century assemblies usually listed as present with their representatives some fifty counts and lords. They could all sit in on sessions of the *Fürstenrat*, even if only two to four of their number could actually debate and vote. See Staatsarchiv Detmold, L 41a IV E 9 vol. 2 for a report on processions, banquets and a vendetta at the 1608 imperial assembly, giving the antics of high society, of interest to the Lippe court.

[42] Staatsarchiv Detmold, L 28 C Section II no. 1.

[43] *Reichstagsakten*, new series, 3, p. 276. [44] *Ibid.*, 7, p. 1368.

murdered in cold blood on his own estate by the Friesen-
hausens. [45]

In 1533 imperial assembly legislation from 1500, 1530 and
1532 against usury was used by the Guelphs against Lippe.
Simon V was accused of increasing the actual capital sum lent
in order to make it seem that he was obeying official maximum
interest rates of 5 and 6 per cent. The argument against usury
was by no means a medieval relic but an economic policy with
territorial sanction at imperial level. The Augsburg imperial
assembly of 1530 diagnosed a sick monetary system in a very
realistic way: [46]

Whereas it has come to our notice that where up to now in the Holy
Empire manifold usurious contracts and the such are made which are
not merely inappropriate but also unchristian, against God and against
justice, in that many are said to be lending a sum of [a thousand]
Gulden [but are only actually lending it] as eight hundred *Gulden*,
yet are demanding more than 5% in the agreement, and are receiving
on repayment more than had been their original capital sum lent; in
the same way there are said to be many who in due time, when they
demand repayment, fix an unreasonably high interest rate to what was
originally a very small capital loan, which capital sum they also increase and thus they alter the original set of figures.

If he was stronger, the debtor bullied the creditor into accepting a lower rate of interest and keeping the actual capital lent.
This the Guelphs did to Count Simon V in 1533 by use of
imperial assembly legislation to sanction their actions, declaring
that Simon was a usurer who had forgotten his noble name and
origin, and that he had acted ignobly. They threatened to
declare that he had lost his noble honour and status. [47]

To the imperial assembly of 1548 Lippe sent two of its noble
councillors to protest against the fines imposed on the county
by Charles V's commissars. In a document that gives an outline
of the policies of the regency government since the death of
Simon V, Lippe argued that it had met all federal commitments

[45] Staatsarchiv Detmold, L 9 vol. 1; L 41a IV E 9 vol. 1.

[46] Staatsarchiv Detmold, L 41a IV B 1. See also a tableau of the simple peasant's
failure to understand capitalism (*Wucher*), G. Franz (ed.), *Quellen zur Geschichte
des deutschen Bauernstandes in der Neuzeit*, Munich, 1963, document 4.

[47] Duke Henry the Younger to Count Simon, 1533, Staatsarchiv Detmold,
L 41a IV B 1; L 92 X nos II–71, Schuldsachen (Welfen), 1510–20. Cf. B. Jarrett,
Social theories of the Middle Ages, London, 1926, pp. 166–7.

and that the county had after all only done its feudal duty by serving Philip of Hesse, although reluctantly and with forces considerably under strength.[48] The religious split was mentioned but Charles V's challenge to return to the old faith was wisely ignored.[49] Lippe desired to bring to the notice of other territories at this assembly the military aggression of Charles V, entailed for the county in a demand for the demilitarization of Detmold castle, but with the exception that it should be open to receive a Habsburg garrison at any time. Having paid fines of 10,000 tlrs and bribes of 1,000 tlrs Lippe complained that Charles V was now demanding a further 8,000 tlrs. Having furthermore given up allegiance to Philip of Hesse, Lippe was still in disgrace and kept waiting for reinvestiture of fiefs directly from the Emperor.[50]

Lippe made a case for its innocence against the tyranny of Charles V. Despite the Emperor's stand on religious issues, Lippe refused to see matters in this light. At stake was the freedom of a small territory which considered itself to have dutifully carried out imperial, federal demands, despite support of Hesse after notification from the Emperor in July 1546 that it was treason to support the Smalkaldic League.[51] Furthermore, this protest was drawn up for Charles V's most docile assembly immediately after his crushing victory over the Protestants.

At the Peace assembly of Augsburg in 1555 Lippe had a representative who signed the conclusion.[52] The county sent its own chancellor to the negotiations of the 1640s that once more led to internal peace. By 1645 Chancellor Tilhen was being instructed by Lippe, Schaumburg, Oldenburg, Delmenhorst, Rietberg, Bentheim, East Frisia and Tecklenburg to lobby in Osnabrück for a separate vote in any reconstituted

[48] Staatsarchiv Detmold, L 41a IV E 9 vol. 1.

[49] 'Wowall mhen nu berichtet wo kay. May. vp dusse herrschupp sunderlichs der religion etwas verbittert vnd myt vngnaden bewogen.'

[50] 'So ist mhen auch wyllich alle de guder so de Graffen tor Lippe van Riche to lenhe hebben, vnd in des Richs Lhenregister befunden to lene toemfangen, de wyll aver Jrer May. vermoge des contracts de hessesschen lene emfangen sollen werden.' Lippe demanded the consent of Landgraf Philip to these proposals.

[51] Staatsarchiv Detmold, L 41a IV E 9 vol. 1, *Reichsacht* threat from Regensburg 7 July 1546 received by Chancellor Bernhard von der Lippe in Detmold on 29 July 1546.

[52] K. Zeumer, *Quellensammlung zur Geschichte der deutschen Reichsverfassung in Mittelalter und Neuzeit*, 2nd ed., Tübingen, 1913, p. 369.

Fürstenrat for the Westphalian counts, which should be quite distinct from the Wetterau comital vote.[53]

By 1653 this separate vote had become a reality, although actual representation depended upon counts' co-operation within their new curia and, more important still, on contribution to the cost of imperial assembly representation. To speed acceptance of a Westphalian comital vote through the federal executives in Vienna and Mainz, twenty-three Westphalian counties and lordships spent 3,500 tlrs in bribes to get the matter through within a month in August 1653. Nineteen *Reichshofräte* each obtained 100 tlrs. The president of this court was given 200 tlrs plus jewellery worth 400 tlrs as a present for his daughter. The imperial chancellor and Mainz chancellor got 100 tlrs and 250 tlrs. This by no means exhausted a list that made little distinction between genuine fees, such as for counsel, secretary and scribe, and honorary or 'speeding up' charges for more politically important officials.[54]

The days of Lippe providing its own imperial assembly representation were now over. When the assembly became permanent after 1663, so did collective representation by the Westphalian counts, but until the 1690s this college lacked financial support to such an extent that the collective vote could not be fully exercised by those who had become members in 1653. The religious issue equally bedevilled its exercise as the Westphalian College of Counts contained Catholic and Protestant members, a split that led, however, only after 1744 to Catholic and Protestant alternative exercise of the vote at Regensburg.[55]

As with any new political organization, there soon developed a fight for internal control of the Westphalian College of Counts between the *potentiores*, those powers like Hanover that demanded control by virtue of admission of Hoya and Diepholz which had long ceased to be natively ruled counties, and actual counties that still had their own dynasties in control, like Lippe and Manderscheid. The struggle over raising Hanover to Electoral status in 1692 reactivated the Westphalian College of Counts

[53] Kesting, 'Geschichte und Verfassung . . .', pp. 177–8, 180.
[54] *Ibid.*, p. 181.
[55] Kesting, *Geschichte und Verfassung*, p. 25; 'Geschichte und Verfassung . . .', pp. 175, 183–4. H. W. von Bülow, *Geschichte und Verfassung des gegenwärtigen Reichstages*, 2, 1792, p. 224.

as every vote in the *Fürstenrat* at Regensburg became worth its weight in gold.[56] As the largest of the still independent counties in this college, Lippe began to play a leading rôle. Lippe tried to negotiate a similar constitution for the college as existed for its neighbours in the Wetterau and Franconia. In 1693 a compromise between the *potentiores* and native rulers was reached whereby the Westphalian counts' vote alternated monthly between them. This gave the Guelphs, Wettiner, Hessians and Hohenzollerns an alternating say with Lippe and Manderscheid (the latter the leaders of the still independent counties and lordships within the college) and also took some account of the religious split as Lippe was Protestant and Manderscheid Catholic. At a meeting of Westphalian counts additional to a circle assembly at Cologne, Friedrich Adolf of Lippe was elected college director for life.[57]

In the eighteenth century Lippe remained one of the chief territories in the direction of the college vote at Regensburg as well as in the administration of the college in Westphalia. Lippe paid the highest single contributions to finance the college and its last director in the 1790s was also once again the ruler of Lippe. It was thus that as the eighteenth century wore on Lippe obtained weekly imperial assembly reports as well as *Reichskammergericht* audit and accounts, and *Reichshofrat* decisions of importance as precedents for administrative law.[58]

The circles took on much routine federal business. The success of each circle as a regional executive depended on the fate of imperial politics at assembly level, but also on the ambitions of the largest territories, which provided the circle directors within each region. Circles also depended on voluntary participation of smaller territories within each region to make imperial assembly legislation more precise and to take regional initiatives from it. There was no question of any territorial rulers giving up their regal powers over their subjects to federal executives, whether at imperial or circle level. This was particularly noticeable at regional level, where circles operated as basically unspecialized consultative bodies for the use of all

[56] Kesting, 'Geschichte und Verfassung . . .', p. 184.

[57] *Ibid.*, pp. 185–6. The leadership, session and voting pattern has been simplified. Kesting has worked it out fully.

[58] Staatsarchiv Detmold, L 41a I–III. Cf. Bader, *op. cit.*

territorial rulers with the general exception of the imperial knights.[59] Effective circle development was an early-sixteenth-century phenomenon which was of vital but sporadic importance to the federal system until the end of the old Empire in the Napoleonic era. During these three centuries most of the ten circles had ceased to function at some time or other but they had also at other times organized federal armies, war taxes and federal executive taxes. They had controlled the currency and co-ordinated inter-territorial economic and judicial policies. They had provided commissions of inquiry, helped the law of distraint and provided a cheap executive in fiscal matters of federal importance.

Although considerable federal legislation went into trying to make the circles compulsory bodies in which nearly all territorial rulers were represented, there was no binding power structure in the units so created. The larger territories, both ecclesiastical and dynastic, may have directed these circles and it was they who wrote out the writs to circle assemblies and generally provided the officials to collect circle taxes and lead circle troops, yet their coercive powers as circle leaders or commanders were strictly limited by the other member territories.

Circles as institutions undoubtedly existed but they were basically unspecialized bodies that depended on the support and enthusiasm of each territorial ruler for imperial policies and federal activities at any one time in early modern Germany. It has to be understood that circles were another, and, because of their scattered but regional and static geography, perhaps the most important manifestation of a federal system that did not undermine the power of diverse territorial units, but instead kept supplying talking-points where those with territorial power could co-operate and resolve their differences on a volun-tary basis. It meant that there was no political discipline outside

[59] For the following survey see P. Casser, 'Der niederrheinisch-westfälische Reichskreis 1500–1806', *Der Raum Westfalen*, 2, pt 2, Münster, 1934, pp. 48–9, and the three Bonn University theses on the Westphalian circle 1648–1713 by Haberecht, Arnold and Isaacson (1933–7). J. J. Moser, *Von der Teutschen Crays-Verfassung*, Frankfurt-am-Main, 1773, especially pp. 507ff., 775–8. F. C. Moser, *Sammlung sämtlicher Crays-Abschiede*, 1–3, Leipzig, 1747–8; *Fränkische Crays-Abschiede 1524–1748*, 1–2, Nuremberg, 1752; *Obersächsische Kreisabschiede*, Jena, 1752. K. Brandi, *Göttingische Gelehrte Anzeigen*, 1898, pp. 787–98.

the territorial sphere, except in times of danger from war, danger both real and imaginary. The amorphous structure of federal politics meant that social forms and legal procedures had to substitute for binding legislation and compulsory execution. It was a lax system that did not aim at uniform control but at its opposite in preserving a diversified *status quo*. In this the circle played a key rôle.

To Lippe the circle meant inter-territorial affairs and a modest form of what developed as foreign affairs among Europe's larger territories. Although territories had been split into 'nations' as the conciliar movement in the church and at the universities had shown, this simplification did not affect a county like Lippe, where there was a basic loyalty to the Emperor but where anyone living outside Lippe, let alone outside the Empire, was a foreigner as well as a neighbour.[60] The Empire was not a national unit, although it may have catered for national feelings especially when it came to federal war. Instead it was a multi-territorial unit where, as in the case of Lippe, many territories were too small to play a strong rôle at imperial court and assembly level. It was thus natural to turn to politics at regional level to solve the problems of territories living together. Here circles were a continuation on a firmer basis of older local and voluntary associations for war, peace and economic regulation.[61] From the 1530s onwards Lippe's sporadic essays into inter-territorial affairs thus had most meaning at Westphalian circle level.

In a memorandum from *c.* 1535–6 in the last year of his reign, Count Simon V complained about federal demands on his county.[62] The four points that were set out for him showed how the Westphalian circle under the direction of Bishop Franz of Münster was already an integral part of the federal, imperial system of government. Lippe complained of being subpoenaed

---

[60] R. W. Southern, *The making of the Middle Ages*, London, 1959, pp. 16–20, illustrates this proto-national element. H. G. Koenigsberger and G. L. Mosse, *Europe in the 16th century*, London, 1968, pp. 212ff.

[61] G. Engelbert, 'Einungen und Landfriedensbündnisse des Spätmittelalters', *Kunst und Kultur im Weserraum*, Münster, 1966, pp. 139–43, 859–71. G. Pfeiffer, 'Die Bündnis und Landfriedenspolitik der Territorien zwischen Weser und Rhein im späten Mittelalter (1180–1512)', *Der Raum Westfalen*, 2, 1, Münster, 1955, pp. 79–139. G. Angermann, 'Die Stellung des Nordöstlichen Westfalens in der Landfriedensbewegung zwischen 1300 und 1350', *Lippische Mitteilungen*, 24, 1955, pp. 160–80. [62] Staatsarchiv Detmold, L 37 XVII 8a.

too much, of receiving too many orders from the Emperor. There were too many fiscal cases running against the county at the *Reichskammergericht*. Münster's tax grant to suppress the Anabaptists, which had been granted at imperial assembly and collected at circle level, had been overpaid by Lippe. Simon refused to pay more to Bishop Franz because other territories had paid correspondingly far less of their quotas than had Lippe. The Bishop's demands for arrears were unfair.[63]

In reply to a new tax demand from the Emperor, Simon sent instructions to his agent at the *Reichskammergericht* to stress once more that although he was fully paid up and had no arrears, all demands were totally beyond his means to pay.[64] Because of this and other imperial tax demands and because no other territory in the circle had given more, Simon asked Bishop Franz to desist from collecting arrears from Lippe subjects by force.

This is the earliest point at which circle affairs in Lippe are traceable from the documents that remain. It already shows a fully fledged regional executive receiving taxes and threatening to ask for more under the control of a director who was crushing a religious rebellion in his own territory with regional, federal support.

From 1537 to 1748 Lippe's circle affairs have been collected together.[65] In Westphalia, circle direction first fluctuated between the Bishops of Münster and the Dukes of Jülich. In the absence of competent rulers in both these territories in the 1590s and first years of the seventeenth century, Count Simon VI of Lippe tried to run the circle as *Kreisobrist* or military leader for Emperor Rudolf II.

In the seventeenth century circle direction was shared, not without conflict and rivalry, between Münster, the Palatinate and Brandenburg, as the Jülich inheritance fell to Wittelsbachs and Hohenzollerns. This tended to place regional affairs in the hands of non-Westphalian rulers and courts. Although Münster and Düsseldorf remained at times the centres of Westphalian affairs, policies were no longer formulated without reference to

---

[63] Simon's scribe claimed 'wa wall syne g[naden] den mesten deell entrichtet dar de van den gemeynen stenden nicht im geliche geplegenn'.
[64] 'Allenthalven baven syner g[naden] vermogen.'
[65] Staatsarchiv Detmold, L 41 vols 1–64.

Bonn and Berlin. This increased the suspicion of territories like Lippe as to the purpose of regional co-operation, when direction could pass so easily into 'foreign' hands just because of native dynastic failure exacerbated by a policy of accumulated bishoprics under younger sons of safe Catholic dynasties.[66]

In the summer of 1538 Bishop Franz demanded fifty knights' service from Lippe to help rout his own mutinous troops. Philip of Hesse supported the Bishop and ordered twenty knights' service from Lippe as the county's overlord. Two Lippe nobles started recruiting and publicized an offer of service from Bishop Franz at 9 fl. a month. The towns were called to Cappel in the heart of Lippe to discuss troop quotas with the regency councillors. The latter declared their open support for Münster and Hesse. They encouraged Lippe subjects to serve under the guarantee of full protection of their property from Münster.[67] They claimed, 'this county is also united to clean out the nest of lordless mercenaries'.[68] Bishop Franz had run out of money. No further federal taxes had been forthcoming from the neighbouring territories whom he thus faced with the problem of dispersing mercenaries that he could no longer afford to pay off.

Lippe was called by Duke Johann of Jülich to its first Westphalian circle assembly in 1537. Encouraged by the regional activities of Bishop Franz to gain support against the Anabaptists, the Westphalian circle now got under way as a conference where member territories could more readily discuss the ways and means of federal policy. The overriding question was how to combat the Turks and to this was added a discussion of the papal proposal to call a council to Mantua.[69] In 1541 Jülich asked Lippe to come to a circle assembly and choose an assessor to send to the *Reichskammergericht* in accordance with arrangements made at the previous imperial assembly. Yet the regency

[66] Casser, *op. cit.*, p. 40; as late as 1784 there were still fifty-one members of the Westphalian circle of which Lippe was the ninth largest.

[67] Staatsarchiv Detmold, L 41 vol. 1, Münster to Count Jobst of Hoya (as regent of Lippe) and to *Drost* Mengersen, Ascension Day, 1538; Philip of Hesse to Detmold, nach cantate, 1538; circular of Werpup and Barckhausen; Detmold regency councillors to Lemgo and Horn towns, and to the countryside (*Landesschup*).

[68] 'Auck dusse Graveschup vereiniget', against 'eyn hupen herloseder Landesknechte'.

[69] Staatsarchiv Detmold, L 28 C II–1; L 41 vol. 1, writ Düsseldorf to Detmold, 14 April 1537.

councillors excused themselves from attendance.[70] Circle directors were exhorted by the imperial assembly in January 1542 to assemble all their members to discuss coinage control and claims for federal tax reductions. This was much more popular and Westphalian territories met at Essen to draft a common policy for a forthcoming imperial assembly in Nuremberg.[71]

In 1542 an attempt was being made to create a regional unit of territories with a common interest at the imperial assembly. The bond was strengthened by appointment of a military staff at circle level. The ten circles were to organize an army against the Turks consisting of 9,000 horse and 48,000 footsoldiers. The territories of the Westphalian circle were expected to provide 1,300 horse and 18,000 foot. In the circle assessment Lippe was charged with 10 horse and 45 foot, yet Lemgo was separately assessed at another 10 horse and 55 foot. The county then withdrew from participation in the circle war effort and serviced its own contingent in Hungary. It was far cheaper that way: Lippe got away with an actual field force of 10 horse and 40 foot. The Lemgo quota was ignored.[72]

A basic weakness of the circle system was revealed. In bypassing the circle authorities Lippe had been able to obtain cheaper conditions of imperial service than through the regional machinery. By April 1542 Jülich was already protesting against Habsburg Burgundian policies, yet the circle assembly that Jülich called and presided over one month later did appoint a military committee and did implement troop musters and money collection in the territories. Even so, the territories that appeared refused to bind themselves to deliver their own troops and taxes to any circle commissariat, using the excuse that it would be unfair to expect them to do this as long as not every territory appeared at the circle assembly and bound itself to do likewise.[73]

The Westphalian circle tried to ascertain its debts on the 1542–3 Turk campaign. It formulated an appropriate arrears policy at an assembly in Cologne in July 1544. Lippe refused to acknowledge the claims on it. It was, however, no fault of the circle system that war was unprofitable, and the territories had

[70] Staatsarchiv Detmold, L 28 C II–1.
[71] Staatsarchiv Detmold, L 37 XVII no. 2, May 1542.
[72] *Ibid.*
[73] Essen assembly conclusion, 15 May 1542, 'weile es eyne gemene werck ist vnd alle geliche betrefft', Staatsarchiv Detmold, L 37 XVII nos 2, 24a.

their own war debts. Lippe continued to owe its commander, Johann Bose, arrears for damage to horses and equipment as late as 1546.[74]

The federal campaign of 1542 did, however, increase the powers of territorial rulers over their territorial Estates and subjects. The regency councillors in Lippe had imperial and circle assembly backing to call their Estates to territorial assembly and goad them into granting the means for the war effort against the Turks. Another precedent was established for taxation as territorial rulers joined forces to make territorial Estates and territorial subjects grant and pay for a common foreign war policy. In Lippe the following writ was issued:[75]

Our friendly service and what more that is dear and good we wish to do. Honourable and steadfast especial good friend.

The Duke of Cleves, Gelderland and Berg etc. on previous demands of the Roman King and also the Emperor's commissars should have written to the Regency Councillors of this County of Lippe and other territories concerning the troops to be sent against the hereditary enemy of the Christian name, saying how the same should be kept and paid.

That is why despite the non-arrival of the Duke's instructions we have agreed to call a territorial assembly at 9 o'clock on the coming Saturday after St. Bartholomew in the village of Donop. We ask you to arrive in Donop on time with the rest of the common country [gemeine Landesschup] who have likewise all been cited, to give advice on the present problem [beswerunge] and to help reach a conclusion to it.

But should you stay away from this territorial assembly, which we do not expect you to do, and our ruler is thereby called to account by the Emperor's commissars and Fiscal, you are cordially informed that we will have protested that any such failure will not be his fault but the fault of those subjects who stayed away. We expect you to show your goodwill in this and avoid all bad counsel.

Circle effectiveness revived after 1555. Territories participated in circle affairs for internal peace and external war. Circle and imperial demands were now discussed in one and the same breath at territorial assembly level in Lippe. At a meeting in

[74] Staatsarchiv Detmold, L 41 vol. 1, Cologne assembly conclusion, 11 August 1544; L 37 XVII no. 2; L 9 vol. 1.
[75] Staatsarchiv Detmold, L 41 vol. 1, writ of 8 August 1542.

Cappel in 1556 the nobles and towns (*Ritter und landschaft*) did not oppose their ruler's appointment as a secondary official in the Westphalian circle but they warned him of costs attached to the post. They approved the publication of a decree from Ferdinand I regulating coinage and wool prices. They granted one unit of land tax for imperial tax payments which they themselves would help to collect.[76]

This shows how territorial, regional and imperial affairs came together and provided motivation for political development at small-state level. Despite the shifting sand of federal expedient, Lippe paid attention especially to circle demands and orders, above all in the second half of the sixteenth, second half of the seventeenth and early eighteenth centuries. Between 1566 and 1598 the Lippe records contain forty conclusions of separate circle assemblies.[77] In 1557 it already suited Lippe to co-operate with the circle in return for protection against local raids from its neighbour, the Count of Rietberg. In December 1557 Bernhard VIII ordered the collection of a capital tax to help pay the Westphalian circle costs in defeating the Count of Rietberg who had broken the imperial land-peace and was soon to die a demented prisoner in Cologne.[78]

Circle military policy meant a circle arrears policy. Whether to punish Rietberg and Grumbach or deplore Dutch and Spanish marauding or provide Geitzkoffler with coin with which to redeem bills of exchange at allegedly favourable rates in the Turkish war of 1592–1605, the circles had more plans than money. In 1583 Simon VI was twice warned to pay circle tax arrears of 1,115 fl. on pain of distraint. He replied that as a secondary circle official he had expenses that should be offset at least by giving him more time to pay his federal taxes.[79]

As early as 1567 a Westphalian circle treasurer had been sending extracts of accounts for specific circle and imperial taxes

[76] 'Landtag in Cappel nach Lichtmesse, 1556', Staatsarchiv Detmold, L 9 vol. 1 folio 223; Knoch Repositur L 9, ad tom. 1 folio 32.

[77] Staatsarchiv Detmold, Knoch L 41. Cf. F. C. Moser, *Sammlung sämtlicher Crays-Abschiede*, who published 64 conclusions of the Franconian circle between 1555 and 1599.

[78] Staatsarchiv Detmold, L 11 IV no. 5a, eighteenth-century copy, authenticated by a similar document in L 11 V no. 1.

[79] Staatsarchiv Detmold, Knoch L 41. F. C. Moser, *Sammlung sämtlicher Crays-Abschiede*, documents 110, 117, 125, 131, 133, 138, circle conclusions as Westphalia made a concerted effort to expel Dutch and Spanish marauders 1597–9.

owed by Lippe.[80] By 1598 imperial accountants in Regensburg were sending lists of all Westphalian tax arrears to member territories. Since 1557 Lippe was alleged to have run up arrears of 10,465 fl. The whole circle allegedly stood at over a million in arrears. The 1567 account did not balance and was in Lippe's disfavour. The 1598 account coincided with Geitzkoffler's attempts to obtain extra money via the circles without resort to imperial assemblies. In the Lippe records federal arrears demands are arbitrary and unconvincing.[81]

Circle militarism always ran short of money. In the later sixteenth century circles were ineffective against Spain and the Dutch. They were never wholly ineffective against the Turks and in fact helped to contain the infidel in the 1540s, 1590s, 1660s and 1680s, thereafter effectively contributing to his defeat. The circles also helped to contain France in the Grand Alliance of the War of the Spanish Succession.[82] Yet, whether at times of defeat or success, arrears policies were the same. Circles were empowered to distrain for arrears by Emperor and imperial assembly in 1664. This is what happened to Lippe under the Westphalian circle directors until the Ryswick Peace.[83] Leopold I's executive rules of 1673 produced a coercive military and fiscal system that Lippe had to follow. Circle directors were the driving force in its execution.[84]

In April 1682 the circle assembly at Duisburg agreed to set up an army. It was proposed and agreed by majority ruling that Westphalian troop contingents of horse, foot and dragoons be ready to make up the imperial army total of 20,000 in one month's time. Colours and arms were standardized. The initial money demand on top of the troop grant was only 32,000 fl. as member territories would supply and service their own troops. This represented no advance on the situation in 1542, despite the wishes of circle directors to rationalize and control the

[80] Staatsarchiv Detmold, L 37 XVII no. 7.

[81] J. Müller, *Zacharias Geitzkoffler 1560–1617*, Vienna, 1938, p. 33. Staatsarchiv Detmold, Knoch L 41; L 41a IV E 9 vol. 2, 'Restanten im Westphälischen Craiss, 24 Januar 1602'. On 1594 and 1598 imperial assembly grants Lippe owed 8,800 fl.

[82] See R. Wines, 'The Imperial circles, princely diplomacy and imperial reform 1681–1714', *Journal of Modern History*, 39, 1967; A. H. Loebl, 'Eine ausserordentliche Reichshilfe', *Sitzungsberichte der phil.-hist. Klasse d. kais. Akad. d. Wiss.*, 153, 1906; and Müller, *op. cit.*

[83] Staatsarchiv Detmold, L 41a IV 207. See Chapter XII for the activities of *Armierte*. [84] Staatsarchiv Detmold, L 41a IV B no. 4.

system. Equally, circle officials' salary arrears were to be paid but no specific grant was made.[85]

Between 1682 and 1697 Westphalian circle troop assessments were increased ninefold and Lippe, which in this period paid in lieu of troops, accumulated only 4,400 fl. arrears on the circle executive account after paying an average of 1,000 fl. a year all through the period. This came on top of the demands made by Leopold I, his commissars and the circle directors as *Armierte* which cost Lippe's rural districts well over 1,000 tlrs a month for winter billets and summer campaigning.[86]

The imperial assembly exercised some degree of control over coinages circulating in the Empire. Since the 1520s it had sporadically issued decrees fixing the price of gold and silver according to the half-pound in weight of the most marketably pure metal. The circles were active as supervisors of territorial mints and they organized regular meetings of member territories where coins were tested and condemned if they were of irregular quality, or were accepted at a fixed rate of exchange according to an imperial standard, on which all existing coin was quoted. Frequent bulletins of exchange rates were published by circle coinage wardens and after circle coinage assemblies, the *Münz-Convente* and *Münz-Probations-Tage*. The imperial assembly of 1566 handed over to the circles as regional authorities control of the ratio of nominal-value small coin to intrinsic-value large coin.[87]

A handbook of 1692 gave tables and reproductions of 1,200 different types of coin likely to be met with in various parts of the Empire.[88] It attempted to assess their value according to quality and weight of precious metal and also the nominal value

[85] 'Conclusum publicat per Gülich', 4 April 1682, Staatsarchiv Detmold, L 37 XVII no. 1.

[86] Staatsarchiv Detmold, L 9 vol. 22 folio 63; L 37 XVII no. 2, 'Simplum Circuli Westphalici'. Cf. 'Verzeichnis ders. H.R.R. Stände nach den zehen Reichs Craissen sambt ihrem monatlich. einfachen Anschlag zum Römerzug', Frankfurt-am-Main, 1659 (British Museum, 301.g.13).

[87] P. Lennartz, *Die Probationstage und Probationsregister des Niederländisch-westfälischen Kreises*, Münster, 1912, pp. 2–3. H. Gebhart, *Numismatische Geldgeschichte*, Leipzig, 1886, pp. 86, 88, over-emphasized the seriousness of small coin as a threat to the stability of money markets. The intrinsic value of coin remained a stabilizing factor that defeated all monetary inflation and profiteering at local, territorial levels. A. Luschin von Ebengreuth, *Allgemeine Münzkunde und Geldgeschichte*, Munich, 1926, pp. 196–234.

[88] Former Franconian circle chief coinage warden L. W. Hoffmann, *Alter und*

of copper small change that each native type of large coin locally supported as legal tender. This necessitated a coinage of account which would cover the whole of the Empire and which could be reckoned at a fixed rate to the half-pounds of pure gold and silver. Such a system the Empire did provide and the circles had to keep it going, with fluctuations according to the market price of precious metal.

Money of account was universally accepted. In the Empire this system operated between the sixteenth and nineteenth centuries on *Reichstalers* for silver and *Gulden* (abbreviated as fl.) for gold. Gold became a prestige currency and silver the standard in the course of the sixteenth and seventeenth centuries. The *Mark* accounting system, based on silver pennies and controlled by tiny, autonomous urban economies, was also not replaced until the end of the sixteenth century in the region around Lippe. Local trade was no longer the backbone of long-distance trade, as towns like Lemgo and Osnabrück struggled with their debased marks, with which they had to try to borrow talers and gulden. This they found increasingly disastrous to their trading positions from as early as the fifteenth up to the seventeenth centuries.[89]

Reichstalers of account were assessed at 90 kreutzer and 72 kreutzer in small silver and alloy rates.[90] This was an adaptation to fluctuating groschen rates of between 24 and 36 to the taler. An attempt to introduce a guldiner at just under 60 kreutzer in the economic crisis of the 1680s was defeated.[91] The

[89] Stadtarchiv Lemgo, Concurse, Kämmereirechnungen. Also *Lippische Regesten*, documents on Lemgo's Hansa trade with the Baltic in the later fourteenth century. F. Friedensberg, *Münzkunde und Geldgeschichte der Einzelstaaten*, Munich, 1926, pp. 44–51, 108–17. W. Tauber, *Geld und Credit im Mittelalter*, Berlin, 1933, on the problems of reissue of coins and honouring of old debts, especially pp. 249–97.

[90] Hoffmann, *op. cit.*, pp. 288, 359–62.

[91] In the 1680s the Empire began a serious armaments policy directed against France just as much as against the Turks. Hoffmann longed for nothing more than a perfect, unchanging system of economics based on stabilized gold and silver supply. Even so he could not help sacrificing his beliefs to 'patriotic' feelings:

'Question: Should actual coins of the Empire remain of the same quality and weight once and for all?

Answer: They should always be of that quality and weight which is fixed by imperial law, but this quality and weight should vary according to what is from time to time most expedient for the safety of the Empire. Especially in wartime,

Neuer Münz-Schlüssel, Nuremberg, 1692. D. Thoman, *Acta Publica Monetaria des Müntz Wesens in Deutschland*, Augsburg, 1692.

problem was that nothing was ever abolished as new expedients arose out of old failures. Yet the complications caused by different regional conversion rates were offset by imperial standard rates, although these could only keep adapting to the bullion market with the consent of the territories at imperial assemblies, and, having no speed of action, could thus exercise little firm control over the price of precious metal. The problem was made worse by the conflict of interests between those territories that mined their own silver and thus needed to keep the price of raw metal high and those like Lippe that produced their own coin for prestige reasons as well as to control their local economies. All territories saw in their local mints a source of quick profit from cheap coin, whilst claiming that their colleagues and neighbours were even greater villains. That meant that money regulation was a full-time federal activity at territorial, circle and imperial level. As with law and war, so in money regulation the territories continued to find worthwhile talking-points at federal levels of politics. Coinage assemblies kept the Empire together as a reality as much as the imperial assemblies convened by the Habsburgs to get money for warfare.

Coinage readjustment was a permanent business and the burden outside the territories themselves fell to coinage wardens in the circles, who co-operated with the larger territories and tried to coerce the smaller ones.[92] In Westphalia a heavier currency compared with the South and the Habsburg lands operated at 9 reichstalers to the half-pound of silver, and the reichstaler = 36 groschen = 216 pfennige = 432 heller, gosslar or sware = 72 kreutzer.[93] This in itself was a vast simplification of the number of actual coins minted, named, circulated and quoted. The same names used in money of

[92] *Ibid.*, pp. 353, 355–6. F. C. Moser, *Sammlung sämtlicher Crays-Abschiede*, 'Recess des Westphälischen Crayses Müntz-Probations-Abschied, 6 October 1596, 2 August 1597'. For a similar complaint see the 1592 *Reichsmünzordnung* discussed in W. A. Shaw, 'The monetary movements of 1600–21 in Holland and Germany', *Transactions of the Royal Historical Society*, 9, 1895, pp. 202–3.

[93] Hoffmann, *op. cit.*, pp. 340, 342. In 1692 the Lippe taler was worth 4 shillings 6 pence, the Lippe groschen one-and-a-half pence, the Lippe pfennig one farthing in sterling of the period.

treasuries must not run out of money, hence they should be allowed to reduce the quality and weight of their coins to enable them to profit by the short-term gain that this involves.' Translated from *ibid.*, pp. 289–90.

account were also used for actual coins in circulation. Coins were also called in by territorial authorities and reminted or counter-marked. This led to further confusion as new coins worth different amounts were reissued with old names and familiar faces.[94]

There was a remarkable stability, however, in foreign exchange rates which should not be masked by instabilities in inter-territorial rates within the Holy Roman Empire itself.[95] In his travels in 1581 and 1584 Leopold von Wedel, a nobleman from Pomerania, noted that he had obtained $1\frac{1}{5}$ gulden for 1 reichstaler in Holland, 4 shillings for it in England and 34 Scots shillings for it north of the Border.[96]

On this, small-coin equivalent values between Germany, Holland, England and Scotland can be worked out, although the guide is hypothetical in that there was no reason for the local purchasing power of a coin to bear any relation to its foreign exchange value. Even so, it gives some idea of early modern money values in relation to each other and not just to the price of bullion. In 1581–4 v. Wedel was charged the following equivalent rates, from which small-coin rates may be deduced, using imperial and Dutch rates of 1 taler (tlr) = 36 groschen = 216 pfennige, and 1 gulden (fl.) = 20 stivers = 180 schillinge, which gives the table as shown:

Empire		*Holland*		*England*		*Scotland*
1 taler	=	$1\frac{1}{5}$ gulden	=	4 shillings	=	34 shillings
1 groschen	=	$\frac{2}{3}$ stiver	=	$1\frac{1}{3}$ pence	=	$11\frac{1}{3}$ pence
1 pfennig	=	$\frac{2}{3}$ schilling	=	$\frac{2}{9}$ pence	=	$1\frac{8}{9}$ pence

The foreign exchange rate was still much the same a century and a half later.[97] It is this remarkable stability that has to be

[94] For a discussion of *Rechnungs- und Zahlmünzen*, H. Grote and L. Hölzermann, *Lippische Geld- und Münzgeschichte*, Leipzig, 1867, pp. 112–19.

[95] The taler was a stable unit, capable of holding its own with the currencies of any other early modern country. Lennartz, *op. cit.*, p. 18.

[96] M. Bär, *Leopold von Wedels Beschreibung seiner Reisen*, Stettin, 1895.

[97] E. Waschinski, 'Zwischenstaatliche Wechselkurse', *Vierteljahrschrift für Sozial- und Wirtschaftsgeschichte*, 47, 1960, pp. 354–62. Hoffmann, *op. cit.*, coinage conversion tables, pp. 337–50. *Encyclopaedia Britannica*, 3rd ed., Edinburgh, 1797, 12, pp. 230–2, 'Universal table of the present state of real and imaginary Monies (or Money of Account) of the World.' By 1797 the reichstaler was still worth 3 shillings 6 pence, although Hamburg held on to the harder rate at 4 shillings 6 pence. Friedensberg, *op. cit.*, pp. 116–17. Between 1667 and 1738 much was

taken into account when quoting actual sums of money from the documents of early modern territories.[98] Inside the Empire territories and circles gave an impression of a monetary instability that was not passed on to neighbouring countries and it was the failure to hold the value of local small change that upset the territorial economies. Larger gold and silver coins were not involved, for talers and gulden were generally safe to handle whereas groschen and pfennige were not.[99] The confusions caused by unstable small coin should not be allowed to obscure the continued hard value of larger coins from the sixteenth century to the eighteenth.[100]

In the Westphalian circle every member had the right to mint its own coins, although that right was exercised only sporadically by the smaller territories. In the sixteenth and seventeenth centuries this involved scrutiny of the activities of 7 bishoprics, 1 complex of principalities, 8 abbeys, 32 counties and lordships, and 8 towns all autonomous on the Westphalian money market alone. During the 1550s and 1560s imperial assemblies began to increase circle powers of control over regional money markets which gave inter-circle coverage in Cologne, Leipzig and Augsburg. By 1566 the circles had obtained the right to report coinage delinquencies among the territories to the Fiscal at the *Reichskammergericht*.[101] Rulers could now be threatened with outlawry for destroying confidence when they minted debased coins. Again it was legislation under Ferdinand I that created the rules upon which an imperial money market could operate by the *Reichsmünz- und Probierordnungen* of August 1559.[102]

[98] Gebhart, *op. cit.*, p. 85.

[99] Friedensberg, *op. cit.*, pp. 114–15, illustrations, 157, 160–2. Staatsarchiv Detmold, L 9 vol. 8 folio 34, Lippe devaluation of small coin. Grote and Hölzermann, *op. cit.*, pp. 202–3.

[100] Friedensberg, *op. cit.*, p. 115. Gebhart, *op. cit.*, pp. 86–9. Thoman, *op. cit.*

[101] Rudolf II's Münzmandat, Prague, 8 August 1596 (British Museum 5604.h.6).

[102] Lennartz, *op. cit.*, pp. 3–6, text in 'Extract Auss allen Reichs- und Deputations-Abschieden / vom Jahr 1356 zu treulicher gehorsamer nachfolge / allen müntzen', Mainz, 1597 (British Museum 5604.h.6), folios 22–40. Gold and silver rates were already being fixed at imperial assembly deliberations in 1442 (folio 1). M. Goldast, *Catholicon Rei Monetariae*, Frankfurt-am-Main, 1620, especially Chapter 7, folios 34–8.

---

done to establish internal coinage stability with fixed regional difference based on the 9 to 10 talers to the half-pound of silver bullion in the Zinna and Leipzig agreements.

The first Westphalian circle coinage meetings were held in late 1566. Rules were laid down for fixing the quality and quantity of local small coins with the co-operation of the money market in Cologne town. Those convicted of importing bad small change into the circle or exporting good small change out of the circle were threatened with confiscation of wealth, mutilation or death. The first Westphalian circle warden was appointed at a basic 50 fl. a year plus 10 tlrs livery and piecemeal rates for each coin test that he carried out. He was paid out of circle executive taxes levied on member territories using the all-purpose *Römermonate* assessments. A determined effort was now made to halt further deterioration of Cologne exchange rates by legislation that allowed coinage checks to become a compulsory circle executive matter.[103]

Success in circle coinage control depended on the co-operation of local territorial rulers and their mintmasters. From February 1567 onwards the money market featured regularly in Westphalian circle assembly discussions. Dealers were appointed to recall bad coin at official discount. The imperial order from 1559 that no one need accept payment of over 25 fl. in small coin was upheld. Results of valuations and condemned coinages were printed and published. The coinage centre of Cologne was reactivated by federal legislation. The weakness of Westphalian circle coinage affairs was that the Burgundian authorities in Brussels would not co-operate, as political differences split the lower Rhineland area and made circle co-operation in any field, let alone in economics, an impossibility. It was not the small-fry that wrecked federal systems, however expedient or voluntary their organization.[104]

This brought out the fundamental weakness of the Westphalian circle. It was excellent to have regional, multi-territorial units but only if they also paid attention to economic geography. This the Burgundian, Westphalian, Electoral Rhenish and Lower-Saxon circles failed to do, although further eastwards on the Elbe the position improved. The Dutch and Netherlands Spaniards contracted out just at a time when these circles were obtaining the legislative powers from Emperors and imperial

---

[103] Lennartz, *op. cit.*, pp. 7–10, 12, 19. Westphalian circle wardens operated between 1566 and 1752 with gaps in 1631–5, 1659–87, 1719–33.

[104] *Ibid.*, pp. 10, 13–14.

assemblies to become really effective in monetary and internal security. Instead of grouping circles around the main arteries of trade in the north-west, the lower Rhine and the lower and middle Weser, the existing territorial power structure fragmented the new regions. The circle system followed suit. Thus the Burgundian circle straddled parts of the Rhine and looked on to the Channel, taking its orders from Spain. The Westphalian circle was landlocked as East Frisia took more of an independent line and looked towards the Dutch in the south-west and the Lower-Saxon hinterland in the south-east. Based on Cologne town as the Westphalian circle's economic centre, the Rhenish hinterland was taken by the Electoral Rhenish circle, as well as the southern Ruhrlands under the Archbishops of Cologne. In the east it had a window on the middle Weser in Lippe, Minden and Schaumburg that upset the trading unity of the Lower-Saxon circle as well as the expansionist plans of Hesse and the Guelphs. The natural centre of the Westphalian circle was thus landlocked Münster. This was conducive to local trade but strangled long-distance trade, as Rhine and Weser were both fragmented and not united by circle as well as territorial boundaries.

The circle structure was thus not designed for economic expansion. It was there to discipline territories within the existing framework of an economic autonomy in the hands of local dynasties and authorities. As such it remained a seemingly weak but essential federal body that watched out for any transgressions of territorial power.

From 1581 each Westphalian mint displayed lists of legal and illegal tender for the public. In 1585 the circle coinage system was used to order a regional devaluation of 15 per cent on member territories' intermediate silver coins. In Cologne this affected the 18 heller coin, containing about three grammes of bullion silver. Circle coinage control was now as effective as it would ever be. From 1571 circle approval from one of four designated circle mints was needed for territories without internal gold and silver mines to mint their own coins. Thus when Lippe started minting again under Simon VI, he furnished himself with a privilege to mint from Rudolf II, circle permission, and a claim that Lippe had silver deposits for which he appointed a mining research team. From 1576 the circle assembly decreed that all mints must notify it in advance of proposed new mintings in an attempt to control the quantity of intrinsic-value to nominal-value coin.[105]

It was thus profitable to send representatives to circle coinage meetings even if the territory concerned had stopped minting, because its support would be canvassed for nominal-value coin quotas by those who were still minting. The circle coinage council of 1591 laid down that of all new coins minted only 10 per cent should be nominal-value small change. This rate varied from year to year but it was extremely restrictive and, as the events of the early 1620s showed, a harsh discipline that encouraged sporadic violation and violent chaos, but not a controlled level of inflation.

In 1604 a Westphalian circle coinage warden explained regional policy to the imperial assembly at Regensburg as the circle was caught between Turk tax arrears demands and pleas for compensation for Dutch and Spanish troop incursions. In 1617–18 all small-change minting was forbidden and circle coinage control in the following years saved the region from the worst effects of violent inflation.

Apart from checking inflation in local coins, the circle tried to control the influx of 'foreign' coins. Here the wardens had to act after the event, that is after the coins had come into their region and were causing a confidence crisis in local trade, for only over-valued coins needed to be dealt with. Thus Portuguese *crusaden* were over-valued in 1618 and had to be re-assessed. By 1627 the circle was ready to forbid foreign coins in an attempt to produce a viable local system of legal tender. In 1656 there was another ban on minting new small change for two years. From the 1660s onwards Westphalia began to co-operate with the Upper-Saxon money market in Leipzig. This gave tighter monetary control at circle and territorial level whilst at the same time allowing official inflation as Cologne devalued to come into line with Leipzig.[106]

In the later sixteenth and seventeenth centuries the member territories of the Westphalian circle made a real effort to control

---

[105] *Ibid.*, pp. 7–11. A. Falkmann, *Beiträge zur Geschichte des Fürstentums Lippe*, Lemgo and Detmold, 1857–1902, 5, pp. 368–78. O. Weerth, 'Der Bergbau bei Falkenhagen', *Lippische Mitteilungen*, 12, 1926, pp. 72–8.

[106] Lennartz, *op. cit.*, pp. 11, 14–17.

the regional money market with their own coins and mints in an attempt to attain power over their subjects' trade and bullion. Thus between 1567 and 1690 thirty-two territorial mints notified their activities to the circle wardens. They minted over 700,000 lb of silver which worked out at an intrinsic value of about 13 million tlrs of account, although the face value will have been considerably higher. Minting of gold was much more restricted and in the same period under 6,000 lb of the metal was used. Leading mints were Cologne town, Liège, Cambrai, Jülich and East Frisia. In the region around Lippe, Ravensberg, Schaumburg and Minden minted between 13,000 and 21,000 lb of silver each. Münster did very badly at under 6,000 lb of silver and Paderborn even worse at well under 2,000 lb. Lippe minted just under 3,000 lb of silver into talers between 1605 and 1616. This cost her just short of 70,000 tlrs and was a speculation that coincided with Simon VI's insolvency and the salvage operations of his eldest son.[107]

Lippe's coinage activity was sporadic and mainly important in the late sixteenth and seventeenth centuries.[108] It was preceded by a long period of local 'soft' currency debasement in the face of 'hard' coin. In Lippe the gulden was worth less than one mark in 1415, by 1500 it stood at 4 marks and by 1550 at 16 marks.[109] The coinage regulation of 1504 shows how Bernhard VII of Lippe tried to safeguard the interests of investors and annuity holders against this inflation of the mark. In that year he issued a coinage decree insisting that all annuities be paid at 18 schillinge to the gulden. In 1504 current rates were in fact $5\frac{1}{4}$ marks to the gulden, and Bernhard was trying to push the clock back to 1440, the last time that the gulden had been worth only 18 schillinge. The problem was caused by lending gulden and receiving payment in marks. It took the greater part of the sixteenth century for debts to be converted to hard coin, and for new contracts to stick to this reality.[110]

[107] *Ibid.*, pp. 68–78, 81. Staatsarchiv Detmold, L 92 Z 1a, Kammerrechnungen, sporadic entries of cost and profit from the mint.

[108] Lennartz, *op. cit.*, pp. 52–3.

[109] Stadtarchiv Lemgo, Urk. Regest no. 820, a table of Gulden to Mark/Schilling conversion rates for use of Lemgo town council in reckoning payments of annuities, 1415–1544, extended to 1552. Grote and Hölzermann, *op. cit.*, pp. 94–9, 121n. Staatsarchiv Detmold, Nachlass Preuss, the reichstaler was worth 15 marks in Lippe in 1592.

[110] *Lippische Regesten*, 2888. Grote and Hölzermann, *op. cit.*, pp. 94–5. Sixteenth-

After 1555 imperial and circle coinage decrees helped to push through a hard coinage policy, epitomized by reichstaler fixing in 1559. Despite the failures of the 1620s it was this hard rate against bullion which continued to be the ideal that imperial and circle coinage decrees tried to uphold. Having gradually got rid of the mark and gone over to the taler in the sixteenth century, there was no further advance in coinage affairs. The taler held good in the next two centuries despite the fact that all German territories debased their coins at some time or other. All still paid attention to a deflationary imperial taler policy.[111]

Taxation and cereals regulation helped to control local monetary supply. At least since the mid-sixteenth century this can be followed in Lippe government.[112] A degree of internal territorial economic planning thus preceded imperial and circle monetary supervision. The tragedy of imperial and circle *Tarifirung* was that it was basically deflationary.[113] Territories' reply to this was coinage delinquency. Thus a territory like Lippe, one-fivehundredth of the imperial whole, went in for its own minting of coin again for the first time in centuries. It tried to control its own money supply in the interests of its own investors, rulers, officials and Estates, like any budding state. No lessons seem to have been learnt from the great age of coinage racketeering that ensued between the collapse and re-establishment of the imperial taler standard, 1598–1623.[114]

In 1617 Lippe mintmaster Tecklenburg presented accounts for 13,900 tlrs of *Schreckenberger*, 18,837 tlrs of *Fürstengroschen* and 18,183 tlrs of *Dreier*. These were of approved circle quality. Yet Lippe had not the self-sufficiency, favourable balance of trade, tight frontier or tariffs to ward off debased coin or to take

---

[111] C. L. Lucius, 'Das im Römischen Reich abermals geschehene Geboth und Verboth der Guldiner', in *Neuer Müntz-Tractat*, Nuremberg, 1692–3, pp. 3–4, refers to Emperor Ferdinand I's *Reichsmünzordnung* of 1559 as still basic doctrine well over a century after its promulgation.

[112] Grote and Hölzermann, *op. cit.*, pp. 153–5. See E. Kittel, H. Stöwer and K. Sundergeld, 'Die älteren Lippischen Landesgesetze und Ordnungen', *Lippische Mitteilungen*, 26, 1957, pp. 48–78. *Lippische Landesverordnungen*, 1. H. Stöwer, *Landschatzregister*, Appendix 4.

[113] C. L. Lucius, 'Denen neuesten . . . Müntz-Mandaten', Nuremberg, 1692–3.

[114] Grote and Hölzermann, *op. cit.*, pp. 123–4, 157–9. Shaw, *op. cit.*, p. 207 lists Lippe as a coinage delinquent in 1608.

---

century practice of accepting new burghers by borrowing hard coin from them and then paying them annuities in debased marks.

up any quantity of it without noticeable losses to all from ruler to labourer.[115]

It is important to notice that it was not necessarily the small territories that caused coinage delinquencies, and certainly they could achieve quantitatively no great disruption to the German economy. The crises of the late 1650s to early 1690s were the fault of big delinquents like Austria and Brandenburg-Prussia, or of heavyweights like Galen of Münster, who issued bad coin under cover as Abbot of Corvey in this period.[116] The fact that there were so many autonomous territorial mints in the early modern Empire did not in itself imply a hopeless and chaotic coinage system, nor was imperial and circle coinage supervision at fault. It was much more serious that the few largest territories could issue bad coin, knowing that they could not be punished with effective economic sanctions by their territorial neighbours. It was not that the Empire had too many small territories to make its federal system work, but rather that it contained too many big territories. Underlying this was always a constricting deflationary economic policy.

The early modern imperial monetary system with all its welter of territorial coinages is often found to be too complicated to include in the main stream of German history. It is taken as yet another example of the 'weak' Empire, another problem that can thereby be dismissed. Yet this currency system was much less complicated than systems today: there was no paper money. Everything centred around the direct supply of gold, silver and copper into people's pockets to keep them consuming and contented, and to keep their trade, manufacture and war going. To do this territories did co-operate and coinage politics were a key factor in keeping territories active in federal, imperial government. Just as no proposals to abolish the Empire have been found among early modern reformers and publicists, so equally nothing has yet been found from contemporaries suggesting that territorial mints be abolished. Reform was a question of improving the existing system and not of altering its basis.

[115] Grote and Hölzermann, op. cit., pp. 157–93, especially p. 179. Stöwer, op. cit., illustration 4.

[116] See Lucius on the Guldiner crisis and his lists and illustrations of bad coin in Neuer Müntz-Tractat. The Lippe coins he deals with were good or modestly debased (25 per cent below imperial standard).

Part Five

Conclusion

XIV

<hr>

The Federal Bond of Empire

<hr>

> Already the Federal Empire was what the lawyers of the
> seventeenth century did not want to believe ... a State
> which had under it other states that were even partly
> independent in terms of international law. In other words
> it is a construction that should not be allowed in theory but
> which does exist in practice but can not be explained by
> using the traditional categories into which states are thought
> to fall.
>
> F. Dickmann in *Historische Zeitschrift*, 208 (1969), p. 144

THE basic problem of early modern German history is that
either studies have been made of the German states as entities
in their own right, or studies have been made showing the
increasing unreality of imperial power in the Holy Roman
Empire. These studies depend on two separate concepts of
German history from the fifteenth to the early nineteenth century. The first is the 'realist' view of individual territories rising
to statehood and sovereignty. The second is the 'idealist' view
of a declining imperial whole, that malingered from crisis to
crisis until Napoleon finally destroyed it.[1]

Our task has been to bring these two views together, and to
modify each by systematically examining specific sources relating to state and imperial-federal affairs.

Yet because of the lack of an early modern German capital
city with comprehensive central archives, the question of recon-
ciling the 'strong statist' with the 'weak imperialist' view of

[1] Cf. F. L. Carsten, *The Origins of Prussia*, London, 1954; *Princes and Parliaments in Germany*, London, 1959. H. J. Cohn, *The Government of the Rhine Palatinate*, Oxford, 1965. Contrast G. Barraclough, *The Origins of Modern Germany*,
Oxford, 1947. Barraclough, *The Medieval Empire*, London, 1950.

early modern German history can be stated only in a piecemeal way by examining the archives of each and every German state in turn. In order to have made a start in this essential and long-overdue task of reinterpreting German political history from the actual day-to-day records, the imperial county of Lippe in eastern Westphalia was chosen.

Lippe was a compact territory, remote from the centres of Habsburg imperial power. It was economically and socially backward, thus it did not produce any unusual state power of its own. It was small but not too insignificant in size and its government remained independent in home affairs until the twentieth century. The greater number of early modern German territories were much more like Lippe than they were like Austria, Brandenburg-Prussia or Württemberg, for example. Thus it is only from a study of such small territories as given generally here for the whole of Westphalia and specifically for Lippe that a full and true picture can be obtained of the effectiveness of the early modern Holy Roman Empire in Germany.

Using the evidence especially of unpublished materials from the county of Lippe we can now summarize our findings in answer to the question of how weak or effective the Holy Roman Empire was as an actual federal government that supervised home affairs for the majority of the states of early modern Germany.

The county of Lippe came under persistent demand to pay federal taxes that had been granted at imperial assemblies for which receipts are still extant. Lippe did not escape the jurisdiction of Habsburg commissars, Westphalian circle directors or Hessian and Guelph expansionist rulers.

The *Reichskammergericht* was essential to this process of federal supervision. It was much more than a law court. It functioned as the chief federal executive, dealing with fiscal, police and security matters, as well as private debt and bankruptcy. It was mainly due to the *Reichskammergericht* that *Fehde* disappeared from the Lippe region during the course of the sixteenth century.

The imperial assembly was essential to Lippe as a court of appeal, as a place where attempts could be made to play one large territory off against the other, thereby achieving continued local independence. This applied especially in the period after 1648. Lippe took a leading part in the Westphalian College of Counts which exercised a collective vote in the *Fürstenrat* of the perpetual imperial assembly.

The county paid careful attention to imperial and circle coinage politics and at least did not mint too debased a coinage in the financial crises of the 1620s and 1680s. Its rulers played a conservative rôle in economics and trade and followed federal orders. Here the Westphalian circle itself took an important part in acting as executive and intermediary between Lippe and the imperial assembly and courts.

The *Reichshofrat* dealt with inheritance disputes between members of the ruling Lippe dynasty in the seventeenth and eighteenth centuries, as well as feudal disputes between Lippe and Paderborn and constitutional squabbles over taxation between territorial nobles and towns.

The *Corpus Evangelicorum* took up the religious conflict between Calvinist Lippe and Jesuit Paderborn from the 1620s to the 1770s. It produced sufficient delay for the letter if not exactly the spirit of the Westphalian Peace to be upheld. That is, it prevented religion from once more destroying the constitution, for after 1648 the Catholic majority in the Empire was still on the offensive, as Lippe learnt to its cost in the affair over Kloster Falkenhagen.

Yet Lippe successfully countered recatholicization attempts by Charles V in 1547-8 and Ferdinand II in 1629-30. Lippe took these matters seriously, and appeared at every important imperial assembly and conference during the later sixteenth and seventeenth centuries.

During the whole period Lippe paid its *Kammerzieler* and brought on average one case every two years to the *Reichskammergericht*. Yet the county was at times threatened with distraint for debt by the Emperor's Fiscal but matters never went beyond this stage except under Leopold I, who made deals with *Armierte* circle directors for military support by farming out to them the federal tax arrears of the *Nichtarmierte*. Demands for arrears were at times without just cause. The territorial town of Lemgo was included as an imperial town in the imperial assessment of 1521. Until the 1660s Lippe had to employ federal lawyers to keep a case pending so that it should not suffer distraint for debt from this cause.

In 1542-3 and 1702-13 Lippe produced its own federal troop contingents within the imperial army to fight the Turks and French. At other times it paid money in lieu of troops. Federal demands were persistent and thus a main cause for rulers to develop Estates' assemblies from the 1530s onwards, as Lippe subjects had to provide the money that the rulers were responsible for paying to federal bodies.

A real weakness of providing only money and not troops was brought out during the seventeenth century when Lippe was exploited by imperial, Swedish, Münster, Brandenburg and Guelph troops. Exactions began in earnest under Tilly after 1623 and continued sporadically under various 'foreign' armies until the Peace of Ryswick in 1697. These war emergencies gave Lippe's rulers and Estates a chance to develop extraordinary taxation, traditionally levied on their tenantry in town and country for funding rulers' excessive debts and for the festivities of his family.

After 1698 the Count of Lippe raised his own federal troop contingent and put an end to military exactions, especially from Westphalian circle directors Brandenburg and Münster with the support of the Habsburgs. But the Estates in Lippe opposed the initial extra expense this entailed. The government had to rule by decree, for the Estates refused to grant money for a standing army in peacetime. There was no fear that the ruler would intimidate them with any soldiers. No such reports were found. The Estates had far too easy an access to the Emperor, *Reichshofrat* and *Reichskammergericht*, as well as to neighbouring territories, and no early modern Lippe ruler ever attempted violence against his Estates.

Owing to Estates' financial opposition, however, the rulers were on the verge of bankruptcy by the 1730s. From this they were saved in the long run by a return to Estates' participation in the granting, levying and assigning of taxes. Leading members of the Estates joined the government in at least a semi-official capacity as the *Landkasse* went into full operation from the later 1740s onwards. Thus by the time of the French Revolution Lippe was a model state with sound finances and with members of the Estates firmly entrenched, either in a passive state of tax freedom, or in a more active position as executive tax-exploiters of the tenantry.

During the sixteenth and seventeenth centuries Lippe adhered closely to *Kaiser, Reich, Kreis, Kammergericht* and *Hofrat*, whose at times conflicting demands necessitated ruler-Estates co-operation in internal Lippian affairs. For the Lippe documents disprove the view that the Holy Roman Empire in early modern times was an ineffective monstrosity. They also question whether in fact an age of absolutism ever existed for this territory. Above all, they show that no ruler in Lippe could for long afford to do without the consent of the Estates to his policies in a host of assemblies and committees which were called throughout the sixteenth, seventeenth and eighteenth centuries.

The political and economic seriousness of Thirty Years' War damage in Lippe has been exaggerated by taking at face value contemporary propaganda designed to ward off further tax demands. Damage there undoubtedly was. Farms were burnt out and the towns were forced to adapt their economies to the hand-to-mouth tactics of billeting and travelling armies. Yet the financial situation was serious before the war years, and the increase in debt during the war was due more to arrears on already existing pre-war debt than to increases of new debt, as there was little wartime credit to be had even in Lemgo, the financial capital of the county. Lippe had little public credit left by 1623 and the war years caused no change here. However, taxation was increased by the war and never decreased again. This benefited rulers, officials and Estates alike, which is at least partly reflected by the stone buildings that went up after 1648, as well as the recovery of court life in various dynastic households.

Lippe central and local governments never lost control over internal affairs. However high the demands of foreign troops of occupation, and those of the *Armierte* in the 1660s to 1690s seem to have been among the highest, the native civil government remained in control. This was largely due to leading members of the Estates co-operating well with chancellery and treasury officials. This applied especially to the 1630s and 1640s when minorities, regency and inheritance disputes set the members of the dynasty against each other, a serious matter whether or not there were occupation troops in the county. It was the skill of Estates' politicians and regular officials that saved the county perhaps from the same fate as Hoya, Diepholz or Schaumburg.

The existence of an independent territory like that of Lippe shows above all the greatest strength of the early modern Empire and the type of federalism that it advocated. In an age still based on property and privilege, the more split-up politics and administration was, the greater the number of people who had at least a chance to get into positions of real responsibility and power. This Empire allowed a very great deal of autonomy to its constituent territories and territorial Estates. No decisions could be wholly autocratic in every territory when there was a two-tiered system, usually watched over by Estates in the territories themselves and by their rulers acting as Estates in the Empire as a whole.

From our evidence we can say without doubt that relations between the county of Lippe and the Holy Roman Empire from the late fifteenth century to the early nineteenth do demonstrate the effectiveness (as shown in the case of one specific territory) of the Holy Roman Empire as a federal government in early modern Europe. This at least shows that our view of early modern German history must be revised. In real terms, therefore, the early modern Holy Roman Empire was something new, a product of fifteenth-century *Reichsreform* and of sixteenth-century German federalism entailed in the fusion of *Kaiser* and *Reich*.[2] Except in the venerable fields of myth and propaganda, this early modern Holy Roman Empire naturally had nothing in common with its forerunner of high medieval times, nor even anything more in common with its chaotic forerunner of later medieval times.[3] It was not a pale reflection of the past but a unique federal solution to the problem of government and

[2] Cf. revisions in H. Angermeier, *Königtum und Landfriede*, Munich, 1966. M. Heckel, 'Staat und Kirche', 'Autonomia und Pacis Compositio', and 'Parität', *Zeitschrift der Savigny-Stiftung für Rechtsgeschichte, Kanonistische Abteilung*, 1956–7, 1959, 1963. F. Dickmann, *Der Westfälische Friede*, Münster, 1965. W. Ebel, *Geschichte der Gesetzgebung in Deutschland*, Göttingen, 1958. W. Fürnrohr, *Der immerwährende Reichstag zu Regensburg*, Regensburg, 1963. C. Haase, *Das Ständische Wesen im Nördlichen Deutschland*, Göttingen, 1964 (an all too brief study modelled on F. L. Carsten's seminal *Princes and Parliaments*).

[3] The view of later medieval chaos has now been revised by Angermeier, *op. cit.*, pp. 3–14, who shows that the continuity between Hohenstaufen and post-Hohenstaufen German crown policies of law and order lay in the use of different means of achieving essentially the same ends.

society at a time when federal solutions were not generally effective or fashionable in large countries like Germany that claimed to be traditional monarchies or Empires.

It is this loose federal system that makes German history so hard to understand in the early modern period. There is no short cut to any national history here. The local elements prevail. They have an identity of their own. They are, however, still parts of a whole, but the way the records survive, as well as the looseness of the federal system, dictates that to understand the whole the parts have first and foremost to be studied in their own right. What has been attempted here must be done with the records of other early modern territories to verify the picture that has emerged from the state of Lippe, that the early modern imperial system provided effective federal government.

Appendix I

Emperors, and Ruling Lords and Counts of Lippe, Fifteenth to Eighteenth Centuries

Emperors

Maximilian I	1493–1519
(Interregnum	Jan.–May 1519)
Charles V	1519–1556
Ferdinand I	1556–1564
Maximilian II	1564–1576
Rudolf II	1576–1612
(Interregnum	Jan.–June 1612)
Matthias	1612–1619
(Interregnum	Mar.–Aug. 1619)
Ferdinand II	1619–1637
Ferdinand III	1637–1657
(Interregnum	April 1657 to Aug. 1658)
Leopold I	1658–1705
Joseph I	1705–1711
(Interregnum	April–Oct. 1711)
Charles VI	1711–1740

Rulers of Lippe

Bernhard VII	1429–1511
Simon V	1511–1536
(Regency	1536–1549)
Bernhard VIII	1549–1563
(Regency	1563–1579)
Simon VI	1579–1613

Simon VII	1613–1627
(Regency	1627–1631)
Simon Ludwig	1631–1636
(Regency—Simon Philip died before attaining the age of	
majority	1636–1650)
Johann Bernhard	1650–1652
Hermann Adolf	1652–1666
Simon Henrich	1666–1697
Friedrich Adolf	1697–1718
Simon Henrich Adolf	1718–1734

Appendix II

The Worms Reichsmatrikel (*federal tax-schedule of the Imperial Assembly*), *May 1521*[1]

This assessment formed the basis of the civil and military tax system of the early modern Holy Roman Empire of the German nation. It could be halved or doubled etc. according to imperial assembly decision, whilst still keeping fixed the proportion of tax in money, horsemen or footsoldiers that each territory was committed to pay to the federal, *Reich* whole. It was possibly one of the simplest, most long-lasting and impressive tax-systems to have ever been worked out. Each entry approximately stands for a separate German state or ruling family, but it is not a complete list of all early modern German territories and high jurisdictions. The system was thus neither perfect nor comprehensive, but those territories that did not or could not contribute were outweighed by those that did, or intended to pay their share of the federal burden. There are some discrepancies in names and spelling in the list (which has here been rendered where possible into English) as well as some unusual omissions and additions.

Assessment for the Roman campaign tax in horsemen and footsoldiers, as well as for upkeep of the Government, and for the Chamber Tribunal in money, 15–17 May 1521.

Horse	Foot		Money (in gulden)
Electors			
60	277	Mainz	600
60	277	Trier	600

[1] After Zeumer, *Quellenkunde* . . . , Document 181.

382

Horse	Foot		Money (in gulden)
60	277	Cologne	600
400	600	Bohemia	—
60	277	Palatinate	600
60	277	Saxony	600
60	277	Brandenburg	600

Archbishops

57	262	Magdeburg (with Halberstadt)	(500)
60	277	Salzburg	500
24	75	Besançon	120
36	150	Bremen (with town)	90

Bishops

36	202	Bamberg	450
45	208	Würzburg	500
2	13	Worms	60
18	60	Speyer	180
15	100	Strasburg	180
30	132	Eichstädt	240
21	100	Augsburg	240
14	60	Konstanz	120
14	28	Hildesheim	60
18	34	Paderborn	120
5	18	Chur	60
—	—	Halberstadt (see under Magdeburg)	120
5	24	Verden	60
34	169	Münster	325
6	36	Osnabrück	60
18	78	Passau	80
14	82	Freising	180
6	24	Chiemsee	60
12	60	Gurk	60
6	24	Seckau	60
5	19	Levant	60
7	42	Basel	60
—	225	(Bishop of Wallis)	—
9	31	Regensburg	70
6	6	Meissen	90
6	6	Naumburg	90

Horse	Foot		Money (in gulden)
6	15	Minden (with town)	60
2	13	Lübeck	60
50	205	Utrecht (with its towns of Utrecht, Deventer, Zwolle, Kampen and Ammersfoort)	325
9	42	Kammin	60
12	19	Schwerin	60
3	13	Geneva	60
22	82	Cambrai	120
19	43	Verdun	120
14	60	Lausanne	60
24	75	Metz	120
9	24	Toul	60
60	190	Liège	400
14	91	Trient	120
14	91	Brixen	120
6	6	Meersburg	150
5	15	Lebus	60
5	15	Brandenburg	60
5	15	Ratzeburg	60
5	15	Slesvig	60
9	33	Havelburg	80

Secular ruling princes

Horse	Foot		Money
60	277	King of Denmark for territories that belong to the German Empire	—
60	277	Duke William of Bavaria / Duke Louis of Bavaria	600
120	600	Archduke of Austria	900
120	600	Duke of Burgundy for territories that belong to the German Empire	900
45	208	Duke George of Saxony (Albertiner)	500
30	115	Duke Frederick of Bavaria's regent, the Palatine Wittelsbachs	250
24	75	Duke Louis of Bavaria, Count of Veldenz	160

Horse	Foot		Money (in gulden)
18	75	Duke John of Bavaria, Count of Sponnheim	120
45	270	Duke of Jülich-Berg	500
45	270	Duke of Cleves-Mark	500
45	208	Margrave Casimir of Brandenburg	500
35	164	Brunswick Guelphs	180
35	164	Brunswick Guelphs	300
12	—	Brunswick Guelphs	60
45	270	Duke of Pomerania and Stettin	500
40	67	Dukes of Mecklenburg	360
15	112	Duke of Lauenburg	180
—	—	Duke of Holstein	240
60	277	Duke of Lorraine	600
60	277	Landgrave Philip of Hesse	600
60	277	Duke of Württemberg	600
8	23	Margrave Bernhard of Baden	$67\frac{1}{2}$
8	23	Margrave Ernest of Baden	$67\frac{1}{2}$
19	48	Margrave Philip of Baden together with Gelderland	135
6	14	Landgrave of Leuchtenberg	100
9	10	Ruling princes of Anhalt	120
9	24	Count Hermann of Henneberg	120
9	24	Count William of Henneberg	120

Foreign ruling princes

Horse	Foot		Money
12	135	Duke of Maas	180
60	277	Duke of Savoy	600
30	94	Ruling Prince of Calin	60

Prelates

Horse	Foot		Money
14	46	Fulda	180
2	9	Hirschfeld	60
5	18	Kempten	180
1	4	Reichenau	60
4	18	Weissenburg	80
6	30	St Gallen	120
2	13	Saalfeld	120

Horse	Foot		Money (in gulden)
5	18	Elwangen	90
19	55	Master of the Teutonic Order	180
14	46	Master of the Knights of St John	120
4	18	Weingarten	120
4	67	Salmannsweiler	250
1	4	Kreuzlingen	60
6	19	Murbach	60
2	6	Walckenried-im-Harz	60
3	13	Schottern	90
2	20	Weissenau	120
4	18	St Blasius	90
5	22	Maulbronn	250
2	9	Corvey with town	120
2	18	Schöffenriedt	120
—	—	Backenried	120
2	10	Rittershausen	70
—	10	Stein-am-Rhein	70
4	18	Schaffhausen	120
4	18	Waldsachsen	120
3	22	Einsiedeln	120
1	8	Rockenburg	120
3	13	Ochsenhausen	155
2	6	Seltz	50
1	13	St Gilgen in Nuremberg	—
3	22	St Maximin	250
2	9	Hünoldhausen	60
2	10	Reckenhausen	60
1	4	St Johann in Turital	60
1	4	Gengenbach	90
1	10	Königsbronn	60
1	10	Rode	60
1	4	Marcktal	90
1	10	St Peter in the Black Forest	60
1	10	Priory of Odenheim	60
2	22	Stablo	120
1	10	Disidis	60
3	13	Rockenhausen	60
2	9	Kintzlingen	60
3	13	Elchingen	180
—	14	Irsee	60
2	9	Blanckenberg	60

Horse	Foot		Money (in gulden)
1	6	St George in Isny	75
1	4	Pfeffers	60
1	10	Abbot of St John	60
—	6	Petershausen in Konstanz	60
1	13	Abbot of Brunnen	—
1	3	Camburg	60
4	67	Keissheim	300
4	45	St Hemeran in Regensburg	160
2	34	Berchtesgarten	90
1	4	Minster in St Georgental	90
1	10	Mönchrode	60
4	45	St Cornelius	160
2	13	Werden/Westfalen	120
—	—	Hernnalbe	—
—	10	Auersberg	—
4	30	Prüm	50
2	18	Echternach	100

Abbesses

Horse	Foot		Money
1	10	Quedlinburg with town	180
2	13	Essen with town	120
—	10	Herford with town	60
2	18	Lower-minster in Regensburg	90
1	13	Upper-minster in Regensburg	90
1	10	Kauffungen	60
1	10	Lindau	90
1	10	Geringerode	—
2	10	Buchau	90
—	9	Rotenmünster	60
—	5	Hegbach	—
—	5	Gutenzell	—
—	55	Baindt	—

Commendories

Horse	Foot		Money
3	13	Koblenz	300
3	13	Alsace	300
3	13	Austria	300
3	13	Etsch region	300

Horse	Foot		Money (in gulden)
		Counts and lords	
2	—	Helfenstein	12
5	10	County Kirchberg (Fugger)	50
3	6	Dissen	30
8	45	Counts of Werdenberg	138
4	18	Counts of Lupfen	60
4	22	Montfort	68
8	45	Fürstenberg	138
2	9	Zimmern	30
1	4	Stoffel-Justingen	14
2	4	Gundelfingen	20
—	4	Eberstein	8
1	3	Geroldseck	6
8	45	Ottingen	138
—	—	Heideck	—
4	45	Rapolstein	114
3	10	Stauffen of Ernfels	38
1	9	Leo of Stauffen	24
2	9	Dirstein	30
2	13	Hohenfels and Reipoltskirch	38
2	9	Sultz	35
6	30	Hohenzöller	96
1	6	Brandis	18
8	45	Owners of the Sonnenberg lands	138
4	22	Truchsess of Waldburg	68
1	4	Castell	14
6	30	Wertheim	96
2	10	Reineck	32
6	30	Albrecht of Hohenlohe	96
2	12	Wolf of Hohenlohe	36
1	4	Owners of the von Weinsberg lands	14
2	10	Schenk Götz of Limburg	32
2	10	Schenk Christof of Limburg	32
2	4	Erbach	20
1	3	Schwarzenberg	12
3	9	Emich of Leiningen	36
2	9	Wecker of Leiningen	30
12	30	Philip of Hanau	—
4	12	Hanau for Lichtenberg	50
—	—	Hanau for Mintzenberg	135

Horse	Foot		Money (in gulden)
30	135	Nassau-Bredau and Tilnburg	460
3	10	Nassau-Wiesbaden and Istein	38
2	12	Nassau-Saarbrücken	40
6	30	Nassau-Weilburg	100
1	4	Nassau-Bilstein	14
4	13	Königstein and Epstein	60
6	30	Isenburg	100
2	8	Nieder-Isenburg with Nymagen and Salm	30
—	—	Metsch and Polheim	—
2	10	Virnberg	32
1	3	Reineck	12
4	20	Philip of Solms	70
3	16	Bernhard of Solms	56
1	—	Wynnenberg	6
3	12	Mörs and Rodemach	45
4	27	Arburg	78
—	—	Finstingen (vacant)	—
—	—	Sarwerden and Lare	—
3	12	Rheingrafen	45
1	4	Oberstein and Falkenstein	14
1	1	Oberstein of Rucksingen	8
2	4	Neuenar	20
3	22	Hurn	62
3	13	Seyne	46
4	12	Bitsch of Liechtenberg	50
1	3	Bitsch and Oschsenstein	14
1	—	Tengen	6
3	12	Rapin	42
12	45	Hardeck	162
1	—	Ber of Hohenstein	6
2	8	Ernest of Hohenstein	6
8	34	Wolkenstein	120
8	34	Schauenberg in the region of the Ens	120
—	—	Sargans	—
10	45	Mansfeld	155
3	12	Stolberg	45
2	—	Beichlingen	15
1	4	Barby and Mulingen	22
3	13	Gleichen	45
1	5	Balthasar of Schwarzburg	16

Horse	Foot		Money (in gulden)
4	14	Gunther of Schwarzburg	53
2	10	Heinrich of Schwarzburg	33
2	12	Gera	30
1	—	Plesse	6
1	3	Reuss von Plauen	12
4	12	Wied-Runkel	48
2	9	Löwenstein	30
2	—	Reinstein	12
20	135	Frisia	390
8	45	East-Frisia (Emden)	138
4	18	Lippe	60
4	30	Oldenburg	84
2	8	Hoya	28
2	10	Westerberg-Leiningen	32
3	16	Waldeck	50
3	13	Losenstein	44
1	4	Diepholz	14
—	—	Landsberg	—
2	9	Steinfurt	30
6	27	Beuten	90
6	27	Bronkhorst	90
1	4	Wittichenstein	14
2	6	Spiegelberg	24
—	—	Reichenstein	—
2	9	Deckelnburg	30
—	—	Schauenburg in Westphalia	—
1	4	Wunsdorf	14
2	6	Ortenberg	24
4	27	Rietberg	78
4	18	Hagen	60
1	2	Leiseneck	10
4	18	Bergen	60
2	9	Salm	30
1	3	Falkenstein	12
—	—	Iselstein	—
2	4	Schönenberg	20
2	9	Degenberg	30
2	—	Owner of Someruff	12
6	27	Dietrich of Manderscheid	90
4	13	Johann of Manderscheid	50
1	4	Manderscheid-Keil	14
2	6	Reifferscheid	24

Horse	Foot		Money (in gulden)
10	45	Ysselstein	150
10	47	Bergen and Walen	194
1	4	Heben	14
1	2	Wildenfels	10
1	4	Dautenberg	14
1	1	Tuwingen	8
6	25	Blankenberg	86
2	4	Krichingen	20
—	10	Rogendorf	20
3	10	Kungseck of Allendorf	32
—	5	Owner of Kungseckerberg	10
4	20	Mersberg	64
1	4	Raniss	14
1	4	Pyrmont	14
—	—	Knights of the Shield of St George in Hegau	—
10	45⎫	Knights of Friedberg and	
4	18⎭	Geilnhausen	—
—	—	Note: Knights who hold fiefs of the Empire	—
—	—	Gortz	—
—	—	Those who have recently become counts and lords, such as Rogendorf, Königseck, Dietrichstein, Ungnad and others	—

Free and imperial towns

20	112	Regensburg	120
40	250	Nuremberg	600
10	90	Rothenburg ob der Tauber	180
4	18	Weissenburg	50
4	36	Schwebischen Werde	90
4	36	Winsheim	180
5	36	Schweinfurt	120
3	13	Wimpfen	130
6	60	Heilbron	240
10	80	Schwebisch-Hall	325
10	80	Nördlingen	325
5	58	Dinkelsbühl	240
29	150	Ulm	600

Horse	Foot		Money (in gulden)
25	150	Augsburg	500
2	13	Giengen	60
1	9	Bopfingen	50
2	18	Aalen	70
5	45	Gemund	150
10	67	Esslingen	325
6	55	Reutlingen	180
2	18	Weil	120
3	40	Pfullendorf	75
4	68	Kaufbeuren	90
10	78	Uberlingen	325
3	18	Wangen	110
4	22	Isny	100
2	18	Leutkirch	90
10	67	Memmingen	325
3	36	Kempten	120
—	10	Buchorn	60
4	67	Ravensburg	180
6	55	Bibrach	180
6	72	Lindau	200
6	72	Konstanz	125
10	180	Basel	325
40	225	Strasburg	550
3	18	Keisersberg	60
5	39	Colmar	180
7	58	Schlettstett	180
6	27	Mulhausen in Alsace	120
3	122	Rottweil	180
8	36	Hagenau	180
2	22	Weissenburg	125
3	31	Obern-Ehenheim	110
1	9	Rossheim	60
3	99	Speyer	325
10	78	Worms	325
20	140	Frankfurt	500
—	22	Friedberg	90
3	31	Geilnhausen	70
—	31	Wetzlar	40
30	322	Cologne	600
20	90	Aachen	260
40	250	Metz	500
7	61	Toul	120

Horse	Foot		Money (in gulden)
10	45	Verdun	120
—	45	Offenburg (Gengenbach, Zell)	150
2	22	Landau	100
—	36	Gengenbach	—
—	22	Zell	—
7	45	Schaffhausen	90
2	9	Kaufmanns Saabrück	120
7	58	Besançon	180
21	177	Lübeck	550
20	120	Hamburg	325
20	100	Dortmund	180
5	50	Niederwesel	180
—	78	Muhlhausen in Thuringia	180
—	78	Nordhausen	180
—	130	Gosslar	205
20	120	Soest	240
7	58	Brakel	60
3	22	Warberg	60
4	22	Lemgo	60
1	9	Durkheim	60
—	15	Verden	60
—	—	Münster in St Georgental	—
3	20	Theuern	120
1	13	Herford	60
2	18	Cambrai	280
2	18	Dussberg	120
—	165	Danzig	350
—	82	Elbingen	120
—	57	St Gallen	180
—	—	Göttingen	120

SIMPLUM Totals

4,202	20,063		51,269

Appendix III

German States and Families in the Imperial Assembly, 1792
(numbered according to voting order within each College)[1]

(1) *College of Electors*

1 Archbishop of Mainz
2 Archbishop of Trier
3 Archbishop of Cologne
4 King of Bohemia

5 Palatine Elector
6 Elector of Saxony
7 Elector of Brandenburg
8 Duke of Brunswick-
    Lüneburg

(2) *College of Ruling Princes*
(A) *Ecclesiastical Bench*

1 Duke of Austria
2 Duke of Burgundy
3 Archbishop of Salzburg
4 Archbishop of Besançon
5 High-master of the
    Teutonic Order
        Bishops of:
6 Bamberg
7 Würzburg
8 Worms
9 Eichstädt
10 Speyer
11 Strasburg

12 Konstanz
13 Augsburg
14 Hildesheim
15 Paderborn
16 Freising
17 Regensburg
18 Passau
19 Trient
20 Brixen
21 Basel
22 Münster
23 Osnabrück
24 Liège

[1] After Zeumer, *Quellenkunde* . . . . , Document 220.

25 Lübeck
26 Chur
27 Abbot of Fulda
28 Abbot of Kempten
29 Prior of Elwangen
30 Master of the Knights of St John
31 Prior of Berchtesgaden

32 Prior of Weissenburg
33 Abbot of Prüm
34 Stablo
35 Corvey
36 Curial vote of the Prelates of Swabia
37 Curial vote of the Prelates of the Rhineland

The curial votes are exercised collectively—
36 by (a) the Abbots and Prelates of

i Salmannsweiler
ii Weingarten
iii Ochsenhausen
iv Elchingen
v Irsee
vi Urspring
vii Kaisersheim
viii Roggenburg
ix Roth
x Weissenau
xi Schuffenried
xii Marchthal

xiii Petershausen
xiv Wettenhausen
xv Zwifalten
xvi Gengenbach
xvii Neresheim
and (b) the Abbesses of
xviii Hegbach
xix Gutenzell
xx Rotenmünster
xxi Baindt
xxii Söflingen
xxiii St George in Isny

37 by

i Kaisersheim
ii Commendory Koblenz
iii Commendories Alsace and Burgundy
iv Odenheim and Bruchsal
v Werden
vi St Ulrich and St Afra in Augsburg
vii St George in Isny (cf. 36 xxiii)
viii St Corneli-Münster
ix St Emmeran in Regensburg

x Essen
xi Buchau
xii Quedlinburg
xiii Herford
xiv Gernrode
xv Niedermünster in Regensburg
xvi Obermünster in Regensburg
xvii Burscheid
xviii Gandersheim
xix Thorn

(B) *Secular Bench*

1 Bavaria
2 Magdeburg

3 Palatinate-Lautern
4 Palatinate-Simmern

5 Palatinate-Neuburg
6 Bremen
7 Palatinate-Zweibrücken
8 Palatinate-Veldenz
9 Saxony-Weimar
10 Saxony-Eisenach
11 Saxony-Coburg
12 Saxony-Gotha
13 Saxony-Altenburg
14 Brandenburg-Onolzbach
15 Brandenburg-Culmbach
16 Brunswick-Celle
17 Brunswick-Calenberg
18 Brunswick-Grubenhagen
19 Brunswick-Wolfenbüttel
20 Halberstadt
21 Vorpommern
22 Hinterpommern
23 Verden
24 Mecklenburg-Schwerin
25 Mecklenburg-Güstrow
26 Württemberg
27 Hesse-Kassel
28 Hesse-Darmstadt
29 Baden-Baden
30 Baden-Durlach
31 Baden-Hochberg
32 Holstein-Glückstadt
33 Saxony-Lauenburg
34 Minden
35 Holstein-Oldenburg
36 Savoy

37 Leuchtenberg
38 Anhalt
39 Henneberg
40 Schwerin
41 Camin
42 Ratzeburg
43 Hirschfeld
44 Nomeny
45 Mömpelgard
46 Arenberg
47 Hohenzollern
48 Lobkowitz
49 Salm
50 Dietrichstein
51 Nassau-Hadamar
52 Nassau-Dillenburg
53 Auersberg
54 East-Frisia
55 Fürstenberg
56 Schwarzenberg
57 Liechtenstein
58 Thurn und Taxis
59 Schwarzburg
60 Curial vote of the Wetterau
counts
61 Curial vote of the Swabian
counts
62 Curial vote of the
Franconian counts
63 Curial vote of the
Westphalian counts

60 by
  i Nassau-Usingen
  ii Nassau-Weilburg
  iii Nassau-Saarbrücken
  iv Solms-Braunfels
  v Solms-Lich
  vi Solms-Hohen-Solms
  vii Solms-Rödelheim
  viii Solms-Laubach
  ix Isenburg-Birstein
  x Isenburg-Büdingen-

Meerholz-
Wächtersbach
xi Stollberg-Gedern-
Ortenberg
xii Stollberg-Stollberg
xiii Stollberg-Wernigerode
xiv Sayn-Wittgenstein-
Berleburg
xv Sayn-Wittgenstein-
Wittgenstein

xvi Wild- und Rheingraf zu
Grumbach
xvii Wild- und Rheingraf zu
Rheingrafenstein
xviii Leiningen-Hartenburg
xix Leiningen-Heidesheim
and Leiningen-
Guntersblum

xx Westerburg Chris-
tophsche Linie
xxi Westerburg Georgische
Linie
xxii Reussen von Plauen
xxiii Schönburg
xxiv Ortenburg
xxv Crichingen

61 by
i Fürst of Fürstenberg
as Count of Heiligen-
berg and Werdenberg
ii Gefürstete Aebtissin zu
Buchau
iii Commendories Alsace
and Burgundy for
Commendory
Aschenhausen
iv Oettingen
v Austria for Menthor
vi Bavaria for Helfenstein
vii Schwarzenberg for
Klettgau and Sulz
viii Königsegg
ix Waldburg
x Baden-Baden for
Eberstein

xi von der Leyen for
Hohen-Geroldseck
xii Fugger
xiii Austria for Hohenems
xiv Traum for Eglof
xv Abbot of St Blasi for
Bondorf
xvi Stadion for Thannhausen
xvii Taxis for Eglingen
xviii von Khevenhüller of
their own persons
xix Kufstein
xx von Colloredo of his
own person
xxi Harrach
xxii Sternberg
xxiii Neipperg
xxiv Hohenzollern

62 by
i Hohenlohe
ii Castell
iii Erbach
iv Löwenstein for Wertheim
v Limburg allodial heirs
vi Nostiz for Reineck
vii Schwarzenberg for Seins-
heim or Schwarzenberg
viii Wolfstein allodial heirs,
namely Hohenlohe-
Kirchberg and Giech
ix Schönborn for Reichelsberg
x Schönborn for Wiesentheid

xi von Windischgrätz for
their own persons
xii von Rosenberg for their
own persons
xiii von Starhemberg (senior
line) for their own
persons
xiv von Wurmbrand for
their own persons
xv von Griech for their own
persons
xvi Grävenitz
xvii von Pückler for their
own persons

63 by
  i Ansbach for Sayn-
      Altenkirchen
  ii Kirchberg for Sayn-
      Hachenburg
  iii Prussia for Tecklenburg
  iv Wied-Runkel for Ober-
      Grafschaft Wied
  v Wied-Neuwied
      (Director of this
      curial college)
  vi Hesse-Kassel and Lippe-
      Bückeburg for
      Schaumburg
  vii Holstein-Gottorp-
      Oldenburg
  viii Lippe
  ix Bentheim
  x King of England for
      Hoya
  xi King of England for
      Diepholz
  xii King of England for
      Spiegelberg
  xiii Löwenstein for Virne-
      burg
  xiv Kaunitz for Rietberg
  xv Waldeck for Pyrmont

  xvi Törring for Gronsfeld
  xvii Aspremont for Reck-
      heim or Reckum
  xviii Salm for Anholt
  xix Metternich for Win-
      nenburg and Bilstein
  xx Anhalt-Bernburg-
      Schaumburg for
      Holzapfel
  xxi Sternberg for Blanken-
      heim and Gerolstein
  xxii Plettenberg for Wittern
  xxiii Limburg-Stirum for
      Gehmen
  xxiv Wallmoden for Gauborn
      and Neustadt
  xxv Quadt for Wickerad
  xxvi Ostein for Mylendorf
  xxvii Nesselrode for Reichen-
      stein
  xxviii Mark for Schleiden
  xxix Schaesberg for Kerpen
      and Lommersum
  xxx Salm-Reifferscheid for
      Dyck
  xxxi Mark for Saffenburg
  xxxii Platen for Hallermünde
  xxxiii Sinzendorf for Reineck

(3) *College of Towns*

(A) *Rhineland Bench*
  1 Cologne
  2 Aachen
  3 Lübeck
  4 Worms
  5 Speyer
  6 Frankfurt-am-Main
  7 Goslar
  8 Bremen
  9 Hamburg
  10 Mühlhausen
  11 Nordhausen
  12 Dortmund
  13 Friedberg
  14 Wetzlar

(B) *Swabian Bench*
  1 Regensburg
  2 Augsburg
  3 Nuremberg
  4 Ulm

5 Eslingen	21 Windsheim
6 Reutlingen	22 Kaufbeuren
7 Nördlingen	23 Weil
8 Rothenburg	24 Wangen
9 Schwäbisch-Hall	25 Isny
10 Rottweil	26 Pfullendorf
11 Uberlingen	27 Offenburg
12 Heilbronn	28 Leutkirch
13 Schwäbisch-Gemünd	29 Wimpfen
14 Memmingen	30 Weissenburg-im-Nordgau
15 Lindau	31 Giengen
16 Dinkelsbühl	32 Gengenbach
17 Biberach	33 Zell-am-Hammersbach
18 Ravensburg	34 Buchhorn
19 Schweinfurt	35 Aalen
20 Kempten	36 Bopfingen

For further information and bibliographies on these states and families, consult *Territorien Ploetz*, vols 1 and 3; *Meyers Lexikon*; and *Der Grosse Brockhaus*.

Maps

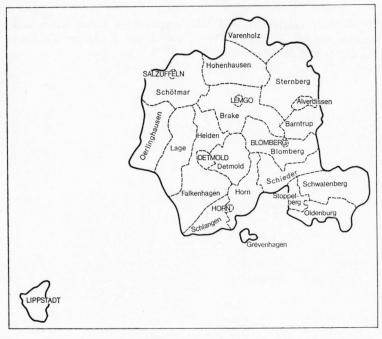

<small>MAP 1</small> *The county of Lippe in 1600*

MAP 2　*The region around Lippe in the seventeenth century*

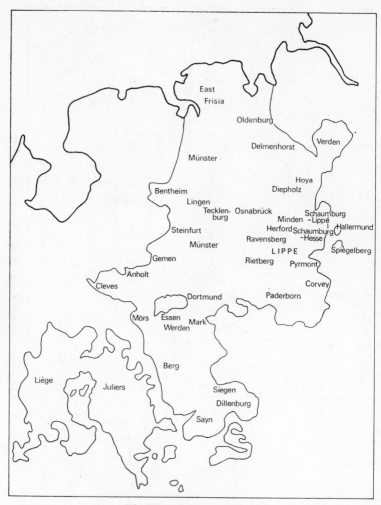

MAP 3 *The Westphalian Circle, 1512–1806*

MAP 4   *The Imperial Circles of 1512*

Bibliography

Sources

Staatsarchiv Detmold
L 1, 4, 6, 8, 9, 10, 11, 12, 16, 28, 29, 37, 41, 41a, 42–9, 52, 56–60, 63, 74, 82, 92, 111, 114. D 71.
Repertoria Knoch, Findbücher, Handschriftensammlung, Bibliothek.

Stadtarchiv Lemgo
Kämmerei, Konkurse, Landkasse, Stadtobligationen und Renten, Urkunden Regest.
Repertoria Hoppe.

St Andrews University Library
German thesis collection.
Lippische Mitteilungen.

Books and articles

ABEL, W., Geschichte der deutschen Landwirtschaft, Stuttgart, 1962.

ADERS, G. and RICHTERING, H., Das Staatsarchiv Münster und seine Bestände, 2, 'Gerichte des Alten Reiches', 2 vols, Reichskammergericht, A–Z, Münster, 1966–8.

Aller des H. R. R. Reichstäge, Abschiede und Satzungen, Frankfurt-am-Main, 1720.

ANGERMANN, G., 'Die Stellung des nordöstlichen Westfalens in der Landfriedensbewegung zwischen 1300 und 1350', Lippische Mitteilungen, 24, 1955.

ANGERMEIER, H., Königtum und Landfriede im deutschen Spätmittelalter, Munich, 1966.

ANON., *Der westpfälische Bauernstand*, Elberfeld, 1843.

ANTZE, C., *Gegenbeleuchtung (contra Clostermeier) im Auftrag der Landstände von Ritterschaft und Städten (bei der Bundesversammlung)*, Minden and Bielefeld, 1819.

ARNDT, J., 'Hofpfalzgrafen-Register', 1, ed. for *Herold*, Neustadt an der Aisch, 1964.

BADER, K. S., 'Die Rechtsprechung des Reichshofrats und die Anfänge des territorialen Beamtenrechts', *Zeitschrift der Savigny-Stiftung für Rechtsgeschichte*, Germanistische Abteilung 65, 1947.

——, *Der deutsche Südwesten*, Stuttgart, 1950.

——, 'Territorienbildung und Landeshoheit', *Blätter für deutsche Landesgeschichte*, 90, 1953.

BADING, T., *Die innere Politik Christof Bernhards von Galen*, Munster, 1912.

BÄR, M., *Leopold von Wedels Beschreibung seiner Reisen*, Stettin, 1895.

——, *Abriss einer Verwaltungsgeschichte des Regierungsbezirks Osnabrück*, Hanover, 1901.

——, *Jobst von Walthausen*, Hildesheim, 1923.

BARGE, F. W., *Die Grafschaft Lippe im Zeitalter der Grafen Friedrich Adolph und Simon Henrich Adolph 1697–1734*, Bonn, 1953 (partly published in *Lippische Mitteilungen*).

BARRACLOUGH, G., *The Origins of Modern Germany*, Oxford, 1947.

——, *The Medieval Empire*, London, 1950.

BAUERMANN, J., 'Die Eigenhörigenkonskription des Amtes Reckenberg', *Westfalen*, 21, 1936.

BAUMGART, P., 'Zur Geschichte der Juden im absoluten Staat', *Vierteljahrschrift für Sozial- und Wirtschaftsgeschichte*, 51, 1964.

BENECKE, G., 'Northwest Germany, Lippe, and the Empire in Early Modern Times' (typescript), St Andrews University thesis, 3 vols, 1970.

——, 'Ennoblement and privilege in early modern Germany', *History*, October 1971.

——, 'Relations between the Holy Roman Empire and the Counts of Lippe as an example of early modern German federalism', *Westfälische Forschungen*, 1972.

——, 'The problem of death and destruction in Germany during the Thirty Years' War', *European Studies Review*, 2, 1972.

——, 'Labour relations and peasant society', *History*, October 1973.

BERENTELG, H., *Der Schmalkaldische Krieg in Nordwestdeutschland*, Münster, 1908.

BERGHAUS, P., *Währungsgrenzen des westfälischen Oberwesergebietes im Spätmittelalter*, Hamburg, 1951.

BEUTIN, L., 'Nordwestdeutschland und die Niederlande seit dem dreissigjährigen Krieg', in *Gesammelte Schriften*, Cologne, 1963.

BIEDERBICK, A., *Der deutsche Reichstag zu Regensburg 1714–24*, Bonn, 1937.

BORGMANN, R., 'Die Türkensteuerliste des Märkischen Amtes Bochum vom Jahre 1542', *Westfalen*, 21, 1936.

BORNHAK, C., *Deutsche Verfassungsgeschichte*, Stuttgart, 1934.

BÖRSTING, H., *Geschichte des Bistums Münster*, Bielefeld, 1951.

BRAND, A., *Die direkten Staatssteuern im Fürstbistum Paderborn*, Münster, 1912.

BRANDIS, R., *Die historische Entwicklung und die heutige Stellung des westfälischen Amtmanns*, Göttingen, 1928.

BRAUBACH, M., *Die Bedeutung der Subsidien für die Politik im spanischen Erbfolgekriege*, Bonn, 1923.

——, 'Holland und die Geistlichen Staaten', *Historisches Jahrbuch der Görresgesellschaft*, 55, 1935.

BRAUER, G., *Die hannoversch-englischen Subsidienverträge 1702–48*, Aalen, 1962.

BRINKMANN, C., 'Charles II and the Bishop of Münster in the Anglo-Dutch War of 1665–6', *English Historical Review*, 21, 1906.

BRINKMANN, R., *Studien zur Verfassung der Meiergüter in Paderborn*, Münster, 1907.

Brockhaus, 16th ed., Wiesbaden, 1955.

BRUNNER, H., *Grundzüge der deutschen Rechtsgeschichte*, Leipzig, 1912.

BRUNNER, O., *Land und Herrschaft*, Vienna, 1939 (4th ed., 1959).

——, 'Deutsches Reich und deutsche Lande', *Zeitschrift für deutsche Geisteswissenschaften*, 3, 1940.

——, *Sozialgeschichtliche Forschungsaufgaben*, Vienna, 1948.

BÜLOW, H. W. V., *Gegenwärtiger Reichstag*, 2 vols, 1792.

——, *Über Geschichte und Verfassung des Corporis Evangelicorum*, 1795.

BUSSE, H. E. 'Der unsterbliche Grimmelshausen', *Badische Heimat*, 22, 1935.

BUTTERWECK, W., *Die Geschichte der Lippischen Landeskirche*, Schötmar, 1926.

CARSTEN, F. L., *The Origins of Prussia*, London, 1954.

——, *Princes and Parliaments in Germany*, London, 1959.

——, 'The causes of the decline of the German Estates' in *Studies presented to the International Commission for the history of representative and parliamentary institutions*, 24, Louvain, 1961.

—— (ed.), *The New Cambridge Modern History*, vol. 5, London, 1961.

CASSER, P., 'Der niederrheinisch-westfälische Reichskreis 1500–1806', *Der Raum Westfalen*, 2, part 2, Münster, 1934.

CLOSTERMEIER, C. G., *Kritische Beleuchtung der von Seiten der Landstände . . . der Bundesversammlung übergebenen Druckschrift*, Lemgo, 1817.

COHAUSZ, A., 'Herford als Reichsstadt und papstunmittelbares Stift' *42 Jahresbericht Historischer Verein Ravensberg*, 1928.

——, 'Ein Jahrtausend geistliches Damenstift Herford', *Herforder Jahrbuch*, 1, 1960.

COHN, H. J., *The Government of the Rhine Palatinate in the 15th century*, Oxford, 1965.

—— (ed.), *Government and Society in Reformation Europe*, London, 1970.

COLLENBERG, R. v., 'Die deutsche Reichsritterschaft', in *Genealogisches Handbuch des Adels* (Glücksburg), 1956.

CONRAD, H., *Liegenschaftsübereignung und Grundbucheintragung in Köln während des Mittelalters*, Weimar, 1935.

—— (ed.), *Recht und Verfassung des Reichs in der Zeit Maria Theresias*, Cologne, 1964.

——, *Deutsche Rechtsgeschichte, 1495–1806*, vol. 2, Karlsruhe, 1966.

CONTZEN, H., *Die Lippische Landkasse*, Münster, 1910.

——, 'Von den lippischen Finanzen im 18. Jahrhundert', *Lippische Mitteilungen*, 9, 1911.

COPEI, F., 'Lemgo und das Reich', *Lippische Mitteilungen*, 15, 1935.

CULEMANN, E. A. F., *Mindische Geschichte*, Minden, 1747–8.

——, *Sammlung der vornehmsten Landesverträge des Fürstentums Minden*, Minden, 1748.

——, *Ravensbergische Merckwürdigkeiten*, 2, Minden, 1749.

——, 'Geographische Beschreibung der Grafschaft Ravensberg (1745)' (ed. G. Engel), *54 Jahresbericht Historischer Verein Ravensberg*, 1948.

DAHL, W., *Die innere Politik Franz Arnolds von Wolff-Metternich zur Gracht, Bischofs von Münster und Paderborn, 1707–18*, Münster, 1910.

DEBES, E., *Das Amt Wartburg*, Jena, 1926.

DEMANDT, K. E., *Geschichte des Landes Hessen*, Kassel, 1959.

DEWALL, H. V., 'Kurzer Abriss der Lippischen Militärgeschichte 1664–1804', *Lippische Mitteilungen*, 31, 1962.

DICKMANN, F., *Der Westfälische Friede*, Münster, 1959.

DIECK, A., 'Lebensmittelpreise in Mitteleuropa und im Vorderen Orient vom 12. bis 17. Jahrhundert', *Zeitschrift für Agrargeschichte und Agrarsoziologie*, 3, 1955.

DISSMANN, T., *Die Landstände der alten Grafschaft Schaumburg*, Kiel, 1938.

DOHMKE, W., *Die Viril-Stimmen im Reichsfürstenrath 1495–1654*, Breslau, 1882.

DONNERBERG, E., *Der Besitz des ehem. Klosters Iburg*, Münster, 1912.

DONOP, W. G. L. V., *Historisch-geographische Beschreibung der Fürstlich Lippischen Landen in Westphalen*, Lemgo, 1790.

DROEGE, G., 'Die finanziellen Grundlagen des Territorialstaates', *Vierteljahrschrift für Sozial- und Wirtschaftsgeschichte*, 53, 1966.

DROOP, F. (ed.), *Annette von Droste-Hülshoff, Ausgewählte Werke*, Berlin, 1925.

EBEL, W., *Geschichte der Gesetzgebung in Deutschland*, 2nd ed., Göttingen, 1958.

EBENGREUTH, A. LUSCHIN V., *Allgemeine Münzkunde und Geldgeschichte*, 2nd ed., Munich, 1926.

EGER, A., *Vermögenshaftung und Hypothek nach fränkischem Recht*, Breslau, 1903.

EHRENKROOK, H. F. V., *Genealogisches Handbuch des Adels*, 1, *Fürstliche Häuser*, Glücksburg, 1951.

EICKHOFF, 'Osnabrückisch-rhedischer Grenzstreit 1524–65', *Osnabrücker Mitteilungen*, 22, 1897.

ELSAS, M. J., *Umriss einer Geschichte der Preise und Löhne in Deutschland*, 1–2, Leiden, 1936–49.

Encyclopaedia Britannica, 3rd ed., Edinburgh, 1797.

ENDEMANN, W., 'Von dem alten Reichskammergericht', *Zeitschrift für deutschen Civilprozess*, 18, Part 2, 1893.

ENGEL, G., *Politische Geschichte Westfalens*, Cologne, 1968.

ENGELBERT, G., 'Einungen und Landfriedensbündnisse des Spätmittelalters', *Kunst und Kultur im Weserraum*, 1–2, Münster, 1966.

—— (ed.), *Fürstin Pauline. Ihr Leben und Wirken*, Detmold, 1969.

ERNST, V., *Die Entstehung des Niederen Adels*, Stuttgart, 1916.

——, *Die Entstehung des deutschen Grundeigentums*, Stuttgart, 1905.

Europäische Stammtafeln, 1, Marburg, 1960.

Extract Auss allen Reichs- vnnd Deputations- Abschieden, Mainz, 1597.

FABER, A. (C. L. Leucht), 'Europäische Staatskanzlei' (available in Library of Historical Institute, Senate House, London University).

FALKMANN, A., *Beiträge zur Geschichte des Fürstentums Lippe*, 1–6, Lemgo and Detmold, 1857–1902.

FEINE, H. E., *Besetzung der Reichsbistümer*, Leipzig, 1921.

FELLNER, R., *Die Fränkische Ritterschaft von 1495–1524*, Berlin, 1904.

FLASKAMP, F., 'Die Anfänge der Wiedenbrücker Patrizierfamilie Wippermann', *Die Glocke*, 30 June 1954.

——, 'Westfälische Bauernhöfe', *Westfälische Forschungen*, 13, 1960.

—— (ed.), *Die Chronik des Ratsherrn Andreas Kothe*, Gütersloh, 1962.

——, 'Eine abseitige Statistik der Grafschaft Lippe', *Lippische Mitteilungen*, 32, 1963.

FRANK, K. F. V., *Standeserhebungen und Gnadenakte für das Deutsche Reich und die österreichischen Erblande bis 1806*, 1, A to E, Schloss-Senftenegg, 1967.

FRANZ, G., *Der dreissigjährige Krieg und das Deutsche Volk*, 3rd ed., Stuttgart, 1961.

——, *Quellen zur Geschichte des deutschen Bauernstandes in der Neuzeit*, Munich, 1963.

——, *Der Deutsche Bauernkrieg*, Munich, 1965.

FRECKMANN, J., *Die Capitulatio Perpetua und ihre Verfassungsgeschichtliche Bedeutung für das Hochstift Osnabrück 1648–50*, Münster, 1906.

FRIEDENSBERG, F., *Münzkunde und Geldgeschichte der Einzelstaaten*, Munich, 1926.

FRITZEMEIER, B., *Die Grafschaft Lippe unter der Regierung Simon Augusts 1734–82*, Göttingen, 1957.

FÜRNROHR, W., *Der immerwährende Reichstag zu Regensburg*, Regensburg, 1963.

GAUL, H., 'Aus der Geschichte von Stadt und Stift Essen', *Beiträge zur Geschichte von Stadt und Stift Essen*, 83, 1968.

GAUL, O., *Schloss Brake und der Baumeister Hermann Wulff*, Lemgo, 1967.

GEBHART, H., *Numismatische Geldgeschichte*, Leipzig, 1886.

GERLACH, F., *Der Archidiakonat Lemgo*, Münster, 1932.

——, 'Die Patrizierfamilie Cothmann in Lemgo', *Lippische Landeszeitung*, Beilagen 1–9, 1951, Beilage 4, 1954.

GERLOFF, W. and MEUSEL, F. (eds), *Handbuch der Finanzwissenschaft*, 1, Tübingen, 1926.

GERMING, J., 'Geschichte der amtlichen Finanzstatistik der Grafschaft Mark', *Jahrbuch des Vereins für Orts- und Heimatkunde in der Grafschaft Mark*, 27, 1912–13.

GLASER, H., *Die Bundesrepublik zwischen Restauration und Rationalismus*, Freiburg, 1965.

GOETHE, *Dichtung und Wahrheit*, 1811–31.

GOEZ, W., *Der Leihezwang*, Tübingen, 1962.

GOLDAST, M., *Catholicon Rei Monetariae*, Frankfurt-am-Main, 1620.

GORGES, M., 'Beiträge zur Geschichte des ehem. Hochstifts Paderborn 1650–61', *Westfälische Zeitschrift*, 50, II, 1892.

GÖTTSCHING, P., 'Justus Möser und der Westfälische Frieden', *Der Friede von Osnabrück*, Oldenburg, 1948.

GRANIER, G., *Der deutsche Reichstag während des Spanischen Erbfolgekrieges*, Bonn, 1954.

GREVE, J., *Das Braugewerbe der Stadt Münster*, Münster, 1907.

GRIESE, G., 'Die Meierhöfe und ihre Entstehung', *47 Jahresbericht Historischer Verein Ravensberg*, 1932.

GRITZNER, *Standeserhebungen und Gnadenakte während der letzten drei Jahrhunderte*, Görlitz, 1881.

GROTE, H. and HÖLZERMANN, L., *Lippische Geld- und Münzgeschichte*, Leipzig, 1867.

GROTHAUS, W., *Die Lage der Eigenbehörigen in Minden-Ravensberg im 18. Jahrhundert*, Münster, 1934.

GRÜLL, G., *Bauer, Herr und Landesfürst. Sozialrevolutionäre Bestrebungen der oberösterreichischen Bauern 1650–1848*, Graz, 1963.

GRÜNBERG, C., 'Leibeigenschaft', *Handwörterbuch der Staatswissenschaften*, 2nd ed., Jena, 1901.

Gründlicher und Wahrhafter Bericht . . . (The Herford Conflict), Rinteln, 1637.

GRUNER, J., *Meine Wallfahrt zur Ruhe und Hoffnung*, Frankfurt-am-Main, 1802.

GSCHLIESSER, O. V., *Der Reichshofrat*, Vienna, 1942.

GUHRAUER, G. E., 'Elizabeth, Pfalzgräfin bei Rhein, Äbtissin von Herford 1667–80', *Raumers Historisches Jahrbuch*, 3rd series, 1, 2.

GÜTHLING, W., 'Die Vermessungen im Siegerland 1717–26', *Westfalen*, 28, 1950.

HAASE, C., *Das ständische Wesen im nördlichen Deutschland*, Göttingen, 1964.

HALLIDAY, A., *A General History of the House of Guelph*, London, 1821.

HANSEN, W., *Lippische Bibliographie*, Detmold, 1957.

HARDING, A., *A Social History of English Law*, Penguin Books, 1966.

HARTUNG, F., 'Die Wahlkapitulationen der deutschen Kaiser und Könige', *Historische Zeitschrift*, 107, 1911.

——, *Volk und Staat in der deutschen Geschichte*, Leipzig, 1940.

HASSELMEIER, H. H., *Die Stellung der Juden in Schaumburg-Lippe 1648–1848*, Bückeburg, 1968.

HAUSER, O., 'Deutsch-englische Missverständnisse', *Geschichte in Wissenschaft und Unterricht*, 18, 1967.

HAY, D., *Europe in the 14th and 15th Centuries*, London, 1966.

HECKEL, M., 'Staat und Kirche': 'Autonomia und Pacis Compositio': 'Parität', *Zeitschrift der Savigny-Stiftung für Rechtsgeschichte*, Kanonistische Abteilung, 1956–7, 1959, 1963.

HEIDEMANN, J., *Die Grafschaft Lippe unter der Regierung des Grafen Hermann Adolf und Simon Henrich 1652–97*, Göttingen, 1957.

——, 'Das lippische Wirtschaftsleben und Finanzwesen in der zweiten Hälfte des 17. Jahrhunderts', *Westfälische Forschungen*, 15, 1962.

HEIDENREICH, J. K., *Das Armenwesen der Stadt Warburg*, Münster, 1909.

HEMPEL, L., 'Heuerlingswesen und Croftersystem', *Zeitschrift für Agrargeschichte und Agrarsoziologie*, 5, 1957.

HENNING, F. W., *Herrschaft und Bauernuntertänigkeit . . . Ostpreussen-Paderborn vor 1800*, Würzburg, 1964.

——, 'Die Verschulding westfälischer Bauernhöfe in der zweiten Hälfte des 18. Jahrhunderts', *Festschrift für W. Abel*, Hanover, 1964.

HERBERHOLD, F., 'Das Ravensberger Urbar von 1550', *Westfalen*, 21, 1936.

—— (ed.), *Das Urbar der Grafschaft Ravensberg von 1556*, Bielefeld, 1960.

HERTZ, F., 'Die Rechtsprechung der höchsten Reichsgerichte', *Mitteilungen des Instituts für österreichische Geschichtsforschung*, 69, 1961.

HILTEBRANDT, P., *Die Römische Kurie und die Protestanten*, Rome, 1910.

HOBSBAWM, H., *The Age of Revolution*, New York, 1962.

HÖMBERG, A. K., *Westfälische Landesgeschichte*, Münster, 1967.

HOFER, E., *Die Beziehungen Mecklenburgs zu Kaiser und Reich 1620–83*, Marburg, 1956.

HOFFMANN, A., 'Die Grundherrschaft als Unternehmen', *Zeitschrift für Agrargeschichte und Agrarsoziologie*, 6, 1958.

HOFFMANN, L. W., *Alter und Neuer Münz-Schlüssel*, Nuremberg, 1692.

HOFFMEYER, L., *Geschichte der Stadt und des Regierungsbezirks Osnabrücks*, 2nd ed., Osnabrück, 1920.

HOLBORN, H., *A History of Modern Germany*, 1, London, 1965.

HOLSCHE, A. K., *Historisch-topographische-statistische Beschreibung der Grafschaft Tecklenburg nebst einigen speciellen Landesverordnungen*, Berlin, 1788.

HONSELMANN, K., 'Der Kampf um Paderborn 1604', *Westfälische Zeitschrift*, 118, II, 1968.

HOPF, *Historischer-Genealogischer Atlas*, Gotha, 1858.

v.d. HORST, *Die Rittersitze der Grafschaft Ravensberg und des Fürstentums Minden*, Berlin, 1884.

HUBATSCH, W., et al., *Die Deutsche Frage (1949–61)*, Würzburg, 1961.

HUNSCHE, F. E., *250 Jahre Landkreis Tecklenburg*, Lengerich, 1957.

HUPP, O., *Schmähbriefe und Schandbilder. Ein Rechtsbehelf aus dem 15. und 16. Jahrhundert*, Munich, 1930.

HUYSKENS, 'Arbeitslohn in Münster im 16. Jahrhundert', *Westfälische Zeitschrift*, 58, I, 1900.

IPSEN, G., 'Die preussische Bauernbefreiung als Landesausbau', *Zeitschrift für Agrargeschichte und Agrarsoziologie*, 2, 1954.

ISRAEL, O., 'Der Bielefelder Kreistag von 1671', *54 Jahresbericht Historischer Verein Ravensberg*, 1947.

JACOB, G., 'Die Hofkammer des Fürstbistums Münster 1573–1803', *Westfälische Zeitschrift*, 115, 1965.

JACOBS, F., 'Die Paderborner Landstände im 17. und 18. Jahrhundert', *Westfälische Zeitschrift*, 93, II, 1937.

JÄGER, H., 'Der dreissigjährige Krieg und die deutsche Kulturlandschaft', *Wege und Forschungen der Agrargeschichte*, Frankfurt-am-Main, 1967.

JARRETT, B., *Social theories of the Middle Ages*, London, 1926.

KAMEN, H., 'The economic consequences of the Thirty Years' War', *Past and Present*, 39, 1968.

——, *The Iron Century*, London, 1971.

KELLER, G., *Kleider machen Leute*, Reclam, 1962.

KELLINGHAN, H., *Das Amt Bergedorf bis 1620*, Göttingen, 1908.

KESTING, H., *Geschichte und Verfassung des niedersächsisch-westfälischen Grafenkollegiums, mit einem Beitrag zur Entwicklung der Kuriatstimmen*, Münster, 1916.

——, 'Geschichte und Verfassung des niedersächsisch-westfälischen Reichsgrafen-Kollegiums', *Westfälische Zeitschrift*, 106, 1956.

KEYSER, E., *Bevölkerungsgeschichte Deutschlands*, 2nd ed., Leipzig, 1941.

——, *Niedersächsisches Städtebuch*, Stuttgart, 1952.

——, *Westfälisches Städtebuch*, Stuttgart, 1953.

KIEWNING, H., 'Der Lippische Fürstenbrief von 1720', *Lippische Mitteilungen*, 1, 1903.

——, *Fürstin Pauline*, Detmold, 1930.

——, *Hundert Jahre Lippischer Verfassung*, Detmold, 1935.

——, 'Das Lippische Landesarchiv in Detmold', *Archivalische Zeitschrift*, 42–3, 1934.

——, *Lippische Geschichte*, Detmold, 1942.

KIRCHHOFF, K. H., 'Die Wiedertäufer in Coesfeld', *Westfälische Zeitschrift*, 106, 1956.

——, 'Die landständischen Schatzungen des Stifts Münster im 16. Jahrhundert', *Westfälische Forschungen*, 14, 1961.

——, 'Landräte im Stift Münster. Erscheinungsformen der landständischen Mitregierung im 16. Jahrhundert', *Westfälische Forschungen*, 18, 1965.

——, 'Exekutivorgane und Rechtspraxis der Täuferverfolgung im Münsterland 1533–46', *Westfälische Forschungen*, 16, 1963.

KITTEL, E., *Geschichte der Stadt Detmold*, Detmold, 1963.

——, 'Die Samtherrschaft Lippstadt', *Westfälische Forschungen*, 9, 1956.

——, *Geschichte des Landes Lippe*, Cologne, 1957.

——, 'Das Kreuzherrenkloster Falkenhagen', *Festschrift G. Schreiber*, Münster, 1963.

——, *Kloster und Stift St. Marien in Lemgo 1265–1965*, Detmold, 1965.

——, STÖWER, H. and SUNDERGELD, K., 'Die älteren Lippischen Landesgesetze und Ordnungen', *Lippische Mitteilungen*, 26, 1957.

KLAVEREN, J. V., 'Die internationalen Aspekte der Korruption', *Vierteljahrschrift für Sozial- und Wirtschaftsgeschichte*, 45, 1958.

——, 'Fiskalismus-Merkantilismus-Korruption', *Vierteljahrschrift für Sozial- und Wirtschaftsgeschichte*, 47, 1960.

KLOCKE, F. V., *Das Patrizierproblem und die Werler Erbsälzer*, Münster, 1965.

KLOCKOW, H., *Stadt Lippe—Lippstadt*, Lippstadt, 1964.

KLÜBER, I. L., *De pictura contumeliosa*, Erlangen, 1787.

KNAUT, M., *Geschichte der Verwaltungsorganisation*, Stuttgart, 1961.

KÖCHER, A., *Geschichte von Hannover und Braunschweig*, 2, Leipzig, 1895.

KOENIGSBERGER, H. G. and MOSSE, G. L., *Europe in the 16th century*, London, 1968.

KOHL, W., *Christof Bernhard von Galen*, Münster, 1964.

KOKEN, H., *Die Braunschweiger Landstände um die Wende des 16. Jahrhunderts*, Kiel, 1914.

KÖLLING, F., 'Hessisch-Oldendorf im dreissigjährigen Kriege', *Schaumburger Heimatblätter*, 1951.

KORTE, F., 'Die staatsrechtliche Stellung von Sitft und Stadt Herford', *58 Jahresbericht Historischer Verein Ravensberg*, 1955.

KRAEMER, H., 'Der deutsche Kleinstaat des 17. Jahrhunderts im Spiegel von Seckendorffs "Teutschem Fürstenstaat"', *Zeitschrift für thüringische Geschichte*, new series, 25, 1922–4.

KRAGEN, N., 'Christlike Ordeninge der Erlyken Stadt Mynden', Lübeck, 1530, reprinted by M. Krieg in *Jahrbuch des Vereins für Westfälische Kirchengeschichte*, 43, 1950.

KRAUSE, H., *System der landständischen Verfassung Mecklenburgs in der zweiten Hälfte des 16. Jahrhunderts*, Rostock, 1927.

KRAWINKEL, H., 'Die Grundherrschaft in Lippe', *Lippische Mitteilungen*, 15, 1935.

KROSCH, W., *Die landständische Verfassung des Fürstentums Lüneburg*, Kiel, 1914.

KUHLMANN, M., *Bevölkerungsgeographie des Landes Lippe*, Remagen, 1954.

KUSKE, B., 'Die Entstehung der Kreditwirtschaft', and 'Das mittelalterliche Deutsche Reich in seinen wirtschaftlichen und sozialen Auswirkungen', *Köln, der Rhein und das Reich*, Cologne, 1956.

LAGARDE, G. de, 'La structure sociale de l'Europe au XIVe siècle', *L'Organisation Corporative du Moyen Age*, 2, 1939.

LAHRKAMP, H., 'Lothar Dietrich Freiherr von Bönninghausen. Ein westfälischer Soldnerführer des dreißigjährigen Krieges', *Westfälische Zeitschrift*, 108, II, 1958.

LAMPE, J., *Aristokratie, Hofadel und Staatspatriziat in Kurhannover*, 1, 2, Göttingen, 1963.

LEESCH, W., 'Die Grafen von Rietberg aus den Häusern Arnsberg und Ostfriesland', *Westfälische Zeitschrift*, 113, 1963.

—— and SCHUBERT, P., *Heimatchronik des Kreises Höxter*, Cologne, 1966.

LENNARTZ, P., *Die Probationstage und Probationsregister des niederländisch-westfälischen Kreises*, Münster, 1912.

LETHE, E. V., *Grenzen und Ämter im Herzogtum Bremen*, Göttingen, 1926.

LETTENBAUER, L., *Gläubiger- und Schuldnerbegünstigung*, Breslau, 1931.

Lippische Landesverordnungen, 1, Lemgo, 1779.

Lippische Regesten, 1–4, Lemgo and Detmold, 1860–8.

LOEBL, A. H., 'Eine ausserordentliche Reichshilfe', *Sitzungsberichte der phil-hist. Klasse d. kais. Akad. d. Wiss.*, 153, Vienna, 1906.

LÖHNEISS, G., *Aulico-Politica*, Brunswick, 1624.

LUCIUS, C. L. (Leucht), *Verboth der Guldiner: Müntz-Tractat: Neueste Müntz-Mandaten*, Nuremberg, 1692–3.

LÜCK, A., 'Die scharfen Exekutionen gegen Kaan und Obersdorf im Jahre 1735', *Siegerland, Blätter des Siegerländer Heimatvereins*, 44, 1967.

LÜCKE, J., *Die landständische Verfassung im Hochstift Hildesheim 1643–1802*, Hildesheim, 1968.

LÜDICKE, R., 'Die landesherrlichen Zentralbehörden im Bistum Münster (1530–1650)', *Westfälische Zeitschrift*, 59, I, 1901.

LÜNIG, J. C., *Teutsches Reichsarchiv*, Leipzig, 1710–22.

LUSSET, F., 'Die Wiedervereinigung Deutschlands von den Nachbarländern aus gesehen', *Geschichte in Wissenschaft und Unterricht*, 16, 1965.

LÜTGE, F., *Die mitteldeutsche Grundherrschaft und ihre Auflösung*, 2nd ed., Stuttgart, 1957.

——, *Geschichte der deutschen Agrarverfassung*, 2nd ed., Stuttgart, 1967.

MAACK, W., 'Kriegsnöte vor 300 Jahren', *Schaumburger Heimatblätter*, 1960–1.

——, *Die Grafschaft Schaumburg*, Rinteln, 1964.

MAIER, H., *Ältere deutsche Staatslehre und westliche politische Tradition*, Tübingen, 1966.

MALLY, A. K., *Der österreichische Kreis in der Exekutionsordnung des Römisch-Deutschen Reiches*, Vienna, 1967.

MANES, A., *Staatsbankrotte*, Berlin, 1918.

MARPERGER, P. J., *Beschreibung der Banquen*, Leipzig, 1723.

MAYER, T. (ed.), *Adel und Bauern*, Leipzig, 1943.

——, *Fürst und Staat*, Weimar, 1950.

MEIER, E. V., *Hannoversche Verfassungs- und Verwaltungsgeschichte 1680–1866*, 1, Leipzig, 1898.

MEIER, K., *Die Standhafte Katarine*, Detmold, 1935.

——, *Die letzte und blutigste Hexenverfolgung in Lemgo 1665–81*, Lemgo, 1949.

——, *Geschichte der Stadt Lemgo*, Lemgo, 1962.

MEINECKE, F., *Machiavellism*, London, 1958.

MEINERS, C., *Geschichte der Ungleichheit der Stände*, Hanover, 1792.

MEININGHAUS, A., 'Vom Adel der Dortmunder Deggings', *Westfalen*, 20, 1935.

Merckwürdige Reichshofrats-Conclusa und Anschlags Protocolle, Frankfurt-am-Main, 1726ff.

MERKL, P. H., *The Origins of the West German Republic* (paperback), New York, 1963.

MERX, O., 'Aus einem westfälischen Kleinstaate', *Westfalen*, 1, 1909.

MEYER, R., 'Die geschichtlichen Grundlagen der westfälischen Landgemeindeordnung vom Jahre 1841', *47 Jahresbericht Historischer Verein Ravensberg*, 1933.

MEYER, W., 'Guts- und Leibeigentum in Lippe', *Jahrbücher für Nationalökonomie und Statistik*, 3rd series, vol. 12, 1896.

Meyers Lexikon, 6th ed., Leipzig, 1908.

MITGAU, H., 'Ständische Daseinsformen genealogisch gesehen', *Gemeinsames Leben 1550–1770*, Göttingen, 1953.

MITTEIS, H. and LIEBERICH, H., *Deutsche Rechtsgeschichte*, 9th ed., Munich, 1965.

MOSER, F. C., *Sammlung sämtlicher Crays-Abschiede*, 1–3, Leipzig, 1747–1748.

——, *Fränkische Crays-Abschiede* (*1524–1748*), 1–2, Nuremberg, 1752.

——, *Obersächsische Kreisabschiede*, Jena, 1752.

MÖSER, J., 'Mitteilungen über die Grenzstreitigkeiten zwischen dem Bischofe zu Osnabrück und dem Grafen von Tecklenburg', *Osnabrücker Mitteilungen*, 2, 1850.

MOSER, J. J., *Teutsches Staatsrecht*, Nuremberg, 1737–54.

——, *Grundriss der heutigen Staatsverfassung*, Tübingen, 1754.

——, *Neues Teutsches Staatsrecht*, Frankfurt-am-Main, 1766–75.

——, *Von der Teutschen Crays-Verfassung*, Frankfurt-am-Main, 1773.

MÜLLER, J., 'Die Verdienste Zacharias Geitzkofflers um die Beschaffung der Geldmittel für den Türkenkrieg Kaiser Rudolfs II', *Mitteilungen des Instituts für österreichische Geschichtsforschung*, 21, 1900.

——, 'Das Steuer und Finanzwesen des Heiligen Römischen Reichs im XVI Jahrhundert', *Neue Jahrbücher für das klassische Altertum, Geschichte und deutsche Literatur*, Leipzig, 1902.

——, *Zacharias Geitzkoffler 1560–1617*, Vienna, 1938.

MÜLLER, W., *Die Abgaben von Todes wegen in der Abtei St. Gallen*, Cologne, 1961.

MUNDT, T., *Geschichte der deutschen Stände*, Berlin, 1854.

MYLIUS, C. O., *Corpus Constitutionum Marcicarum*, Berlin, 1737–55.

Neue und vollständigere Sammlung der Reichsabschiede, Frankfurt-am-Main, 1747.

NEUMANN, W., 'Die Türkeneinfälle nach Kärnten', *Festgabe H. Steinacker*, Munich, 1955.

NICHTWEISS, J., *Das Bauernlegen in Mecklenburg*, Berlin, 1954.

NITZSCH, K., 'Die ravensbergische Territorialverfassung bis 1535', *17 Jahresbericht Historischer Verein Ravensberg*, 1903.

OHE, H. J. v.d., *Die Zentral- und Hofverwaltung des Fürstentums Lüneburg* (*Celle*) *und ihre Beamten 1520–1648*, Celle, 1955.

OHNSORGE, W., 'Zum Problem: Fürst und Verwaltung um die Wende des 16. Jahrhunderts', *Blätter für deutsche Landesgeschichte*, 88, 1951.

OLPP, T., 'Die Stellung der Mindener Bischöfe zur Reformation', *Jahrbuch des Vereins für Westfälische Kirchengeschichte*, 48–50, 1956–7.

PAPE, R., 'Überblick über die Geschichte der Stadt Herford', *Herforder Jahrbuch*, 1, 1960.

PETERSOHN, J., *Fürstenmacht und Ständetum in Prenssen während der Regierung Herzog Georg Friedrichs 1578–1603*, Würzburg, 1963.

PFEIFFER, G., 'Die Bündnis und Landfriedenspolitik der Territorien zwischen Weser und Rhein im späten Mittelalter 1180–1512', *Der Raum Westfalen*, 2, part 1, Münster, 1955.

PHILIPPI, F., 'Zur Osnabrücker Verfassungsgeschichte', *Osnabrücker Mitteilungen*, 22, 1897.

——, *Landrechte des Münsterlandes*, Münster, 1907.

PLANITZ, H., *Grundzüge des deutschen Privatrechts*, Berlin, 1931.

——, *Das deutsche Grundpfandrecht*, Weimar, 1936.

——, *Quellenkunde der deutschen, österreichischen und schweizer Rechtsgeschichte einschliesslich des deutschen Privatrechts*, Graz, 1948.

PLÖTHNER, R. L., 'Erbregister über das schriftsäßige Ritterguth zu Clodra 1669', *Zeitschrift des Vereins für thüringische Geschichte*, 29, new series, 1931.

PRINZ, J., *Das territorium des Bistums Osnabrück*, Göttingen, 1934.

PÜTTER, J. S., *Historische Entwicklung der heutigen Staatsverfassung des Teutschen Reichs*, 3 parts, 2nd ed., Göttingen, 1788.

PUTTKAMER, E. V., *Föderative Elemente im deutschen Staatsrecht seit 1648*, Göttingen, 1955.

Quellen zur Neueren Geschichte, no. 17, Bern, 1951.

RANKE, L. V., *Deutsche Geschichte im Zeitalter der Reformation*, 1, Munich, 1914 ed.

RAUCH, K., *Traktat über den Reichstag im 16. Jahrhundert. Eine offiziöse Darstellung aus der Kurmainzer Kanzlei*, Leipzig, 1905.

——, *Kapitalerhöhung aus Gesellschaftsmitteln und ihre Besteuerung*, Marburg, 1950.

REDLICH, F., *De Praeda Militari. Looting and Booty 1500–1815*, Wiesbaden, 1956.

——, *The German Military Enterpriser and his Task Force*, 2 vols, Wiesbaden, 1964–5.

REHKER, H., 'Die landesherrlichen Verwaltungsbehörden im Bistum Osnabrück 1553–1661', *Osnabrücker Mitteilungen*, 30, 1905.

Reichstagsakten, old series, 2nd ed., Göttingen, 1956ff., new series, Gotha, 1893ff.

REINERT, R., *Die Besonderheit der preussischen Städtischen Verwaltung*, Münster, 1968.

REMBE, H., *Die Grafen von Mansfeld in den Liedern ihrer Zeit*, Halle, 1885.

RENGER, R., *Landesherr und Landstände im Hochstift Osnabrück in der Mitte des 18. Jahrhunderts*, Göttingen, 1968.

RITTER, M., 'Zur Geschichte der deutschen Finanzverwaltung im 16. Jahrhundert', *Zeitschrift des Bergischen Geschichtsvereins*, 20, 1884.

ROSENKRANZ, G. J., 'Die Verfassung des ehem. Hochstifts Paderborn', *Westfälische Zeitschrift*, 12, 1851.

ROSENTHAL, E., 'Die Behördenorganisation Kaiser Ferdinands I', *Archiv für österreichische Geschichte*, 69, 1887.

ROSSBERG, A., *Die Entwicklung der Territorialherrlichkeit in der Grafschaft Ravensberg*, Leipzig, 1909.

RÖSSLER, H. (ed.), *Deutscher Adel 1430–1555*, Darmstadt, 1965.

ROTHERT, H., *Das tausendjährige Reich der Wiedertäufer zu Münster 1534–5*, Münster, 1947.

——, 'Ein Artländer Bauer zur Zeit des grossen Krieges', *Der Friede von Osnabrück*, Oldenburg, 1948.

——, *Westfälische Geschichte*, 1–3, 2nd ed., Gütersloh, 1962.

Sammlung der Reichsabschiede, Frankfurt-am-Main, 1747.

SANDER, P. and SPANGENBERG, H., *Urkunden zur Geschichte der Territorialverfassung*, Stuttgart, 1922–6; reprinted Aalen, 1965.

SCHACHT, 'Der leibhaftige Teufel in Herford', *46 Jahresbericht Historischer Verein Ravensberg*, 1931.

SCHAER, F. W., *Graf Friedrich Christian zu Schaumburg-Lippe*, Bückeburg, 1966.

——, 'Der Absolutismus in Lippe und Schaumburg-Lippe. Überblick und Vergleich', *Lippische Mitteilungen*, 37, 1968.

SCHAFMEISTER, K., *Herzog Ferdinand von Bayern, Erzbischof von Köln als Fürstbischof von Münster 1612–50*, Münster, 1912.

SCHATEN, *Annales Paderbornenses*, II, Neuhaus, 1693.

SCHAUROTH, *Sammlung aller Conclusorum ... des Corporis Evangelicorum*, 1–3, Regensburg, 1751.

SCHLESINGER, W., *Die Herrschaft der Herren von Schönburg*, Münster, 1954.

SCHMELZEISEN, G. K., *Polizeiordnungen und Privatrecht*, Münster, 1955.

SCHMIDLIN, J., 'Christof Bernhard von Galen und die Diözese Münster nach seinen Romberichten', *Westfalen*, 2, 1910.

SCHMIDT, A., 'An welchen auswärtigen Schulen und Hochschulen haben Angehörige der Grafschaft Lippe bis zum Beginn des 19. Jahrhunderts ihre Ausbildung gesucht?', *Lippische Mitteilungen*, 15, 1935.

SCHMIDT, G., *Die alte Grafschaft Schaumburg*, Göttingen, 1920.

SCHMIDT, H., *Lippische Siedlungs- und Waldgeschichte*, Detmold, 1940.

SCHMITT, C., *Die Diktatur*, 3rd ed., Berlin, 1965.

SCHMITZ-ECKERT, H. G., 'Die Hochstift-Münsterische Regierung von 1574–1803', *Westfälische Zeitschrift*, 116, I, 1966.

SCHMITZ-KALLENBERG, L., 'Des Grafen Simon VI Gesandtschaftsreise', *Lippische Mitteilungen*, 4, 1906.

SCHNATH, C., *Die Herrschaften Everstein, Homburg, und Spiegelberg*, Göttingen, 1922.

SCHNATH, G., *Geschichte Hannovers*, 1, Hildesheim, 1938.

SCHNEE, H., *Die Hoffinanz und der moderne Staat*, 1–3, Berlin, 1953–5.

——, 'Stellung und Bedeutung der Hoffinanzier in Westfalen', *Westfalen*, 34, 1956.

SCHÖNING, A., *Der Grundbesitz des Klosters Corvey im ehem. Lande Lippe*, 1–3, Detmold, 1958–60.

SCHÖTTKE, G., 'Die Stände des Hochstifts Osnabrücks unter dem evangelischen Bischof Ernst August von Braunschweig—Lüneburg 1662–98, *Osnabrücker Mitteilungen*, 33, 1908.

SCHRÖDER, R. and KÜNSSBERG, E. V., *Lehrbuch der deutschen Rechtsgeschichte*, 1–2, 6th ed., Leipzig, 1919–22.

SCHULTEN, A., *Die Hodegerechtigkeit im Fürstentum Osnabrück*, Münster University thesis, 1909.

SCHULZ, H., 'Johanna Charlotte, Markgräfin von Brandenburg-Schwedt, Äbtissin des Reichsstifts Herford 1729–50', *Herforder Jahrbuch*, 1, 1960.

SCHWERIN, C. V., *Deutsche Rechtsgeschichte*, Leipzig, 1912.

SECKENDORFF, V. L. V., *Teutscher Fürsten-Staat*, Frankfurt-am-Main and Hanau, 1656; 5th ed. with additions, 1678.

SELLERT, W., *Über die Zuständigkeitsabgrenzung von Reichshofrat und Reichskammergericht*, Aalen, 1965.

SHAW, W. A., 'The monetary movements of 1600–21 in Holland and Germany', *Transactions of the Royal Historical Society*, 9, 1895.

SICKEN, B., *Das Wehrwesen des fränkischen Reichskreises 1681–1714*, 1–2, Nuremberg, 1967.

Siedlungskundliche Entwicklung. Die Gemeinden Bokel und Druffel, Gütersloh, 1968.

SMEND, R., *Reichskammergericht, Geschichte und Verfassung*, 1, reprint, Aalen, 1965.

SOUTHERN, R. W., *The making of the middle ages* (paperback), London, 1959.

SPANGENBERG, C., *Die Geistliche Haustafel*, Wittenberg, 1556.

——, *Mansfeldische Chronik*, Eisleben, 1572.

——, *Adels Spiegel*, Schmalkalden, 1591.

SPANGENBERG, H., 'Beiträge zur älteren Verfassungs- und Verwaltungsgeschichte des Fürstentums Osnabrück', *Osnabrücker Mitteilungen*, 25, 1900.

SPANNAGEL, K., *Minden und Ravensberg unter brandenburg-preussischer Herrschaft 1648–1719*, Hanover, 1894.

STEGEMANN, E., 'Die Grafschaft Lippe im dreissigjährigen Krieg', *Lippische Mitteilungen*, 3, 1905.

STEIMEL, R., *Kleine Geschichte des deutschen Adels*, Cologne, 1959.

STÖWER, H. (ed.), 'Die Lippische Amtsordnung vom 11. März 1536', *Lippische Mitteilungen*, 26, 1957; 31, 1962.

—— and VERDENHALVEN, F., *Salbücher der Grafschaft Lippe von 1614 bis etwa 1620*, Münster, 1969.

STULZ, J., 'Ausschusstag der fünf niederösterreichischen Lande in Wien 1556', *Archiv für Kunde österreichischer Geschichtsquellen*, 8, Vienna, 1852.

STÜNKEL, R., *Rinteln im dreissigjährigen Kriege*, Rinteln, 1952.

STUPPERICH, R., 'Heinrich von Braunschweig und Philipp von Hessen im Kampf um den Einfluss in Westfalen 1530–5', *Westfälische Zeitschrift*, 112, I, 1962.

STÜVE, C., 'Das Finanzwesen der Stadt Osnabrück bis zum Westfälischen Frieden', *Osnabrücker Mitteilungen*, 11, 1876.

SUERBAUM, A., 'Der Zehnte im Landkreis Osnabrück vom späten Mittelalter bis zur Ablösung', *Osnabrücker Mitteilungen*, 70, 1961.

SUGENHEIM, S., *Geschichte der Aufhebung der Leibeigenschaft und Hörigkeit in Europa*, St Petersburg, 1864.

SÜVERN, W., *Brake, Geschichte des Schlosses und der Gemeinde*, Lemgo, 1960.

—— (ed.), 'Letzter Wille und Lebenslauf des Grafen Otto zur Lippe-Brake vom Jahre 1636', *Lippische Mitteilungen*, 30, 1961.

TACK, W., 'Aufnahme, Ahnenprobe und Kappengang der Paderborner Domherren im 17. und 18. Jahrhundert', *Westfälische Zeitschrift*, 96, II, 1940.

TAUBER, W., *Geld und Kredit im Mittelalter*, Berlin, 1933.

TELLENBACH, G., 'Vom karolingischen Reichsadel zum deutschen Reichsfürstenstand', in *Adel und Bauern*, Leipzig, 1943.

Territorien Ploetz, 1, Würzburg, 1964.

TESSIN, G., 'Wert und Grösse Mecklenburgischer Rittergüter zu Beginn des dreissigjährigen Krieges', *Zeitschrift für Agrargeschichte und Agrarsoziologie*, 3, 1955.

THEUERKAUF, G., 'Das Lehenswesen in Westfalen', *Westfälische Forschungen*, 17, 1964.

THIEME, H., 'Die Funktion der Regalien im Mittelalter', *Zeitschrift der Savigny-Stiftung für Rechtsgeschichte*, Germanistische Abteilung, 1942.

THOMAN, D., *Acta Publica Monetaria des Müntz Wesens in Deutschland*, Augsburg, 1692.

TREUE, W., 'Das Verhalten von Fürst, Staat und Unternehmer', *Vierteljahrschrift für Sozial- und Wirtschaftsgeschichte*, 44, 1957.

TÜMMLER, H., 'Ein Bedeverzeichnis des Distriktes Buttelstedt vom Jahre 1333', *Zeitschrift des Vereins für thüringische Geschichte*, 29, new series, 1931.

TÜMPEL, H., *Minden-Ravensberg unter der Herrschaft der Hohenzollern*, Bielefeld, 1909.

TURBA, G., 'Verhaftung und Gefangenschaft des Landgrafen Philip v. Hessen 1547–50', *Archiv für österreichische Geschichte*, 82, 1895.

TURNER, S. E., *A Sketch of the Germanic Constitution*, New York, 1888.

VERDENHALVEN, F., *Alte Masse, Münzen und Gewichte*, Neustadt, 1968.

VERSPOHL, T., *Das Heerwesen des Münsterschen Fürstbischofs Christof Bernhard von Galen 1650–78*, Hildesheim, 1909.

Verzeichnus ders. H. R. R. Stände nach den zehen Reichs Craissen, Frankfurt-am-Main, 1659.

VÖLKER, A. J., *Die innere Politik des Fürstbischofs von Münster, Friedrich Christian von Plettenberg 1688–1706*, Hildesheim, 1908.

VOORT, H., 'Burgmannen zu Bentheim', *Osnabrücker Mitteilungen*, 76, 1969.

VOSS, A., 'Die Grundherrschaft im Altenautale. Ein Beitrag zur Geschichte des Bauernstandes im Paderborner Lande', *Westfälische Zeitschrift*, 92, II, 1935.

——, 'Patrimonialgerichte im Paderborner Land', *Westfalen*, 21, 1936.

VRIES, R. de, *Die Landtage des Stifts Essen*, Münster, 1934; also in *Beiträge zur Geschichte von Stadt und Stift Essen*, no. 52.

WALDER, E. (ed.), *Der Westfälische Friede*, Bern, 1952.

WALLTHOR, A. HARTLIEB V., *Die landschaftliche Selbstverwaltung Westfalens*, 1, Münster, 1965.

——, 'Die Verfassung in Altwestfalen als Quelle moderner Selbstverwaltung', *Westfälische Forschungen*, 9, 1956.

WASCHINSKI, E., 'Zwischenstaatliche Wechselkurse aus dem letzten Viertel des 16. und im ersten Drittel des 18. Jahrhunderts', *Vierteljahrschrift für Sozial- und Wirtschaftsgeschichte*, 47, 1960.

WEBER, C. L., 'Die Anfänge der Statistik in der ehem. Grafschaft Mark bis zum Jahre 1609', *Jahrbuch des Vereins für Ortsgeschichte in der Grafschaft Mark*, 23, 1908–9.

WEDDIGEN, P. F., *Historisch-geographisch-statistische Beschreibung der Grafschaft Ravensberg*, 1–2, Leipzig, 1790.

WEDDIGEN, T., 'Die freien Höfe und Häuser, die Exempten oder Eximirten', *10 Jahresbericht Historischer Verein Ravensberg*, 1895.

WEERTH, O., *Die Grafschaft Lippe und der Siebenjährige Krieg*, Detmold, 1888.

——, 'Der Bergbau bei Falkenhagen', *Lippische Mitteilungen*, 12, 1926.

WERNHAM, R. B. (ed.), *The New Cambridge Modern History*, vol. 3, London, 1968.

Der Raum Westfalen, 2, part 2, Münster, 1933; 2, part 1, Münster, 1955.

WIEDEN, H. b. d., *Fürst Ernst*, Bückeburg, 1961.

——, *Schaumburgische Genealogie*, Bückeburg, 1966.

——, 'Die Erhebung des Grafen Ernst von Holstein-Schaumburg in den Fürstenstand 1619', *Schaumburg-Lippische Mitteilungen*, 18, 1967.

WIGAND, P., 'Rietberger Landrecht 1697', *Archiv für Geschichte und Altertumskunde Westphalens*, 5, Lemgo, 1831–2.

——, *Provinzialrechte Paderborn und Corvey*, 1–3, Leipzig, 1832.

——, *Provinzialrechte Minden Ravensberg etc.*, 2, Leipzig, 1834.

WINES, R., 'The imperial circles, princely diplomacy and imperial reform 1681–1714', *Journal of Modern History*, 39, 1967.

WITTICH, W., *Ländliche Verfassung Niedersachsens und Organisation des Amts im 18 Jh.*, Strasburg, 1891.

WÖHRMANN, O., *Elizabeth von der Pfalz*, Herford, 1921.

WOLF, R., 'Der Einfluss des Landgrafen Philipp des Grossmütigen von Hessen auf die Einführung der Reformation in den Westfälischen Grafschaften', *Jahrbuch des Vereins für Westfälische Kirchengeschichte*, 51–2, 1958–9.

WREDE, G., 'Familienforschung und Hofgeschichte', *Westfalen*, 18, 1933.

——, *Die Westfälischen Länder, 1801, Eine Übersichtskarte*, Münster, 1953.

ZEUMER, K., *Quellensammlung zur Geschichte der deutschen Reichsverfassung in Mittelalter und Neuzeit*, 2nd ed., Tübingen, 1913.

ZUHORN, W., 'Stammtafel Meinders', *Ravensberger Blätter*, 1907.

ZWIEDINECK-SÜDENHORST, H. von, *Deutsche Geschichte im Zeitraum der Gründung des Preussischen Königtums*, 2 vols, Stuttgart, 1894.

Index

STUDIES IN SOCIAL HISTORY

Editor: HAROLD PERKIN
Professor of Social History, University of Lancaster

Assistant Editor: ERIC J. EVANS
Lecturer in History, University of Lancaster

◇◇

ANCIENT CRETE: A Social History from Early Times until the Roman Occupation	R. F. Willetts
CHILDREN IN ENGLISH SOCIETY, VOL. I: From Tudor Times to the Eighteenth Century	I. Pinchbeck & M. Hewitt
CHILDREN IN ENGLISH SOCIETY, VOL. II: From the Eighteenth Century to the Children Act 1948	I. Pinchbeck & M. Hewitt
CHURCHES AND THE WORKING CLASSES IN VICTORIAN ENGLAND	K. S. Inglis
EDUCATION IN RENAISSANCE ENGLAND	Kenneth Charlton
ENGLISH LANDED SOCIETY in the Eighteenth Century	G. E. Mingay
ENGLISH LANDED SOCIETY in the Nineteenth Century	F. M. L. Thompson
ENGLISH PARISH CLERGY ON THE EVE OF THE REFORMATION	P. Heath
FROM CHARITY TO SOCIAL WORK in England and the United States	Kathleen Woodroofe
HEAVENS BELOW: Utopian Experiments in England, 1560–1960	W. H. G. Armytage
A HISTORY OF SHOPPING	Dorothy Davis
THE IMPACT OF RAILWAYS ON VICTORIAN CITIES	J. R. Kellett
THE ORIGINS OF MODERN ENGLISH SOCIETY, 1780–1880	H. Perkin